NAVIGATING THE CRISIS
IN THE CHURCH

NAVIGATING THE CRISIS IN THE CHURCH

Essays in Defense of Traditional Catholicism

by
Stephen Kokx

Foreword by
Archbishop Carlo Maria Viganò

Printed in the United States of America
© 2024 Stephen Kokx
St Peter's Press

Cover image by Rembrandt van Rijn, 1606–1669.
"The Storm on the Sea of Galilee"

Please send inquiries to
StPetersPress@proton.me

ISBN 979-8-9877771-5-2 (Paperback)
ISBN 979-8-9877771-3-8 (e-Book)

Cover design by Michael Schrauzer
Typesetting by Kenneth Lieblich

To the Wulffe family

"Seek and you shall find."
— Matthew 7:7

"The truth will set you free."
— John 8:32

ACKNOWLEDGMENTS

A special thanks is extended to those persons who have allowed me to share my thoughts with the world on their platforms. Any useful insights I have ever made are completely God's doing. I take credit only for my sins. The following individuals are particularly appreciated for having helped me in various ways over the past eleven years. I thank them for allowing me to republish here articles that first appeared on their websites: Josh Mercer of CatholicVote.org; Louie Verrechio of akaCatholic.com; Mike and Lisa Austin of Magnificat Media; Brian McCall and Matt Gaspers of Catholic Family News; and Steve Jalsevac and John-Henry Westen of LifeSiteNews. Additional gratitude is extended to Kenneth Lieblich and Michael Schrauzer for typesetting and designing the cover of this book, respectively. Fr Ambrose, Fr Timothy Hoopes, Evan Stambaugh, Jack Bingham, Mark Pestana, PH.D, Sean Johnson, S.D. Wright, and most especially Stephanie Mader also deserve praise for their editorial recommendations. I am eternally indebted to Archbishop Carlo Maria Viganò, who speaks with the voice of the shepherd, for endorsing this project. Many of the essays in this book have been edited from their original publication for brevity and/or stylistic purposes.

TABLE OF CONTENTS

Chapter IV: The Second Vatican Council

Chapter V: Traditional Catholicism

PART 2 – STATE

Chapter VI: Catholic Social Teaching

Chapter VII: US Politics

Chapter IX: Culture

Chapter x: Family Life

FOREWORD

This collection of articles by Stephen Kokx entitled *Navigating the Crisis in the Church: Essays in Defense of Traditional Catholicism* is a precious opportunity for Catholics to lean out, so to speak, over the abyss of horrors and deviations that the conciliar church—today further evolved into a synodal church—has been digging for decades between the Hierarchy and the faithful. As Stephen Kokx rightly points out in the second part of the book, a similar gulf has been created between rulers and citizens, demonstrating that these divisions originate from the same errors and serve the same purposes.

The problem that unites these times of apostasy in the civil and religious spheres is the crisis of authority. If, in fact, society and the Church are unrecognizable today, compared to what the former was until the French Revolution and the latter up until the Second Vatican Council, we owe it to a radical subversion of the power of those who govern both. This subversion is what constitutes the very essence of the Revolution, that is, of that subversive process that attacks the divine order—the κόσμος willed by God in Creation—in order to replace it with the infernal χάος. The apostasy of the angelic spirits headed by Lucifer was revolutionary; so was the sin of Adam and Eve, tempted by the Serpent. Revolution is everything that does not recognize the Supreme and Eternal Lordship of Our Lord Jesus Christ, both in temporal things removed from His Kingship and in spiritual things from which its artificers would like to exclude the Eternal High Priest.

The enmity between the race of the Woman and the race of the Serpent is irreconcilable, because it is based on the irreconcilability between light and darkness, between God and Satan. An irreconcilability that does not confront us with a dualistic vision of the world, in which Good and Evil eternally face each other as two sides of the same coin, but in which the omnipotence of God allows the Enemy—who is and remains a creature—to act in the history of the human race to test each of us and ensure that we can deserve the eternal reward. The awareness of the provisional nature of Evil and the inexorable victory of Good allows us to face current events—even the most terrible and painful—*sub specie aeternitatis*, that is, considering them in their theological dimension, knowing full well that the power granted to Satan will not exceed even by a moment the time established by God.

When, therefore, we observe the rebellion of the nations against the Lordship of Christ the King, and the still more unheard-of and absurd rebellion of the Catholic Hierarchy against Christ the Pontiff, we must consider them in their ontological provisionality: only in this way do we understand why the wicked seem to be in a hurry to attain their ends in both civil and ecclesiastical matters. They know well that the time of trial is limited, and that the more they seem to prevail over the good, the nearer the end of their dissolving action becomes. The Heads of State and Government of Western countries subservient to the New World Order and the criminal plan of Freemasonry know this; Their accomplices who have infiltrated the Church to make her the handmaiden of globalism know this. If we see them speeding up their moves, it is because they know—perhaps more than we do—that the *redde rationem* is approaching and that their power is about to end.

Stephen Kokx's articulated examination considers the crisis of the Church and that of the State in parallel, dividing it into the two parts that compose this work, and this certainly has the merit of rationalizing the duplicity of what is happening on these two fronts, showing their coherence and interdependence. The apostasy of the rulers of the nations would not be possible without an apostasy of the Hierarchy of the Catholic Church, for exactly the same reason that the prosperity and concord of States is not possible where Religion does not animate the lives of citizens with Grace. That is why, with a supernatural outlook, what is happening today is in some way necessary and logical, if there can be a logic in the delirious project of going against God.

One of the most terrible aspects of the Enemy's action is precisely this obstinacy in evil, even knowing that he has no chance of overcoming the Almighty. But is not this, on closer inspection, what constitutes the folly of rebellion against God? Is not νέμεσις the inescapable punishment for the ὕβρις that defies the Divine Majesty? This vertigo on the edge of the abyss, which blinds the minds of Satan and his servants with pride, drives them to do evil knowing full well that they have no hope of victory, but rather knowing their eternal destiny of despair and damnation. *Quos Deus perdere vult dementat prius:* God drives mad those whom he wants to lose, because only madness can lead them to choose eternal death instead of the beatific vision of the Most Holy Trinity. But it is a madness that does not take away the will to evil but rather makes it more dangerous, because the prospect of a damned eternity leads to irrational and destructive gestures.

But if it is foolish to think that we can usurp the royal crown of Christ in the government of the State, it is still more foolish to believe that we can snatch the Tiara of the High Priesthood away from Him in the government of the Church. This is why the "pontificate" of Jorge Mario Bergoglio is destined to sink into general execration, and with it the new Iscariot who, for thirty pieces of silver, has delivered Our Lord—in His Mystical Body—to the globalist Sanhedrin. The *passio Ecclesiae* is in fact nothing but the completion in the members of the Passion of its Head, and just as two thousand years ago the scribes and elders of the people preferred to submit to the power of a pagan Empire in order not to lose the power they held over the Jews, so today we see the high priests of the Bergoglian Sanhedrin allied with the Masonic and technocratic elite, and a new Caiaphas accuses those who oppose him of blasphemy and reveals their foul complicity with the enemies of Christ.

In this relentless battle, the people are victims of authority: the citizens are victims of the civil authority and the faithful are victims of the religious authority. A corrupt and perverted authority that, because of its ability to be blackmailed—now amply demonstrated by scandals of unprecedented gravity—continues to obey the wicked and, ultimately, obeys Satan. As Stephen Kokx points out, both citizens and the faithful feel alienated from their civil and ecclesiastical rulers, abandoned by those who should defend them, and indeed struck and persecuted by them as enemies.

But if these tribulations constitute the sifting that each one of us—as an individual and as part of the social and ecclesial body—must pass through in order to prove ourselves worthy of Blessed Eternity and merit to celebrate the triumph with Christ, we must also believe that this trial will have an end and that the Lord will grant us the graces necessary to face it without succumbing, and indeed to overcome it victoriously with Him. Conversely, those who have sided with the Enemy can only see that the end is nearer, just as the punishment that awaits them also draws near.

Until eleven years ago there were those who still believed that the Hierarchy had fallen into an unfortunate misunderstanding, and that it did not really want to prostitute the Bride of the Lamb by making her the concubine of the world. There were those who thought that the world was not an enemy, and that some concession on marginal points could prevent the Church from fighting with the world, even as the world waged war against Her. Today those illusions have been disavowed and shown in their inanity by the evidence of the Hierarchy's deliberate complicity with the enemies of Christ: today it is no longer possible to attribute good faith to those who knowingly deprive the clergy and faithful of the spiritual weapons with which to face the confrontation, while they tear down the walls of the Citadel and let in those who besiege it.

How, then, can we face this test? First of all, with a supernatural spirit, understanding that we are facing an epochal clash that involves not only men, but also the infernal powers *quae militant adversus animam.* In the second place, we must pray and act that the authority vested in civil rulers and pastors may once again be an expression of the authority of Christ, which he possesses by divine right both by lineage conquest. In the third place, it is in-dispensable to lay the foundations for a universal reform of the customs and faith of the people—both citizens and faithful alike—in such a way that the errors and betrayals that humanity has perpetuated for at least two centuries may be healed by a return to the divine order—that is, the κόσμος—marked by the conversion of souls and the restoration of the harmony of all things in Christ: *instaurare omnia in Christo*. There is, in fact, a universal harmony willed by the Creator and Redeemer, in which the temporal and spiritual spheres are complementary and not enemies, in which science and faith are sisters as daughters of the same Lord, in which our freedom is fulfilled not in rebellion but in conforming our will to that of God: *fiat voluntas tua sicut in coelo et in terra*. If each of us belongs to the Lord and has His glory and eternal salvation as our sole purpose, the societies of which we are members will also enjoy the benefits, beginning with the Church.

I hope that reading this volume will open the eyes of many, enabling its readers not only to understand the nature and gravity of the present crisis, but also and above all to begin a work of resistance and opposition animated by the supernatural love of both God and neighbor.

+ Carlo Maria Viganò, Archbishop

I was not always a Traditional Catholic. In fact, I did not always attend Mass. For a variety of reasons, I stopped going to church for two and a half years in college despite graduating from a Catholic grade school and high school. I was more or less convinced that when it came to certain political and moral issues, the Church was woefully out of touch and didn't have all the answers, so I was going to decide for myself what to believe. It wasn't until my senior year of college that God inspired me, through different friends, to research what the Church teaches and why She teaches it.

My first wake-up call came after reading various public figures who held different political views than I did. At the time, I was watching the mainstream media for hours on end. I simply resolved to familiarize myself with those who the press said were spreading "disinformation." I wanted to see for myself if they were as fraudulent as they were made out to be.

I immediately started visiting websites, buying books, and watching as many television shows I could that featured "conservative" commentators. After several short weeks, I realized—much to my surprise—that I actually agreed with them on a number of issues. I soon came to view the liberal journalists and organizations I previously supported as the enemies not only of the United States but of the Church itself. I began to understand that they were advancing a sinister agenda directly opposed to Catholic doctrinal, moral, and social teachings.

More than a few of my friends were shocked that I so drastically and so suddenly changed my perspective. After all, I campaigned and voted for Barack Obama just one year earlier in 2008. I did the same for Democratic Senator John Kerry during his own presidential bid in 2004. Some of those relationships were damaged beyond repair as a result of my apostasy.

When it came to my faith, I began to read Pope Benedict x vi and Catholic author George Weigel. I also started watching videos of Fr Robert Barron and acquainted myself with the Michigan-based Acton Institute, an internationally known think tank that analyzes economics and cultural events from a Biblical perspective.

Before I knew it, my entire worldview was flipped on its head. The Church was drawing on more than a thousand years of philosophical and theological insights for Her positions. I simply couldn't find a way to disprove them. My naive complaints couldn't hold a candle to what I was learning. It became apparent that it was me, and not the Church, who was in the wrong, and that it was I who needed to change.

⋟

After completing my undergraduate degree, I moved to Illinois in January 2010 to study at Loyola University Chicago. I realized after just several days that I had very little in common with my pro-LGBT classmates and instructors. While most of them were entirely friendly people, I was the lone "conservative Catholic" in the entire program.

Although I didn't grasp everything that term implied back then (nor did I understand all the theological battles taking place among the clergy), I knew the Church was under attack by forces wanting to change Her teachings and that I needed to defend them in whatever way I could.

It's not hard to guess what conservative Catholics generally believe. Among other things, they steadfastly support the Church's teachings against homosexual "marriage," abortion, transgenderism, and similar issues. Conservative Catholics also tend to consider John Paul II one of if not the greatest popes in Church history. Some even refer to him as "St John Paul the Great." Mother Teresa and Pope Benedict XVI are likewise held in high esteem, as is the Divine Mercy devotion. Many conservative Catholics read the *National Catholic Register* and watch EWTN and Fox News.

While conservative Catholics admit that there are many problems in the Church today, they think the solution will come when bishops implement the Second Vatican Council in the way it was allegedly intended. The so-called spirit of Vatican II that dissident clergy got carried away by in the 1970s and 80s is responsible for the massive drop off in vocations and shuttered parishes and schools, not the Council itself, many argue. Catholics simply need to be re-catechized on what made Vatican II the historic accomplishment it really was. The Latin or "Extraordinary Form" of the Mass might be fine for those who are "attached" to it, many conservatives also maintain, but a reverent *Novus Ordo* liturgy is also beautiful and can even "enrich" the Latin Mass.

When I was attending Loyola, I was hired as an intern for the Archdiocese of Chicago, which was run by Francis Cardinal George (1937–2015). Many conservatives considered him to be one of the most intellectually gifted, orthodox churchmen in the United States. He was often compared to German Cardinal Joseph Ratzinger (1927–2022), i.e., Benedict XVI.

Thanks to persons who God put into my life at that time, I started making connections with like-minded individuals, including professors, bloggers, and public intellectuals. I also attended symposiums and academic gatherings organized by conservative Catholics that promoted the view that limited government, market-based economics, "Judeo-Christian values," and the principles of America's founding could save Western Civilization.

꙳

When I moved back to West Michigan in 2011, I rented a room at a friend's house on the south side of the town I grew up in. He was working at a bank while I was hired as a part-time political science instructor at two community colleges. On weekends, my friend would lead Sunday school at the diocesan church down the road. One day, he discovered that the book the priest was making him teach from included a quote from Mother Teresa that seemed rather odd.

"Hey, look at this," he said. "She doesn't want non-Catholics to be Catholic. She just wants Muslims 'to be a better Muslim' and Hindus 'to be a better Hindu.'"[1]

"Really?" I replied. "That doesn't seem right."

Puzzled, my friend asked his priest how those remarks lined up with Christ's command to go forth and teach all nations the Gospel. We also contacted some of our closest Catholic friends from college to see what they thought.

"Christ's words are no doubt true," the priest replied, "but the Church today practices ecumenism and inter-religious dialogue. The popes are simply asking Catholics to not proselytize and instead be witnesses to their faith. We need to find visible unity with our separated Christian brothers, not criticize them. Just do what the popes do and you'll be fine."

Our friends re-iterated those remarks, though oddly warned us to "not go down" that rabbit hole.

"Just know the Holy Spirit is guiding the Church," they said.

We were rather confused by these remarks, as our main concern had not been addressed. What we were hearing basically amounted to "sit down, be quiet, and do what you're told." Given that the Catholic religion is one of both faith and reason, we looked elsewhere for answers.

In the weeks that followed, my friend and I came across a handful of videos about ecumenism, Vatican II, the Latin Mass, and similar topics on YouTube. I had only vaguely heard about the Latin Mass growing up and assumed the English-language liturgy I had been attending my entire life was the same

---

1 This quote is confirmed by Mother Teresa's biographer Navin Chawla, author of *Mother Teresa: The Authorized Biography*, Element Books, 1991. See the following article: "'I convert you to be a better Hindu, a better Christian, a better Muslim,'" The Economic Times, September 5, 2016, https://web.archive.org/web/20201112013658/https://economictimes.indiatimes.com/blogs/et-commentary/73995/

thing but just in a different language. It didn't take long to learn how wrong I was, as the two have completely different rubrics, prayers, readings, feast days, and more! Sadly, I came to learn that the reason why the Vatican created the new, watered down Mass in the 1960s was because it wanted to improve relations with Protestants.

As far as ecumenism goes, I didn't have a clue about what that entailed. In fact, when my friend and I watched those videos for the first time, I told him, "these are all conspiracy theories. That one bishop is talking about Freemasonry. He thinks the Church is 'infiltrated' and that the world is run by a shadow government trying to corrupt Her doctrines. Why are we wasting our time on this? This is the devil trying to get us to doubt Our Lord's promises!"

Despite my initial negativity, I wanted to better understand what the Church taught on those subjects. Simply putting my head in the sand wasn't an option. Furthermore, I did not possess a great grasp of Church history, especially of the Second Vatican Council, which was held from 1962 until 1965 in St Peter's Basilica. Nor was I aware of everything John Paul II did. In fact, in one of the videos I watched, he was praying at the tomb of Mahatma Gandhi, a Hindu. John Paul bizarrely referred to him as a "hero of humanity" and claimed his example could lead to a "new world order" based on "a civilization of love."[2]

"Maybe John Paul *is* doing things his predecessors didn't," I began to wonder. "But how could that be? Jesus said the gates of hell won't prevail against the Church. Whatever the truth is, I'll pray that God will lead me to it."

From that moment on I was determined to get to the bottom of "conservative Catholicism."

One of the first books I read that started me on the road out of conservative Catholicism and into Traditional Catholicism was *The Popes Against Modern Errors.* Published by TAN Books in 1999, it is a collection of encyclicals and other papal letters issued before Vatican II.

Although I already knew who Pope Leo XIII was, most of the other names in that book—Gregory XVI, Pius IX, St Pius X, and Pius XI—were totally foreign to me. Rarely, if ever, did any of the conservative Catholic authors and media personalities I looked up to reference them in their articles, interviews, books, and speeches. I also couldn't recall a single high school or

2 John Paul II, Address On Occasion of The Visit to The Funerary Monument of Raj Ghat Dedicated To Mahatma Gandhi, Delhi, India, February 1, 1986, Vatican website, https://www.vatican.va/content/john-paul-ii/en/speeches/1986/february/documents/hf_jp-ii_spe_19860201_raj-ghat.html

college instructor who alluded to them. Everything I knew about the Church began and ended with the Second Vatican Council, John Paul II in particular.

Of the many documents included in that book, Leo's 1891 *Rerum Novarum* was most familiar to me as it was constantly being praised by mainstream Catholic writers for its insights on economics. At the same time, none of them had ever mentioned *Humanum Genus*, his 1884 encyclical where he accused Freemasonry of being a "fatal plague" on society because its "ultimate purpose" is the "destruction of holy Church" and "the utter overthrow of that whole religious and political order of the world which the Christian teaching has produced."

And here I was thinking Freemasons were just nice old men who helped build hospitals!

I also had not come across Leo's 1888 encyclical *Libertas Praestantissimum*, which repudiated separation of Church and State, condemned the principle that "every man is free to profess … any religion or none," and taught that "it is contrary to reason that error and truth should have equal rights."

"Why doesn't anyone on EWTN talk about this?" I asked my friend in anger. "This is hard hitting and exactly how the Church should be speaking today."

I was also unaware of Pope Gregory XVI's 1832 encyclical *Mirari Vos*. It denounced not only what he called the "perverse opinion" that one can obtain salvation "by the profession of any kind of religion" but also "the freedom to publish any writings whatever and disseminate them." The Church opposes "immoderate freedom of opinion, license of free speech, and desire for novelty" because they lead to the "corruption of youths" and "contempt of sacred things and holy laws," he explained.

As an American, I was shocked the first time I read those words, as the United States Constitution wholeheartedly affirms the opposite. I never considered our founding principles to be anything other than universal truths.

Gregory's remarks also stand in contrast to *Dignitatis Humanae*, Vatican II's document on religious liberty that claims "religious communities should not be prohibited from … [showing] the special value of their doctrine" in public.[3]

In totality, those pope's teachings were uniquely penetrating, decidedly counter-cultural, and stunning in their breadth and scope, not to mention politically incorrect and anti-ecumenical. Although many of them are referenced in the essays in this book, you should research them on your own as their tone and tenor are far different than anything the authorities in Rome have produced since Vatican II.

---

3 *Dignitatis Humanae*, 4, 1965, Vatican website, https://www.vatican.va/archive/hist_councils/ii_vatican_council/documents/vat-ii_decl_19651207_dignitatis-humanae_en.html

My astonishment reached new heights when I discovered *Mortalium Animos*, which is commonly published in English under the title "On Fostering True Religious Unity."

Written in 1928 by Pope Pius XI, that encyclical taught the exact opposite of what Mother Teresa was quoted as saying in my friend's Sunday School textbook. Below is one of its most widely referenced sections:

> It is clear why this Apostolic See has never allowed its subjects to take part in the assemblies of non-Catholics: for the union of Christians can only be promoted by promoting the return to the one true Church of Christ of those who are separated from it, for in the past they have unhappily left it.

"What is going on?" I asked my friend during dinner one evening. "Pius XI says Catholics are not allowed to participate in 'assemblies' with non-Catholics. But John Paul and Benedict have been doing that for decades! Many bishops also partake in prayer vigils with Protestants and light menorahs with Jewish Rabbis during Advent. How is this permitted if he banned these activities?"

"He is also teaching that non-Catholics need to 'return' to the 'true Church of Christ,'" my friend replied. "That's not what Father told me last month after Sunday school. Nor is that what our college buddies said. They just told us the Church needs to seek 'visible unity' with Protestants. *Mortalium Animos* is calling for their full-on conversion. Do you know if others are aware of these discrepancies?"

※

Neither of us knew exactly what to think at first. Again, we were basically flying blind. As we had done before, we reached out to the most well-educated Catholics we knew. We approached those conversations with an open mind as if there was an obvious explanation for the stark contrast in what popes, saints, and churchmen before the 1960s taught and what their successors put forth in the decades that followed. To our dismay, our inquiries were met with immediate hostilities.

"Are you more Catholic than the pope?" we were told on several occasions. "John Paul and Benedict aren't promoting anything un-Catholic. They recognize we are all children of God on different stages of this journey to heaven. Non-Catholic Christians are loved by Jesus as much as you and I. You are correct to say that Jesus is 'the Prince of Peace' but the Church officially endorsed ecumenism and religious liberty for all at the Second Vatican Council.

Have you even read its documents?"

Others we knew—even those we were closest to—accused us of acting like Protestants and schismatics, seemingly for nothing more than asking questions.

Exasperated, we turned to those whose hands we had put our faith in years before.

"Surely the leaders of the 'conservative Catholic' movement will be able to explain all this," I said to myself.

My friend and I quickly got to work scouring the internet and conducting an extensive study of pre-Vatican II teachings, as well as the Council's documents themselves. In totality, we read hundreds of essays and books by its most ardent supporters and outspoken critics. Sure enough, what we found mirrored the remarks made by our friends and the priest at the parish down the road.

"The Council implicitly taught that the united church of the future will not come about by a capitulation of the other churches and their absorption into Roman Catholicism," Fr Avery Dulles (1918–2008) boldly asserted in the 1970s.[4] "A basic unity … must replace the idea of conversion, even though conversion retains its meaningfulness for those in conscience motivated to seek it," Fr Joseph Ratzinger wrote in 1966.[5] "We are not trying to make converts," Cardinal Richard Cushing of Boston (1895–1970) shockingly stated in a book published in 1963 at the height of Vatican II.[6]

Other quotations my friend and I came across contained similar remarks. "The deliberate targeting of another Christian or group of Christians for the sole purpose of getting them to reject their church to join another, is not allowed," a press release issued by the United States Conference of Catholic Bishops in 2009 stated. "Some people may feel called in conscience to change from one tradition to another, but 'sheep stealing' is unacceptable."[7]

I quickly learned that this collective disobedience to *Mortalium Animos* was not confined to a handful of clergy; it was actively being promoted by

4 Quoted in "Progressivist Document of the Week: Avery Dulles on the Pan-Religion of Vatican II," Tradition in Action, May 26, 2005, https://www.traditioninaction.org/Progressiv-istDoc/A_005_Dulles_Millennium.htm

5 Josef Ratzinger, *Theological Highlights of Vatican II*, Paulist Press; Rev. ed. edition, 2009, p. 114

6 Rev. Walter M. Abbott, *Twelve Council Fathers*, The Macmillan Company, First Edition, New York, New York, January 1, 1963, p.154

7 Fr Leo Walsh, "USCCB News Release: Christian Unity A Goal, But Won't Happen Overnight, Says USCCB Official In Ecumenism, Interreligious Affairs," United States Conference of Catholic Bishops, September 18, 2009, http://web.archive.org/web/20100109094244/https://www.usccb.org/comm/archives/2009/09-182.shtml

the Vatican itself. God is "at work in us," John Paul II said in an address to Anglicans, Protestants, and the Orthodox during the "Week of Christian Unity" in 1997. He also insisted that "ecumenical developments" should give them "a foretaste of the joy that full communion will bring when it is finally achieved."[8] Benedict XVI repeated that message in 2012. "The Week of Prayer for Christian Unity is in itself one of the most effective expressions of the impetus the Second Vatican Council gave to the search for full communion among all Christ's disciples," he said.[9] Pope Francis has echoed this attitude during his own tenure. In May 2015, he welcomed to the Vatican a delegation from the Lutheran Church of Sweden. He scandalously referred to their leader, Antje Jackelén, as an "archbishop." He also called her his "esteemed sister."[10] That same month, he sent a message to an ecumenical meeting in the United States where he claimed that despite their theological differences, Evangelicals, Orthodox, Lutherans, and Catholics "are one."[11] Barring a miracle, his successor will continue this same mistaken approach.

⁂

For many Catholics today, forging "unity" with "non-Catholic Christians" is far from controversial. After all, Vatican II instructs them to do that, and to be a "conservative" in these times means to be faithful to the Council. *Unitatis Redintegratio*, the Council's document on ecumenism, explicitly states that non-Catholic "ecclesial communities" can "enrich" the "Church of Jesus Christ." *Lumen Gentium* likewise claims that Christ's Church "subsists in the Catholic Church." It also maintains that "many elements of sanctification and truth are found outside of its visible structure." These "elements" are "gifts properly belonging to the Church of Christ" and "impel towards catholic unity."

Taken collectively, Vatican II argues that there is an entity larger than the Catholic Church called "the Church of Christ" and that baptized Catholics, Protestants, and other self-identified Christians are among its members. Catholics should therefore not act "polemically" towards them (i.e., point

8 John Paul II, General Audience During Week of Prayer for Christian Unity, January 22, 1997, Vatican website, https://www.vatican.va/content/john-paul-ii/en/audiences/1997/documents/hf_jp-ii_aud_22011997.html

9 Benedict XVI, General Audience, January 18, 2022, Vatican website, https://www.vatican.va/content/benedict-xvi/en/audiences/2012/documents/hf_ben-xvi_aud_20120118.html

10 John-Henry Westen, "Pope Francis Creates Anticipation for Intercommunion Between Catholics and Lutherans," LifeSiteNews, October 27, 2016, https://www.lifesitenews.com/news/pope-francis-creates-anticipation-for-intercommunion-between-catholics-and/

11 Francis, Video Message on the Occasion of the Day of Christian Unity, Vatican website, May 23, 2015, https://www.vatican.va/content/francesco/en/messages/pont-messages/2015/documents/papa-francesco_20150523_videomessaggio-giornata-unita-cristiana-phoenix.html

out their errors and seek to convert them) but instead work for "visible unity" with "all Christians" so "the Church of Christ" can be fully realized.

Since 1965—the year the Council ended—this novel way of viewing the Church has been adopted in Catholic schools, seminaries, dioceses, and by all who hold high-ranking offices in Rome. To oppose it in any way is to earn immediate ostracization. Pope Francis, in keeping with his predecessors, has shown that he fully embraces it. "Proselytism is solemn nonsense, it makes no sense," he infamously remarked in October 2013.[12] In 2016, while visiting the nation of Georgia south of Russia, he said it is a "very grave sin against ecumenism" for Catholics to try to convert the Orthodox.[13] While still a cardinal, Francis, whose real name is Jorge Mario Bergoglio, urged Pentecostal minister Tony Palmer to not become a Catholic despite the fact that he expressed a great interest in doing so.[14] The Church needs "bridge-builders" to other communities, he told Palmer at the time. Bergoglio made similar remarks in October 2016 during a meeting with Lutheran pilgrims at the Vatican. "It is not licit that you convince them of your faith; proselytism is the strongest poison against the ecumenical path,"[15] he told an 8-year-old girl who asked about converting her friends. In saying this, he was merely being faithful to the Council, but disobedient to Christ's command to "make disciples of all nations."[16]

It became painfully obvious to my friend and I that the Vatican's approach toward non-Catholics since the 1960s was entirely at odds with what it was before. Below are just a few of the many additional references we came across back then. They serve as clear and undeniable proof that conservative Catholic claims that there is "continuity" between the Council and what the Church taught previously is a complete fallacy.

12 Michael Haynes, "Pope Francis Condemns 'Serious Sin' of 'Proselytism' But Has 'No Explanation' For Vocations Crisis," LifeSiteNews, January 16, 2023, https://www.lifesite-news.com/news/pope-francis-condemns-serious-sin-of-proselytism-but-has-no-explanation-for-vocations-crisis/

13 Claire Chretien, "Pope: It's a 'Very Grave Sin' for Catholics to Try to Convert Orthodox," LifeSiteNews, October 4, 2016, https://www.lifesitenews.com/news/pope-very-grave-sin-for-catholics-to-try-to-convert-orthodox/

14 Michael Haynes, "Pope Francis Has a Long Record of Telling People Not to Convert to Catholicism," LifeSiteNews, April 5, 2022, https://www.lifesitenews.com/news/pope-francis-has-a-long-history-of-discouraging-people-from-entering-the-catholic-church/

15 Jan Bentz, "Pope Again Criticizes 'Proselytism': 'It Is Not Licit That You Convince Them of Your Faith'," LifeSiteNews, October 19, 2016, https://www.lifesitenews.com/opinion/pope-to-teen-girl-proselytism-is-the-strongest-poison-against-the-ecumenica/

16 Matthew 28: 19–20

If "those who are separated from Us … humbly beg light from heaven, there is no doubt … they will recognize the one true Church of Jesus Christ and … enter it," Pius XI wrote in 1928.[17] "Those who are divided in faith or government cannot be living in the unity of the true Church of Jesus Christ," Pius XII affirmed in 1943.[18]

Popes of the 19th century said the same thing. In 1899, Leo XIII consecrated the human race to the Sacred Heart of Jesus. The prayer he composed for that occasion begged Christ to be a king to those who are "deceived by erroneous opinions, or whom discord keeps aloof, and call them back to the harbor of truth and unity of faith, so that soon there may be but one flock and one shepherd."[19]

The First Vatican Council, which took place from 1869 until 1870, likewise declared that "the whole multitude of believers should be held together in the unity of faith and communion."[20]

The popes before the Second Vatican Council would have therefore rebuked in the harshest terms possible the Council's strange new definition of the Church of Christ. For them, the "Church of Christ" was synonymous with "the Catholic Church." Like every pope before them, they understood that when Christ prayed "that they all may be one,"[21] He was praying that all men would be Catholic.

Priests and other clergy who lived before Vatican II knew non-Catholics were not in communion with the Church. "Christ established a definite Church to last for the rest of time … and that definite Church of Christ is the Catholic Church. To her men must return," American priests Frs. Leslie Rumble and Charles Carty taught in their popular three-volume *Radio Replies* books in the 1930s and 40s.[22] The series bears the endorsement of Bishop Fulton Sheen (1895–1979). "Separation from the visible Body of Christ is separation from the presence and assistance of the Holy Ghost Who inhabits it," 19th century English Cardinal Henry Edward Manning (1808–1892) likewise

---

17 Pius XI, *Mortalium Animos*, 13, 1928, Vatican website, https://www.vatican.va/content/pius-xi/en/encyclicals/documents/hf_p-xi_enc_19280106_mortalium-animos.html

18 Pius XII, *Mystici Corporis Christi*, 22, 1943, Vatican website, https://www.vatican.va/content/pius-xii/en/encyclicals/documents/hf_p-xii_enc_29061943_mystici-corporis-christi.html

19 "Prayer of Consecration to the Sacred Heart by Pope Leo XIII," Catholic News Agency, https://www.catholicnewsagency.com/resource/55304/prayer-of-consecration-to-the-sacred-heart-by-pope-leo-xiii

20 Session 4, July 18, 1870, First Dogmatic Constitution on the Church of Christ, no. 4

21 John 17: 21

22 Fr Leslie Rumble and Fr Charles Carty, *Radio Replies, Third Volume*, TAN Books and Publishers, Rockford, Illinois, 1942, Reprinted 1979, p.65

said.[23] He also advised Catholics to "choose your friends from among the friends of God. Be not united with any that are separated from Him."[24] Far from inventing his own ecclesiology, Cardinal Manning was simply repeating what St Paul wrote in his Second Letter to the Corinthians: "Do not bear the yoke with unbelievers ... what fellowship hath light with darkness?"[25]

Philippine Cardinal Luis Tagle was therefore entirely correct to admit in 2015 that "the understanding of [the] Church changed radically" at Vatican II.[26]

‏❧

For many Catholics who have never read what the popes who lived before the 1960s said, there can be a certain amount of confusion in seeing just how diametrically opposed they are to what those who came after them have taught. This can be rather unsettling at first. It certainly was for me.

Many times, the initial reaction Catholics will have is to say that while there "appears to be differences" between the pre- and post-Vatican II magisterium, trying to understand the complexities of it all is above their level of expertise. "I'm not a theologian. I just need to stay in a state of grace. I can't worry about this," many well-intending laity who attend diocesan churches have told me over the past eleven years. "I'll pray for the pope and just trust my priest."

Others, usually those who are more educated, will try to rationalize the obvious discontinuities by saying something along the following lines:

> To suggest there is a rupture between the Council's documents and what the preceding popes taught is to make oneself the authority of what passes for tradition. The Council was overseen by the Holy Spirit. Christ promised the gates of hell will not prevail against His Church. If you think the Vatican is at odds with previous popes then you need to re-examine more closely what is being put forth. To be Catholic is to obey the pope!

While it is true that not everyone is obligated to read everything published by the popes before, during, and after the Council to save their soul, what

23 Cardinal Henry Edward Manning, *The Blessed Sacrament*, The Neumann Press, Long Prairie, Minnesota, 1992, p.30

24 Henry Cardinal Edward Manning, *Sin and Its Consequences*, TAN Books and Publishers, Rockford, Illinois, 1986, p.66

25 2 Corinthians, Chapter 6:14–15

26 Joshua McElwee, "Cardinal Tagle: Church should not look to 'idealized past' with nostalgia," National Catholic Reporter, May 22, 2015, https://web.archive.org/web/20150612093622/http://ncronline.org/news/global/cardinal-tagle-church-should-not-look-idealized-past-nostalgia

is undeniable is that Catholics have a duty to know their faith as best they can. "Be ready to explain to everyone who asketh you a reason for the hope which is in you," 1 Peter 3:15 says. Put another way, God has created us to live in these times for a reason, and that reason is to take up the heavy cross of trying to understand the perplexing situation of officials in Rome since the 1960s saying and doing the exact opposite of their predecessors.

Catholics today must realize that they have to make a choice, a choice as to what they are going to follow. Will they, like many conservative Catholics, submit to the novel teachings of the Council and in so doing put themselves in direct disobedience to the popes who reigned before the 1960s? Or will they, as Traditional Catholics do, obey the popes and magisterium prior to then and consequently oppose those who are and have occupied positions of power in the Vatican since the close of the Council? This is not a both/and scenario but an either/or one.

The gravity of this dilemma is made all the more clear by the following quotations, which support the argument that there has been a real, substantive change in what passes for the Catholic religion since the 1960s.

In his 2018 book *The Disputed Teachings of Vatican II*, Fr Thomas Guarino rightly admits that "the Council represents a significant volte-face on ecumenism." Pius XI's *Mortalium Animos* "casts doubt on the entire ecumenical enterprise," he writes. It "forbids Catholics from engaging in the movement." On the other hand, Vatican II's *Unitatis Redintegratio* "warmly welcomes ecumenism." The "discontinuity between the two documents is the source of consternation for some Catholics." [27]

John Paul himself told Lutherans visiting the Vatican in 1999 that the "common spiritual space is larger than many of the denominational barriers that still separate us." [28] He also once praised Protestant heretic Martin Luther (1483–1546) for having a "deep religiosity." [29]

Similarly, Bishop Robert Barron on his popular *Word on Fire* website has admitted that he always had a "certain fascination" with Luther and

27 Quoted in "The Vatican and the Ecumenical Movement: From Stern Condemnation to Enthusiastic Approval," Novus Ordo Watch, July 1, 2022, https://novusordowatch.org/2022/07/vatican-ecumenical-movement-condemnation-approval/

28 John Paul II, Address to the President of the World Lutheran Federation, December 9, 1999, Vatican website, https://www.vatican.va/content/john-paul-ii/en/speeches/1999/december/documents/hf_jp-ii_spe_09121999_lutheran-fed.html

29 Letter to Cardinal Giovanni Willebrands, In Commemoration of the 500th Anniversary of Matin Luther's birth, October 13, 1983, Vatican website, https://www.vatican.va/content/john-paul-ii/it/letters/1983/documents/hf_jp-ii_let_19831031_card-willebrands.html. Also see Henry Kamm, "Pope Praises Luther In An Appeal For Unity on Protest Anniversary," New York Times, November 6, 1983, https://www.nytimes.com/1983/11/06/world/pope-praises-luther-in-an-appeal-for-unity-on-protest-anniversary.html

that he has been reading his books, speeches, and sermons for many years. Luther is "cantankerous, pious, very funny, shockingly anti-Semitic, deeply insightful, and utterly exasperating," Barron embarrassingly confesses. His writings "crackle with life and intensity." He was "a mystic of grace" who was arguably "right to express his ecstatic experience of the divine love" in his "distinctive way."[30]

Before going any further, imagine if a prominent public figure like a president or a governor praised a mass murderer for something they wrote in years past. There would be outrage across the country and an increasing number of lawmakers would call on him to resign. But this is exactly what Barron has done. Luther was a killer, and a killer of the worst kind: he was a destroyer of souls whose poisonous ideas led—and still lead—countless persons away from the Catholic faith and into the arms of the devil.

The great pontiffs who were alive when Luther was spreading his heresies knew this. They rebuked him in the harshest way possible. "We likewise condemn, reprobate, and reject completely the books and all [of his] writings and sermon[s]," Pope Leo x declared in his 1520 bull *Exsurge Domine.* His ideas are "heretical, false, scandalous, or offensive to pious ears." Luther's essays are to be "burned publicly and solemnly." No Catholic may "read, assert, preach, praise, print, publish, or defend them," he added. Against the Roman Church, Leo further declared, "lying teachers are rising, introducing ruinous sects, and drawing upon themselves speedy doom. Their tongues are fire … full of deadly poison. They have bitter zeal, contention in their hearts, and boast and lie against the truth."

Imagine if we had a pope (or bishops) who spoke like this today! Oh, what a great treasure we have been deprived of.

At any rate, Fr Francis Sullivan (1922–2019), who was not a Traditionalist, acknowledged in 1983 that "on several important issues the council clearly departed from previous papal teaching."[31] The liberal co-authors of the 1969 book *Dissent in and For the Church* also correctly recalled that Pius XII repeatedly taught that the Mystical Body of Christ was "identical with the Roman Catholic Church." They also observed that Vatican II "produced a different teaching" on that subject, namely, that "the mystical body of Christ cannot be simply identifiable with the Roman Catholic Church."[32]

30 Bishop Robert Barron, "Looking at Luther With Fresh Eyes," Word on Fire, June 13, 2017, https://www.wordonfire.org/articles/barron/looking-at-luther-with-fresh-eyes/

31 Francis A. Sullivan, sj, *Magisterium: Teaching Authority in the Catholic Church,* Mahwah, NY: Paulist Press, 1983, p. 157

32 Charles Curran, Robert Hunt, etc., *Dissent in and For the Church: Theologians and Humanae Vitae,* Sheed & Ward, New York, 1969, p. 80

Catholics today are thus being told that not only were Pius XII, Leo X, and all of the other pre-Vatican II popes flat out wrong in their magisterial teachings but that the Holy Ghost can somehow inspire the Church to teach something She previously condemned. This is simply not possible according to the dogma of the indefectibility of the Church. As Vatican I affirms, "This See of St Peter always remains unblemished by any error, in accordance with the divine promise of Our Lord and Savior to the prince of His disciples." St Pius X also observed in 1908 that "to follow and obey the Successor of St Peter with the greatest faith" is of the "highest importance to the safeguarding of Catholic truth.[33]

Since Vatican II did not follow and did not obey the Successors of St Peter who reigned in the years, decades, and centuries prior to the Council, Catholics today are not obligated to follow or obey *it*.

❧

There is much more that can be said about the Council and the rotten fruit it has produced over the past six decades. An exhaustive presentation of everything it touched on is not practical for this introduction, as many of those topics are discussed in Chapter IV. Still, a shortened explanation as to what it truly "accomplished" seems helpful in order to set the stage for the essays herein.

In brief, Vatican II was a Color Revolution in the Catholic Church. It is the seven-headed hydra that acts as the font from which many of the problems in our time flows. As it is often said: "So goes the Church, so goes the world."

The Second Vatican Council could have been a grand and glorious event that ushered in a new Christendom in the post-World War II era had it put love of God instead of human respect and earthly prestige first. But it did the opposite. Among other things, Vatican II should have consecrated Russia to the Immaculate Heart of Mary and condemned the scourge of atheistic communism. It should have also upheld Scholastic theology, anathematized neo-modernism, and aggressively defended the Social Kingship of Christ by launching a more concerted counter-revolution based on the principles of Catholic Action as laid out by the popes in the late 19th and early 20th centuries. Finally, it should have carefully revised its liturgical practices while inviting Jews and non-Catholics in the East and West to return to the Barque of Peter.

Instead, Vatican II gave the world and its most powerful interest groups whatever they wanted. "The Second Vatican Council will be an act of charity

33 St Pius X, *Tuum illud*, 1908, Quoted in "Newman Reader," The National Institute for Newman Studies https://newmanreader.org/canonization/popes/acta10mar08.html

to our separated brethren—Orthodox, Anglicans, and Protestants," Belgian Cardinal Leo Suenens (1904–1996) once admitted.[34] For the Russians and the Orthodox, the Council embraced collegiality and refused to mention communism by name. For the Western World, the United States in particular, it endorsed religious liberty. For the Jews, it declared that their covenant with God has not been abrogated and that they are not collectively responsible for the death of Christ.[35] For Protestants, Vatican II elevated the laity while diminishing the priesthood. It also refused to issue a stand alone document on Mary and adopted a number of Luther's reforms for its new Mass. Lastly, for Freemasons and the rest of mankind, the Council made dialogue and concern for human dignity its primary focus.

To put it in as blunt terms as possible, Vatican II was a theological vasectomy that stripped the Church of its virility. In place of a relatively healthy and vibrant institution, it installed a cancer-stricken, emaciated body double, a counterfeit puppet church that today acts as the spiritual arm of the New World Order by lending its imprimatur to international institutions and corrupt individuals who are imposing a globalist, social justice-driven agenda.

What seems to have happened from 1962 until 1965 was the setting up of a false religion inside the juridical structures of the Church by men whose ideas were condemned by multiple popes before the Council. Had these spiritual adulterers erected worship centers of their own, they would be on the verge of dying out by now. But like any adaptive parasite that feeds off its host for survival, they continue to live on *within* the Church's institutions by passing themselves off as Catholics and by promoting and covering up for one another. They retain power by indoctrinating laity with the myths told by their liberal forefathers about how the Council was a return to the "sources" of the "early Church" that brought about a much needed "updating."

This newly created Conciliar Church, which now calls itself a "Synodal Church," is a subservient colony of the planet's international elite. It has been given the same task as the Roman soldiers who were commissioned by the Sanhedrin to stand guard over the entombed Body of Christ to prevent it from rising. It mocks, spits in the face of, and attacks Traditional Catholicism with help from a supportive Deep State as well as secular and Catholic news outlets. Well-placed allies in politics also ensure that Tradition is not spoken about in a positive light. Accusations of being "rigid," "schismatic,"

---

34 Rev. Walter M. Abbott, *Twelve Council Fathers,* The Macmillan Company, First Edition, New York, New York, January 1, 1963, p. 41

35 Pontifical Commission for Religious Relations with the Jews, "The Gifts of God Are Irrevocable," December 10, 2015, See https://www.ewtn.com/catholicism/library/gifts-of-god-are-irrevocable-2478

"anti-Semitic," and "promoting conspiracy theories" are some of the more common—though entirely baseless—smears used to pressure laity and clergy today so they do not leave the Conciliar concentration camp they have been unknowingly imprisoned in.

Regrettably, the many falsehoods spewed by Vatican II apologists on a daily basis have succeeded in brainwashing otherwise innocent Catholics into thinking the Council really was an unleashing of the Holy Spirit and that what they adhere to today is a more robust version of the faith than the so-called "pray, pay, and obey" variant their parents and grandparents practiced.[36] In truth, when laity walk into Catholic churches and diocesan schools today, what they are being given is not the real faith but a deracinated, toothless, knockoff version.

≥

Most Catholics are wholly unaware that this is what has happened in the Church. It takes a special grace from God to understand it. As Archbishop Carlo Maria Viganò has explained, the Conciliar Church is a "subversive organization born almost imperceptibly from the Council and which in these sixty years has almost totally eclipsed the Church of Christ by occupying her highest levels and usurping her authority." [37]

In many ways, this is the grandest illusion in the history of the world. Satan has tricked Catholics into following a false religion by turning their virtue of obedience against them. Yet God did not fail to foresee this. Not only does Scripture instruct us to "test all things"[38] and to not follow even "an angel from heaven"[39] if it does not preach the Gospel, the Holy Ghost has raised up multiple men in recent decades to help us through this crisis.

"In the measure in which the Pope, the bishops, priests or faithful adhere to this new church, they separate themselves from the Catholic Church," French Archbishop Marcel Lefebvre (1905–1991), the founder of the Traditionalist Priestly Society of St Pius X (SSPX), once remarked.[40] "It is, therefore, a strict

36 "Researcher says days of Catholics who 'pay, pray and obey' are gone," Catholic Review, Archdiocese of Baltimore, January 19, 2012, https://www.archbalt.org/researcher-says-days-of-catholics-who-pay-pray-and-obey-are-gone/

37 Archbishop Carlo Maria Viganò, "Abp Viganò Blasts 'Total Self-Referentiality of the 'Conciliar Church' in Response to Papal Homily," Catholic Family News, October 28, 2022, https://catholicfamilynews.com/blog/2022/10/28/abp-vigano-blasts-the-total-self-referential-ity-of-the-conciliar-church-in-response-to-papal-homily/

38 1 Thessalonians 5:21

39 Galatians 1:8

40 Quoted in Bishop Tissier de Mallerais, "Is There A Conciliar Church?" Dominicans of Avrille, Originally published as hand-written letter of Archbishop Lefebvre to friends on July 29, 1976, reproduced in Sel de la Terre, Number 36, p.10, https://dominicansavrille.us/is-

duty for every priest who wants to remain Catholic to separate off from this Conciliar Church for as long as it does not rediscover the Tradition of the Church and of the Catholic Faith."[41]

Bishop Bernard Tissier de Mallerais, who was one of the four priests Archbishop Lefebvre consecrated in 1988 against the Vatican's wishes, echoed those remarks in 2012. "The irregularity is not ours. It is that of Rome. A Modernist Rome. A Liberal Rome that has renounced Christ the King. A Rome that had been condemned in advance by all popes up until the eve of the Council," he said. He also clarified that "we [the SSPX] do not want any compromise with this religion, any risk of corruption, not even any appearance of conciliation, and it is this appearance that our so-called 'regularization' would give us."[42]

Archbishop Viganò has similarly stated that Catholics today are "authorized in conscience to revoke our obedience to someone who, presenting himself as pope, is in reality acting like the Biblical wild boar in the Lord's vineyard."[43]

To repeat, many well-meaning and zealous souls are not aware of even 1/10th of what the Council did or said, partly because it produced sixteen ambiguously written documents totaling hundreds of pages in length. Far fewer Catholics know what the Church taught before the 1960s, so they just go along with what this bishop, that priest, or some lay author or social media influencer says about it, having never been made aware of the fact that what those persons are telling them is, as Chapter IV will show, the end result of a liberal *coup d'etat* carried out by dissident clergy.[44]

Despite the good intentions of many priests and laity who are trying to make the best of the awful situation in the Church by putting a positive spin on the Council and by "giving the benefit of the doubt" to the obviously heretical remarks of those who wield power in Rome these days, such efforts amount putting lipstick on a pig. Archbishop Viganò spoke the truth when he observed that "not a single one of the Saints, Doctors of the Church, or Popes, up to and including Pius XII... would approve anything of what is

there-a-conciliar-church/
41 Archbishop Marcel Lefebvre, *Spiritual Journey*, Angelus Press, Kansas City, Missouri, 2011, p.17
42 Augustinus, "Bishop Tissier de Mallerais: "The Irregularity Is That Of Rome, A Modernist Rome," Rorate Caeli, June 13, 2012, https://rorate-caeli.blogspot.com/2012/06/bishop-tissier-de-mallerais.html
43 Archbishop Carlo Maria Viganò, "Aspicite nobis illusiones," Exsurge Domine, December 27, 2023, https://exsurgedomine.it/231209-aspicite-fra/
44 See Robert Nugent, *Silence Speaks: Teilhard de Chardin, Yves Congar, John Courtney Murray, and Thomas Merton,* Paulist Press, January 3, 2011 and Barry Hudock, *Struggle, Condemnation, Vindication: John Courtney Murray's Journey toward Vatican II,* Liturgical Press, Collegeville, Minnesota, 2015.

currently happening in the Vatican."[45] The Council "should be forgotten 'as such and en bloc.'"[46]

꧁

The goal of the essays contained in this book is twofold. First, to help Catholics see the crisis in the Church for what it is so they can know how to respond to it. Second, to provide future historians with a time capsule so that when the dust has settled on this tragic period in the Church's history Catholics will be able to look back and recognize the extent of the errors God allowed to be spread by those claiming to be His representatives on earth. An autopsy report, in other words, is needed so generations yet unborn will know how great the devil's influence was and the lengths true followers of Our Lord went in order to preserve the faith. It is my hope that Catholics in the decades ahead will not allow similar mistakes to be made if it be within their ability and God's will to prevent them from happening again.

The title of this book is *Navigating the Crisis in the Church: Essays in Defense of Traditional Catholicism*. It may rightly be wondered: what does the "crisis" in the Church consist of beyond what has already been said? Moreover, what is "Traditional Catholicism" and what should faithful Catholics do in these times?

Father Mattias Gaudron of the Society of St Pius x argues that the crisis is due to, among other things, a lack of belief. Not only are "the number of those who consider themselves to belong to the Church diminishing, but even the majority of those who are officially members of the Church no longer hold the Catholic faith!" he has said. He also contends that when a man loses his faith he "no longer believes that he is called to moral perfection." He will then "inevitably yield ... more and more to the unregulated pleasures of this life." This is evident, he recalls, in the fact that the behavior of Catholics today "differs little from that of the children of this world." This is all caused by what he calls "the crisis of the clergy."[47]

St Alphonsus Liguori (1696–1787) is one of my favorite saints. He had

45 Archbishop Carlo Maria Viganò, "Archbishop Viganò: Every saint and Doctor of the Church would stand against today's Vatican," LifeSiteNews, November 6, 2023, https://www.lifesitenews.com/opinion/archbishop-vigano-every-saint-and-doctor-of-the-church-would-stand-against-todays-vatican/

46 Matt Gaspers, "Abp Viganò to Sandro Magister: 'I Do Not Find Anything Reprehensible in Suggesting We Should Forget Vatican II," Catholic Family News, July 6, 2020, https://catholicfamilynews.com/blog/2020/07/06/abp-vigano-to-sandro-magister-i-do-not-find-anything-reprehensible-in-suggesting-we-should-forget-vatican-ii/

47 Fr Matthias Gaudron, *The Catechism of the Crisis in the Church,* Angelus Press, Kansas City, Missouri, 2010, pp. 5–6

such an impact on me when I was a younger man that I wrote a book about him in my late thirties.[48] In 1732, he founded the Redemptorist Order to help the most abandoned souls living in the desolate Italian countryside. There are many parallels between the work he did in those isolated areas and the thankless efforts Traditional clergy are doing now for small groups of devout Catholics in remote locations and in dilapidated Mass centers across the world.

Among other things, St Alphonsus was acutely aware of the connection between the sanctity of the priest and the holiness of the laity. "The good morals and the salvation of the people depend on good pastors," he once wrote. "If there is a good priest in charge of the parish, you will soon see devotion flourishing and people frequenting the Sacraments and honoring the practice of mental prayer. Hence the proverb: like pastor, like parish."[49]

In a private letter, Alphonsus noted that, "if, by chance, for our great misfortune, we should get a pope that does not have the glory of God as his sole purpose, the Lord will not help him greatly and things from their present condition will go from bad to worse."[50] He also said that if a pope were to be "manifestly and exteriorly heretical" he would be "deposed" of his office "by Jesus Christ" and the Church would declare that he had fallen from his pontificate.[51]

It is as if he was speaking for our own time!

Fr Gaudron makes the additional point that the crisis today is distinct from those of the past because it is "the highest [authorities]" in the Vatican who have "unleashed this crisis, who maintain it, and who prevent the implementation of effective measures of its resolution." He further argues that while there have been immoral popes in previous centuries "never, as in our times, have errors and the public negation of truths of the Faith been spread abroad thanks to the tolerance, approbation, and even the active effort of the Roman authorities and the episcopate throughout the world. This is the peculiar characteristic of the current crisis."[52]

48 Stephen Kokx, *St Alphonsus for the 21st Century: A Handbook for Holiness*, St Peter's Press, September 2023

49 Jean-Baptiste Chautard, *The Soul of the Apostolate*, TAN Books, Rockford, Illinois, 2008, p.41

50 Quoted in Father John Zuhlsdorf, "A saint on the wretched condition of the Church while waiting for a new Pope to be elected.," Fr Z's blog, February 17, 2013, https://wdtprs. com/2013/02/a-saint-on-the-wretched-condition-of-the-church-while-waiting-for-a-new-pope-to-be-elected/

51 Quoted in "On the Deposition of the Pope—continued (Part 2 of 2)," Dominicans of Avrille, Originally published in *Le Sel de la Terre*, No. 90, Fall 2014, https://dominicansavrille. us/on-the-deposition-of-the-pope-part-2-of-2/

52 Fr Matthias Gaudron, *The Catechism of the Crisis in the Church*, Angelus Press, Kansas City, Missouri, 2010, p.8

≈

As has already been shown, two of the main "errors" being "spread abroad" by "the highest authorities" in the Vatican are 1) the Council's heretical understanding of Christian unity and 2) its blasphemous redefinition of what constitutes "the Church of Christ." Many of the essays in this book, especially those in Chapter 11, expose the sacrilegious practices that have been carried out as a result of those changes.

A third error is religious liberty, a subject that took me more than three years of intense and determined study in the face of a mountain of misinformation and empty platitudes from conservative Catholics to fully comprehend. Time does not allow me to discuss all the twists and turns involved in that particular journey, but one episode is worth drawing attention to before concluding this admittedly lengthy preface.

In 2012, the friend I was living with emailed me a video of George Weigel during an appearance on Raymond Arroyo's EWTN program *The World Over.* A young man had called into the show asking about the Kingship of Christ. Weigel's response confirmed my worst fear: that there wasn't anything conservative about "conservative Catholicism."

"The state is incompetent to make theological judgments ... it does not have the capacity to make the judgment that Christ is King," Weigel shamelessly remarked. "A state that could say 'Christ is King' is a state that could say 'Charles III' or 'George VI' [is King] or [that] Oprah Winfrey is Queen," he further chortled. "As John Paul II would say, as the Second Vatican Council would say ... that's simply not the business of the state."[53]

I pulled out my copy of Pius XI's 1925 encyclical *Quas Primas* and found a section I had underlined several times before: Christ's "kingly dignity demands that the State should take account of the commandments of God and of Christian principles, both in making laws and in administering justice," it read.

Leo XIII likewise taught that the state is obligated by its own lights to recognize Christ's sovereignty over it. His 1885 encyclical *Immortale Dei* notes the following:

> The State, constituted as it is, is clearly bound to act up to the manifold and weighty duties linking it to God, by the public profession of religion. Nature and reason, which command every individual devoutly to worship God in holiness ... bind also the civil community by a like law. For, men living together in society are under the power of God no less

---

53 The New Cafeteria, "George Weigel mocks the Social Kingship of Christ on EWTN - The World Over," May 3, 2009, https://www.youtube.com/watch?v=LqZ2ybiDlaw

than individuals are, and society, no less than individuals, owes gratitude to God who gave it being and maintains it and whose ever bounteous goodness enriches it with countless blessings.

Leo's teachings were affirmed by his successor St Pius X in 1905. "The Creator of man is also the Founder of human societies, and preserves their existence as He preserves our own. We owe Him, therefore, not only a private cult, but a public and social worship to honor Him." It is a "pernicious error" to believe "the State must be separated from the Church."[54]

Despite these unambiguous declarations being part of the Church's ordinary and universal magisterium, their complete opposite has been embraced in the post-Vatican II era thanks to *Dignitatis Humanae*, the Council's document on religious liberty.

"States must be secular. Confessional states end badly. That goes against the grain of history," Jorge Bergoglio said in a 2016 interview where he echoed comments made by his predecessors Joseph Ratzinger and Karol Wojtyła. "I believe that a version of laicity accompanied by a solid law guaranteeing religious freedom offers a framework for going forward."[55]

Even a cursory glance at the cultural and political landscape over the past half-century indicates that this arrangement cannot and has not prevented the proliferation of heresy and sin. Either Christ reigns or chaos does. There is no middle ground. Archbishop Lefebvre knew this. He once said that, "in the lands of 'liberty,' the so-called people's democracies, there is really the tyranny of democracy. There is no longer [the] question of truth or error … experience has shown the contrary: it is easier to do evil than good … that is why, when one grants this liberty, it is error that gains."[56]

Aside from the disastrous consequences *Dignitatis Humanae* has had on Catholic countries across the world since the close of the Council, equally egregious was how its proponents basically lied to get it approved.

I myself was always told *Dignitatis Humanae* represented a "development" rooted in the "dignity of the human person" and that previous papal teachings on religious liberty and Church-State relations could be ignored because

54 St Pius X, *Vehementor Nos*, 3, 1906, Vatican website, https://www.vatican.va/content/pius-x/en/encyclicals/documents/hf_p-x_enc_11021906_vehementer-nos.html

55 Gerard O'Connell, "Pope in La Croix interview: The State Must Respect People's Consciences" America Magazine, May 17, 2016, https://www.americamagazine.org/content/dispatches/pope-la-croix-interview-state-must-respect-peoples-consciences

56 Archbishop Marcel Lefebvre, *Against the Heresies*, Angelus Press, Kansas City, Missouri, 1997, p.168

they were written in an "impulsive" manner and for a particular "historical context" that no longer exists.

Fr John A. Coleman sj of Loyola Marymount University has admitted that while *Dignitatis Humanae* "evokes" a "development of doctrine, it fails to state and justify any explicit theory of development of doctrine."[57] British theologian Fr Aiden Nichols o p is of a similar opinion. *Dignitatis Humanae* "occasions a genuine difficulty for orthodox Catholics. ... it is not immediately apparent how to reconcile its acknowledgement of the traditional teaching about the Christendom State with its development of the teaching about the freedom of the act of faith."[58] Liberal US priest Fr John Courtney Murray (1904–1967), who was one of the documents' main architects, also drew attention to the theological problems it presented. In 1967, just two years after the Council, he said "the course of the development between the *Syllabus of Errors* (1864) and *Dignitatis Humanae Personae* (1965) still remains to be explained by theologians."[59]

Despite noble attempts in recent years by men wanting to show how this profound change actually was an organic evolution of doctrine, none of them have been able to do so.[60] Perhaps this is because, as Vatican ii foot soldier Kenneth Whitehead (1930–2015) confessed in a moment of candor in 2011, the "Council Fathers were evidently prepared to take the risk of allowing some [theological] loopholes in the interests of establishing the general principle of freedom from coercion in matters of religious belief and practice."[61]

Well, the mainstream church today is reaping what the Council's "loopholes" sowed. The Priestly Society of St Pius x was entirely correct to point out in 2012 that the dire situation Catholics are facing from secular governments across the world today stems directly from the Council's decision to no longer defend the Kingship of Christ.

57 John A. Coleman, sj "Religious Liberty," America Magazine, November 28, 2005, http://www.americamagazine.org/issue/552/article/religious-liberty

58 Moyra Doorly and Fr Aidan Nichols, o p, *The Council in Question: A Dialogue with Traditional Catholicism*, t a n Books, Charlotte, North Carolina, 2011, p.102

59 Quoted in Michael Davies, *Archbishop Lefebvre and Religious Liberty*, t a n Books and Publishers, Rockford, Illinois, p.13. First cited in Rev. Walter M. Abbot, *The Documents of Vatican ii*, America Press, 1967, p.673

60 Archbishop Charles Chaput described *Dignitatis Humanae* as having "profoundly changed" Church teachings in his book *Render Unto Caesar*, Doubleday, New York, 2008, p.129. See Gregory Dubois, "'A Failure to Achieve the Impossible': Critiquing Prof. Thomas Pink's explanation of religious liberty," WM Review, December 29, 2023, https://wmreview.co.uk/2023/12/29/a-failure-to-achieve-the-impossible-prof-thomas-pink-is-wrong-about-religious-liberty-heres-why/

61 Kenneth Whitehead, *Affirming Religious Liberty: How Vatican ii Developed the Church's Teachings To Meet Today's Needs*, Society of St Paul / Alba House, 2010, p.53

US bishops who attended Vatican II "thought that cozying up to the liberal establishment would bring to the American Church peace," the Society said in a statement. But, "as it was not based upon Truth, it was ultimately a false peace and doomed to fail." As a result, "we are today witnessing the fulfillment of the famous quip 'the revolution eats it own.' We are now face-to-face with the outcome of the American bishops' support of religious liberty as they are being coerced to jettison the Church's moral teachings." It is "tragic" that Vatican II "did not heed" the warnings of the Traditionalists who "vigorously fought the errors" of those who composed *Dignitatis Humanae*.[62]

⁂

Philosopher Alasdair MacIntyre once wrote that "contemporary debates within modern political systems are almost exclusively between conservative liberals, liberal liberals, and radical liberals."[63] The same can be said for debates in the mainstream Church following the Second Vatican Council. Jorge Bergoglio and many of the Cardinals and bishops he has appointed are unabashed "radical liberals." John Paul II, Benedict XVI, and their supporters could be considered "conservative liberals" of varying degrees.

How do we know this? They themselves admit it. "The problem of the 1960s was to acquire the best expressed values of two centuries of 'liberal' culture…and purify [them]," Josef Ratzinger said in 1984.[64] "The Church is indebted to the early liberal Catholics," the aforementioned Cardinal George wrote in 2009.[65] Robert Barron, who is seen by many as one of the most "orthodox" thinkers in the American Church, has observed that when he was a young bishop, Karol Wojtyła (i.e., John Paul II), was one of the leading "progressive" voices at the Council and that he fought against the "keepers of the traditional, scholastic form of Catholicism."[66] Barron has also stated that John Paul had "zero interest in reviving pre-conciliar conservatism."[67]

62 "Our First, Most Cherished Liberty: problematic," SSPX - District of the USA, April 17, 2012, https://web.archive.org/web/20210309204214/https://sspx.org/en/news-events/news/our-first-most-cherished-liberty-problematic-706

63 Alasdair MacIntyre, *Whose Justice? Which Rationality?*, University of Notre Dame Press, Notre Dame, Indiana, 1988, p.392

64 Quoted in Archbishop Marcel Lefebvre, *They Have Uncrowned Him*, Angelus Press, Kansas City, Missouri, 2003, pp. xvi, 76, 220–221

65 Cardinal Francis George, *The Difference God Makes: A Catholic Vision of Faith, Communion, and Culture*, The Crossroad Publishing Company, New York, October 1, 2009, p.165

66 Bishop Robert Barron, "Yves Congar and the Meaning of Vatican II," Word on Fire, June 29, 2012, https://www.wordonfire.org/articles/barron/yves-congar-and-the-meaning-of-vatican-ii/

67 Quoted in T.S. Flanders, "Bishop Barron and the 'Unhappy' Renewal of the 'Trad' Movement," One Peter Five, October 24, 2019, https://onepeterfive.com/bishop-barron-un-

What many Catholics today don't realize is that those who are considered "conservatives" are not really conservatives. In fact, they and their "radical liberal" counterparts both want to preserve the last liberal revolution: Vatican II. As Fr Gaudron has explained: "The conciliar popes generally pass for conservatives because they continue to defend certain principles of the natural law that the modern world rejects, and because, in doctrinal matters, they seek to restrain the more radical of the modernist theologians."[68]

Those who are held up as conservatives today have never been shy about their desire to smuggle their liberal ideology into the bosom of the Church. As such, they should be identified as "neoconservatives," "neo-modernists," or "neo-Catholics" in contrast to Traditional Catholics who steadfastly uphold the anti-liberal teachings of the popes before the Council. Archbishop Viganò has explained the difference in the following way:

> Conservatism wants to 'preserve' the outward appearances of Tradition, without the doctrinal substance that makes it alive. Conservatism is the attitude of those who criticize the excesses of the Synodical Church but are careful not to question its causes, which are to be found in Vatican II. Conservatism is really a 'suicidal attitude' because it creates an artificial 'dogmatic box,' made of Novus Ordo ad orientem with Roman chasubles and Gregorian chants... [and] of selected quotations of some conciliar documents, accidentally not contrasting with the Catholic Magisterium of all time.[69]

His Excellency's point is best understood when one considers that in 1791 Pope Pius VI declared that "it is not fitting that the Church of God be changed according to the fluctuations of worldly necessity."[70] In 1864, Blessed Pius IX likewise condemned the notion that "the Roman Pontiff can, and ought to, reconcile himself, and come to terms with progress, liberalism and modern civilization."[71] Their successors, clearly inspired by the Holy Ghost, repeated these magisterial pronouncements in the decades that followed. "Formal

happy-trad/

68 Fr Matthias Gaudron, *The Catechism of the Crisis of the Church*, Angelus Press, Kansas City, Missouri, 2010, p.33

69 Archbishop Carlo Maria Viganò, "You have heard it, 'A conservative is someone who clings to something and does not want to see beyond it,'" X, May 17, 2024, https://x.com/CarloMVigano/status/1791401441938092453

70 Pope Pius VI, *Quod Aliquantum*, 1791

71 Blessed Pius IX, *The Syllabus of Errors*, 80, 1864, Papal Encyclicals, https://www.papalencyclicals.net/pius09/p9syll.htm

denunciations of liberalism in whole or part, appeared in Pius IX's *Syllabus of Errors* (1864), and in Leo XIII's *Immortale Dei* (1885), *Libertas Praestantissimum* (1888), *Longinque Oceani* (1895), and *Testem Benevolentiae* (1899)," Cardinal George has noted.[72]

Yet, in 1982, Cardinal Ratzinger boasted that Vatican II's *Gaudium et Spes* acted as a "counter-Syllabus" that "represents an attempt to reconcile the Church with the world as it had become after 1789."[73] Cardinal Paul-Émile Léger (1904–1991), who served as Archbishop of Montreal from 1950 until 1967, complained like an ill-tempered child in 1963 when he said "if we do not take steps to do more about achieving rapprochement between the Church and the modern world, we are in danger of finding ourselves considered unrealistic and irrelevant."[74] He ultimately got his wish, but the modern world still considers the Church's teachings not worth listening to.

Princeton Professor Robert P. George succinctly summarized the prevailing post-conciliar attitude when he claimed in a 2001 book that Catholics today "not only may, but must, be liberals of a different type" and that a "sound understanding of the teachings of modern popes ... and of the First and Second Vatican Councils requires the abandonment of key positions associated with" a "type of conservatism" that "used to be widely held by Churchmen and by faithful Catholics." To "be a good Catholic one must be a kind of old-fashion liberal."[75]

Before closing this preface by commenting on what Traditional Catholicism consists of and discussing how this book seeks to defend it, I want to say a few quick words about a forgotten figure in US Catholic history. I reference his insights at length in Chapter VI but a brief note here is fitting given Professor George's blasphemous comment above.

One of the greatest American theologians who ever lived was Fr Clifford Fenton, CSSR (1906–1969). Among other things, Fr Fenton correctly predicted that the Church was going to be "very badly hurt" by Vatican II, an event he attended as an assistant to Italian Cardinal Alfredo Ottaviani, the Secretary

---

72 Cardinal Francis George, *The Difference God Makes: A Catholic Vision of Faith, Communion, and Culture*, The Crossroad Publishing Company, New York, October 1, 2009, pp.162–163

73 Quoted in *Principles of Catholic Theology*, Ignatius Press, San Francisco, 1987, pp.381–382

74 Rev. Walter M. Abbott, *Twelve Council Fathers*, The Macmillan Company, First Edition, New York, New York, January 1, 1963, p. 48

75 Robert George, *The Clash of Orthodoxies: Law, Religion, and Morality in Crisis*, ISI Books, Wilmington, Delaware, 2001, pp. 231–236

of the Vatican's powerful Holy Office, which was entrusted with upholding the integrity of the Church's doctrinal teachings.[76] Fr Fenton observed in his diary that Vatican II "seems to be entirely liberal." He also said he "always thought that this Council was dangerous. It was started for no sufficient reason." He additionally remarked that "this is going to mark the end of the Catholic religion ... it would seem Christ is abandoning His Church."[77]

Fr Fenton would be considered a Traditional Catholic were he alive today. During his life, he served as the Dean of the School of Sacred Theology at The Catholic University of America in Washington DC. A pupil of famed Thomistic theologian Fr Réginald Garrigou-Lagrange, OP (1877–1964), he was one of the most respected priests in the entire country, having been an editor for the widely-read *American Ecclesiastical Review* starting in the 1940s and ending in 1963. For his service to the Church, he received multiple awards from the Vatican.

Fr Fenton was keenly aware of the harmful ideas being promoted by liberals before the Council. He wrote in his journal that the Church during the first half of the 20th century was "being run by men who have no concern whatsoever for the purity or the integrity" of Catholic doctrine. He also said that "since the death of St Pius X, the Church has been directed by weak and liberal popes, who have flooded the hierarchy with unworthy and stupid men."[78]

And so it has been until the present day! Motivated by their hatred for Tradition, both "conservative liberals" and "radical liberals" openly celebrate the cancelation of the faith of our fathers at the Council.

"Many of the ideas [St Pius X] railed against would become standard theology by the time of Vatican II," left-wing writer Michael Sean Winters once proudly declared on the dissident website *National Catholic Reporter*.[79]

George Lindbeck (1923–2018), a Lutheran who attended the Council as an "observer," would have agreed with Winters. In 1994, he told George Weigel in an interview for the neoconservative magazine *First Things* that efforts taken by Pius XII in the 1950s to re-affirm St Pius X's traditionalist theology were aimed at silencing progressive theologians who later exerted great influence over the Council. "The Catholic anti-Modernist campaign of the early

76 "Explosive! The Personal Diaries of Mgr. Joseph Clifford Fenton—Modernism & Vatican II," Novus Ordo Watch, April 17, 2014, https://novusordowatch.org/2014/08/diaries-mgr-joseph-clifford-fenton/

77 Ibid.

78 Ibid.

79 Michael Sean Winters, "First Things' Matthew Schmitz needs church history lesson," National Catholic Reporter, December 4, 2017, https://www.ncronline.org/opinion/distinctly-catholic/first-things-matthew-schmitz-needs-church-history-lesson

twentieth century had created a situation in which a very rigid and biased interpretation of Thomas emerged," he alleged. Pius XII's encyclical *Humani Generis* "was intended to say 'No' to the sorts of approaches represented by the *nouvelle theologie*" that was being promoted by the liberals at the time. "It reinforced the position of the regnant powers in the congregations and the academy, who used the encyclical to make the *nouvelle theologie* people *personae non gratae*. Which meant that the encyclical reinforced the anti-Modernist style of dealing with exploratory theology."[80]

Weigel himself, who is wrongly seen a reliable source for sound Catholic teaching these days, complained in a 2015 essay that the "anti-Modernist denunciations" issued by St Pius X "damaged reputations and destroyed careers in an attempt to enforce a narrow form of Catholic intellectual life." He also grumbled about what he called "the below-the-belt machinations that followed [Pius XII's] 1950 encyclical *Humani Generis*."[81]

Earlier it was asked: What is Traditional Catholicism? Simply put, Traditional Catholicism is the belief and practice of the Catholic religion as it was believed and practiced up until Vatican II. "Pass not beyond the ancient bounds which thy fathers have set," Proverbs 22:28 warns. Traditional Catholics take this seriously.

It is not hard to guess what those who adhere to Traditional Catholicism generally believe. Among other things, they defend all of the Church's traditional doctrinal, moral, theological, social, and related teachings. Traditional Catholics also tend to have a high regard for Archbishop Marcel Lefebvre, Pope St Pius X (1835–1914), Pope St Pius V (1504–1572), St Thomas Aquinas (1225–1274), and similar figures throughout the Church's 2,000 year history, as opposed to just the past six decades.

Having a devotion to the Sacred Heart of Jesus and Our Lady of Fatima is also common in Traditional-minded communities, as is the observance of Ember Days and abstaining from meat on Fridays throughout the year. Many Traditional Catholics tend to watch and read influencers, authors, and clergy who discuss Freemasonry, end-times prophesies, and the intensely-debated topic of whether any or all of the authorities in Rome following Vatican II are actual popes given their many deviations from and outright rejection of

80 George Weigel, "Re-Viewing Vatican II," First Things, December 1994, https://www.firstthings.com/article/1994/12/re-viewing-vatican-ii

81 George Weigel, "Progressive Catholic Authoritarianism: An Enduring Problem," First Things, July 1, 2015, https://www.firstthings.com/web-exclusives/2015/07/progressive-catholic-authoritarianism-an-enduring-problem

what came before. Traditional Catholics would likely agree that Vatican II is the root cause of the crisis (and not merely its alleged poor implementation). More than a few would agree with Archbishop Viganò when he says that Jorge Bergoglio "has proven beyond a reasonable doubt that he is acting as an emissary of the Deep Church to discredit the Papacy and the Catholic Church, and this is repugnant to the role assigned by Christ to St Peter and his Successors."[82]

"Trads" as they are sometimes called often disagree on how best to respond to the crisis in the Church. Some give more weight to obedience than adherence to Tradition. They struggle, in other words, to know just how much they should follow, be silent about, or speak out against those who are restricting the Latin Mass and implementing other anti-traditional practices. Accusations of "schism" are frequently hurled at those who resist such measures in an overt or "aggressive" manner, like preaching against the Council's errors from the pulpit or consecrating bishops and ordaining priests without papal or diocesan approval, which has become a necessity today.

Oftentimes, debates arise over whether some should even be considered Traditionalists, or if the terms "neo-Traditionalist" and "semi-Traditionalist" are more fitting. Usually, those discussions revolve around whether one thinks Vatican II is in rupture with the past, whether you should attend the Novus Ordo Mass or receive any of the revised sacraments, and what one makes of the "recognize and resist the popes" argument.[83]

While intra-Traditionalist disputes are not dealt with directly in this book, it is worth recalling that Tradition itself *is the faith* and that it alone has the right to reign in the Vatican. The Judas' currently occupying the Dicasteries and offices in Rome have no legitimate claim to the positions they hold. The battle for those who attend the Latin Mass cannot be over the Mass *per se*. It must be over Vatican II. Modernists know this, and have known it for five decades, which is why they hijacked the Council and created a new, Protestanized liturgy. Their relentless attacks on the Latin Mass in recent years are nothing less than bald-faced attempts to eradicate the faith it represents.

Those who identify as Traditionalists but seek approval from the Conciliar Church—especially on condition that they accept in some way Vatican II and/or the Novus Ordo Mass—are living in a state of contradiction. They

82 LifeSiteNews Staff, "Archbishop Viganò: Bergoglio is acting as an emissary of the deep church to discredit the papacy," LifeSiteNews, January 4, 2024, https://www.lifesitenews.com/news/archbishop-vigano-bergoglio-is-acting-as-an-emissary-of-the-deep-church-to-discredit-the-papacy/

83 See here "No, Catholics Can't "Recognize and Resist": Response to One Peter Five," Novus Ordo Watch, December 13, 2021, https://novusordowatch.org/2021/12/no-recognize-resist-sammons-one-peter-five/

act like those Christians who offered a pinch of incense to the Roman emperors in exchange for not being put to death. But the Catholic religion and the neo-modernist imposter that the Vatican passes off for it these days are diametrically opposed to one another. Catholics cannot merely be "attached" to the smells and bells of the traditional liturgy, which repudiates the Council and everything it teaches. To do so is to rely on emotion instead of reason and on subjectivism instead of standing on principle.

After the pro-Latin Mass Diocese of Campos, Brazil made a deal with the Vatican in the early 2000s, then-SSPX Superior General Bishop Bernard Fellay commented that Rome is seeking to put Tradition in a "cage" at the "ecumenical zoo" in the name of "ecclesiastical pluralism."[84] He was right! Traditionalists today must recognize that the heretics in the Vatican are theological terrorists who want to destroy the last remaining vestiges of the pre-Vatican II Church and that they mustn't be negotiated with. In other words, Traditionalists shouldn't be concerned with obtaining permission from them for their ministry. Instead, they should seek to persuade them—and the rest of the conciliar laity and hierarchy—to realize they are not Catholic and that they need to convert to the one true faith.

Whatever the future of the Latin Mass and the various groups and priests who offer it will be, the United States' Federal Bureau of Investigation is spying on most of them thanks to encouragement from the Jewish-run Anti-Defamation League and the anti-Catholic Southern Poverty Law Center, which considers "Radical Traditionalism" to be a "hate group."[85] These and similar topics will be discussed in detail in Chapter V.

84 Bishop Bernard Fellay, Address at St Vincent de Paul Catholic Church, Kansas City, Missouri, November 10, 2004. Transcript available at "The Conference: What Catholic Need to Know," *Angelus Magazine*, November 2004, http://www.angelusonline.org/index.php?section=articles&subsection=show_article&article_id=2351
85 James Comey, "The FBI and the ADL: Working Toward a World Without Hate," Anti-Defamation League National Leadership Summit, Washington, DC., April 28, 2014, https://www.fbi.gov/news/speeches/the-fbi-and-the-adl-working-toward-a-world-without-hate. "The Society of St Pius X: Mired in Anti-Semitism," Anti-Defamation League, March 20, 2009, https://www.adl.org/resources/news/society-st-pius-x-mired-anti-semitism. Abraham Foxman, "Latin Mass Cause for Concern," Anti-Defamation League, July 11, 2007, https://extremismterms.adl.org/resources/news/latin-mass-cause-concern. "12 Anti-Semitic Radical Traditionalist Catholic Groups," Southern Poverty Law Center, January 16, 2007, https://www.splcenter.org/fighting-hate/intelligence-report/2007/12-anti-semitic-radical-traditionalist-catholic-groups. Stephen Kokx, "FBI whistleblower releases docs showing agency is surveilling 'Radical' Latin Mass Catholics," LifeSiteNews, February 8, 2023, https://www.lifesitenews.com/news/fbi-doc-suggests-agency-is-surveilling-radical-traditional-catholics-in-virginia/. Stephen Kokx, "Catholic media outlet named in FBI report slams 'dystopian' Latin Mass surveillance," LifeSiteNews, February 9, 2023, https://www.lifesitenews.com/news/catholic-media-outlet-named-in-fbi-report-slams-dystopian-latin-mass-surveillance/

ↂ

Before ending these introductory remarks, it must be mentioned that neo-conservatives and other apologists for the Vatican II religion like to claim that the squabbles found among Traditionalists indicate that they are outside the Church and that they do not have unity in the faith. Consequently, they accuse them of not only being schismatics who are causing scandal to others but endangering their own souls as well. While popular, these arguments fall flat on their face for several reasons.

First, Our Lord Himself told the Apostles that He was going to be arrested and put to death, and that this would cause them to go their separate ways. "I will strike the shepherd, and the sheep of the flock shall be dispersed," He said in the Gospel of Matthew.[86] To those with eyes to see and ears to hear, this is precisely what has happened since the Council. Just as the Apostles fled after Our Lord's betrayal, and just as St Peter was absent from the passion and foot of the cross, so too are the successors of Peter and the Apostles absent from this second crucifixion of Our Lord's Mystical Body. As a result, faithful Catholics have been left to fend for themselves to find and support clergy who echo the voice of the shepherd until God sees fit to bring this crisis to an end by giving them a Traditional pope, the only authority on earth who can truly "unite the clans."

Second, mainstream parishes are themselves divided. Indeed, there is hardly a diocese in the United States, maybe even the world, that doesn't have a Protestant-style mega-church, a new age "Catholic community," a pro-LGBT parish, and a conservative-leaning priest who occasionally permits Communion on the tongue while kneeling. What's more, there are many clergy in good standing with Rome who promote female ordination, who support homosexuality, are homosexuals themselves, who give Communion to persons in adulterous relationships, and who invite non-Catholics to perform pagan ceremonies in their churches. These are serious matters that violate the heart of the Catholic religion.

Third, the Vatican says one thing one day, does the opposite the next, and exacts punishment on those who refuse to go along with it. One doesn't even know what to submit to at times. Rome has thus become the primary source of disunity for Catholics. Traditionalists who read its forked tongue declarations and study its ambiguously-written statements and erratic behavior simply cling to what was taught before the madness began in the 1960s because they see in it clarity that can help them remain loyal to Christ. Some friends of mine have said that the situation is analogous to innocent children trying to

---

86 Matthew 26:31

avoid a drunk father beating them with a belt. Traditionalists, in other words, are the victims of division, not its cause. They are merely doing their best to maintain their faith in uncharted territory as heresy flows uninterrupted from the Chair of St Peter day after day.

Lastly, the "popes" since the Council are not in communion with those who came before them. It is not "judgmental" to say this. Basic reason and observable reality tells us this is true. On the whole, those who have wielded power in Rome since the Second Vatican Council have made it abundantly clear by their deeds and convoluted documents—almost none of which cite anything before Vatican II on a routine basis—that objectively speaking they despise the Traditional (i.e. Catholic) faith. This necessarily places them outside the Church and in schism with their saintly predecessors. To be considered out of communion with them is, as the leaders of the SSPX said in a letter to Rome in 1988, "a mark of honor and a sign of orthodoxy before the faithful," who "have a strict right to know that the priests who serve them [are] not in communion with a counterfeit church."[87]

⁂

Several of the essays I first published in 2013 at the age of twenty-six are included in this book. They took the standard neoconservative position that confusion over remarks made by Jorge Bergoglio during his initial months in office could be attributed to a biased media and pessimistic laity purposefully seeing the worst in what he was saying. By the grace of God, it didn't take long to understand that was not happening every time he spoke. Chapter I reveals how quickly I realized he was pushing a more nefarious agenda.

Some of the great anti-liberal Catholics who helped me escape the Conciliar Church have already been mentioned. I have encountered many others as well. All of them should be more widely appreciated. Many are referenced in Chapter VI. A short summary of who they are and the impact they had on me seems useful before closing these remarks. But be warned: you will not find these heroic souls mentioned in diocesan classrooms or sermons. Nor are they written about by mainstream Catholic book publishers, or brought up on conservative podcasts and radio shows. Why? Because they represent the faith as it was in its pre-Vatican II glory. They far outrank the pseudo-intellectuals held up as the standard bearers for Catholic orthodoxy in these times.

Fr Felix Sarda y Salvany (1844–1916) was a Spanish priest whose book *Liberalism is a Sin* exposes the real errors of neoconservatism. His writings

---

87 "Open Letter to Cardinal Gantin, Prefect of the Congregation for Bishops," Society of St Pius X - District of Asia, July 6, 1988, https://www.sspxasia.com/Documents/Archbishop-Lefebvre/Archbishop_Lefebvre_and_the_Vatican/Part_I/1988-07-06.htm

helped me realize that organizations like the Acton Institute, men like George Weigel, and their many allies in academia, politics, and even the Vatican were just repeating the views of progressive clergy who lived in the 18th and 19th centuries who had already been condemned by the Church. With Fr Salvany's insights, I was also able to see that prominent neo-Catholics in the United States were guilty of spreading what Leo XIII called the "heresy of Americanism."[88]

Nineteenth century French author Louis Veuillot (1813–1883) and 20th century British scholar Michael Davies (1936–2004) were immensely helpful in aiding my understanding of Traditional Catholic teaching on Church-State relations and religious liberty. Fr Clifford Fenton's essays in the *American Ecclesiastical Review* were an immense help as well. Davies' writings on Vatican II and *Dignitatis Humanae* specifically answered dozens of questions I had that the Council's most popular defenders were simply not addressing.

Irish priest Fr Denis Fahey (1883–1954) and his books on organized naturalism, international finance, and the Kingship of Christ were also instructive. American lay writers Carol Robinson (1911–2002) and Ed Willock (1916–1960), co-founders of *Integrity* magazine in the 1940s, helped me see contemporary politics through a truly Catholic lens. Their writings inspired me to withdraw my support from neoconservatives in Washington DC who have turned the faith into an offshoot of classical liberalism and a footstool for Zionism and the Republican Party. The many writings, lectures, and letters of Archbishop Lefebvre, Bishop Richard Williamson, and other Traditionalists have also been formative.

Unsurprisingly, some of these figures—and others like them—have been whitewashed from Catholic history books. "To the victor go the spoils," it is often said. And the liberal winners of Vatican II have waged an effective war that has hidden these lions of doctrine, these heroes of the faith, from ordinary Catholics. But no lie can live forever. Thanks to the growth of Tradition in recent years, these men are now being appreciated by a larger audience. They represent the long line of anti-liberal, integralist Catholic political and Thomistic theological thought that runs counter to the neo-Catholic and neo-Traditionalist intelligentsia class that serves as the unofficial Gestapo of the Deep Church by policing what is and isn't allowed to reach the ears of the faithful.

In time, all Catholics will understand that the individuals listed above—despite having varying opinions on an array of topics—were, by and large, right all along. Of course, that may not happen this year, or next year, or even 10

---

years from now. Only God knows how long this current Babylonian Captivity will last and whether our martyrdom is the price He will charge for it to come to an end. Regardless, all of them would have agreed with 19th century English Bishop John Cuthbert Hedley (1837–1915) when he said, "the religion of Jesus Christ—which Catholicism alone adequately presents to the world—is intended to take possession of every heart, to influence all the actions of men, and to be the grand rule and arbiter in all the world's concerns, whether public or private, whether social, commercial, or political."[89]

❧

The day will soon come when all of the gatekeeping efforts, slick marketing campaigns, well-funded inter-religious organizations, and ecumenical alliances and political partnerships that keep the Matrix-like, Conciliar Church running will come to a crashing end; the software it relies on has too many glitches, and it cannot continue to deceive souls indefinitely. A "red pill" moment is coming. You and I may not all be around to see it, but when it does, it will be a glorious rebirth for the Catholic religion.

Already diocesan seminaries and parishes are closing at breakneck speed while Traditional-minded ones are experiencing a massive uptick in interest and attendance. God is clearly pouring out His graces on simple though devout souls, many of whom are still trapped in the Vatican II Church but are slowly coming to realize, despite perhaps not being able to identify specifically what it is yet, that something has gone terribly wrong since the 1960s.

As the mask begins to slip on the Conciliar lie, neo-modernists in the Vatican will continue to lash out. *Traditionis Custodes* and the "excommunication" of Archbishop Viganò are two of the most recent instances of this. Deep State Vatican allies in the media and politics may also join in the persecution by blackmailing, framing, and even imprisoning Traditionalists simply for resisting what St Pius X called the "movement of apostasy being organized in every country for the establishment of a One-World Church."[90]

In some ways, the situation we now face is comparable to the sinking of the Titanic. The Conciliar Church is taking on water and the hour is getting late. Some Traditionalists jumped off right after it hit the iceberg, Vatican II—not a few of whom did not have life preservers on. Others made flotation devices out of small-knit communities of zealous souls. They have

89 Quoted in Bishop John Cuthbert Hedley, OSB, "Union Among Catholics: A Bishop and His Flock," Tradidi, https://web.archive.org/web/20200922063425/http://tradidi.com/union-among-catholics/

90 St Pius X, *Notre Charge Apostolique*, 1910, Papal Encyclicals, https://www.vatican.va/content/leo-xiii/la/letters/documents/hf_l-xiii_let_18990122_testem-benevolentiae.html

miraculously survived to the present day with prayer, penance, and trusting in God's providence. Still others, like the Society of St Pius X, are in life boats and not as susceptible to the freezing water or the waves crashing up against them. At the same time, indefectibility is promised to the Church alone. And some would argue that cracks and even holes are starting to appear in some Traditionalist vessels. As the Conciliar ship starts to sink at a faster rate than before, those who are too close are going to be sucked to the bottom with it. Both prudence and wisdom are needed to know what to do.

Before he died in 1991, Archbishop Lefebvre gave his most mature thought on the matter in an interview with *Fideliter* magazine. "We would have to re-enter this Conciliar Church in order, supposedly, to make it Catholic? That is a complete illusion! It is not the subjects that make the superiors, but the superiors who make the subjects," he explained.[91] Archbishop Lefebvre's final position on relations with Rome, which is discussed more in Chapter V, was thus:

> We do not have the same outlook on a reconciliation. Cardinal Ratzinger sees it as reducing us, bringing us back to Vatican II. We see it as a return of Rome to Tradition. We don't agree; it is a dialogue of death. I can't speak much of the future, mine is behind me, but if I live a little while, supposing that Rome calls for a renewed dialogue, then, I will put conditions. I shall not accept being in the position where I was put during the dialogue. No more. I will place the discussion at the doctrinal level: 'Do you agree with the great encyclicals of all the popes who preceded you? Do you agree with *Quanta Cura* of Pius IX, *Immortale Dei* and *Libertas* of Leo XIII, *Pascendi Gregis* of Pius X, *Quas Primas* of Pius XI, *Humani Generis* of Pius XII? Are you in full communion with these Popes and their teachings? Do you still accept the entire Anti-Modernist Oath? Are you in favor of the social reign of Our Lord Jesus Christ? If you do not accept the doctrine of your predecessors, it is useless to talk! As long as you do not accept the correction of the Council, in consideration of the doctrine of these Popes, your predecessors, no dialogue is possible. It is useless.[92]

91 Archbishop Lefebvre, "One year after the Consecrations: An interview with Archbishop Lefebvre," July-August 1989, *Fideliter* magazine, SSPX, https://sspx.org/en/one-year-after-consecrations-30335

92 Archbishop Lefebvre, "Interview with Archbishop Lefebvre Given to *Fideliter* Magazine," November-December 1988, SSPX Asia, https://www.sspxasia.com/Documents/Archbishop-Lefebvre/Archbishop_Lefebvre_and_the_Vatican/Part_II/1988-11.htm

Traditional Catholics should not fear the situation they find themselves in. The saints longed to live in these times. The opportunities God is giving them to show their love for Him are seemingly in greater abundance now than in any other period in Church history.

Before entering a war, one must know one's enemy, and not only the enemy beyond one's borders but those within it as well. This book seeks to expose both the hirelings and wolves in sheep's clothing inside the Church's structures and the legates and servants of Satan outside of them in the political realm. Oftentimes, there is overlap between the two.

In some ways, what is happening reminds me of what Pius XI wrote to German priests in 1937. "The priest's first loving gift to his neighbors is to serve truth and refute error in any of its forms," he said. "Failure on this score would be not only a betrayal of God and your vocation, but also an offense against the real welfare of your people and country."[93]

The duty of pastors today must be to warn their flock about the dangers of Vatican II and to instruct them on the great need to embrace Tradition. They must also never shy away from ripping the mask off evil in the secular world.

Clergy should also take the advice of Fr Francis J. Connell (1888–1967). Fr Connell was one of Fr Fenton's closest collaborators in the 1940s and 50s. In a memo written to the Vatican in 1951, Connell said that the "most effective means toward preserving the Church from harm and promoting its apostolic activity will be found in a more ardent zeal on the part of bishops and priests and in a more faithful observance of God's laws by Catholics." If "all priests fulfilled their duty conscientiously in this matter, there would be three times as many converts in the United States annually as there are at present."[94]

Catholics should likewise heed the wisdom of Pius XII, who, in 1958, the year that he died, said, "when new dangers threaten Christians and the Church … We—like Our Predecessors in bygone days—have turned in prayer to the Virgin Mary, our loving Mother, and have urged the whole flock entrusted to Our care to place itself confidently under her protection."[95]

Bishop Fulton Sheen spoke with similar ardor and clarity before Vatican II. "If I were not a Catholic, and were looking for the true Church in the world today, I would look for the one Church which did not get along well with

93 Pius XI, *Mit Brennender Sorge*, 36, Vatican website, https://www.vatican.va/content/pius-xi/en/encyclicals/documents/hf_p-xi_enc_14031937_mit-brennender-sorge.html

94 Fr Joseph A. Komonchak, et al., "'The Crisis in Church-State Relationships in the U.S.A.' A Recently Discovered Text by John Courtney Murray." *The Review of Politics*, Volume 61, no. 4, 1999, pp. 710 -713, JSTOR, http://www.jstor.org/stable/1408404

95 Pius XII, *Meminisse Iuvat*, 1, Vatican website, https://www.vatican.va/content/pius-xii/en/encyclicals/documents/hf_p-xii_enc_14071958_meminisse-iuvat.html

the world," he once wrote in a book published in 1938. "I would look for the Church which the world hates."[96]

Well, the world certainly hates Tradition. It most certainly does not hate the Vatican II Church. In fact, it partners with it on a regular basis.[97]

While it is true that global forces have opposed at various times the men who have worn the papal vestments since the 1960s, what those individuals adhered to was what might be described as "decaffeinated Catholicism," one that was far less bold than the original blend brewed before the Second Vatican Council. The following remarks of Cardinal Francis George are quite telling in that regard. "At the funeral of Pope John Paul II, the whole world assembled in St Peter's Square in Rome." It was "there to honor a peacemaker" and to worship "the God of peace to whom Pope John Paul II had totally given himself." God was "forging a new unity among his creatures."[98] *National Catholic Register* likewise reported that "Kings, queens, presidents … cabinet ministers and ambassadors representing more than 140 nations sat off to one side of Pope John Paul's casket." On the other side were "representatives of the Orthodox, Oriental, Anglican, Protestant and US evangelical communities. Ten Jewish and 10 Muslim organizations sent delegations, as did Buddhists, Sikhs and Hindus."[99]

When Archbishop Lefebvre died in 1991, *The New York Times* published a dismissive obituary describing him as a "stubborn Frenchman" who held "extreme right-wing views" and who took a "rebellious course."[100] When one

96 Frs. Leslie Rumble and Charles Carty, *Radio Replies, First Volume*, TAN Books and Publishers, Rockford, Illinois, 1938, Reprinted 1979, p.ix

97 Michael Haynes, "Pope Francis receives Bill Clinton and George Soros' son in private Vatican visit," LifeSiteNews, July 6, 2023, https://www.lifesitenews.com/news/bill-clinton-and-george-soros-son-privately-received-by-pope-francis-at-vatican/. Michael Haynes, "Pope Francis appoints population control activist Jeffrey Sachs to Pontifical Academy of Social Sciences," LifeSiteNews, October 25, 2021, https://www.lifesitenews.com/news/pope-francis-appoints-population-control-activist-jeffrey-sachs-to-pontifical-academy-of-social-sciences/. Elizabeth Yore, "Bergoglio prefers dialogue with globalists and communists than with Catholics," LifeSiteNews, December 15, 2023, https://www.lifesitenews.com/opinion/bergoglio-prefers-dialogue-with-globalists-and-communists-than-with-catholics/. Diane Montagna, "Vatican hosts youth conference with pro-abortion UN activists," LifeSiteNews, November 8, 2019, https://www.lifesitenews.com/news/vatican-hosts-youth-conference-with-pro-abortion-un-activists/. Pete Baklinski, "'I invited him': Vatican official defends giving speaking slot to pro-abortion Bernie Sanders," LifeSiteNews, April 8, 2016, https://www.lifesitenews.com/news/meddling-in-us-politics-vatican-defends-invite-of-abortion-extremist-bernie/.

98 Francis Cardinal George, *God in Action*, Doubleday Religion, United States, First Edition, 2011, p. 211

99 "John Paul II: 'Standing at the Window of the Father's House," National Catholic Register, April 17, 2005, https://www.ncregister.com/commentaries/john-paul-ii-standing-at-the-window-of-the-father-s-house

100 Steven Greenhouse, "Archbishop Lefebvre, 85, Dies; Traditionalist Defied the Vatican,"

compares that send off to the one received by John Paul, the following words of Our Lord in the Gospel of St John take on new significance: "If the world hates you, know that it has hated me before it hated you. If you were of the world, the world would love its own; but because you are not of the world, but I chose you out of the world, therefore the world hates you."[101]

For two millennia, Traditional Catholicism has produced saints, fostered vocations, enkindled prayer, and inspired holiness. The Novus Ordo religion can lay claim to none of these over a sustained period of time. In fact, it has produced the exact opposite. As Christ said in the Gospel of Matthew, "by their fruits you shall know them."[102] The goal of Traditional Catholics in the United States—and across the world for that matter—must be the safeguarding of the faith and helping others to see the truth about the current crisis. They should also provide financial, material, and spiritual support to clergy who are defending the faith in this historic moment. Let us take up that arduous task with the same joy and love that Our Lord had when he redeemed mankind by his death on the Cross more than 2,000 years ago.

Stephen Kokx • October 2024

The New York Times, March 26, 1991, https://www.nytimes.com/1991/03/26/obituaries/archbishop-lefebvre-85-dies-traditionalist-defied-the-vatican.html
101 John 15: 18–19
102 Matthew 7:16

PART 1

CHURCH

CHAPTER I: POPE FRANCIS

IS POPE BENEDICT'S RESIGNATION A CATASTROPHE?

During a 2012 visit to a Rome-based community for senior citizens, Pope Benedict told residents that they are "an asset to society, even in suffering and disease."[1]

If only someone had whispered those words in his ear last month, he may not have announced his resignation three weeks ago.

Most commentators have spent the past several days praising Benedict's "humble" and "courageous" decision to become the first pope to willfully abdicate the papacy in over 600 years. Very few have voiced disagreement with it. But an essay published in *La Croix*, the semi-official daily newspaper of the French Church, has been getting some attention for doing precisely that.

The column in question is written by Pierre Dulau and Martin Steffens, two professors of philosophy.[2] "This resignation by the pope is a catastrophe," they plainly argue. "It is an event that is rarely found in history, a fact that, in its symbolic violence, is a portrait of our time." They continue:

> The Papacy is, in the West, the very last function of which it is commonly accepted by all that it engages the one who entered it 'up until death.' This 'till death' means at least two things. First, that human life is not its own goal: our life has no meaning if not linked to a greater life to which we may, in justice, sacrifice everything—exactly as the love of the spouses, 'till death' as well, takes its meaning from beyond itself, in a promise that does not cease existing.
>
> This 'till death' recalls consequently that the pope, a 'pontiff,' is the arch that links Earth to Heaven, that is, by the threshold of death, finite life to infinite life. A pope who resigns is a bridge that decides not to reach the other side where promise lies, [a destination] of which it is the assurance, and that leads there all those who left the point of departure.

1 Benedict, Address to the Community of Sant'Egidio Home for the Elderly, Rome, November 12, 2012, Vatican website, https://www.vatican.va/content/benedict-xvi/en/speeches/2012/november/documents/hf_ben-xvi_spe_20121112_viva-anziani.html

2 Pierre Dulau and Martin Steffens, "The Pope's Abandonment is a Catastrophe," La Croix, February 19, 2013, https://www.la-croix.com/Archives/2013-02-19/OPINION-Pierre-Dulau-et-Martin-Steffens-professeurs-agreges-de-philosophie-L-abandon-du-pape-est-une-catastrophe-_NP_-2013-02-19-912951

> To rupture this arch by way of a unilateral decision means to join hands with the global movement of non-commitment that strikes the entire Western symbolic order. Parenthood? Yes, but if we are in the mood for it, as long as we are in the mood for it. Marriage? Yes, if I can get divorced. To be in charge? Why not, if that does not deprive me of my right to happiness...
>
> There where a word is given that opens the door of life to something greater than itself, there also that word is broken, mocked, relegated as an old oddity. And even a pope should resign? A CEO or a president may resign. A pope is fired by death.

Although I don't entirely agree with the assertion that Benedict's decision to step down is a "catastrophe," count me among those who think Dulau and Steffens marshal a very strong argument as to why popes shouldn't be resigning.

Count me also among those who don't think it would be wise for Benedict to retire and, as some Catholics have suggested, start writing books and essays. I mean, didn't he cite a deterioration in mental strength as the reason for his abdication?

Sure, having a pope who is incapable of effectively managing the Church would likely lead to chaos and disarray. But there's a reason why fewer than a dozen men have resigned the papacy over the course of the past 2,000 years. It would be unwise to think that what Benedict has done should become the new normal.

CatholicVote • February 28, 2013

AN OPEN LETTER TO THE COLLEGE OF CARDINALS: WHAT I WANT IN A CHURCH

Several polls released over the past few weeks indicate a growing chasm between lay Catholics and Church leadership on key moral and doctrinal issues.[3]

Many have interpreted the results to mean that the Church needs to change its teachings on homosexuality, married priests, and similar issues in order to stay relevant in an ever-changing world.

That more Catholics want the Church to be more "inclusive" when it comes

---

3 Jawed Kaleem, "New Pope Survey Finds US Catholics Think Church is Out Of Touch, Must Change Course," Huffington Post, March 8, 2013, https://www.huffpost.com/entry/new-pope-survey-catholics_n_2832598

to gay "marriage," contraception, and women's ordination is undeniable. But is abolishing centuries of teaching the right thing to do just because that's what some laity want?

In the not so distant past I considered myself a supporter of many liberal causes. To my eternal shame, I voted for John Kerry and Barack Obama for president in 2004 and 2008, respectively. Looking back, I can honestly say I was more influenced by the secular aspects of my political views than by official Catholic teaching, of which I was only vaguely familiar with.

In light of this recent polling data, I feel compelled to let the hierarchy know that not all Catholics, especially those of us who are of the Millennial generation, disagree with the Church's doctrines. Many of us love the faith just the way it is. Below is an open letter I wish to send to them as they gather to select the next pope.

Dear College of Cardinals,

I, along with millions of other Catholics, are praying for you as you prepare for the upcoming conclave, set to begin March 12. Choosing a new pope is a monumental task, one that will require the help of the Holy Spirit. In this time of great upheaval, I pray that you take into account all the needs of the Church at this time.

As you may have heard, many of the people who sit in your pews disagree with you on important issues. I do not share in their disagreements.

At the same time, there are areas in the Church that do need improvement. In a spirit of meekness and humility, I with to express to you what I believe those areas are. It is not my goal to demand anything, but it is my intention to ask you to consider these suggestions while deciding on the future of our beloved Church.

First, I do not want a Church that placates to the demands of the world. I want a Church that respects Tradition. I want a Church that acknowledges prayer and sacrifice are more powerful ways to bring people to God than worldly-minded reforms. I also want a Church that stands firm on the belief that we must conform to God's will, and not He to ours. Unlike so many in my generation, I reject the view that the Mystical Body of Christ as an oppressive, intolerant, and sexist institution.

What I also want is a Church that doesn't discard teachings that have been handed down for centuries in an attempt to curry favor with interest groups or other religions. There are a number of new-age churches that do precisely this, and they fail miserably because of it.

If the Church truly respects the will of God, it will stay true to His teachings in perpetuity. What this looks like, practically speaking, is a Church that a) encourages monthly, if not weekly, confession b) teaches the Baltimore Catechism instead of "the spirit of Vatican II" c) makes it easier for laity to live out the corporal as well as spiritual works of mercy and d) prepares its followers to combat and correct the errors of the modern world.

I also want a Church that recognizes the sacredness of the Mass. I probably differ from most Catholics in that I prefer attending the Traditional Latin Mass. When I go to the *Novus Ordo* on occasion, I don't want to see altar girls, guitars, and immodestly dressed Eucharistic ministers. I also don't want to attend Mass in a building that looks like a skyscraper or where the altar looks like it came from IKEA and the chalice bought on sale at Target.

Furthermore, I want a Church that unabashedly preaches the word of God. There is much good that can come from inter-religious dialogue, but endless discussions with those who deny Christ is the Son of God does have its limits. There was only One Church founded by Jesus Christ, and that Church is the Catholic Church. I want a Church that is unafraid to proclaim this truth and to convert others to it. I do not want one that preaches a watered-down version of its teachings because it fears being politically incorrect.

Ultimately, I want a Church that lives out the teachings it professes. In other words, I want a Church that preaches the Gospel while readily acknowledging it has not always lived up to the Gospel's teachings. If the past ten years have taught Catholics anything, it's that the Church needs to do a better job of cracking down not only on abusive priests, but on dissident theologians, progressive professors, wayward seminaries and colleges, and left-wing politicians who misrepresent or speak out against the Catholic faith. This might even require excommunications.

And finally, because we are all God's children, I want a Church that improves its outreach to persons suffering from same-sex attraction by providing them with sound, orthodox guidance so they too can learn how to live chaste, holy lives and get to heaven.

With the sincerest devotion, humility, and respect, I ask that you take into account the aforementioned concerns as you begin the conclave on March 12th.

Pax Christi,
Stephen Kokx

CatholicVote • March 8, 2013

I PRAY POPE FRANCIS IS THE RIGHT MAN FOR THE JOB

The College of Cardinals elected Argentinean Archbishop Jorge Mario Bergoglio to the Papacy this month. He was the runner-up at the 2005 conclave. Bergoglio has been described by almost everyone as a humble, down to earth defender of the faith who can bridge the gap between Latin America—where roughly 40% of the world's Catholics reside—and the parts of the world where Catholicism is in decline.

As expected, many Catholic commentators are telling us that the man now known as Francis is a "reformer" and a "true man of God."

I don't know if there was anyone who the Cardinals could have chosen that wouldn't be considered a "man of God." And I hate to rain on everyone's parade, but what evidence is there that Bergoglio was a "reformer"? As CatholicVote contributor Pia de Solenni recently admitted, "we don't know much about how he ran the chancellery in Buenos Aires."[4]

I'm willing to give the benefit of the doubt to persons more familiar with this pope than I am, but it seems to me that many of them are simply making the absurd claim that Archbishop Bergoglio's decision to ride the subway to work—and to live in a simple apartment in Argentina—says something about how he will manage the Roman Curia.

To be sure, early reports indicate Francis has historically been an outspoken critic of gay "marriage," birth control, and other issues that Mass-attending Catholics support.[5] That's great news. But what I'm more interested in is where he stands on internal Church issues. In particular, has he implemented *Summorum Pontificum*—Pope Benedict's decree on the Extraordinary Form of the Mass—in his archdiocese? Is he a supporter of all things Vatican II? Where does he stand on Catholic-Jewish, Catholic-Muslim, and Rome-SSPX relations? And does he actually have a track record of disciplining abusive and progressive priests?

The answers to these questions will become evident in the weeks and months ahead, as his past writings are being translated into English this very moment. His homilies and daily activities will also give us a better sense of who he is and what he believes.

Given the brief amount of time we've had to get to know Pope Francis, I think its fine that Catholic media outlets focus on his life story and report

---

4 Pia de Solenni, "Shoe Leather Evangelization," CatholicVote, March 14, 2013, https://www.catholicvote.org/shoe-leather-evangelization/

5 LifeSite Staff, "Pro-life leaders say Pope Francis will inspire the world to 'promote the culture of life,'" LifeSiteNews, March 13, 2013, https://www.lifesitenews.com/news/pro-life-leaders-say-pope-francis-will-inspire-the-world-to-39promote-the-c/

on how he's the *type* of person we would want as our pope. But to be quite honest, I'm having a hard time understanding how this 76-year-old, seemingly unknown Cardinal was who Pope Benedict had in mind to succeed him when he stepped down. After all, most Catholics have been publicly saying that the Church is in need of a youthful and vigorous leader. Francis is definitely not that.

I could be wrong, and I won't presume to know better than the Cardinals themselves, but only time will tell if Francis is the right man for the job. I pray that he is.

CatholicVote • March 15, 2013

WHAT POPE FRANCIS REALLY SAID ABOUT ATHEISTS

Pope Francis raised a lot of eyebrows Wednesday after saying all people who do good works, including atheists, are going to heaven. At least, that's how the *Huffington Post* interpreted his Wednesday morning homily:

> Pope Francis rocked some religious and atheist minds today when he declared that everyone was redeemed through Jesus, including atheists...
> Of course, not all Christians believe that those who don't believe will be redeemed, and the Pope's words may spark memories of the deep divisions from the Protestant reformation over the belief in redemption through grace versus redemption through works.[6]

Apparently, the *Huffington Post* doesn't understand the difference between redemption and salvation.

Reuters interpreted the pope's comments in a similar way:

> Atheists should be seen as good people if they do good, Pope Francis said on Wednesday in his latest urging that people of all religions—or no religion—work together...
> He told the story of a Catholic who asked a priest if even atheists had been redeemed by Jesus.
> 'Even them, everyone,' the pope answered, according to Vatican Radio.
> 'We all have the duty to do good,' he said. 'Just do good and we'll find

6 "Pope Francis Says Atheists Who Do Good Are Redeemed, Not Just Catholics," Huffington Post, May 22, 2013, https://www.huffpost.com/entry/pope-francis-good-atheists_n_3320757?ref=topbar

a meeting point,' the pope said in a hypothetical conversation [with a priest]...

Francis' reaching out to atheists and people who belong to no religion is a marked contrast to the attitude of former Pope Benedict, who sometimes left non-Catholics feeling that he saw them as second-class believers.[7]

No more than an hour went by and an inquisitive Presbyterian friend of mine emailed me with a link to the *Huffington Post* story with the following question: "So doing good on its own is enough for salvation in Catholicism?" In response, I sent him two links that clarified the pope's words. The first was a blog post by Fr Dwight Longenecker. Here is what he wrote:

The Pope is simply affirming certain truths that any somewhat knowledgeable Catholic will uphold.

First, that Christ died to redeem the whole world. We can distinguish his redemptive work from the acceptance of salvation. He redeemed the whole world. However, many will reject that saving work. In affirming the universality of Christ's redemptive work we are not universalists. To say that he redeemed the whole world is not to conclude that all will be saved.

Secondly, the Pope is also affirming that all humans are created in God's image and are therefore created good. Yes, created good, but that goodness is wounded by original sin.

Thirdly, he is affirming that all men and women are obliged to pursue what is beautiful, good, and true. Natural virtue is possible—even obligatory, but natural virtue on its own is not sufficient for salvation. Grace is necessary to advance beyond natural virtue to bring the soul to salvation. The Pope does not say atheists being good on their own will be saved. He says they, like all men, are redeemed by Christ's death and their good works are the starting place where we can meet with them—the implication being 'meet with them in an encounter that leads eventually to faith in Christ.'[8]

---

7 Reuters, "Atheists Are Good if They Do Good, Pope Francis Says," May 22, 2013, https://web.archive.org/web/20130703112502/http://uk.reuters.com/article/2013/05/22/uk-pope-atheists-idUKBRE94L0V120130522

8 Fr Dwight Longenecker, "Did Pope Francis Preach Salvation by Works??" Patheos, May 23, 2013, https://www.patheos.com/blogs/standingonmyhead/2013/05/did-pope-francis-preach-salvation-by-works.html

The second link I sent him was from *Catholicism.org's* Brian Kelly, who was writing in response to a *Catholic Online* article that had a headline that read: "Pope Francis says atheists can do good and go to heaven too!" Here is what Mr Kelly said:

> Pope Francis did not say that an atheist who does naturally good things can be saved if he dies an atheist. Yet that is the impression given by Catholic Online's half truth headline...
>
> The Pope... simply reminded the faithful that there can be, and is, goodness, or natural virtue, outside the Church. And that Christ's death on the Cross redeemed all men. He paid the price so that every man could come to God and be saved.
>
> If *Catholic Online* is insinuating that Pope Francis has 'reformed' the irreformable dogma, outside the Church there is no salvation, then that is shameful and disingenuous.[9]

At the end of the day, could Pope Francis have been a little clearer about what he was trying to say? Sure. That's the risk of delivering off-the-cuff sermons. The real fault, I think, lies with the theologically-illiterate press corps, whose understanding of basic Catholic doctrine is so infinitesimal that it is increasingly unable to report on the Catholic Church without completely embarrassing itself.

CatholicVote • May 23, 2013

PUTTING POPE FRANCIS IN CONTEXT

This is really getting old, isn't it? Instead of courageously guiding his sheep through the landmine-ridden battle field that is the modern world, the Bishop of Rome, with his latest head scratching remarks about atheists, proselytism, and following one's conscience, is making life for members of the Church Militant infinitely more difficult as they attempt to save non-Catholics from the fires of hell.

In the days following Cardinal Bergoglio's elevation to the papacy, we were told that he is a "man of God" and that his humility—as exemplified by his reliance on public transportation while living in Buenos Aires—would serve

---

9 Brian Kelly, "Dreadful Misleading Headline of Catholic Online Pins Heresy on Pope," Catholicism.org, May 23, 2013, https://catholicism.org/dreadful-misleading-headline-of-catholic-online-pins-heresy-on-pope.html

CHAPTER I: POPE FRANCIS

as "a breath of fresh air" for the overly-bureaucratized Church hierarchy. Resisting the urge to jump on the cult of personality bandwagon that has unfortunately characterized the papacy in recent decades, I argued that we don't really know anything about this man from South America, and that it is ludicrous to assume we can glean insight into how he will run the Curia based on his love of riding the subway. I kindly suggested that it would be wise for Catholics to simply "pray that Pope Francis is the right man for the job" instead of building him up into a sort of Catholic superhero who may turn out to be the complete opposite of what people think he is.

Six months into Francis' reign and it is safe to say that Jorge Bergoglio is the same liberal Jesuit he was before he was named the Vicar of Christ, and that the College of Cardinals knew exactly who they were choosing to succeed Pope Benedict.

The most troubling aspect of the pope's recent comments about atheists to Fr Antonio Spadaro SJ and Italian journalist Eugenio Scalfari is that he has made these sorts of disturbing statements before. While talking with Pius XII-hating Jewish Rabbi Abraham Skorka in their 2010 book *On Heaven and Earth*, Bergoglio said the following:

> When I speak with atheists, I will sometimes discuss social concerns, but I do not propose the problem of God as a starting point, except in the case that they propose it to me. I do not approach the relationship to proselytize or convert the atheist. I respect him...nor would I say his life is condemned.[10]

In *Conversations with Jorge Bergoglio: His Life in His Own Words*—a text with a forward written by Skorka—the former Archbishop of Buenos Aires said: "We are looking for a reconciled diversity...I do not think we can, at the moment, consider uniformity, or complete unity, but we can consider a reconciled diversity that implies walking together, praying and working together, and seeking unity in the truth."[11]

These scandalous comments are rarely brought up by the mainstream Catholic media, which has strangely failed to inform us about anything Jorge Bergoglio said or did before he was named the latest successor of St Peter. Perhaps they know he has a leftist past?

---

10 Jorge Mario Bergoglio and Abraham Skorka, *On Heaven and Earth: Pope Francis on Faith, Family, and the Church in the Twenty-First Century*, Image Books, New York, 2015, Originally published in Spanish in 2010, p.12

11 Sergio Rubin and Francesca Ambrogetti, *Pope Francis: Conversations with Jorge Bergoglio*, Putnam, New York, 2013, pp. 227–228

Whatever the case, Francis' words today provide us with evidence that he is far more interested in promoting a "brotherhood of man" than converting non-Catholics to the one true faith. They also allow us to conclude that he was not taken out of context when, in a homily delivered back in May, he seemed to say that atheists only need to do do good if they want to get into heaven—even though Scripture directly refutes the possibility of this ever happening.[12]

Francis' interviews are also not done, as some suggest, in a joking, half-hearted manner. While speaking with Eugenio Scalfari, an 89-year-old atheist, Francis intentionally de-emphasized the unchangeable teaching of the Church that says all people are obligated to form their consciences according to the Catholic faith and that the Church is required to go forth and baptize all nations.

Is he wholly unfamiliar with Christ's teaching to baptize all nations? Or does he reject it outright?

Some commentators say Francis is simply presenting the doctrines of the Church in a new, fresh sort of way with his own "linguistic flair" and that the ambiguity he speaks with is what we should expect going forward.

Hogwash.

Francis is not putting the Church's teachings forward in a new way. He is purposefully ignoring them altogether. Introducing atheists to a lukewarm, watered-down version of Catholicism is the direct opposite of Christian charity. Just look at the Gospel. Jesus didn't chase after the rich man, invite him over for tea, get to know what his childhood was like, learn how much he disagrees with Scripture, and then tell him that if he wants to gain eternal life that instead of giving away everything he owns all he has to do is sell 3/5[ths] of his possessions. No. Our Lord let him go on his way after He firmly told him the truth and that He realized his message wasn't being received. He kicked off the dust from his shoes, in other words, and moved on to others who were open to his message.

In order to mop up the mess Pope Francis is leaving behind as he reaches out to everyone who isn't a supporter of the Latin Mass and Traditional Catholic teachings, a literal cottage industry of papal apologists has emerged. Eager to prove their devotion to the person who currently occupies the throne of St Peter, a small cadre of bloggers, priests, and arm chair-theologians have seen to it to repeatedly assert that Pope Francis' statements are within the limits of the Church's magisterium, and that the rest of us are just a bunch of angry Traditionalists who need to "take a breath" and "relax."

12 Romans 1:20

Relying on the goodwill they've built up with their audiences over the past many years, these powerful though intellectually dishonest Pharisees have put themselves in a vulnerable spot, as their entire reputation is now contingent upon the hope that Catholics will blindly buy into their claim that all this confusion can simply be attributed to a biased press corps and a few translation errors. By invoking this deceptive strategy, these con artists allow themselves to worm their way out of ever having to truly explain the errors of Francis' remarks while accusing Traditionalists of being schismatic after coming to the obvious conclusions about him and stating them publicly.

Letting Francis Speak For Himself

Inasmuch as the mainstream media is incompetent on a number of issues, they are not as mentally handicapped as the Catholic propaganda "news" industry makes them out to be. They can, after all, read and write.

And unlike some in the Catholic press corps (which is proving itself to be nothing more than an army of blind followers willfully following blind prophets), secular journalists have gone to school for their profession. They may not all possess Bachelor's degrees in theology, but then again, neither do most Catholics. At some point, blaming the secular media will become an ineffective strategy. You can only cry wolf so many times until you lose all credibility.

Simply stated, Pope Francis is not being taken out of context in his interviews. Nor is he trolling the media, as one contributor to *First Things* has embarrassingly argued. This is a man who has been a priest for over four decades. He knows what he is saying. "What the mouth speaketh the heart believeth," Scripture says.[13] If the pope cannot talk freely in an interview without deviating from approved Catholic doctrine on a regular basis, then the crisis in the Church has reached an entirely new level. He is not a guest lecturer at some community college. He is the leader of a church with over a billion souls. It's his duty to provide them with clear teachings and to denounce the errors of the world that threaten their faith.

Although the majority of the arguments establishment Catholic media outlets are going along with this circus, there have been more than a few individuals who want to keep their integrity intact during this troubling papacy. Noted natural law theorist Germain Grisez, who is not a Traditionalist by any means, recently wrote the following:

---

13 Luke 6:45

Pope Francis [has] said some things that I do not understand. I'm afraid [he] has failed to consider carefully enough the likely consequences of letting loose with his thoughts in a world that will applaud being provided with such help in subverting the truth that it is his job to guard as inviolable and proclaim with fidelity.[14]

Fr Michael Orsi, a research fellow at Ave Maria School of Law, has likewise argued that Francis' words "have caused [damage] for the pro-life movement and [to] those who are trying to defend marriage as being between a man and a woman. His remarks have effectively given a sword to those who want to stifle [those voices]."[15]

Continuing to Make Excuses

That Catholics are jumping through linguistic hula-hoops in order to assure the faithful that Francis' words fall within Tradition is a major problem. Giving the pope the benefit of the doubt is one thing, but even he needs to be corrected when he speaks in a questionable manner. As St Thomas Aquinas once wrote: "There being an imminent danger for the faith, prelates must be questioned, even publicly, by their subjects."

Be that as it may, the majority of Catholic bloggers seem to think St Thomas is just plain wrong. As it stands currently, the overwhelming majority of them prefer not to correct, but rather to defend the pope's confusing rhetoric by telling us *what they think he meant to say* instead of telling us *what he actually said*. They simply won't let the man speak for himself!

In a column that appeared on *The Catholic Thing* website, Robert Royal, who regularly appears on EWTN, astonishingly wrote: "Most ordinary people won't be able to distinguish between what Francis is talking about—an overbearing proselytism—and a proper effort to convert."[16] Royal then argues that John the Baptist and the rest of the Apostles weren't aggressive proselytizers and that they never stepped on non-Catholic's toes when it came to converting them.

How risible!

14 Michael Sean Winters, "Germaine Grisez on Pope Francis," National Catholic Reporter, October 1, 2013, https://www.ncronline.org/blogs/distinctly-catholic/germaine-grisez-pope-francis

15 Michael Orsi, "The Pope's Blurred Red Lines," The Washington Times, September 26, 2013, https://www.washingtontimes.com/news/2013/sep/26/orsi-the-popes-blurred-red-lines/

16 Robert Royal, "The Heart of Bergoglio," The Catholic Thing, October 2, 2013, https://www.thecatholicthing.org/2013/10/02/the-heart-of-bergoglio/

Writing for *Patheos*, Fr Dwight Longenecker argued: "What [Pope Francis] probably meant was that the kind of religious emotional blackmail that is sometimes used to gain converts is useless."

Seriously? Do you know any Catholic who has relied on a "religious emotional blackmail" strategy to convert non-Catholics? What planet am I on? Is this really the level folks have stooped to?

Yet another blogger insanely called on Catholics to plug their ears and put their head in the sand because, "if a Catholic is opposed to the Holy Father's teaching, he or she should either 1) take the concern privately to a priest or bishop who will decide whether to take it to the Holy See, or 2) remain prayerfully silent trusting that if the truth really is at stake, it will ultimately prevail."[17]

Traditional Catholicism Condemns Francis

No man is above the teachings of the One, Holy, Catholic and Apostolic Church. As we are told in 2 John 1:10: "If anyone comes to you and does not bring this doctrine, do not receive him in your house or even greet him." The Bible is replete with instructions similar to this.

We also know that Paul corrected Peter and that we are not to be captivated, as Colossians 2:8 states, "with an empty, seductive philosophy according to human tradition." Silence, in other words, is not an option when souls are at stake. Sorry, neocatholic bloggers!

What the first several months of Francis' papacy tells us is that the Church in the post-Vatican II era is not unlike what its proponents allege the Church of the pre-Vatican II era was known for: docility, obedience, clericalism, and silence.

Self-appointed papal-explainers-in-chief love to look down on "Radical Traditionalist" Catholics. They act like we don't have the mental capacity to understand what the pope is actually saying. They also lecture us to remain "silent" about our concerns. They then tell us to pray, obey, and "trust" that everything will turn out just fine. When we don't comply with their demands, and proceed to point out how unnerving it is, for example, to hear President Obama say how "hugely impressed" he is with Pope Francis, we are labeled schismatics and are uninvited to speak at prominent conferences. Priests and bishops who see the problems with Francis are also pressured to stay silent. What irony it is to see the dictatorship of relativism Pope Benedict so frequently condemned has found its way into the Church.

At the outset of this article, I mentioned that in the days immediately

17 Stacy Transancos, "The Head-Slapping Criticism of Pope Francis," Catholic Sistas, October 1, 2013, https://www.catholicsistas.com/pope-francis-criticism/

following Francis' election I wrote a column arguing that instead of building him up into something he might not be it is best to simply pray that Jorge Bergoglio is the right man for the job. Having now lived through six months of questionable statements, ambiguous remarks, and problematic pronouncements, it seems we will all have to pray harder for this man from South America. A lot harder.

Unpublished • October 1, 2013

FRANCIS AND THE SULTAN

Cardinal Jorge Mario Bergoglio chose the name Francis in honor of St Francis of Assisi. Catholics on E W T N could barely contain themselves in the days after the 2013 conclave when they learned of this. The following comment (or some variation of it) was mentioned almost every five minutes on that network: "God told St Francis to 'go and rebuild my Church.' Pope Francis will go and do the same. I can't wait to see how he does it!"

That was then. This is now.

Earlier this week, Pope Francis welcomed Ahmed el-Tayyib and a small band of merry Mohammedans to the Vatican. El-Tayyib is the grand Imam of an Islamic center in Egypt that five years ago cut off relations with Rome because Pope Benedict x v i rightly pointed out that certain teachings of Islam are wrong.

Fine by me. After all, what does endless "dialogue" with erroneous cults accomplish anyway? It's certainly not Biblical to engage in such behavior. More often than not, a false notion of human respect develops between the two "dialoguing" parties, resulting in a worldly friendship that ignores the person in error's eternal well being.

During their meeting, Francis told the Imam that "the meeting is the message."

I wonder: just what is "the message"?

As far as I can tell, "the message" is "you're okay, I'm okay. Let's put aside doctrine and come together in fraternal brotherhood. We are all God's children. We will go forward slowly."

How utterly Masonic.

This is par for the course for Pope Francis, who just a couple years ago told Muslims not to embrace Jesus Christ but rather to cling to "the faith that your parents instilled in you."

After their meeting, the Vatican told the media that Francis and El-Tayyib discussed the need for the "the world's great religions to show a common commitment to peace in the world."[18]

Here's my question: How can there be a true commitment to peace if the "the world's great religions" reject the Prince of Peace, Jesus Christ?

St Francis of Assisi knew the answer to that question. That's why, when he ventured to meet with sultan Malek al-Kamil in 1219, he preached to him the truths of the Catholic faith—*the world's* "one great religion." Dialogue, as it has been practiced by the Church since Vatican II, would have been viewed by him as wholly un-Catholic.

Rebuild my Church? Pope Francis has done nothing of the kind and until he returns to Tradition, the Church will remain in ruins.

Magnificat Media • May 25, 2016

POPE FRANCIS' ABU DHABI SPEECH IS MORE MASONIC THAN CATHOLIC

Pope Francis' visit to Abu Dhabi, the capital of the United Arab Emirates (UAE), in February was a disaster for the Catholic Faith. So was the downplaying, ignoring, and attempts to explain away his un-Catholic remarks by mainstream Catholic media personalities.[19]

Not once during his lengthy speech at the UAE's Human Fraternity meeting did Francis mention the Most Holy Name of Jesus—the name which the devil hates to hear, demons hide in terror of, and whose name priests invoke to cleanse possessed souls.

Instead, the pope spoke generally about "the Creator" and "the Merciful One" while imploring listeners to build a world founded not on the Social Kingship of Christ but on "fraternity" (mentioned 15 times), "brotherhood" (mentioned 13 times), and "justice" (mentioned 9 times).

Some Catholics might think emphasizing what Catholics have in common with Muslims—as well as other persons who believe in a higher power but are not followers of Christ—is what any responsible Successor of St Peter would do in the modern, globalized age.

18 Nicole Winfield, "Pope Embraces Al-Azhar Imam in Sign of Renewed Relations," Associated Press, May 23, 2016, https://apnews.com/general-news-dd502c6bd1eb446eaa646e-20242564cf

19 Father John Zuhlsdorf, "Francis Signed Document Saying That God Willed The 'Pluralism and Diversity of Religions.' What's Up With That?" Fr Z's Blog, February 5, 2019, https://wdtprs.com/2019/02/francis-signed-document-saying-that-god-willed-the-pluralism-and-diversity-of-religions-whats-up-with-that/

"Francis is a public figure. He has a duty to maintain good relations with the different peoples of the world," one often hears.

This pope-as-globetrotting-politician-in-chief attitude forgets several key aspects of the Catholic religion.

First, rounding off the edges of our faith to pursue common political cause with non-Catholics was the chief mistake of the Americanists in the United States in the 1890s. They were rightly condemned by Leo XIII for this error.

Second, the primary duty of the pope is to teach Catholicism in its fullness by rebuking falsehoods and clarifying the truth, come what may.

Third, while the pope can obviously play a leading role in maintaining a certain level of natural harmony among nations, he cannot do so at the expense of the faith. He is obligated first and foremost to preach the Gospel, in season and out (2 Timothy 4:2), and to accept the persecution that may result knowing full well that Christ was also hated by the world (John 15:18–19) for teaching the truth.

Lastly, God desires all men to be Catholic. It would be the height of absurdity to say the pope should temporarily pause this mandate to proselytize all nations because the world has plunged itself headlong into heresy. If anything, such a situation should compel him to be an even more zealous missionary for souls.

Christ, Not Fraternity, Safeguards Peace

If the Church today was led by a holy pope, those who attended Francis' speech in Abu Dhabi would have been encouraged to leave behind their false ideas and to embrace the Catholic religion. Quite obviously, this did not happen.

Far from emulating St Francis of Assisi, who, in the 13th century, tried to convince Sultan al-Kamil to follow Our Lord, Pope Francis told his audience that "today, we too in the name of God, in order to safeguard peace, need to enter together as one family into an ark which can sail the stormy seas of the world: the ark of fraternity."[20]

In other words, forget Jesus Christ. Forget the sacraments. Stay where you are. Human fraternity is our guide!

But how can men have peace without the Prince of Peace? It is a fool's errand to propose such a policy. Not only does Psalm 127 tell us that those who build without the Lord "labor in vain," Pope Pius XI, in his 1925 encyclical *Quas Primas*, taught that only when men recognize "both in private and in

20 "Pope to UAE: Address to Fraternity Conference—Full Text," Vatican News, February 3, 2019, https://www.vaticannews.va/en/pope/news/2019-02/pope-francis-uae-global-conference-human-fraternity-full-text.html

public life, that Christ is King, society will at last receive the great blessings of real liberty, well-ordered discipline, peace and harmony."

Basic Catholic teaching also holds that the Catholic Church is the Ark of Salvation, and that it is within *that* vessel which men are meant to "sail the stormy seas of the world." True and lasting peace only occurs when men enter *that* ark, and not into the rickety, glued-together paddle boat Modernist Rome is constructing with the enemies of God. The Jesus-free project that Francis' Masonic-inspired remarks speak about is doomed from the start.

Christ Wants All Men to be Catholic

Despite Francis' contention that they are "brother and sisters," Catholics and Muslims aren't either of these in any real sense.

Ephesians 2:3–5 tells us we are all born "children of wrath." It is through Baptism that we are liberated from Satan and become part of the true People of God. Put another way, Baptism is what makes us leave behind the "human family" and become part of the supernatural "Body of Christ."

Islam denies all this. It rejects Original Sin. It rejects the divinity of Jesus Christ and it condemns the teaching that God is three-in-one. It also does not venerate Mary the way she is supposed to be venerated. Brothers and sisters typically honor the same mother. But it is clear that Catholics and Muslims do not do this.

Francis' assertion that "the desire to affirm oneself and one's own group above others" is "the enemy" of fraternity is also offensive. His claim that "each belief system is called to overcome the divide between friends and enemies" is equally detestable.

Perhaps there is a translation error here, but since when do Catholics believe the "great pearl" (Matthew 13:46) of faith that they possess is just one of the many "belief systems" of the world? Did the great martyrs of the past die for a mere "belief system"? Of course not. As Pope Pius IX wrote in *Qui Pluribus* in 1846, "the Christian faith is the work of God." Islam, on the other hand, is not.

God Does Not Will a Diversity of Religions

The pope's monstrous betrayal of the Gospel is made worse by his signing of a "Document on Human Fraternity for World Peace and Living Together" with Sheikh Ahmed al-Tayeb, the Grand Imam of Al-Azhar in Cairo.

Waxing and waning about what tomorrow's worldwide utopia will look like, the document astonishingly declares that "the pluralism and the diversity of religions, color, sex, race and language are willed by God in His wisdom, through which He created human beings. This divine wisdom is the source from which the right to freedom of belief and the freedom to be different derives."

Whatever happened to the rights of God? What about God's claim over His creatures to be worshipped according to the manner He desires? Wasn't a diversity of languages punishment for the Tower of Babel?

What this document essentially amounts to is Jesus standing next to Mohammed and co-authoring a statement that declares the two of them are just old friends, and that everyone in the world is free to follow or reject either of them.

Despite the document's obvious assertion that religious pluralism is "willed by God," more than a few neoconservative Catholics jumped into action to tell us what the pope was probably, really, trying to, sort of, actually say on that subject.

"We must seek a way to understand this without it sounding like heresy," Fr John Zuhlsdorf ridiculously argued on his blog. "If you read the statement to mean that by God's positive or active will there are a multiplicity of religions, that's an error."

"Were one to choose," he went on, to read the document as saying "God willed a diversity of religions not just by His permissive will but by His active, positive will," then "[t]hat would be contrary to reason and the Catholic Faith."[21]

Wait, what? It's the *reader's fault* for not understanding this noxious document in the way it is plainly written? Imagine taking this sort of approach while you were in school.

"I the student must seek to understand how Mr Nethercott's claim that 2+2=5 isn't wrong. Although last year Mr Brand said 2+2=4, maybe he has some deep insight that can enlighten me. If I don't come up with how to reconcile these two teachings, then I am the one in the wrong and not my teachers."

Catholic University of America professor Chad Pecknold trotted out another worn-out neocon strategy when he told the U.K.-based *Catholic Herald* that, "in the context of the document, the Holy Father is clearly referring not to the evil of many false religions, but positively refers to the diversity of religions only in the sense that they are evidence of our natural desire to know God."

"A diversity of religions can be spoken about as permissively willed by

21 Fr John Zuhlsdorf, "PODCAzt 169: Bp Athanasius Schneider on 'The Only God-Willed Religion," Fr Z's Blog, February 8, 2019, https://wdtprs.com/2019/02/podcazt-169-bp-athanasius-schneider-on-the-only-god-willed-religion/

God without denying the supernatural good of one true religion," he added.[22]

Sorry. This "permissive will" nonsense is not what Francis' document speaks about. A Dominican theologian speaking anonymously to LifeSiteNews recently clarified Church teaching on this exact point.

"God permits non-Catholic religions to exist; but permitting something is not a way of willing it, it is a way of not willing to prevent it. Thus God permits many innocent people to be killed, but He does not will it," he rightly noted.[23]

Catholic author Taylor Marshall also picked up on the absurdity of what the blogosphere was saying. He tweeted the following: "We faithful shouldn't have to jump through theological hoops in order to make the Pope of Rome sound like an orthodox Catholic. Most of us are fatigued by it. I tried it for years. 'Context! Mistranslation! Well it could mean this!' No more #popesplaining."

There is no divine duty imposed on Catholics to read something clergy say in a particular way so it doesn't "sound like heresy." The "truth will set you free" (John 8:32) is our only guide. If what a priest, bishop, cardinal or even pope puts forth is obviously against the faith, it deserves to be challenged and if necessary rebuked and corrected.

Placing the burden of understanding Francis' heterodox remarks so that the so-called "hermeneutic of continuity" isn't violated—as Fr Zuhlsdorf is attempting to do here—is a cheap, intellectually dishonest way of avoiding the crux of the matter. It's a not-so-subtle form of gaslighting that emanates from fear and a lack of fortitude.

Vatican 11 is the Real Culprit

As noted by Professor Roberto de Mattei, at the heart of Francis' statement lies the core teachings of Freemasonry—liberty, equality, and fraternity.[24]

Whereas Freemasonry holds that man has no need of Baptism and has a natural right to religious liberty, Catholicism teaches that error has no rights and that he is obliged to conform his conscience to the religion established by Jesus Christ.

22 Chad Pecknold, "Pope Signs Document Saying God Wills Religious Pluralism," Catholic Herald, February 5, 2019, https://catholicherald.co.uk/news/2019/02/05/pope-signs-declaration-saying-god-wills-religions-pluralism-what-does-this-mean/

23 Diane Montagna, "Pope Francis under fire for claiming 'diversity of religions' is 'willed by God,'" LifeSiteNews, February 5, 2019, https://www.lifesitenews.com/news/pope-francis-under-fire-for-claiming-diversity-of-religions-is-willed-by-go/

24 Diane Montagna, "Pope seems to 'overturn' Gospel in statement with Grand Imam: Church historian," LifeSiteNews, February 6, 2019, https://www.lifesitenews.com/news/popes-claim-that-god-wills-many-religions-seems-to-overturn-gospel-church-h/

Whereas Freemasonry says that all men—and religions—are equal, and that politics should be separated from and totally independent of religion, Catholicism affirms that it alone is the one true faith and that the state is obliged to recognize its dependence on Jesus Christ.

Moreover, whereas Freemasonry claims that all men are "brothers" united by a fraternal bond under "the Grand Architect of the Universe," Catholicism teaches that men become spiritual brothers after being incorporated into the Mystical Body of Jesus Christ through baptism under the divine paternity of a Trinitarian God.

When one reads Francis' remarks—and the statement he signed with the Grand Imam—it is clear he is espousing Freemasonic principles.

On his plane ride back to Rome, Francis admitted the document he signed was inspired by the Second Vatican Council.

"From the Catholic point of view, the document does not pull away one millimeter from Vatican II, which is even cited a few times. The document was made in the spirit of Vatican II."[25]

Catholics must continue to insist that Pope Francis embrace Tradition. They must call upon him to give up the Council, its Masonic-inspired teachings, and affirm his brethren in the faith of our fathers.

Fr Davide Pagliarani, the Superior General of the Society of St Pius X, has been exemplary on this issue in recent months. Below are just a few of the comments he has made as of late:

- "It is the duty of the Pope to transmit faithfully the Deposit of Faith. The Pope must therefore put an end to the terrible crisis that has shaken the Church for the last 50 years."[26]

- "The Pope should declare the decree on religious liberty erroneous and correct it accordingly. We are convinced that one day a Pope will do just that, and return to the pure doctrine that was the reference before this Council."[27]

- "The questions of religious liberty, ecumenism, and the divine constitution of the Church were all dealt with by Popes prior to the Second

25 Pope Francis, "Full Text of Pope Francis' In-Flight Press Conference From Abu Dhabi," Catholic News Agency, February 5, 2019, https://www.catholicnewsagency.com/news/40492/full-text-of-pope-francis-in-flight-press-conference-from-abu-dhabi
26 "It Is Inconceivable That The Church Was Mistaken for Two Millenia," FSSPX. News, December 15, 2018, https://fsspx.news/en/news-events/news/it-inconceivable-church-was-mistaken-two-millennia-43158
27 Ibid.

Vatican Council. It suffices to revive their teachings."[28]

• "Collegiality places the Church in a permanent situation of a quasi-council...this revolutionary doctrine is fundamentally contrary to the monarchical nature of the Church."[29]

• "One day, a Pope...will take things in hand and all that needs to be corrected, will be corrected."[30]

Let us pray Pope Francis heeds the advice given to him by Fr Pagliarani. Not only for our sake, but for his own.

Catholic Family News • February 15, 2019

POPE FRANCIS ATTACKS THE KINGSHIP OF CHRIST

If you ask your local *Novus Ordo* priest or bishop about the Social Kingship of Christ chances are you'll be greeted with a blank stare looking back at you. Such is the sad reality of living in a post-*Dignitatis Humanae* world where seemingly everyone thinks that everyone has a God-given right to reject the religion God himself said was the only way to eternal salvation.

Despite the fact that the vast majority of Catholic clergy a) don't know b) don't care or c) are too lacking in courage to preach about the Social Kingship of Christ, Our Lord remains the sovereign ruler of the entire universe.

Fr Brian Harrison, an Australian-born priest, is clued in on this. In a recent essay for *OnePeterFive,* he reminded Pope Francis about it.

Before discussing his article, I'd like to call to mind that in a wide-ranging interview with *La Croix* on May 9th, Francis said the following:

States must be secular. Confessional states end badly. That goes against the grain of history. I believe that a version of laicity accompanied by a solid law guaranteeing religious freedom offers a framework for going forward. We are all equal as sons (and daughters) of God and with our personal dignity.[31]

28 Ibid.
29 "An Exclusive Interview With Father Davide Pagliarani," FSSPX.News, December 28, 2018, https://stas.org/en/news-events/news/exclusive-interview-father-davide-pagliarani-43460
30 Ibid.
31 Gerard O'Connell, "Pope in La Croix Interview: The State Must Respect People's Consciences," America Magazine, May 17, 2016, https://www.americamagazine.org/content/dis-

I commented on the those remarks in this space a couple weeks ago. Here is what I wrote:

Has there ever been a pontiff who so despised not only the un-changeable Catholic doctrine that Christ is King of all the Universe but also the Divine Mandate to go forth and teach all nations the Catholic faith as Francis does?

One wonders if he has ever read the *Syllabus of Errors,* which condemns the notion that 'the Church ought to be separated from the State, and the State from the Church.' Has he also ever studied Pope St Pius x's *Vehementer Nos,* which teaches that it is an 'absolutely false' and 'most pernicious error' to say the State 'must be separated from the Church?'

In his article for *OnePeterFive,* Fr Harrison said something similar to my own remarks. Here are his words:

Over a century ago, Pope Leo xiii already acknowledged that American-style church-state separation (then fairly benign) was acceptable in countries with predominantly non-Catholic populations. However, he and all the popes taught that, as a matter of doctrinal principle, the nation or state has no more right than the individual to proclaim its independence from God and his revealed word. It is not morally entitled to say, 'As a civic community we have no duty to worship and honor God, or to follow any specific religious creed in our laws and policies.'

Fr Harrison continues:

In response to the growing secularization of Western society, this doctrine of Christ's social kingship was classically expounded by Pope Leo xiii in *Immortale Dei* (1885), 'On the Christian Constitution of States,' and by Pius xi in his 1925 encyclical *Quas Primas...* Both these encyclicals are referenced in their entirety in the final (1997) edition of the Catechism of the Catholic Church in its exposition of the First Commandment (cf. last footnote to #2105). In this sub-section, headed 'The Social Duty of Religion and the Right to Religious Liberty,' the ccc also cites two affirmations of Vatican Council ii. One is that a just religious liberty leaves intact 'the traditional Catholic doctrine on the moral duty of individuals and societies to the true religion and the

patches/pope-la-croix-interview-state-must-respect-peoples-consciences one Church of Christ.' (Just before they voted on this text, the Council Fathers were told by the official relator that these words from article 1 of the Declaration on Religious Liberty were to be understood as reaffirming the duty of the 'public power' [*potestas publica*] to recognize Catholicism as the true religion.) The other citation comes from the Decree on the Apostolate of the Laity, #13, affirming that citizens should strive to "infuse the Christian spirit into the mentality and mores, laws and structures, of the communities in which [they] live" (#2105, emphasis added in both citations).

While Fr Harrison is certainly right to highlight the fact that Vatican II mentions, at least in passing, the Social Kingship of Christ, I would quibble with the way he seems to claim that there is continuity with pre- and post-Vatican II teaching on the matter.

The portion of *Dignitatis Humanae* (DH) where it says the traditional teaching has been "left intact" was inserted into the document at the last minute by Paul VI. It was more or less a throwaway line that didn't change the fact that once *DH* was approved, the Church, from that point on, would hold that every man, in the name of his dignity, has a right to publicly proclaim blasphemy, even in Catholic nations.

If you read *DH* and its various paragraphs in their proper context, you realize that it says even in countries where an established religion reigns (i.e. where the Kingship of Christ is recognized) false religions also have a right to be publicly professed. In essence, if Christ gets to reign, so does Mohammed, Luther, and the like. This inevitably leads to the dissolution and undermining of the Social Kingship of Christ. I'll address that question more in a future post. For now, let's revisit Fr Harrison's essay:

> It's true that the historical record of confessional Catholic States has been far from stainless: it has often been marred not only by excessive intolerance of minorities, but also by harmful government interference in church affairs. But in this fallen world, disestablishment eventually turns out to be worse, as we are now finding out the hard way in the apostate West. For once the Catholic Church is no longer legally recognized as the authentic interpreter of morality, even the natural moral law becomes perverted and finally jettisoned.

He continues by saying:

> Taken in their most natural sense, the Pope's first four words cited above

go directly against the Catholic doctrine of Christ's social kingship. Francis doesn't merely say that in today's pluralistic and secularized Western society it may now sometimes be more pastorally prudent for the Church, even in traditionally Catholic countries, not to insist on the exercise her divinely-bestowed right to be legally recognized as the true religion (cf. Vatican ɪɪ, Gaudium et Spes, #76). No, his assertion that States have a duty to disavow any religious confession is unqualified. It would therefore be pretty hard to give a 'hermeneutic-of-continuity' reading to these words—one that would plausibly harmonize them with the doctrine of Christ's Social Kingship that we've summarized above. Indeed, this doctrine has been so neglected and forgotten in recent decades that I wonder how much the Holy Father knows about it. His view, unfortunately, seems to be that the Church simply got it wrong when she promoted Catholic confessional states right through the post-Constantine era; and that only in the late 20th century has she finally learned that Church/State separation, along the lines pioneered by the U.S.A., is really the best arrangement for all nations—even those with large Catholic majorities.[32]

This is precisely what I wrote a couple weeks ago! Here is what I said:

The core idea behind [the Pope's] naive theory is that of Integral Humanism—the belief that a society infused by a wide assortment of Christian, Jewish, Muslim and all sorts of 'religious' values is all that is needed for a country to flourish.

How wrong this view was. And still is! The aggressive secularism we experience in much of the West today is due to the fact that the Church went silent on the Social Kingship of Christ and turned over the public square to men who had no understanding (hatred?) of original sin or spiritual warfare and sanctifying grace. The entire idea of 'Integral Humanism' is a fiction. History has proven that a state always has an established religion. Today, that religion is secular humanism (i.e. Liberalism). Pope Francis is living in the past. It is secular states that end badly.

The pope is beyond confused about this issue. We should pray for him.

Magnificat Media • May 31, 2016

32 Fr Brian Harrison, "Does Pope Francis Understand the Kingship of Christ?" One Peter Five, May 26, 2016, https://onepeterfive.com/pope-francis-understand-social-kingship-christ/

IS THE AMAZON SYNOD BEING USED TO SET UP A FALSE CHURCH?

The Amazon Synod is almost over. It's probably going to be a disaster for the Church. Just how much destruction it leaves in its wake is up to God. In all likelihood, the synod's final document will rely on ambiguous language with footnotes galore. Then again, its authors may be more brazen than they have in years past. After all, who is going to stop them?

To be sure, previous encyclicals written by Francis, as well as the documents of Vatican II, will be cited in whatever the event's organizers conjure up. The Council of Trent? Probably not so much.

Pope Francis' sermon at the synod's opening Mass in St Peter's gave Catholics a clue as to how the gathering would proceed. In his remarks, he spoke about how the fire of the Gospel needs to spread and should not be "smothered by the ashes of fear."

He then called on bishops to not have a "concern for defending the status quo." In typical liberal fashion, he also remarked that "the Church is always on the move" and that she mustn't have a "spirit of timidity."[33]

Perhaps the most egregious part of his remarks was when he seemed to characterize the teaching of the Catholic faith to pagan tribes as a form of colonialism.

Laying the Groundwork for Schism

The real reason the Amazon Synod is taking place is so liberal clergy in various parts of the developed world (Germany especially) can point to the exceptions that will likely be made for married priests and female "deacons" in the Amazonian region. They will then introduce these "pastoral reforms" in their own countries, citing the need for the Church to stay relevant.

These changes will result in the creation of radically distinct national churches that are so different from one another that the term "catholic"—which means "universal"—will no longer be an accurate way to describe the Roman Church. "Fractured" and "regional" will be more appropriate.

Eventually, progressives at the Vatican will seek to force their revolutionary agenda onto the remaining holdout "conservative" countries. Naturally, those who resist will be accused of schism.

Ultimately what seems to be taking place is that a false church that

33 Francis, Homily, Mass for the Opening of the Synod, October 6, 2019, https://www.vatican.va/content/francesco/en/homilies/2019/documents/papa-francesco_20191006_omelia-sinodo-amazzonia.html

promotes a man-made, humanistic religion is supplanting the One, Holy, Catholic, and Apostolic one. It is not difficult to wonder if the gates of Hell have prevailed against this Church and that Christ was a liar when he said they wouldn't.

By no means! What we are living through is the Church entering what the Catechism calls her "final trial," a period of time that will "shake the faith of many believers."[34]

It is the duty of Catholics today to seek out and cling to the few remaining clergy who are faithful to Christ's teachings, wherever they may be. As a wise bishop once told me, "Watch and pray, watch and pray, 15 decades every day."

LifeSiteNews • October 22, 2019

CATHOLIC MEN WHO THREW 'PACHAMAMA' IDOL INTO TIBER DESERVE PRAISE

Modernists have predictably gone berserk over news that the Pachamama idol has been tossed into the Tiber River near the Vatican. Some have decried the act as "racist" and "xenophobic." These accusations are wholly off base for a number of reasons.

First, no one at the Vatican seems to know what this thing even is. At best it's a symbol of "Mother Earth." But isn't Mary our true mother? The 5th glorious mystery is the Coronation of the Blessed Virgin as Queen of Heaven and Earth, not the coronation of nature itself! The only "mother" that should be honored inside a Catholic Church is the Mother of God.

Second, Italian journalist Andrea Tornielli has claimed that the statue is "a traditional symbol for indigenous peoples representing the bond" they have with the environment. [35] Okay. What does that have to do with the Catholic faith?

In the United States, a football is a "traditional symbol" of one of the most popular ways American families come together on Sundays. Should St Peter's house a pigskin that was thrown by Tom Brady in the Super Bowl in honor of that? Of course not. Just because some people somewhere in the world believe something is sacred, doesn't mean Catholics should act like it is.

34 Catechism of the Catholic Church, para. 675, Quoted in https://www.usccb.org/sites/default/files/flipbooks/catechism/178/

35 Andrea Tornielli, "Saint John Henry Newman and the Statuettes Thrown Into the Tiber River," Vatican News, October 22, 2019, https://www.vaticannews.va/en/vatican-city/news/2019-10/john-henry-newman-statuettes-thrown-in-tiber-river.html

Third, some have said this object is a fertility goddess and that it represents "life." What does that even mean? Why, moreover, would something like that share a space with icons, statues, and paintings of Saints who died as martyrs for the Catholic faith?

I don't understand how it's "racist" or "an act of theft" to remove from a Catholic Church a piece of timber that's not a Catholic symbol and holds no spiritual value. It simply doesn't belong there. Justice demands it be tossed out.

The Blessed Virgin Crushes the Head of Pachamama

Placing this carving in the Church of Santa Maria in Traspontina was obviously done out of respect for the Amazonian people. But what about the fact that God has a right to not have His house defiled? Since when does cordiality with indigenous tribesmen trump the duties we owe the Holy Trinity?

It seems the real reason leftists are upset with this act of heroism is that they've been reminded that there are Catholics who still believe, and are willing to defend, the claim that Catholicism is the only true religion.

They have also been reminded that aboriginal peoples and their cultures are objectively deficient. Consider the following remarks of Pope Leo XIII in 1892. He was speaking about the now universally hated Christopher Columbus:

By his toil...hundreds of thousands of mortals have, from a state of blindness, been raised to the common level of the human race, reclaimed from savagery to gentleness and humanity; and, greatest of all, by the acquisition of those blessings of which Jesus Christ is the author, they have been recalled from destruction to eternal life.[36]

The Church has always rejected the ideology of multiculturalism that is supported by those who roam the halls of power in the Vatican. It has always taught that when Christ said "go forth and teach all nations," he was instructing his apostles to replace the various pagan traditions of the unbelieving world.

Moreover, when Mary appeared to Juan Diego in the 1500s, she was, in effect, "tossing out" the barbaric practices of the aboriginal people and charitably welcoming them into the true faith.

If we follow the logic of those who are angry with this praiseworthy act of protest, we should view Our Lady of Guadalupe as a sort of theological terrorist guilty of violating the first commandment of inter-religious dialogue.

36 Leo XIII, *Quarto Abuente Saeculo*, On the Quadricentennual of Christopher Columbus, July 16, 1892, Vatican website, https://www.vatican.va/content/leo-xiii/en/encyclicals/documents/hf_l-xiii_enc_16071892_quarto-abeunte-saeculo.html

Far from being a hate crime worthy of contempt, those who threw this object into the Tiber have performed a most admirable spiritual work of mercy. In an age where blending false religions with the true one is an all too common occurrence, I tip my cap to them. Bravo gentlemen.

LifeSiteNews ◆ October 23, 2019

VATICAN GOES DARK FOR EARTH HOUR, SYMBOLIZING MEMBERSHIP IN 'CHURCH OF ENVIRONMENTALISM'

On Sunday, March 26, St Peter's Basilica turned off its lights for "Earth Hour." Somewhere, Pachamama is smiling.

Earth Hour began in 2007 in Australia when more than 2.2 million people denied themselves electricity for a whopping 60 minutes of their day in the name of protecting the climate. Presumably, they returned to their normal (sinful?) energy consumption rates immediately thereafter.

The Vatican has participated in this quasi-pagan act of mortification every year since at least 2009.

The United Nations—which Paul VI said in 1965 people look to as mankind's "last hope for peace"[37]—has been one of Earth Hour's biggest cheerleaders. Its inquisitors have successfully coerced nearly every global landmark into supporting it. The Eiffel Tower, Moscow's St Basil's Cathedral, and even Rio De Janero's Christ the Redeemer Statue have all dimmed their lights in recent years.

Last month, Fox News host Tucker Carlson delivered a stinging rebuke of what he called "the church of environmentalism." He was speaking about the way liberals have turned care for creation into a modern day religion.

Carlson's remarks so impressed former Apostolic Nuncio to the United States Archbishop Carlo Maria Viganò, that His Excellency published a 2,400-word essay reflecting on them. Here is a snippet of what he wrote:

> Carlson recalls that the American Constitution prohibits any state religion, but for some time the governing Democratic Party has imposed on the American people the globalist cult, with its green agenda, its woke dogmas, its condemnations and cancel culture, its priests of the World Health Organization, and its prophets of the World Economic Forum. A religion in all respects, all-encompassing not only for the life of the

37 Paul VI, Address to the United Nations, October 4, 1965

individuals who practice it, but also in the life of the nation that publicly confesses it, adapts laws and sentences to it, and inspires education and every governmental action around it.[38]

The symbolism of the Vatican's participation in Earth Hour cannot be over-stated, especially as Rome's policies increasingly overlap with the eco-fascist measures advanced by the sinister forces behind the Great Reset. As Arch-bishop Viganò notes in his essay, the "apostasy of the Catholic hierarchy" has resulted in Roman clergy worshipping "Mother Earth" alongside the "high priests" and "prelates" of the World Economic Forum.

Instead of holding a Holy Hour of Reparation for the many sins our debauched age commits every day, the Vatican has chosen here to engage in a blasphemous act of ecological penance taken straight from the Satanic catechism of the un-holy trinity of Klaus Schwab, George Soros, and Bill Gates.

The Church is the Mystical Body of Christ. Its members, as Matthew 5:14 states, are "the light of the world." Since Vatican II, the Church has turned off those lights by no longer preaching that it is the one true religion and that all souls must come to embrace it's teachings.

By participating in Earth Hour, She shows, in a symbolic way, that She is now a fully fledged adherent of what Archbishop Viganò has rightly called the "globalist cult, with its green agenda."

When Our Lord said to His followers, "let your light shine before men," the post-Vatican II Church responds, "only if doesn't harm the environment."

How shameful.

LifeSiteNews • March 27, 2023

US BISHOP: POPE FRANCIS SHOULD 'SUPPORT,' NOT CRITICIZE AMERICAN CATHOLICS

Bishop James Conley is urging Pope Francis to support American bishops, and not criticize them, as rumors swirl that the Pontiff will visit New York City to speak at the United Nations this fall.

Conley, 69, has led the Diocese of Lincoln in Nebraska since 2012. He is

---

38 Archbishop Carlo Maria Viganò, "Abp Viganò: The globalist New World Order has the marks of the 'Antichurch of Satan,'"LifeSiteNews, February 17, 2023, https://www.lifesitenews.com/opinion/abp-vigano-the-globalist-new-world-order-has-the-marks-of-the-antichurch-of-satan/

generally considered one of the more conservative bishops in the US. In the past, he has defended the Church's teachings on refusing Communion to pro-abortion politicians and has pushed back against the pro-LGBT efforts of dissident clergy.[39] He has also warned about the dangers of the German "Synodal Path."[40]

On May 15, Conley published an article for *The Catholic Thing* website calling on Francis to acquaint himself with "the real terrain of American Catholic life." Conley noted that Francis' verbal attacks on devout Catholics have had a negative impact overall.[41]

"Francis is not without critics. His past comments about 'backward-looking' and 'reactionary' attitudes in American Catholic life have caused resentment among some faithful Catholics," Conley wrote. "And his view of Church leadership in the United States—often perceived as negative—has perplexed American bishops who, as a body, have a long record of loyalty and generosity to the Holy See."

Conley added that, "men in our country who accept an appointment as bishop today, are, by and large, men who know full well that they will suffer." They "need—and they deserve—encouragement, clarity, and support from the man who holds the Office of Peter. Pope Francis can provide all three."

For the past twelve years, Conley has led Catholics in praying the Stations of the Cross outside a Planned Parenthood center on Good Friday. He has also repeatedly conducted a Eucharistic procession around the same facility.

In his essay, he notes that he himself previously served as a member of the Vatican's Congregation (now Dicastery) for Bishops. The group is responsible for recommending priests to the pope as future bishops. Pro-LGBT Chicago Cardinal Blasé Cupich has served on the Dicastery since 2016. In 2022, Francis appointed three women to the organization.[42]

39 Matt Lamb, "US bishops praise Abp Cordileone's 'compassionate' decision to bar Pelosi from Holy Communion," LifeSiteNews, May 23, 2022, https://www.lifesitenews.com/news/dozens-of-bishops-share-support-for-abp-cordileones-pelosi-holy-communion-ban/. Raymond Wolfe, "Two more bishops condemn Cdl. McElroy's attack on Catholic moral teaching," LifeSiteNews, February 22, 2023, https://www.lifesitenews.com/news/two-more-bishops-condemn-cdl-mcelroys-heterodox-push-for-radical-inclusion/

40 Michael Haynes, "Over 70 bishops warn German bishops that 'Synodal Path' will lead to 'schism,'" LifeSiteNews, April 12, 2022, https://www.lifesitenews.com/news/over-70-bishops-write-to-german-bishops-warning-that-synodal-path-will-lead-to-schism-dead-end/

41 Bishop James Conley, "On the ministry of America's bishops," Southern Nebraska Register, May 24, 2024, https://www.lincolndiocese.org/op-ed/bishop-s-column/17846-on-the-ministry-of-america-s-bishops

42 Deborah Castellano Lubov, "Pope names three women to Vatican's Dicastery for Bishops," Vatican News, July 13, 2022, https://www.vaticannews.va/en/pope/news/2022-07/pope-francis-names-three-women-to-vatican-dicastery-for-bishops.html

Conley recalled that the abuse crisis has diminished the prestige of being a bishop but that "brother bishops" are still "faithful to the Church" and "unquestionably loyal to Pope Francis, which makes his ambiguities and seeming criticisms difficult to understand."

As reported by LifeSite previously, Francis has frequently expressed great antipathy toward Traditional Catholics living in the United States. At various times since the 2013 conclave, he has remarked that conservative and Tradition-minded American Catholics are "reactionary," "rigid," and, as he said during an interview with *60 Minutes* earlier this month, that they have a "suicidal attitude."[43]

The current Apostolic Nuncio to the United States, Frenchman Christophe Pierre, was criticized in November 2023 for belittling younger clergy who offer the Latin Mass and wear the traditional cassock.[44] In 2019, Francis likewise accused young men who wear traditional priestly attire of harboring "moral problems" and "imbalances."[45] Francis' most infamous interaction with an American cleric was in November 2023 when he unceremoniously dismissed Bishop Joseph Strickland from his post in Tyler, Texas without a clear explanation.

The Traditional Priestly Society of St Peter has its Our Lady of Guadalupe Seminary in Denton, Nebraska, which about 12 miles southwest of Lincoln.

LifeSiteNews • May 27, 2024

ARGENTINA'S PRESIDENTIAL FRONT-RUNNER: FRANCIS HAS 'AFFINITY FOR MURDEROUS COMMUNISTS'

Libertarian economist Javier Milei says he is Catholic. But that didn't stop him from telling Tucker Carlson last week that he believes Pope Francis has

43 Michael Haynes, "Pope Francis belittles devotion to the Latin Mass as a 'nostalgic disease' during Jesuit meeting," LifeSiteNews, May 9, 2023, https://www.lifesitenews.com/news/pope-francis-belittles-devotion-to-the-latin-mass-as-a-nostalgic-disease-during-jesuit-meeting/. Michael Haynes, "Pope Francis says 'conservative' bishops have 'suicidal attitude' during 60 Minutes interview," LifeSiteNews, May 17, 2024, https://www.lifesitenews.com/news/pope-francis-says-conservative-bishops-have-suicidal-attitude-in-60-minutes-interview/

44 Stephen Kokx, "US Apostolic Nuncio receives blowback for slamming the cassock, Traditional Latin Mass," LifeSiteNews, November 3, 2023, https://www.lifesitenews.com/news/us-apostolic-nuncio-receives-blowback-for-slamming-the-cassock-traditional-latin-mass/

45 Dorothy Cummings McLean, "Pope criticizes young traditional priests' clothes: Cassock suggests 'moral problems," LifeSiteNews, September 27, 2019, https://www.lifesitenews.com/news/pope-criticizes-young-traditional-priests-clothes-cassock-means-moral-problems/

NAVIGATING THE CRISIS IN THE CHURCH

a soft spot for tyrannical world leaders.

"He has an affinity for murderous communists. He's lenient to the entire left even when they are true criminals," he exclaimed.

Milei, 52, is the leading candidate for the presidency of Argentina, Pope Francis's native country. He sat down for a wide-ranging conversation with Carlson for his "Tucker on X" program last week. Among other topics, the two spoke about Donald Trump, socialism, and abortion, which Milei called "murder."

Regarding Francis, Milei said that "the pope plays politics. The pope plays politics." He "has a strong political influence. And he has shown a great affinity for dictators such as Castro and Maduro."

Carlson has previously pointed out that Western elites are profiting from the 124% inflation rate that is currently crippling Argentina's economy, and that they are seeking to prevent Milei, a self-described "anarcho capitalist," from coming to power when elections are held in October.

Milei often touts his Catholicism publicly, but he also studies the Torah. He visits with Rabbis and possesses what has been described as a "fascination" with Judaism as well. He also wants to move Argentina's embassy in Israel from Tel Aviv to Jerusalem.

Aside from his strange personal beliefs, Milei's remarks about Francis are spot on. Several years ago, Francis struck a deal with the Chinese Communist Party that basically gave its leaders control over the appointment of bishops in their country. He also notably failed to bring up human rights abuses while visiting Raul Castro in Cuba in 2015.[46] He previously met with Raul's atheist brother Fidel, whom he did not encourage to convert to Catholicism. Rather, they talked about the environment.[47]

LifeSite has extensively documented Francis's troubling remarks about communism since his elevation to the papacy ten years ago. In 2014, Francis said "communists are closet Christians."[48] Two years later, he told atheist journalist Eugenio Scalfaro that communists "think like Christians."[49] In 2015,

---

46 David McLoone, "Pope Francis says he has 'human relationship' with former Cuban communist dictator Raul Castro" LifeSiteNews, July 13, 2022, https://www.lifesitenews.com/news/pope-francis-says-he-has-a-human-relationship-with-communist-cuban-dictator-raul-castro/

47 Stephanie Kirchgaessner and Jonathan Watts, "Pope Meets Fidel Castro In 'Intimate and Familiar' Encounter," The Guardian, September 20, 2015, https://www.theguardian.com/world/2015/sep/20/pope-francis-meets-with-fidel-castro-cuba-visit

48 Phillip Pullella, "Pope Says Communists Are Closet Christians," Reuters, June 29, 2014, https://www.reuters.com/article/us-pope-communism/pope-says-communists-are-closet-christians-idUSKBN0F40L020140629/

49 Eugenio Scalfari, "Pope Francis: 'Trump? I do not judge. I care only if he makes the poor suffer," La Repubblica, November 11, 2016, https://www.repubblica.it/vatica-

he accepted a communist hammer and sickle with a crucified Christ on it from Bolivian President Evo Morales.[50] Now-deceased American Catholic journalist George Neumayr published a book in 2017 that noted Francis "tends to speak of communism in benign terms." He was absolutely right.

LifeSiteNews • September 19, 2023

WHAT WOULD ST ALPHONSUS SAY ABOUT FRANCIS' CRITICISMS OF 'RIGID' SEMINARIANS?

Pope Francis made headlines last week when he complained about priests not receiving a "humanistic formation."

"We need normal seminarians, with their problems, who play soccer, and who don't go to the neighborhoods to dogmatize," he told staffers for the Spain-based Catholic newspaper *Nueva Vida*. "I don't like rigidity because it is a bad symptom of the inner life," he added.

Francis didn't elaborate on what he meant by "rigidity." Nor did he provide a specific example of who in the Church is guilty of "dogmatizing" others.

He proceeded to warn that seminaries should not be "ideological kitchens." Rather, they need to "train pastors" who are not "trapped in a theology manual, unable to get into trouble and make theology move forward."[51]

After having listened to these petulant outbursts for 10 years now, it's not hard to figure out who Francis has in mind, despite his refusal to name names. He's referring, of course, to those who steadfastly remain loyal to the deposit of faith and who oppose his sinister efforts to undermine the Church's traditional teachings and liturgy.

Francis' animus, simply put, is directed at those who take seriously Proverbs 22:28: "Pass not beyond the ancient bounds which thy fathers have set."

Francis is Wrong When it Comes to 'Rigidity'

Two questions come to mind. One: are Francis' remarks a fair description of what is actually taking place in the Church? Two: what sort of training should

no/2016/11/11/news/pope_francis_trump-151810120/

50 John-Henry Westen, "VIDEO: Pope Francis' record on communism is dangerously ambiguous," LifeSiteNews, April 23, 2019, https://www.lifesitenews.com/blogs/video-pope-francis-record-on-communism-is-dangerously-ambiguous/

51 "Pope Francis to New Life: 'I Am a Victim of the Holy Spirit," Vida Nueva, April 8, 2023, https://www.vidanuevadigital.com/2023/08/04/el-papa-francisco-a-vida-nueva-soy-una-victima-del-espiritu-santo/

seminarians receive anyway?

Personally speaking, I'm unaware of any traditional-minded seminary that bans young men from at least some recreation, soccer included. Nor do I know any that would qualify as an "ideological kitchen," whatever that means. All the seminarians I've met who are enrolled in the SSPX, FSSP, and other houses of formation are entirely "normal" and receive a standard course of study. All they want to do is serve God faithfully by giving their lives to prayer and sacrifice.

While left-wing theologians may swoon over Francis' cartoonish characterizations, his words are quite devoid of any real substance. Was St Thomas Aquinas, for instance, "trapped in a theology manual" when he was a student, or when he was writing the *Summa*? Was St Patrick of Ireland "rigid" when he "dogmatized" inhabitants of the Emerald Isle with the Catholic faith?

There is no doubt that papal apologists will say that all Francis was "trying to get at" is that priests can't be so obsessed with doctrine that they forget they are dealing with real people in real time who need real pastoral care. Sure, but that forgets the ugly truth that since 2013 Francis has waged a relentless war on those doctrines!

Francis' chastising of those who oppose moving theology "forward" is also just a polite way to express his wholesale disgust for Catholics who refuse to muddy the waters of sin with him. To use an analogy, he wants to spread gray paint over a canvas where previously there was only black and white. And he attacks those who are trying to prevent him from doing so.

St Alphonsus Would Not Agree with Francis

St Alphonsus Liguori founded the Redemptorist Order in 1732. He is believed to be one of the best-selling spiritual authors of all time due to the vast number of translations, editions, and re-printings that his publications have gone through. His book *The Dignity and Duties of The Priest* explains in great detail how priests should be formed.

"Withdraw from worldly conversations and amusements ... think of nothing but prayer and frequenting the sacraments, and be nowhere but at home and in church," he writes. "One day of amusement, a word from a friend ... suffices to bring to nought all our resolutions of retiring from the world."

He goes on: "All is folly: feasts, theaters, parties of pleasure, amusements—these are the goods of this world, but goods which are filled with the bitterness of gall and with sharp thorns."

"Keep perfectly recollected, detaching ourselves from everything of this world," he further adds. "We ought during this time to think of nothing but prayer, and frequenting the sacraments. ... Let him who will not do so, but contracts himself with pastimes, be persuaded that he will without doubt lose his vocation."

St Alphonsus concedes that seminarians need not always speak on serious topics. "Laugh, amuse yourself, speak even on entertaining subjects," he notes, "but preserve recollection, by interiorly making occasional acts of the love of God, or petitions for His graces."

I could go on, as I just wrote a book on his spiritual teachings that is set to come out later this month.[52] But the point should be obvious: Francis' advice for training seminarians stands in marked contrast to the wisdom of St Alphonsus. My tip for rectors of seminaries across the world? Listen to Alphonsus and not to Francis if you want real priests who will follow in the footsteps of Christ.

LifeSiteNews • August 11, 2023

ARCHBISHOP VIGANÒ: 'FALSE PROPHET' BERGOGLIO IS GUILTY OF 'ALL-OUT APOSTASY'

Archbishop Carlo Maria Viganò delivered a powerful address to the "Is the Pope Catholic?" conference this past weekend, stating that Jorge Mario Bergoglio is a "false prophet" who fits the description of the one spoken about by the prophet Daniel during the time of the "final persecution" of the Church.

Organized by Dr Edmund Mazza, the online event was streamed on You-Tube on Saturday, December 9. It featured an array of speakers discussing whether or not Francis is actually the pope, a topic that Archbishop Viganò noted has emerged after a decade of "[Bergoglian] horrors" that are "worse than those we have witnessed in the last sixty years."

Liz Yore, co-host of LifeSite's Faith & Reason show, was among those who addressed the conference. Fr Paul Kramer and blogger Ann Barnhardt also appeared. Kramer has written multiple books on the papacy, including, *On the True and False Pope: The Case Against Bergoglio.*

Archbishop Viganò's 50-minute message (which was cut down, Mazza told LifeSite, to 34 minutes for the livestream) is a clear-eyed assessment of the Church and state today. Among other things, His Excellency commented on current events in Gaza, called out the "heresy" of Zionism, and mentioned Epstein Island and how Israeli intelligence officials blackmail Western politicians in order to control them.

52 Stephen Kokx, *St Alphonsus for the 21st Century,* St Peter's Press, September 2023

He also said that "we have all sorts of hair-splitting about the distinctions between formal and material heresy, none of which do the least thing to impede Bergoglio's destructive action." We "cannot behave as if we were resolving a question of a point of Canon Law. No. The Lord is being outraged, the Church is being humiliated, and souls are being lost because a usurper remains on the Throne."

At the same time, he emphasized that "what we cannot do, because we do not have the authority, is to officially declare that Jorge Mario Bergoglio is not Pope. The terrible impasse in which we find ourselves makes any human solution impossible."[53]

A Defect of Consent

His Excellency's remarks were similar to his previous "Vitium Consensus" message on October 1. In those comments, he argued that Catholics should consider the possibility that Jorge Bergoglio obtained the office of the papacy with a "criminal intention" to "carry out a coup d'état within the Church and bring the prophet of the Antichrist to the Throne of Peter." Viganò doubled down on those claims Saturday by mentioning that a "Luciferian intelligence" is at work in Rome these days:

> We know that John Podesta was working on behalf of Hillary Clinton and Obama—and the globalist elite in general—to promote a 'colored revolution' within the Church that was supposed to oust Benedict XVI from the papacy, elect an ultra-progressive pope, and substantially modify the Catholic Magisterium by making it accept the demands of the Agenda 2030: gender equality, the introduction of gender ideology and LGBTQ+ doctrine, the democratization of Church governance, collaboration in the neo-Malthusian project of the Great Reset, cooperation on immigrationism, and cancel culture.
>
> It seems clear to me that this subversive project has found perfect realization in the appointment of Bergoglio—and I use the word 'appointment' deliberately—and that it is confirmed by his consistent pattern of acts of governance and magisterial teaching, both public and private, over the course of this most inauspicious decade.

53 Since this statement, His Excellency has called Bergoglio an "anti-pope." He has also said that he should "be judged as a heretic and schismatic and removed from the throne which he has unworthily occupied ... since a heretic is unable to assume the Papacy." See https://www.lifesitenews.com/opinion/archbishop-vigano-i-accuse-bergoglio-of-heresy-and-schism/ and https://www.lifesitenews.com/news/archbishop-vigano-bergoglio-is-an-anti-pope-benedicts-resignation-was-certainly-invalid/

Bergoglio is the Source of Division

Bishop Athanasius Schneider of Kazakhstan and Professor Roberto de Mattei of the Lepanto Foundation have issued public statements expressing disagreement with various aspects of Viganò's arguments in recent weeks. His Excellency pushed back against their criticisms.

"[Bergoglio's] heterogeneity to the papacy is now evident and perceived both by the simple faithful as well as by a large part of the clergy, and even by certain fringes of the media," Viganò recalled. "The consensus and support for the Argentine Jesuit comes significantly from the ultra-progressive and pro-heretical wing that sponsored his election: all notorious members of the deep church and closely-linked to the homosexual and pedophile lobby of the deep state." The "objection that accusing the 'reigning Pontiff' of heresy or apostasy could cause division and scandal is belied by the evidence of the division and scandal that is already widely present in the ecclesial body precisely because of Bergoglio's heresy and apostasy," he continued. "The intention to harm the Church by acting on behalf of an enemy power is not compatible with the acceptance of the papacy, and there is therefore a defect of consent given by the will of the one elected—confirmed by his words and deeds over the last ten years."

The Abomination of Desolation

On July 1 of this year, Archbishop Viganò established the Exsurge Domine organization after initially supporting the U.S.-based Coalition for Canceled Priests. He remarked on X earlier this month that he "disassociated" himself from the Coalition privately in 2021 due to the behavior of the organization's co-founder Fr John Lovell, who has since been removed for alleged reckless personal, financial, and managerial decisions. Viganò has subsequently founded Exsurge Domine USA to assist religious and clergy who live in America and has established a house of formation in Italy.

During his remarks Saturday, Archbishop Viganò also alluded to the writings of St Robert Bellarmine, a Jesuit born in the 16th century. A Doctor of the Church, Bellarmine's *De Romano Pontifice* is often referenced for its opinions on how a pope could lose his office. His Excellency said that although many Catholics can see the chaos being sown by the Vatican today, they are not drawing the necessary conclusions.

"For them, it is permissible to criticize Bergoglio, but only on the condition that one never criticizes the conciliar idol [Vatican II], the untouchable fetish of the Montinians," he said. "Bergoglio's heresy and apostasy" is "the tip of the iceberg of a much worse and more widespread crisis of the Hierarchy and of the Clergy that began sixty years ago and has now almost reached its peak," Viganò further explained. Vatican II, he added, was "rightly defined by its own architects as 'the 1789 of the Church.' John XXIII, Paul VI, John Paul I, John Paul II and Benedict XVI did not fail to emphasize how the revolutionary and Masonic principles—liberté, égalité, fraternité—could in some way be shared and made their own by Catholicism."

Viganò then reiterated that the Church is not dealing with a situation where "a pope adheres to one specific heresy" but instead she is confronted with something far worse.

No Doctor of the Church has ever contemplated the possibility of an apostate pope or of an election falsified and manipulated by powers avowedly hostile to Christ, because such an enormity could only happen in a unique and extraordinary context such as that of the final persecution foretold by the Prophet Daniel and described by Saint Paul. Our Lord's admonition *videritis abominationem desolationis*—when you shall see the abomination of desolation (Matthew 24:15)—is to be understood as such precisely because of its absolute uniqueness.

The Society of St Pius X

His Excellency also brought up, twice, the priestly Society of St Pius X, which was founded by French Archbishop Marcel Lefebvre (1905–1991) in 1970. In the past, Viganò has praised Lefebvre for preserving the faith following the Second Vatican Council. On Saturday, he seemed to issue something of a warning to the group.

"The *vexata quaestio*—'Is Bergoglio Catholic?'—is addressed from many different angles according to differing criteria stemming from various cultural heritages," he stated. "The traditional scholastic point of view; the moderate and conciliar, or, we could say, the Montinian point of view; and the one that wavers, so to speak, between the two shores, recognizing Bergoglio as Pope although being *de facto* canonically independent from him (I'm referring to the SSPX)."

"But we must recognize that today it is possible to share, along with many priests and laity, a feeling of serious unease and grave scandal due to the cumbersome presence of the Argentine Jesuit," he added. "The Hierarchy limits itself to demonstrating either cowardice or complicity with the tyrant, and the few discordant voices do not dare to draw the necessary conclusions in the face of the heresies and nonsense of the tenant of Santa Marta."

"And here we come to the *punctum dolens*," he continued, "that is, the great contradiction that unites the proponents of Vatican II with its historical opponents—the Society of St Pius x *in primis*—in wanting to proceed with an evaluation of objectively extraordinary facts using ordinary norms of evaluation." He then remarked:

> As I have often said, it seems to me that some commentators are more concerned about the doctrine of the papacy than with the salvation of souls, so that they find themselves preferring to be governed by a heretical and apostate pope rather than recognizing that a heretic or an apostate cannot be at the head of the Church to which, as such, he does not belong...
>
> Our task must not be to engage in the abstract speculations of canonists, but to resist with all our strength—and with the help of God's Grace—the explicitly destructive action of the Jesuit Argentine, refusing with courage and determination any collaboration, even indirect collaboration, with him and his accomplices.

A Masonic Ambassador Who Must Be Resisted

His Excellency concluded his message by stating that Catholics can be "morally certain" that "the tenant of Santa Marta is a false prophet." As such, they are "authorized in conscience to revoke our obedience to" him, as he is acting like a "Biblical wild boar" who "has no care for the sheep."

> [St Robert] Bellarmine could never have imagined that an emissary of Freemasonry could go so far as to be elected pope with the purpose of demolishing the Church from within, usurping and abusing the very power of the papacy itself against the papacy. Nor could he have imagined that a hypothetical pope would surpass mere heresy and embrace all-out apostasy.

"'The Bergoglio problem,'" he further said, "cannot be solved by ordinary means: no society can survive the total corruption of the authority that governs it." As long as "society and the Church continue to be held hostage by the enemies of Christ the King and His Most August Mother, we will not be able to hope for the end of this most painful trial, because we will not have made the necessary choice of sides that the Lord expects of us in order to make us sharers in His total and definitive triumph over Satan."

LifeSiteNews • December 12, 2023

CHAPTER II: WAYWARD CLERGY

POPE BENEDICT WAS RIGHT TO TARGET DISSIDENT NUNS

One of the most popular stories being discussed in anti-Catholic circles right now is the decision of the Vatican's Congregation for the Doctrine of the Faith (CDF) to chastise the Leadership Conference of Women Religious (LCWR). The LCWR is a type of trade association that represents roughly 80% of the 57,000 women religious in the United States.

The CDF has just issued a years-long report that criticized the group for "scant regard for the role of the magisterium." It also accused them of promoting "certain radical feminist themes," and of not providing proper doctrinal formation.[1]

Sister Jeanine Gramick is the founder of New Ways Ministries, a dissident, pro-LGBT organization that was officially condemned by Pope Benedict in 1999. In an interview with MSNBC host Lawrence O'Donnell, Gramick complained that "the government of the Catholic Church is very totalitarian."

"Women come from a different conception of church from the Vatican" but "in a totalitarian institution, there is no disagreement," she said.[2]

Other progressive voices spoke out as well.

"What's left to say? By now the whole world has heard the Vatican is going to take care of those uppity, radical feminist nuns," groaned Phyllis Zagano of the *National Catholic Reporter*.[3]

Pope Benedict XVI "fails to [acknowledge] that Jesus was obeying God while also radically disobeying the religious leaders and laws of his time," Jamie L. Manson argued.[4]

1 Congregation for the Doctrine of the Faith, "Doctrinal Assessment of the Leadership Conference of Women Religious," Vatican website, April 18, 2012, https://www.vatican.va/roman_curia/congregations/cfaith/documents/rc_con_cfaith_doc_20120418_assessment-lcwr_en.html

2 Tim Graham, "MSNBC's O'Donnell: Obama Isn't Comparable to Stalin or Hitler, Actually Pope Benedict Is!" NewsBusters, April 20, 2012, https://web.archive.org/web/20120427235447/http://newsbusters.org/blogs/tim-graham/2012/04/20/msnbcs-odonnell-obama-isnt-comparable-stalin-or-hitler-actually-pope-ben

3 Phyllis Zagano, "The Vatican and the LCWR," National Catholic Reporter, April 25, 2012, https://www.ncronline.org/blogs/just-catholic/vatican-and-lcwr

4 Jamie Manson, "LCWR: A Radical Obedience to the Voice of God In Our Time," National Catholic Reporter, April 23, 2012, https://www.ncronline.org/blogs/grace-margins/lcwr-radical-obedience-voice-god-our-time

Others have said that this amounts to "bullying" women religious. For a more sober analysis of the situation, here's George Weigel, official biographer of Pope John Paul II:

> Yes, many sisters continue to do many good works. On the other hand, almost none of the sisters in LCWR congregations wear religious habits; most have long since abandoned convent life for apartments and other domestic arrangements; their spiritual life is more likely to be influenced by the Enneagram and Deepak Chopra than by Teresa of Avila and Edith Stein; their notions of orthodoxy are, to put it gently, innovative; and their relationship to Church authority is best described as one of barely concealed contempt.[5]

In his book *Justice in the Church: Gender and Participation*, Fr Benedict M. Ashley OP points out that "it is risky to presume that what is just in a democratic state is just for every human community without taking into account of what is unique for each."[6]

"All members" of "the Christian community" are "equally children of God by baptism" but "there is also a variety of functions" they perform, he also remarked.[7] In other words there is a hierarchy of superior and inferior offices comprised by persons who are "personally equal" yet "functionally unequal."

Sr. Gramick and her feminist confrères are unwilling to accept this.

The Congregation for the Doctrine of the Faith should be commended, not castigated, for its work. As St Paul wrote in his letter to the Romans, Christians need to "take note of those who create dissensions and difficulties. For such persons do not serve our Lord Christ, but their own appetites, and by fair and flattering words they deceive the hearts of the simple-minded."

RenewAmerica • April 29, 2012

CARDINAL KOCH IS WRONG TO SAY CATHOLICS DON'T NEED TO CONVERT THE JEWS

While speaking at Cambridge University recently, Cardinal Kurt Koch, the

5 George Weigel, "The Vatican and the Sisters," National Review Online, April 23, 2012, https://web.archive.org/web/20120427075139/http://www.nationalreview.com/articles/296811/vatican-and-sisters-george-weigel

6 Fr Benedict M. Ashley OP, *Justice in the Church: Gender and Participation*, The Catholic University of America Press, United States, 1996, p. 2

7 Ibid, p.17

CHAPTER II: WAYWARD CLERGY

president of the Pontifical Council for Promoting Christian Unity, said the following: "We have a mission to convert all non-Christian religions' people [except] Judaism. It is very clear that we can speak about three Abrahamic religions but we cannot deny that the view of Abraham in Jewish and the Christian tradition and the Islamic tradition is not the same."[8]

At first glance, the Cardinal's remarks look to be an echoing of Christ's words in the Gospel of Matthew: "Going therefore, teach ye all nations." In reality, the Cardinal said nothing of the sort. In fact, he contradicted Christ's instructions.

For one, the term "non-Christian" is different than "non-Catholic." Before Vatican II, the Church held that Baptists, Calvinists, Lutherans, etc. belonged to heretical sects. After the Council, those religions were described as "ecclesial communities" who's members are "separated brethren." Accordingly, Christ's prayer in John 17:21 "that all may be one" was re-interpreted to mean "all Christians should come together in visible unity" without non-Catholics needing to convert to Catholicism.

The traditional understanding of Christian unity was that those who 1) are under the governance of the pope 2) adhere to the Catholic faith and 3) participate in the same sacraments are united in Christ's Church. Anyone who dissents from any of these three categories cannot be considered one with Her.

Early 20th century Catholic author Hilaire Belloc (1870–1953) explained this in the following manner:

> There is no such thing as a religion called 'Christianity'—there never has been such a religion. There is and always has been the Church, and various heresies proceeding from a rejection of some of the Church's doctrines by men who still desire to retain the rest of her teaching and morals. But there never has been and never can be or will be a general Christian religion professed by men who all accept some central important doctrines, while agreeing to differ about others. There has always been, from the beginning, and will always be, the Church, and sundry heresies, either doomed to decay—or like Mohammedanism—to grow into a separate religion. Of a common Christianity there never has been and never can be a definition, for it has never existed.[9]

8 John Shammas, "Pope Francis Top Adviser Says Christians 'Have a Mission' to Convert ISIS Terrorists," May 24, 2016, Mirror, https://www.mirror.co.uk/news/world-news/pope-francis-top-adviser-says-8037093

9 Hillaire Belloc, *The Great Heresies*, 1938, Quoted in "The Modern Phase," Catholic Culture, https://www.catholicculture.org/culture/library/view.cfm?recnum=4745

As far as Cardinal Koch saying that Catholics do not have a mission to convert the Jews, well, one may simply respond by quoting Pope Pius XII's encyclical *Mystici Corporis*, which recalls that the Old Testament has been fulfilled and is no longer valid:

> By the death of our Redeemer, the New Testament took the place of the Old Law which had been abolished; then the Law of Christ together with its mysteries, enactments, institutions, and sacred rites was ratified for the whole world in the blood of Jesus Christ. For, while our Divine Savior was preaching in a restricted area—He was not sent but to the sheep that were lost of the House of Israel—the Law and the Gospel were together in force; but on the gibbet of His death Jesus made void the Law with its decrees fastened the handwriting of the Old Testament to the Cross, establishing the New Testament in His blood shed for the whole human race. 'To such an extent, then,' says St Leo the Great, speaking of the Cross of our Lord, 'was there effected a transfer from the Law to the Gospel, from the Synagogue to the Church, from the many sacrifices to one Victim, that, as Our Lord expired, that mystical veil which shut off the innermost part of the temple and its sacred secret was rent violently from top to bottom.'

Put another way, the Old Law has been abolished. As Hebrews 8:13 says, "In speaking of a new covenant, he makes the first one obsolete. And what is becoming obsolete and growing old is ready to vanish away." The Jews, simply stated, must embrace Jesus Christ if they want to be saved. One hopes the Vatican will understand this again and strive to convince them to embrace the one true faith.

Magnificat Media • May 25, 2016

ANGLICANS PROFANE ST PETER'S BY HOLDING HERETICAL PRAYER SERVICE

On Monday, March 13, a group of Anglicans sang Evensong (the equivalent of Catholic Vespers) in St Peter's Basilica. David Moxon, an Anglican "archbishop" who runs the Anglican Center in Rome, presided over the sacrilegious event. Pope Francis was not in attendance.

That this blasphemous ceremony was conducted in St Peter's makes it all the more wicked. Indeed, one has to wonder just what religion the bishops and cardinals who participated in this service belong to. Certainly not the religion of St Paul, who in Greece exposed the errors of the pagans. Nor the religion of St Augustine, who debated the wayward Donatists. And most definitely not the religion of the Council of Trent, which anathematized those who reject the primary of the Petrine Office, as Anglicans do.

The erroneous theology that motivates Catholics to hold these sorts of ecumenical events is premised on Vatican II's teaching that Catholics and Protestants need only seek "visible unity," the argument being that so long as you are baptized and profess Jesus Christ as the savior of mankind then in a certain way you are already part of Christ's Church—there is no need for conversion.

This novel theory is, quite simply, not Catholic. When Our Lord prayed that all of His followers "may be one," what He meant was that all of his followers would be united in the same doctrines, the same sacraments, and under the same pope. In other words, He desired that all men would be Catholic. In no way did His prayer for unity mean He wanted Catholics to band together into a loose confederation with Anglicans, Baptists, Lutherans, and others while agreeing to disagree on doctrine.

In these perverse times, many Catholics today express a desire to go back to the "good old days" of John Paul II and Benedict XVI. That's a foolish statement if there ever was one. Francis is simply bringing to its logical conclusion the revolutionary concepts introduced at the Second Vatican Council. He is simply following in the footsteps of his immediate "conservative" predecessors, both of whom promoted ecumenism and indifferentism with their Assisi gatherings. The only difference now is that Francis has his foot all the way down on the accelerator and the car is going 88 miles per hour instead of 55.

The only question that remains is: Who will rebuke Peter to his face and speak out against this abominable event? Will a Traditional bishop stand up for the rights of God and condemn it? Or will they remain silent under the claim of being "prudent"? Time will tell. Until then, it seems the laity must defend the faith.

Magnificat Media • March 24, 2017

CATHOLICS REFUTE JAMES MARTIN'S CLAIM THAT 'MARRIED' LESBIAN JUDGE WHO WAS DENIED COMMUNION IS VICTIM OF 'DISCRIMINATION'

Pro-gay Jesuit priest Fr James Martin is arguing that a pastor in West Michigan is guilty of "discrimination" for asking a lesbian judge in a same-sex "marriage" to not present herself for Holy Communion. Hundreds of Catholic laity and several prominent Catholic clergy have taken to social media to refute his ridiculous arguments.

Martin, who was ordained in 1999, is one of the most well-known promoters of normalizing homosexuality in the Church. In years past, he has expressed support for homosexual couples kissing during the sign of peace at Mass.[10] A LifeSite petition urging American bishops to ban him from their dioceses has acquired more than 18,000 signatures.

In a Facebook post published yesterday, Martin expressed outrage over Fr Scott Nolan's decision to refuse to administer county judge Sara Smolenski the Eucharist. He argued that priests like Nolan are singling out "married LGBT people" because they fail to also deny Communion to other Catholics who don't live by the Church's moral teachings. The Church's rules, he added, "must be applied across the board, not selectively, and not simply to one group of people."[11]

Smolenski has repeated Martin's claims during her many public appearances recently. While speaking with CNN this weekend, she said, "this feels like selective discrimination. Why choose gay people, and why now?"[12]

Three weeks ago, Martin met via Skype with Smolenski and a small group of her fellow parishioners at St Stephen's Catholic Church to discuss his LGBT-affirming book, *Building a Bridge*. The event was not hosted on parish property as per the request of Fr Nolan, who is the priest at St Stephen's.

Fr Dwight Longenecker pushed back against Fr Martin's arguments in an essay on his personal website *Standing on My Head*.

"By attempting a marriage with a woman, Ms. Smolenski publicly, formally and irremediably denied the Catholic teaching about marriage," he wrote. "A

10 Claire Chretien, "Eight extreme things Fr James Martin just said about Catholics and gay 'marriage,'" LifeSiteNews, September 21, 2017, https://www.lifesitenews.com/blogs/eight-extreme-things-fr.-james-martin-just-said-about-catholics-and/
11 James Martin, Facebook, December 1, 2019, https://www.facebook.com/FrJamesMartin/posts/pfbid02DRifsPsVmof9621aCQL8UAUGpzFAx4qYVsd7uFzeajGHk4KNRK8rP-pwAgcAuBrj1l
12 Monica Haider, "Catholic Diocese Denies Gay Michigan Judge Communion," CNN, December 1, 2019, https://www.cnn.com/2019/11/30/us/gay-michigan-judge-communion/index.html

same-sex marriage is not simply 'not following church teachings' it is rejecting church teachings and doing so formally and publicly."

This "is not at the same level of commitment as a couple using birth control or IVF or someone committing fornication," he continued. "All these sins are private sins and can be repented of [but] in a same-sex marriage…they are saying by their words and actions, 'Gay sex is not a sin [and] the Catholic Church is wrong and I am publicly, formally declaring that I reject the Catholic Church's teaching.'"[13]

Fr Thomas Petri, a Dominican priest who teaches at the Dominican House of Studies, published his response to Martin on Twitter this morning.

"Once again, Father Martin fails to distinguish between sinful choices that are private from sinful choices that are public and obstinately held to. It's as if he's never read or understood Canon 915," he explained. "Basically, when you commit a mortal sin, it's up to you to go to confession before you receive Holy Communion. But when you go public and insist the sin is fine or not a sin, then the Church's ministers must deny you the Sacrament because you're now publicly not in communion."

Several priests in the Grand Rapids Diocese have also come forward with support for Nolan. Last Wednesday, hundreds of Catholics from across the diocese flocked to St Stephen's for his 6:30pm evening Mass. The church was overflowing with attendees. The Bishop of Grand Rapids, David Walkowiak, expressed his support for Nolan as well in a public letter just days after Smolenski went to the press with her grievances.[14]

Yesterday, Smolenski attended a pro-LGBT Methodist church in Grand Rapids with her "wife." The two participated in an "inclusive communion" service featuring bread and wine. Local media covered the scandalous event.[15] The Catholic Church teaches that Catholics are are not to receive communion at Protestant churches as it is not the Body and Blood of Our Lord Jesus Christ. Smolenski recently told local NBC affiliate WOOD-TV 8 she considers herself a lifelong Catholic.

LifeSiteNews • December 2, 2019

---

13 Dwight Longenecker, "Answering Fr James Martin SJ," DwightLongenecker.com, December 1, 2019, https://dwightlongenecker.com/answering-fr-james-martin-sj/

14 Stephen Kokx, "Bishop sides with priest who denied 'married' lesbian judge Communion," LifeSiteNews, November 27, 2019, https://www.lifesitenews.com/news/bishop-sides-with-priest-who-denied-married-lesbian-judge-communion/

15 Whitney Burney, "Church Has Inclusive Communion, Invites Gay Judge," WOODTV.com, December 1, 2019, https://www.woodtv.com/news/grand-rapids/church-has-inclusive-communion-invites-gay-judge/

BISHOP BARRON'S CONGRESSIONAL PRAYER REFLECTS HIS MISGUIDED APPROACH TO EVANGELIZATION

There's no denying that Bishop Robert Barron is a popular figure both inside and outside the Church. Aside from his calm manner of speaking and encyclopedic knowledge—good luck trying to find an interview where he doesn't quote G.K. Chesterton or St Thomas Aquinas—his ability to discuss a wide variety of issues has won him admiration from many who do not follow Our Lord.

In recent years, Barron has appeared on commentator Dave Rubin's You-Tube channel. He's also been interviewed by Canadian psychologist and best-selling author Jordan Peterson. In a way, he has become the in-house spiritual guru for these politically incorrect though hugely popular social media celebrities.

But there are many question marks that surround Barron's smooth-talking brand of New Evangelization. His prayer last Wednesday on the floor of the US House of Representatives was the latest instance of that. Here is what he said:

Let us Pray. Oh God, source of all justice, You summoned everyone who works in this chamber to walk the path of righteousness, to foster life, and liberty, to care, especially for the poorest and most vulnerable in our society. Free these servants of yours Oh, Lord, of all those attachments to wealth or power or privilege or fame that would prevent them from following the course you have set out for them. Make them mindful of a time when they first heard your voice and followed it with idealism and enthusiasm. Illumine their minds, direct their wills, stir up in them a holy passion for doing what is right despite the cost. Give them the knowledge that whenever they strive for justice, they are pleasing to you. And shower, Oh Lord, your choicest blessings upon our country. Amen.

A few things stand out. The bishop's failure to make the sign of the cross, or even mention the name of Jesus Christ, was a major error. Moreover, talking about "justice" and "righteousness" is fine and all, but there's nothing distinctly Catholic about this payer.

One also can't help but notice that Barron placed his pectoral cross safely inside his coat pocket, seemingly so non-Catholics wouldn't be offended by it.

The entire affair reminded me of Matthew 10:33: "He that shall deny me before men, I will also deny him before my Father who is in heaven."

Barron has long been a critic of what he calls "dumbed down" Catholicism. He likes to say that Catholics should bring their faith into the public square. These facts alone make his avoidance of the simplest expressions of our religion all the more baffling.

If Barron had listened to his own advice, he might have quoted from Pope Pius XI's encyclical *Quas Primas*, which states that "it would be a grave error … to say that Christ has no authority whatever in civil affairs, since, by virtue of the absolute empire over all creatures committed to him by the Father, all things are in his power."

A History of Avoiding the Truth?

Unfortunately, this is not the first time Barron has sidestepped some of the "hard teachings" of the Catholic faith.

During an interview with Ben Shapiro last year, Barron was asked what the Church teaches on who gets into heaven. Instead of reminding Shapiro, a Jew, that Jesus Christ is "the Way, the Truth, and the Life," he said Christ was the "privileged route" to salvation, a claim that is wholly at odds with Church doctrine.

Fortunately, many Catholics took to Twitter and elsewhere on the internet to inform Shapiro he'd been given faulty information.

Another example was in 2017 when Barron appeared on the aforementioned Dave Rubin's podcast. During their conversation, he argued that he wouldn't be in favor of rolling back same-sex "marriage" laws because, he alleged, doing so would probably do more harm than good. Not once did he remind his host, who is an active "married" homosexual, that the Church believes sodomy is a sin.

Despite the entirely reasonable criticisms that faithful Catholics made about Barron's performance in that interview, His Excellency defended his actions on Facebook by explaining that, "my aim in the Rubin Report interview was to show its secular viewers that there is a lot more to Christianity than the 'pelvic issues.'"

Let Your 'Yes' Be 'Yes' and Your 'No' Be 'No'

It is sometimes difficult to see just how Barron's outreach to not only atheists but to the Rubin, Peterson, and Shapiro crowd is ever going to pay off. Presumably, he's trying to meet them "where they are" and to get them to think about deeper issues over time. But in doing so, he's frequently failing to give them the fullness of Catholic doctrine.

Come to think of it, I'm not sure this shrewd strategy ever results in the conversion of souls to Christ. It's possible there are such instances. But when does His Excellency plan on bringing up the "hard truths" of the Catholic faith to these particular men in public? In other words, when does he think it is the right time to talk about the Catholic religion being the religion all souls must embrace?

In my estimation, Barron's approach rarely produces the fruit it promises. Moreover, whenever I read the saints, they seem to take a wholly different, more hardline strategy in teaching the faith. Jordan Peterson appears to be more aware of that than Barron is. During an interview with Barron earlier this year, Peterson scolded the Church (and was perhaps intending to scold Barron himself) when he said Catholic clergy aren't doing enough to make people amend their ways.

"We're afraid of hurting people's … feelings in the present and willing to absolutely sacrifice their well-being in the future," he exclaimed. "And that's the sign of a very immature and unwise culture, because the reverse should be the case."

"If you really love someone, you can't tolerate when they are less than they could be," Peterson pressed on. "When someone comes into the Church, and, it's all forgiveness, there's no care there … what the hell are you doing?"[16]

Bishops Should Preach the Truth in Season and Out

While preaching the Gospel can be done in a variety of ways, what seems to be happening with Barron is that he's becoming too focused on finding the lowest common denominator with non-Catholics. In doing so, he is forgetting how simple the Holy Spirit is and how it can stir up in a soul the grace of God when it hears, straightforwardly, the unvarnished truth.

On Tuesday of last week, His Excellency met with a small group of lawmakers from both parties on Capitol Hill after his prayer in the House chamber. He apparently told them he would not discuss the "hot button issues" of abortion or homosexual "marriage" and that instead he wanted to make them think about the first time they wanted to get involved in "the vocation" of public service.

Catholic News Agency reported that Barron did indeed avoid abortion and marriage in his behind closed doors conversations with them because he felt those issues could distract from "really deep and abiding points of contact between what I call the spiritual condition and political tradition."[17]

16 Jordan Peterson, "Bishop Barron: Word on Fire," YouTube, https://www.youtube.com/watch?v=cXllaoNQmZY

17 Matt Hadro ,"Bishop Barron Goes to Washington," Catholic News Agency, October 30, 2019, https://www.catholicnewsagency.com/news/42682/bishop-barron-goes-to-washington

This wishy-washy, sentimental attitude is woefully inadequate for these diabolical times. My guess is that whatever Bishop Barron said to those lawmakers has already been forgotten and that it will make no lasting impact on the way they conduct themselves going forward.

What might have actually made them reflect seriously on their "vocation" is a message reminding them that they will be judged "more strictly" (James 3:1) than others and that they will gain admission to heaven only if they lived in accordance with Christ's laws—and whether they used their state in life to help others do the same.

But my guess is that sort of approach is too confrontational for Bishop Barron's style of "evangelization." Let's pray that changes.

LifeSiteNews • November 6, 2019

CARDINAL CUPICH PUSHES CLIMATE AGENDA, FAILS TO MENTION NAME OF JESUS AT PARLIAMENT OF WORLD'S RELIGIONS EVENT

Liberal Cardinal Blase Cupich urged attendees at this year's Parliament of the World's Religions to be more mindful of forming their consciences, but not in accordance with the truths of the Catholic faith.

"To be properly formed, a conscience needs to be sensitized, to be aware of others and of all creation," he argued. It can do this by "cultivating awareness and respect for others."

Cupich has been one of the most outspoken clerics in the United States when it comes to promoting climate ideology. He has also often equated social justice issues like gun control and care for the environment with moral evils like abortion.

While neglecting to mention the name of Jesus Christ even once in his remarks, Cupich told his audience of mostly non-Catholics that a "sensitized conscience" will "heed" the advise of Pope Francis' encyclical *Laudato Si.* Cupich further told the crowd that he supports the group's Fifth Directive of its so-called Global Ethic, which is titled, "Commitment to a Culture of Sustainability and Care for the Earth."

Pope Leo XIII Would Not Have Allowed Cupich's Appearance

More than 6,500 representatives of various forms of pagan and non-Catholic sects were present at the scandalous gathering, which was held at the

McCormack Place conference center in Chicago, Illinois, earlier this week. The event was coordinated by Wiccan priestess Phyllis Curott.

The Parliament's first meeting was held in 1893, also in Chicago. Cardinal John Gibbons of Baltimore controversially attended that gathering with several liberal US clergy, all of whom later came to be associated with what then-Pope Leo XIII called "the heresy of Americanism."[18]

In 1895, two years after conservative priests voiced their opposition to the meeting, Leo condemned the conference and forbade Catholics from attending future ones out of fear it would give the impression the Church viewed other religions to be true or good in themselves.

Cupich told his audience this week that he was "grateful" to help advance "the mission of this respected organization to cultivate harmony among the world's religions and spiritual communities." He also said that he sees "the spark of the Divine Will alive here today" and that this spark "informs us and engages my conscience and urges me to redouble my commitment to defend and support the freedom of all."

On Tuesday, a "climate repentance ceremony" was held at the gathering. A speaker from the left-wing Anti-Defamation League also addressed attendees. She called for a greater need to police free speech online. Various non-Catholic speeches and rituals were performed at the event as well.

What About 'De-Humanizing' Traditionalists?

Cupich used his speech to address what he called certain "unfortunate" aspects of "technological advances."

"It is very easy to seek out and talk with those who we find most agreeable [online]," he said. "Rarely or never listening to those who oppose our views can harden our positions."

"Through algorithms meant to keep us in touch with like-minded individuals and causes, technology has made dialogue across differences even less likely. We're also finding that those outside of our growing silos become easier to vilify and dehumanize as 'the others.'"

Perhaps forgetful of the repeated name-calling Pope Francis has used against so-called "rigid" Traditionalists, Cupich called on attendees at this year's Parliament to "never ... fall into the temptation to demonize and de-humanize those who disagree with us."

"Religious and cultural differences do not separate us here today," he insisted. "In fact, they pull us together in an effort to conscientiously address

---

18 Pope Leo XIII, *Testem Benevolentiae Nostrae*, January 22, 1899

the challenges we face in ensuring freedom, rights and dignity for all."

"You testify loudly," he added, "to a growing consciousness in our world that we are all interconnected. If we hope to advance the causes of peace and justice in the world, we must continue to seek out forums like this to connect with one another in recognition of our differences and diversity," he concluded.

It's astonishing to see how much love and appreciation Cupich, and Pope Francis for that matter, have for heretics and how little they care for Catholics who attend the Traditional Latin Mass.

LifeSiteNews • August 19, 2023

CHICAGO CATHOLICS BLAST CUPICH FOR CLOSING CHURCHES DURING COVID: 'BETRAYAL OF CHRIST'

The St Charles Borromeo Society has issued a statement denouncing Cardinal Blase Cupich's government-approved plan to re-open Catholic churches for the Chicago Archdiocese.[19]

"Cardinal Cupich has blithely yielded the Authority of the Church and subjugated the primacy of her worship to laws of man" it reads. His plan is "insidious" and a "betrayal of Christ."

Cupich released his proposal earlier this week, though public Masses in Chicago have been cancelled since mid-March, when he closed all schools and churches. He has also forbidden "any public celebrations, even outside including live Stations of the Cross on Good Friday" during Holy Week.[20]

The St Charles Borromeo Society has been holding prayer vigils outside Holy Name Cathedral on Fridays starting at 12:00pm for the last month. On Good Friday, they protested that churches were not deemed "essential" during COVID-19.[21]

The Society, which was co-founded by Lisa Bergman, a graduate of the

19 "Reopening Resources," Archdiocese of Chicago, UPDATED: March 17, 2022, https://web.archive.org/web/20220318192447/https://www.archchicago.org/pl/coronavirus/reopening

20 "The Archdiocese of Chicago Distributed the Following Guidelines and Policies to Clergy and Parish Staff," Archdiocese of Chicago, March 19, 2020, "https://www.archchicago.org/en/statement/-/article/2020/03/19/the-archdiocese-of-chicago-distributed-the-following-guidelines-and-policies-to-clergy-and-parish-sta-1

21 Stephen Kokx, "Chicago Catholics pray outside cathedral on Good Friday to protest church closings during COVID-19," LifeSiteNews, April 10, 2020, https://www.lifesitenews.com/news/chicago-catholics-pray-outside-cathedral-to-show-churches-must-be-considered-essential-during-COVID-19/

University of Notre Dame who runs St Augustine Academy Press, reached out to Cupich previously to discuss their ideas on how to re-open churches. But Cupich's office was predictably not interested in meeting with them.

In his announcement letter, Cupich said his plan was made in conjunction with Illinois' pro-abortion Democratic Governor J.B. Pritzker. "There have been moments in history when governments and rulers have persecuted Christians and banned their public worship. This is not one of them," he alleged. Bergman wholeheartedly rejects that claim.

"He replaces what has been heroically defended for thousands of years with the absurd perception that the Mass and the Sacraments are less necessary and more potentially dangerous than grocery stores, gas stations, hardware stores, take-out restaurants, laundries, the postal service, and construction trades, all of which are having no trouble observing CDC regulations," she said.

"This monstrous...betrayal of Christ and His Church...normalizes the narrative that the Church is secondary and must abase itself as though it were merely a place of recreation," she added.

In April, Bergman, along with Society co-founders Joe and Ann Scheidler of Pro-Life Action League, were joined by more than 30 Catholics in praying the rosary at the Cathedral. One woman brought a sign that read, "Cardinal Cupich: Please Restore the Sacraments." Another said, "400 inside Costco, why not 20 in Church?"[22]

Scheidler forwarded LifeSite the letter that she, her husband, and Bergman sent to Cupich asking him to intervene with Governor Pritzker so restrictions on churches could be lessened. The letter says, in part, that "we Catholics need to get back to a real, present Mass and to receive Jesus in the Blessed Sacrament...many of our churches are large enough that we could easily follow the social distancing protocols."

The Society has since launched a website called OpenOurChurches.org to amplify its message. Bergman previously told LifeSite that "the sacraments are wellsprings of grace for the Church" and that even during times of plagues and persecution from unjust rulers, Catholics went to great lengths to flee to them for spiritual health. "We must do what we can to unshackle our Church and allow the healing waters of the Sacraments to flow once more," she said. Only then will She "stand once more as the beacon of hope for all amidst the darkness of fear, rather than hiding that light under a bushel."

LifeSiteNews • April 2020

22 Stephen Kokx, "Chicago Catholics urge Cdl. Cupich to help ease state restrictions so churches can re-open," LifeSiteNews, April 24, 2020, https://www.lifesitenews.com/news/chicago-catholics-urge-cdl-cupich-to-help-ease-restrictions-on-church-closings/

SWISS BISHOPS' PRESIDENT CALLS FOR
ORDINATION OF WOMEN AHEAD OF SYNOD

The president of the Swiss Bishops' Conference has made the heretical claim that the Catholic Church should ordain women.

As reported by *Swissinfo* this past weekend, Bishop Felix Gmür told Swiss media outlet *NZZ am Sonntag* earlier this month that the Church needs to update its approach.

"The subordination of women in the Catholic Church is incomprehensible to me. Changes are needed there," Gmür said.

Gmür, who is scheduled to attend the upcoming Synod on Synodality in Rome, also called for married priests.

"Celibacy means that I am available to God. But I believe that this sign is no longer understood by society today," he remarked. "The time is ripe to abolish celibacy. I have no problem at all imagining married priests."[23]

The unchangeable teaching of the Catholic Church since its founding by Jesus Christ is that only men can receive Holy Orders because they, being males like Our Lord was, offer to God the Sacrifice of the Mass *in persona Christi.*

"Only to the apostles, and thenceforth to those on whom their successors have imposed hands, is granted the power of the priesthood, in virtue of which they represent the person of Jesus Christ before their people, acting at the same time as representatives of their people before God," Pope Pius XII taught in his encyclical *Mediator Dei* in 1947.

Christ Himself also purposefully chose only males to be His apostles, thereby denying the possibility that women could ever be ordained.

As previously reported by LifeSite, in 2017, Gmür approved a priest who had been convicted of sexually abusing several adolescent boys from 1999 until 2010 to serve at a parish in Riehen.[24] The priest had previously been put in pretrial detention for over a month and was ordered to pay a fine of 4,000 Swiss francs ($4,386 US dollars). Instead of keeping him sidelined, Gmür rehabilitated him, arguing that he deserved a second chance. The priest eventually withdrew his nomination after legal documents related to his sentencing were leaked to the public.

---

23 "'It's Time to Abolish Celibacy,' Says President of Swiss Bishops' Conference," Swissinfo, September 24, 2023, https://www.swissinfo.ch/eng/business/it-s-time-to-abolish-celibacy-says-president-of-swiss-bishops-conference/48835488

24 Maike Hickson, "Top swiss bishop approves convicted child abuser as parish pastor," LifeSiteNews, January 21, 2019, https://www.lifesitenews.com/blogs/top-swiss-bishop-approves-convicted-child-abuser-as-parish-pastor/

LifeSite journalist Maike Hickson has reported that Gmür is "known for his rather progressivist and lax views." In 2019, Gmür praised initiatives in Switzerland that sought to legalize same-sex civil "marriage."[25] On Christmas Eve 2020, he told *NZZ* that he could imagine "a woman standing at the altar."[26] Switzerland is home to some of the most notoriously left-wing, dissident clergy in the entire world. In 2020, women in the Swiss Diocese of Basel were discovered putting on vestments, standing at the altar, and essentially simulating a Catholic Mass.[27] Earlier this month, Bishop Joseph Maria Bonnemain of Chur decided not to punish two women who attempted to concelebrate at Catholic Mass in 2022. Instead, he opted to issue a "formal reprimand."[28]

The Synod on Synodality is scheduled to begin October 4 and run until October 29. It will reconvene for its final session in October of 2024. Speculation from Vatican experts is that the role of women in the Church will be a major point of discussion at the gathering.

LifeSiteNews • September 25, 2023

DISSIDENT GROUP OF US PRIESTS DENIED TABLE AT EUCHARISTIC CONGRESS

The most notorious group of left-wing clergy in the United States has been denied a place at the upcoming July 17–21 Eucharistic Congress in Indianapolis.

On Tuesday, the ultra-liberal Association of US Catholic Priests (AUSCP) announced that they have repeatedly asked for a table at the event since last summer but that they were recently told there is no room remaining.

"A month ago, we were assured that display space was available if we acted swiftly—and we responded immediately. One week ago (June 25) ... we were

25 Jeanne Smits, "Swiss diocese officially applauds govt's efforts to legalize same-sex 'marriage,'" LifeSiteNews, September 11, 2019, https://www.lifesitenews.com/news/swiss-diocese-officially-applauds-govts-efforts-to-legalize-same-sex-marriage/

26 Pete Baklinski, "Top Swiss bishop: 'I can very well imagine women standing at the altar,'" LifeSiteNews, January 4, 2021, https://www.lifesitenews.com/news/top-swiss-bishop-i-can-very-well-imagine-women-standing-at-the-altar/

27 Martin Bürger, "Women regularly simulate Catholic Mass in Swiss diocese," LifeSiteNews, July 28, 2020, https://www.lifesitenews.com/news/women-regularly-simulate-catholic-mass-in-swiss-diocese/

28 Andreas Wailzer, "Heterodox Swiss bishop declines to punish women who attempted to concelebrate at Mass," LifeSiteNews, September 12, 2023, https://www.lifesitenews.com/news/heterodox-swiss-bishop-declines-to-punish-women-who-attempted-to-concelebrate-at-mass/

informed that all display spaces had been taken, even the one that had been assured," the group said in a press release.[29]

The AUSCP was founded in 2011. Claiming to draw inspiration from the Second Vatican Council, it supports married clergy, "women priests," the normalization of homosexuality in the Church, pro-LGBT political policies, and numerous other positions at odds with immutable Catholic teaching.[30] Last month, from June 24–27, the AUSCP held its 13th annual meeting in Lexington, Kentucky. Local ordinary, Bishop John Stowe, served as retreat director.

The renegade group's website lists as one of Stowe's past accomplishments his "criticism" of Nick Sandmann and other pro-life students from Covington Catholic High School who wore "Make America Great Again" hats at the 2019 March for Life.[31] At the time, scores of mainstream media outlets falsely depicted Sandmann mocking liberal Native American activist Nathan Phillips. Parents were furious with Catholic clergy for throwing Sandmann and his friends under the bus in order to curry favor with the press.[32]

Attendees at this year's AUSCP meeting were mostly white elderly men and women. Photos of the event indicate almost none of them wore clerical attire. Former LifeSite video reporter Jim Hale confronted several of the group's members at their 2021 meeting in Minneapolis in the Archdiocese of St Paul and Minneapolis, which is run by Bernard Hebda. Instead of answering Hale's simple questions about homosexual "marriage," they lashed out and berated him while pushing his camera.[33]

Left-wing Jesuit priest Thomas Reese, who is 78, delivered an address at this year's gathering. Reese attended a brunch at the White House with

29 Paul Leingang. "Why the AUSCP is not at the Eucharistic Congress," AUSCP, July 2, 2024, https://auscp.org/why-the-auscp-is-not-at-the-eucharistic-congress/

30 Michael Hichborn, "US Catholic priests conspiring to create 'priestless parishes' run by 'deaconnesses'," LifeSiteNews, November 28, 2017, https://www.lifesitenews.com/opinion/us-catholic-priests-conspiring-to-create-priestless-parishes-run-by-deaconn/. Michael Hichborn, "Dissident priest group backed by prominent bishops demands Catholic 'priestesses'," LifeSiteNews, June 25, 2019, https://www.lifesitenews.com/opinion/dissident-priest-group-backed-by-prominent-bishops-demands-catholic-priestesses/

31 John Stowe, "Wearing a Trump hat? That's not exactly pro-life, says Catholic Bishop John Stowe," Lexington Herald Leader, February 20, 2019, https://www.kentucky.com/opinion/op-ed/article224984305.html

32 Lisa Bourne, "Parents are right to be angered by bishops' rash judgement of Covington boys," LifeSiteNews, January 25, 2019, https://www.lifesitenews.com/blogs/catholic-parents-are-right-to-be-angered-by-bishops-rash-judgement-of-covin/

33 Michael Haynes, "WATCH: Priests at dissident meeting berate LifeSite reporter for questioning them on Church teaching," LifeSiteNews, June 22, 2021, https://www.lifesitenews.com/news/priests-at-dissident-meeting-berate-lifesite-reporter-for-questioning-them-on-church-teaching/

pro-abortion Joe Biden on St Patrick's Day in March. He has previously expressed support for homosexual clergy and "women deacons."[34] In May, he promoted a video that insinuated Biden was handpicked by God to serve as the president.[35]

The AUSCP also screened a documentary about heterodox 20th century priest Teilhard de Chardin and honored pro-LGBT Santa Fe Archbishop John Wester with its John XXIII Award. Wester serves as the group's liaison to the US bishops' conference. Chicago Cardinal Blase Cupich, Washington, DC, Cardinal Wilton Gregory, and San Diego Cardinal Robert McElroy, among others, have spoken at its events previously.

Stowe was widely criticized by faithful Catholics last month for doubling down on his support for a gender-confused 39-year-old woman named Nicole Matson who is living as a "diocesan hermit" in his diocese under the name "Brother Christian Matson."[36]

"Bishop John Stowe... accepted his profession and is grateful to Brother Christian for his witness of discipleship, integrity and contemplative prayer for the Church," the Lexington diocese said in a statement referring to the bearded and balding Nicole as a man, contradicting Catholic teaching.

The National Eucharistic Congress is backed by the United States Conference of Catholic Bishops. On Friday, July 19, LifeSite is sponsoring a Traditional Eucharistic Revival at Victory Field also in Indianapolis, with speakers including John-Henry Westen, Michael Hichborn, Father James Altman, and canceled priest Father Jeffrey Fasching. The event will feature the Traditional Latin Mass at 11:30 a.m.

LifeSiteNews • July 3, 2024

34 Thomas Reese, "Yes, there are lots of good gay priests," National Catholic Reporter, December 8, 2016, https://www.ncronline.org/blogs/ncr-today/yes-there-are-lots-good-gay-priests. Thomas Reese, "Women deacons? Yes. Deacons? Maybe," National Catholic Reporter, August 12, 2016, https://www.ncronline.org/blogs/women-deacons-yes-deacons-maybe

35 "Catholic priest promotes video claiming 'God made Biden'," LifeSiteNews, May 27, 2024, https://www.lifesitenews.com/episodes/catholic-priest-promotes-video-claiming-god-made-biden/

36 LifeSiteNews Staff, "Diocese of Lexington doubles down on referring to female 'hermit' as 'he,' 'Brother'," May 21, 2024, https://www.lifesitenews.com/news/diocese-of-lexington-doubles-down-on-referring-to-female-hermit-as-he-brother/

'SERVANT OF FREEMASONRY': ARCHBISHOP VIGANÒ REBUKES BISHOP WHO APPROVED PAGAN RITUAL AT CATHEDRAL

Archbishop Carlo Maria Viganò has issued a stinging rebuke of an American bishop who allowed a pagan ritual to be performed inside his cathedral earlier this month.

In a X post published last Friday, Viganò condemned the scandalous event and referred to the prelate who permitted it as a "squalid official of the ecumenical religion."

"The shamanic ceremony … constitutes a sacrilegious act that desecrates the Cathedral of the Diocese of Superior (WI) on the very day on which the Holy Chrism is consecrated," His Excellency declared. "This makes Bishop [James] Powers, present at the rite, responsible for a very serious sacrilege and for the scandal caused to those present. This is not a Successor of the Apostles, but a servant of Freemasonry."

Archbishop Viganò is the former Apostolic Nuncio to the United States. His courageous and sharply worded commentaries on Vatican and international affairs have won him many admirers in recent years, even non-Catholics. He recently opened a house of formation in Italy for aspirants to the priesthood so they would not be "subjected to the blackmail of having to accept the errors of Vatican II or the deviations of Bergoglio in order to exercise their ministry."

In his X post, Viganò did not hold back in his criticism of Powers, who was tapped to lead the diocese, located in northwest Wisconsin, by Pope Francis in 2015.

"The way [Powers] celebrates Mass reveals his total alienation from the Divine Mysteries," His Excellency remarked. "What is 'comforting'—so to speak—is to see that the participants in the profanations of the Bergoglian sect are almost all of advanced age (especially the shamans, who are truly pathetic). The generation of Vatican II, sterile and senescent, is heading towards the sunset."[37]

Powers previously served as the diocesan administrator under Bishop Peter Christensen, who oversaw the diocese since 2007 until he was reassigned to Boise, Idaho. In 2020, Christensen banned priests from offering Mass facing the tabernacle.[38] He also outlawed Communion rails.[39]

---

37 Archbishop Carlo Maria Viganò, "'Powers of abomination," X, March 22, 2024, https://x.com/CarloMVigano/status/1771193561867866496

38 Dorothy Cummings McLean, "Did US bishop plagiarize blog in directive banning priests from saying Mass ad orientem?" LifeSiteNews, April 9, 2020, https://www.lifesitenews.com/news/did-us-bishop-plagiarize-blog-in-directive-banning-priests-from-saying-mass-ad-orientem/

39 Dorothy Cummings McLean, "US Bishop forbids priests to say Mass facing tabernacle,

In December 2023, Powers issued a statement in support of *Fiducia Supplicans*, a Vatican document calling for blessings of homosexual couples. "The blessing is simply an encouragement to those involved that they may be open to God's love and find joy in their call to holiness," he misleadingly claimed at the time.[40]

During the ceremony, four women dressed in Native American attire stood around the altar and simultaneously turned to the north, east, south, and west while a person at the pulpit implored help from "the creator" to grant them "strength and courage... to perceive the sacredness of life, of mother earth, and all creation."

LifeSite reached out to the Superior diocese for clarity on the event. LifeSite wanted to know who the women were, what their religious beliefs are, and what they were chanting. LifeSite also sought an explanation as to how the ritual didn't violate the 1983 Code of Canon Law, which holds that an altar "must be reserved for divine worship alone, to the absolute exclusion of any profane use."[41] It also teaches that "sacred places are violated by gravely injurious actions done in them with scandal to the faithful."[42]

LifeSite was informed by Dan Blank, the director of administrative services, that diocesan offices had a "snow day" due to bad weather. He said he would confer with those who were copied on the email in order to "determine a reply, if any." LifeSite has not received a response from the diocese as of the publication of this story.

Hundreds of Catholics attended the liturgy, officially known as the Chrism Mass, where holy oils are anointed by the bishop for priests to use for sacraments. Video evidence suggests most every priest in the diocese was present. Members of the Knights of Columbus and many young people attended as well. It is not readily known if the women who performed the ritual conduct it every year, were invited this year only, or are a regular fixture at other churches in the diocese. *Catholic Family News'* managing editor Matt Gapers expressed outrage about the ceremony in an X post as well. "Bishop James Powers invited those present to 'repent from your sins and to dispose yourselves' to receive the Apostolic Blessing—after allowing

bans Communion rails," LifeSiteNews, April 2, 2020, https://www.lifesitenews.com/news/us-bishop-forbids-priests-to-say-mass-facing-with-people-bans-communion-rails/

40 "Bishop Powers Statement on Pastoral Blessings," Diocese of Superior, December 19, 2023, https://files.ecatholic.com/5291/documents/2023/12/Bishop%20Powers%20Statement%20on%20Pastoral%20Blessings.pdf?t=1703087007000

41 Code of Canon Law, c. 1239, §1, Vatican website, https://www.vatican.va/archive/cod-iuris-canonici/eng/documents/cic_lib4-cann1205-1243_en.html

42 Code of Canon Law, c. 1211, Vatican website, https://www.vatican.va/archive/cod-iuris-canonici/eng/documents/cic_lib4-cann1205-1243_en.html

a non-Christian ritual in the sanctuary," he said.[43]

Deacon Nick Donnelly of England likewise remarked: "The heresy of Bergoglianism in six words: Latin Mass banned; Pagan rituals encouraged."[44]

A priest who resides in the Superior diocese and offers the Latin Mass exclusively but who was not at the ceremony spoke to LifeSite on condition of anonymity. He said the ritual was "tragic" in that it was an "abomination of desolation" that effectively makes Powers a "minister of Satan."

"They invoked foreign deities with strange emblems, dancing, and incantations to consecrate the altar to Pachamama and the forces of darkness. This is an act of spiritual fornication carried out by the representatives of the Mystical Body of Christ, making it a grievous sin," the priest said.

"The bishop defiled his soul and this diocese by forcing his priests, who stood by in silence, to approve of it," he added. "They have collectively reconsecrated this diocese to Satan by an act of apostasy of unanimous consent that now permits demons to come and go as they please wherever they please, even in churches. They have deceived their sheep, presenting evil as good, and defiled the altar and the Cathedral itself, which now requires an exorcism."

The priest further remarked that:

The oils that were 'made holy' at this un-worthy liturgy were approved by an entire group of clergy in the state of mortal sin. These very oils will be used in all sacraments for the next year, defiling all who receive them. Never has anyone heard of such an indescribable sin as what took place here, and because the Vatican has been encouraging this all over the world, laity think it is just an ecumenical gesture of mercy. The truth is, there is nothing on earth so unmerciful as to condemn to eternal fire your whole body of clergy, and all of your sheep. This makes them the ministers of Satan, and like him, murderers of souls.

LifeSiteNews • Mar 27, 2024

THE USCCB MISUNDERSTANDS OUR LADY OF GUADALUPE

History, Winston Churchill once said, is written by the victors. Ever since the close of the Second Vatican Council, Liberal Catholics (also known as

43 Matt Gaspers, "Scenes from the Chrism Mass in Christ the King Cathedral," X, March 22, 2024, https://x.com/MattGaspers/status/1771345133239259489
44 Nick Donnelly, "The heresy of Bergoglianism in six words," X, March 23, 2024, https://x.com/ProtecttheFaith/status/1771441412174688295

"neoconservative Catholics") have relied on two main strategies to ensure laity remain obedient to their "victory" at the Council.

Aside from teaching the lie that the Church before the 1960s was "legalistic" and "rigid," one of the primary tactics Liberal Catholics rely on is to draw the attention of laity to certain encyclicals (and popes) while ignoring others—a sort of purposeful cafeteria Catholicism, if you will. Or, as blogger Gabriel Sanchez once put it, "a hermeneutic of selectivity."[45]

In the Liberal Catholic hall of fame of pre-Vatican II papal documents rests Pope Leo XIII's *Rerum Novarum* and Pius XI's *Quadragesimo Anno.* Of themselves, these are great encyclicals. Neither has anything to do with what ails the Church today. My point in bringing them up is this: when is the last time you heard someone in the mainstream Catholic media, a bishop, or even a pope, refer to any of the other encyclicals these two Vicars of Christ, who collectively reigned for more than 40 years, ever produced?

Indeed, show me a youth minister or RCIA director that assigns Pope Leo's *Humanum Genus* (his encyclical on Freemasonry) or Pius XI's *Mortalium Animos* (his encyclical on Christian Unity) for homework and I'll show you someone about to lose their job.

The Significance of Quas Primas

Of all the pre-Vatican II encyclicals that Liberal Catholics disdain, perhaps none draws their ire as much Pius XI's 1925 *Quas Primas*, which is on the Social Kingship of Christ.

Readers of this blog know all too well what *Quas Primas* says, so I needn't bother you with all its details. What needs drawing attention to, however, is that Friday, December 11th was the 90th anniversary of its publication.

And how, one might wonder, did Rome celebrate that grand occasion? With silence.

Dead. Silence.

Instead of reminding the corrupt leaders in the world that, as *Quas Primas* teaches, "only when men recognize, both in private and in public life, that Christ is King, will society at last receive the great blessings of real liberty," the Vatican celebrated that beautiful anniversary by literally saying nothing.

Actually, I take that back. Rome did say something about Our Lord last week. On Thursday December 10th, the Commission for Religious Relations with the Jews published a 10,000 word document about how their "covenant"

---

45 Gabriel Sanchez, "A Reflection on St Pius X and Contemporary Approaches to Catholic Social Teaching," The Josias, January 16, 2015, https://thejosias.com/2015/01/16/a-reflection-on-st-pius-x-and-contemporary-approaches-to-catholic-social-teaching/

is still valid and that followers of Judaism don't need to acknowledge Jesus Christ as the Messiah.[46] Pius XI must be spinning in his grave!

Our Lady Does Not Support Religious Liberty

This past weekend was the Feast of Our Lady of Guadalupe. I do not believe these two events—the 90th anniversary of *Quas Primas* and the feast of Our Lady—are un-related.

In 1517, Martin Luther nailed a piece of paper to the door of Castle Church in Wittenberg, Germany. That Satanic-inspired event resulted in the destruction of Christendom and the plunging of Europe headlong into errors that are still afflicting the world to this day.

Our Blessed Mother, who is always one step ahead of the prince of this world, knew what was to come. As if to say, "Lucifer, you have no power here," she appeared, just 14 years later, to Juan Diego in Guadalupe, Mexico. In doing so, she won over about the same number of, if not more, souls than those who left the Church due to Luther's heresies.

Prior to Our Lady's appearance to Juan Diego, Latin America was a pagan hell hole where human sacrifice and worship of "Mother Nature" was the norm. In revealing herself to the region's inhabitants, Our Lady obliterated those barbaric practices, thereby putting herself at odds with "religious liberty." The message she conveys is essentially this:

> I alone am your Queen and Christ alone is your King. We desire to be adored, publicly, by you, our children. Religious pluralism is not pleasing to us. God is a jealous God who wishes all men to be Catholic. He desires nations to acknowledge their complete and utter dependence upon Him in the one religion He has established.

America is a Pagan Land in Need of Conversion

Today, we live in a country that is not that different from the one Our Lady of Guadalupe appeared to. The United States is an increasingly irreligious place. It also unapologetically promotes human sacrifice in the form of abortion. How should the US Bishop's respond to this?

If we are to take anything away from our Blessed Mother's apparition, it is that Catholic clergy must provide the men of our age with the teachings of the one true faith. The natural law is not enough. It was only after converting

---

46 Louie Verrechio, "Recent Document on Jews Merely a Symptom," akaCatholic.com, December 11, 2015, https://akacatholic.com/recent-document-on-jews-merely-a-symptom/

to Catholicism that the natives stopped massacring their own.

Yet the United States Conference of Catholic Bishops (USCCB) failed to support that mission last week. On Our Lady of Guadalupe's Feast Day, they issued a Tweet calling on their followers to "pray to Our Lady of Guadalupe, patroness of the Americas, for the protection of our religious liberty." Translation:

> Dear Catholics, ask Mary to enlighten the minds of the bloodthirsty, evil politicians who rule over us to give us the freedom to build soup kitchens and perform acts of charity. Let us not demand too much! We just need to more earnestly beg the enemies of the Holy Trinity who run the world to let us have the liberty to serve mankind!

In essence, the men who occupy the offices of the Church have opted to become Oliver Twist!

Although the bishops didn't mention it in their Tweet, it is a doctrine of our faith that every nation of the world owes obedience to Jesus Christ. Why is that the case? Because he purchased all men with His blood when he died on the cross for them. The public square is His and His alone, in other words. Anything that is not from Him, as Pius XII once wrote, is "an error, and the same rights, which are objectively recognized for truth, cannot be afforded to error."[47]

Is Co-Existence What Christ Desires?

Since the Protestant Revolt, nation after nation has been overrun with heresy. Men and women show by their words and deeds that they don't want anything to do with the Catholic faith.

Instead of fighting back like Our Lady of Guadalupe did, worldly-minded Churchmen (like those at the USCCB) have chosen to simply co-exist with our pagan rulers, preferring to fight for the crumbs of "religious liberty" instead of reclaiming the public domain for God.

Louis Veuillot, a famous 19th century French author, exposed the absurdity of this position in his book *The Liberal Illusion* in the following way:

> Imagine a king deposed from his throne, the last, best hope of his conquered fatherland, who was suddenly to declare that he considered himself justly deposed and that he only aspired to enjoy his personal

---

47 Pius XII, Discourse to the Tribunal of the Sacred Roman Rota, October 6, 1946, https://www.vatican.va/content/pius-xii/it/speeches/1946/documents/hf_p-xii_spe_19461006_roman-rota.html

possessions, according to the laws governing all citizens, beneath the protection of the very men who were plundering his subjects.

The king we imagine would disgrace himself in vain. No one would believe him. Those to whom he offered to sell his rights and his honor would tell him: Are you mad!? You are king!

We would be doing worse, and for that reason people would be even less inclined to believe us.

Veuillot adds that eventually Liberal Catholics "will lend a hand to persecuting the true Catholics, and in so doing they will become apostates."[48] Has this not come true today?

Let us follow neither the advice nor the example of the USCCB, but instead that which was provided to us by of Our Lady of Guadalupe. Let us never cease proclaiming the Social Kingship of Christ to the pagan world around us, just as she did, so that it will leave its evil practices behind.

akaCatholic.com • December 16, 2015

48 Louis Veuillot, *The Liberal Illusion*, Angelus Press, Kansas City, Missouri, 2005, pp. 59–61

CHAPTER III: THE LATIN MASS

THE INFERIORITY OF THE *NOVUS ORDO* MASS

A few weeks ago a young man by the name of Benedict Turvill wrote an article for the U.K.-based *Catholic Herald*. The title of his essay was, "Why young Catholics love the Extraordinary Form."[1]

Ostensibly speaking on behalf of all "young Catholics," Turvill praised "the purity and beauty" of the "Extraordinary Form" but also extolled the "appealing" "structural simplifications" and "versatility" of the *Novus Ordo* Mass.

"The Latin, the Gregorian chant, the priest facing *ad orientem* and even the Roman biretta are ingredients in a spiritual feast that represents an oasis of replenishing beauty from the madness of the modern world," he wrote.

"I love the Extraordinary Form because it is so unashamedly and distinctively Catholic," he added. "It represents a brave and missionary faith willing to take on the world, and affirm our identity in so doing."

I'm not sure what to make of this. A "spiritual feast"? A "brave and missionary" faith? Well-catechized Catholics would say that what makes the Latin Mass "distinctively Catholic" is its prayers and use of symbols (the altar rail, receiving communion kneeling and on the tongue, etc.) to reflect the faith it defends. As the saying goes, *"lex orandi, lex credendi"* ("how we pray, is how we believe").

When one reads Mr Turvill's essay, it is not difficult to discern that he, like many young Catholics, is simply enchanted by its reverence. This is confirmed by what he says about the new Mass: "It would be wrong to assume that solemnity, beauty and spiritual armor cannot be found within the rich folds of the *Novus Ordo* Mass."

Like many neo-Traditionalists, Turvill seems scared of appearing "triumphalistic" or "judgmental" so he feels compelled to say that both liturgies have their pros and cons and that they can somehow enrich each other. But the *Novus Ordo* was not an organic development that took place over hundreds of years bearing many fruits, as the Latin Mass is. It was literally concocted out of thin air with the help of six non-Catholics less than 60 yeas ago. It's aim was not to better express the truths of Catholicism, but to suppress them so

---

1 Benedict Turvill, "Why Young Catholics Love the Extraordinary Form," Catholic Herald, September 4, 2016, https://catholicherald.co.uk/why-young-catholics-love-the-extraordinary-form/

inter-religious dialogue could take place. As Archbishop Annibale Bugnini, the architect of the *Novus Ordo*, once said: "we must strip from our Catholic prayers and from the Catholic liturgy everything which can be the shadow of a stumbling block for our separated brethren that is for the Protestants."[2] Plainly stated, the "Extraordinary Form" and the "Ordinary Form" reflect two different religions.

What's Wrong With the Novus Ordo?

High ranking Vatican officials in the 1960s did not agree with Turvill's assessment that there is "solemnity, beauty and spiritual armor" in the new Mass. Cardinal Alfredo Ottaviani, the long-time Secretary of the Holy Office, once famously wrote that "the *Novus Ordo* represents, both as a whole and in its details, a striking departure from the Catholic theology of the Mass as it was formulated in Session XXII of the Council of Trent."[3]

Once can't help but wonder if Mr Turvill has ever read Ottaviani's critique of the Mass he believes is such a treasure.

Cardinal John Heenan was the Archbishop of Westminster from 1963 until 1975. He echoed Ottaviani's remarks when he said that if the Church were to offer the *Novus Ordo Missae*, she would "soon be left with a congregation mostly of women and children."[4]

Has this not come true today?

It is also worth noting that "reverence" of itself is not what makes something Catholic. What makes something Catholic is its theology, ecclesiology, and doctrinal conformity to Tradition. The Latin Mass does this, clear and unambiguously. The *Novus Ordo* does not.

For more than a thousand years the Latin Mass has acted as a veritable saint-producing factory. The *Novus Ordo* lends itself to liturgical abuses and has driven countless persons away from the faith instead of helping them live holy lives. It's time to stop thinking one isn't better than the other.

Magnificat Media • September 20, 2016

---

2 L'Osservatore Romano, March 19, 1965

3 Cardinal Alfredo Ottaviani, "A Brief Critical Study of the Novus Ordo Missae," Angelus Press, First printed1969, https://angeluspress.org/blogs/catholic-doctrine/a-brief-critical-study-of-the-novus-ordo-missae

4 Aaron Taylor, "Fatherless Churches," First Things, January 15, 2014, https://www.firstthings.com/web-exclusives/2014/01/fatherless-churches

TRADITIONAL CATHOLICS ATTEND 'PARKING LOT MASS' AMID COVID LOCKDOWNS

Hundreds of Catholics from across Michigan flocked to the small town of Allendale this weekend to attend from inside their vehicles the only public Mass offered in the entire western side of the state.

Fr David Gillilan of the Society of St Pius X (SSPX) endured chilly 30 degree temperatures Sunday as he offered what some are calling a "parking lot Mass" from a wooden altar set up on the porch of the rectory behind St Margaret Mary's Chapel.

While no sermon was given and the choir didn't sing, those who went to the Mass said it was as reverent and as holy as any other liturgy.

"It was sort of like Ireland and the old Mass rocks," one man who knelt on the concrete outside during the service said. "It was a pretty cool experience."

The SSPX is a pious union of more than 600 traditional Catholic priests. Founded in Switzerland in 1970, the group maintains that the crisis in the Church is a direct result of the Second Vatican Council. It also claims that "supplied jurisdiction" allows its priests the freedom to operate outside the authority of diocesan bishops.

On a normal weekend, St Margaret Mary's sees upwards of 200 laity at its Sunday morning Mass. According to one of the ushers who helped direct cars this weekend, Sunday's liturgy saw an increase of more than two dozen new attendees.

One of the possible reasons for the uptick is that Catholics not only in West Michigan, but throughout the United States, have been left without access to the sacraments thanks to every American bishop canceling public Masses in their dioceses due to the COVID-19 outbreak.

In order to maintain the spiritual well-being of their parishioners, many Catholic priests in the US are resorting to drive-thru confessions, outdoor adoration, and broadcasting Mass online.

Fr Jürgen Wegner is the district superior of the Society of St Pius X's American district. He released a statement on March 14 indicating the SSPX is offering a "continuous Mass" for protection during the pandemic. He also said Society-run chapels in the US would "follow the lawful government orders" but also promised that they would make priests available as best they can.[56]

5 Fr Jurgen Wegner, "Letter from Fr Wegner Regarding US District and COVID-19 Coronavirus," SSPX.org, March 14, 2020, https://sspx.org/en/news/letter-fr-wegner-regarding-us-district-and-COVID-19-coronavirus-23671

6 Stephen Kokx, "Society of St Pius X cancels 'most public Masses' in U.S., promises to make priests available as needed," LifeSiteNews, April 3, 2020, https://www.lifesitenews.com/

Fr Gillilan told LifeSite he does not know for certain if another parking lot Mass will be necessary. During his sermon at the Saturday evening liturgy, he preached about how the Church has lived through far worse times but that this outbreak should remind Catholics to be grateful for the sacraments and to not take them for granted.

LifeSiteNews • March 24, 2020

LIFESITE JOURNALISTS REACT TO FRANCIS' 'CRUEL,' 'HATEFUL' *MOTU PROPRIO TRADITIONIS CUSTODES*

Editor's note: LifeSite journalists were asked so share their thoughts on Traditionis Custodes, *a motu proprio released by Pope Francis on July 16, 2021 that greatly restricted the Latin Mass. Below is the statement I provided for that article.*

Far from being pastoral or merciful, *Traditionis Custodes* is a declaration of war by cunning forces in the Church aligned with the diabolical New World Order. It is the logical next step in the liberal agenda aimed at doing away with all that is unabashedly and unapologetically Catholic.

Ultimately, the document is a lashing out by a dying group of elderly churchmen against those who have refused and continue to refuse to go along with their syncretistic, modernist religion that the Deep State and corporate media help promote.

Catholic faithful now wait to see which clergy will defend them from these wolves in sheep's clothing. God gave us the great gift of Archbishop Marcel Lefebvre after the Second Vatican Council. Archbishop Viganò today seems to be carrying his message forward. We need to pray that more shepherds will recognize the truth in His Excellency's words and for them to continue to offer the Traditional Mass, regardless of what any authority in the Church says.

Nevertheless, despite the great harm this decree will do, one can perceive in it the hand of God, who always brings good out of evil. As with the Great Reset and the COVID scamdemic, this attempt to crush that which has created and sustained saints for centuries is laying bare the true intentions of those who have set themselves up on the side of Satan and his counter-church. This monstrous assault on Catholics who practice the true faith is being allowed

news/priestly-society-of-st-pius-x-cancels-public-u.s-masses/

by the Almighty for His eventual glorification.

Catholics everywhere now have the duty to openly resist Peter to his face and to educate themselves, and others, on the traitorous deeds being perpetrated against them. God doesn't want unthinking drones who obey what these usurpers are imposing on them. He wants souls to "test all things" and to "hold fast to the traditions," as Scripture says.

We have been born into these times as an invitation by God to carry these heavy crosses. I pray that Catholics—both laity and clergy—will take them up with the same joy and steadfastness that earlier generations (and Christ Himself) did no matter the persecution, or martyrdom, they will face in the years ahead for doing so.

LifeSiteNews • July 19, 2021

CARDINAL CUPICH SUGGESTS JOHN PAUL II WOULD SUPPORT FRANCIS' CRACKDOWN ON THE LATIN MASS

Pro-LGBT Cardinal Blase Cupich of Chicago is arguing that John Paul II would have supported the Vatican's widely-criticized decision to greatly restrict the Traditional Latin Mass.

In an article for *America* magazine this week, Cupich accused Catholics angry with Francis' crackdown on the more than 1,500-year-old liturgy of not only opposing the will of God and of "undermining" the Holy See, but of pitting themselves directly against Francis' Polish predecessor.

"Over my 50 years as a priest and 25 as a bishop, I have seen pockets of resistance to the Council's teachings and reforms, especially the refusal to accept the restoration of the liturgy," Cupich complained. "St John Paul II challenged this resistance head on in his apostolic letter on the 25th anniversary of Vatican II's *'Constitution on the Sacred Liturgy.'"*

Cupich also claimed that John Paul would have endorse Francis' 2021 motu proprio *Traditions Custodes*, as well as his rescript published last week that requires bishops to obtain permission from the Dicastery for Divine Worship before allowing the celebration of the Latin Mass in their dioceses.

Cupich's essay has been republished in Italian by the Vatican's daily newspaper *L'Osservatore Romano*, a strong indication that Francis supports it and fully intends to continue down the path of canceling the Latin liturgy.

Francis is the True Enemy of the Latin Mass

It cannot be denied that John Paul was a man of the Council. He robustly defended its liberal policies and held a number of bizarre theological views that came out of it, especially its overt emphasis on the dignity of man. Read his 1979 encyclical *Redemptor Hominis* for proof of that.

At the same time, he was not entirely hostile to the concerns of those who attended the Latin Mass. For one, he attempted to resolve with significant energies the situation of French Archbishop Marcel Lefebvre in the 1980s. Cardinal Joseph Ratzinger, who served as the Prefect of the Congregation for the Doctrine of the Faith under him, worked with Lefebvre to remedy their differences for several years. Their efforts ultimately lead to an agreement, in principle, for Lefebvre's Society of St Pius X (SSPX) to have one bishop. After that arrangement fell through, Lefebvre consecrated four bishops in May of 1988 against Rome's wishes, at which time John Paul established the Pontifical Commission *Ecclesia Dei* so former SSPX priests could say the Latin Mass under the Vatican's purview.

Four years earlier, in 1984, John Paul's Congregation for Divine Worship and the Discipline of the Sacraments issued a letter permitting bishops to grant a Latin Mass indult in their dioceses under certain circumstances.

While these facts don't take away from the likely ulterior motives John Paul had for carrying these actions out (nor do they minimize the many liturgical abuses and other scandalous behaviors that occurred during his reign), they do seem to indicate he did not have the same level of antipathy toward the traditional Mass that Francis, who abolished *Ecclesia Dei* altogether in January 2019, does.

Ignoring Liturgical Abuses

One of the great ironies of Cupich's essay is that for all his references to the need for Catholics to celebrate the "unique expression" of the Roman Rite, he himself has permitted, and even encouraged, a wide array of sacrilegious liturgical practices in his Archdiocese.

At Old St Pat's Church in June 2022, a "married" homosexual couple delivered a sermon on the alleged merits of legalized sodomy. Cupich took no action.[7] At Holy Family "Catholic Community" in the same month, parishioners

---

7 Matt Lamb, "Homosexual couple gives 'Gospel reflection' at Chicago parish Mass," Life-SiteNews, June 21, 2022, https://www.lifesitenews.com/news/homosexual-couple-gives-gos-pel-reflection-at-chicago-parish-on-fathers-day/

broke out into song and dance as bubbles were blown in the air.[8] Meanwhile, dissident priest Fr Michael Pfleger has conducted Protestant-like "worship services" at his South Side St Sabina's Church for decades without penalty.

What's more, in November 2022, the music director at the Holy Name Cathedral physically assaulted the leader of a Rosary rally supporting the Latin Mass on the steps outside.[9] That altercation took place just months after Cupich banned the Institute of Christ the King Sovereign Priest from publicly offering Latin Masses.[10] Cupich's autocratic approach has put himself at odds with neighboring Bishop Thomas Paprocki, who has expressed strong reservations with Francis' latest crackdown on the Latin Mass.

Cupich has also pit himself against fellow Vatican II cheerleader Bishop Robert Barron, who recently shocked Traditionalists by allowing the Society of St Pius x to offer Mass at a college chapel in the Diocese of Winona–Rochester in Minnesota.

The Latin Mass Is The Future

Cupich's claim that the *Novus Ordo Missae* is a bright shining "fruit" of the Second Vatican Council is particularly laughable, as Latin Mass churches are not only bursting with young families but boasting high weekly-attendance rates and experiencing a massive uptick in vocations.

Diocesan parishes, on the other hand, are being shuttered at breakneck speed due to declining membership and a lack of priests to service them.[11] Cupich himself has had to sell off several properties in recent months. That doesn't sound like a "golden age" in church history to me, as he recently described it.[12]

8 Matt Lamb, "Layman giving homily and dancing included at Archdiocese of Chicago parish Mass," LifeSiteNews, June 8, 2022, https://www.lifesitenews.com/news/layman-giving-homily-and-dancing-included-at-archdiocese-of-chicago-parish-mass/

9 Matt Lamb, "Chicago cathedral's music director attacks Catholic praying the rosary in support of Latin Mass," LifeSiteNews, November 7, 2022, https://www.lifesitenews.com/news/chicago-cathedrals-music-director-attacks-catholic-praying-the-rosary-in-support-of-latin-mass/

10 Maike Hickson, "Cdl. Cupich bans Institute of Christ the King from saying public Masses, confessions in Chicago," LifeSiteNews, August 1, 2022, https://www.lifesitenews.com/blogs/cdl-cupich-bans-institute-of-christ-the-king-from-saying-public-masses-confessions-in-chicago/

11 Fr John Zuhlsdorf, "These numbers suggest a seriously unhealthy Church. UPDATED," Fr Z's Blog, February 27, 2023, https://wdtprs.com/2023/02/these-numbers-suggest-a-seriously-unhealthy-church/

12 Jack Bingham, "Cdl. Cupich says we are in a 'golden age' of the Church. He is right, but for the wrong reasons," LifeSiteNews, July 29, 2022, https://www.lifesitenews.com/blogs/cdl-cupich-says-we-are-in-a-golden-age-of-the-church-he-is-right-but-for-the-wrong-reasons/

As a member of the Dicastery for Divine Worship, Cupich should be aware of the historical documents governing the Church's liturgical life. Yet, by taking steps to relegate the Latin Mass to the dustbin of history, he, like others who have attempted to displace the traditional liturgy with what Archbishop Viganò has called "The Montinian Mass," shows a profound level of ignorance of—or perhaps purposeful disdain for—St Pius V's 1570 papal bull *Quo Primum*, which declares that the Roman Missal shall "remain always valid and retain its full force" and that "superiors, administrators, canons, chaplains, and other secular priests, or religious, of whatever title designated, [are not] obliged to celebrate the Mass otherwise than as enjoined by Us."

History will not be kind to His Eminence nor to any pope or bishop who stifles the Latin Mass.

LifeSiteNews • March, 2, 2023

KENTUCKY BISHOP REMOVES TWO LATIN MASS PRIESTS FROM PUBLIC MINISTRY

The bishop of Covington, Kentucky removed from public ministry two beloved priests who offer the Traditional Latin Mass.

Parishioners at Our Lady of Lourdes in Park Hill were recently informed by Father Shannon Collins that he and Fr Sean Kopczynski were stripped of their faculties by their ordinary, John Iffert.

Collins and Kopczynski belong to the Missionaries of St John the Baptist, a "public association of the faithful" that was erected by Iffert's predecessor Roger Foys in the Covington diocese in 2019. The group is currently training several young men for the priesthood.

Aside from preaching retreats, Collins and Kopczynski provide the traditional sacraments to laity at Our Lady of Lourdes and at the Oratory of the Holy Family, which is located 28 miles southwest in Union, Kentucky.

Our Lady of Lourdes was established as a "quasi-parish" reserved for the exclusive celebration of the Traditional Mass in 2016. In 2017, Foys conducted a dedication ceremony of the property. In 2018, he elevated it to the status of "personal parish," writing in a public statement that "its members have distinguished themselves by their piety, generosity, and love for the Lord and His Church."

LifeSite has learned that Collins was removed for preaching a "divisive sermon" several months ago that the diocese says undermined "unity" in the Church. In the sermon, Collins refers to the Novus Ordo liturgy as being "largely against the old order of things." He also recalled that "not only was the Mass changed but every single sacramental ritual was changed."[13] LifeSite has also learned that Collins refused to concelebrate a Novus Ordo Mass with Iffert.

LifeSite emailed Laura Keener, the Diocese of Covington's communication director, to inquire about other details related to the removal, as well as what the future of the Missionaries will be. She directed LifeSite to a diocesan statement released on January 17.

In that statement, Iffert said that Collins had maintained that the Novus Ordo "is 'irrelevant,' preserves 'literally nothing of the old,' and that the reform of the liturgy was motivated by hatred toward traditional Catholics and the ancient liturgies of Rome."

Iffert then stated that Collins and Kopczynski "maintain these errors and refuse the opportunity to renounce them." He subsequently declared that this "disqualifies them from being granted permission to publicly celebrate" the Latin Mass.

When the news of his cancelation went public, Collins received praise from numerous Catholics on social media for his many forceful, spiritually rich sermons, which are widely available on YouTube. They decried the move as yet another attack on Traditional Catholicism under Francis. "I used to listen to the sermons from these priests all the time, this is very sad," author and podcaster Kennedy Hall posted on X. Others made similar remarks.

LifeSiteNews • January 17, 2024

CARDINAL MÜLLER SAYS IT IS 'CHILDISH' FOR BISHOPS TO CANCEL LATIN MASS PRIESTS

During a recent appearance on EWTN's *The World Over* with Raymond Arroyo, German Cardinal Gerhard Müller lamented the "childish behavior" of "some bishops" who are attacking the Latin Mass in an effort to curry favor with the Vatican.

What "is needed [is] more sensibility, pastoral sensibility, [for] those priests and faithful who prefer the Latin Mass," His Eminence remarked.[14]

13 Complicit Clergy, "Is this the Homily that Resulted in the Cancellation of Two Kentucky Priests?" Rumble, March, 2024, https://rumble.com/v47sr6c-is-this-the-homily-that-resulted-in-the-cancellation-of-two-kentucky-priest.html
14 EWTN, "The World Over January 25, 2024 | RESISTANCE TO FIDUCIA SUPPLICANS: Cardinal Gerhard Müller," YouTube, January 25, 2024, https://www.youtube.com/

Müller, 76, was named Prefect of the Congregation (now Dicastery) for the Doctrine of the Faith by Pope Benedict x v i in 2012. He held that position until 2017 when he resigned under Pope Francis, whom he has accused of issuing "some statements" that are "formulated in such a way that they could be reasonably understood as material heresy."[15]

Müller was asked by Arroyo to share his reaction to the recent cancellation of Fathers Shannon Collins and Sean Kopczynski of the Missionaries of St John the Baptist by Bishop John Iffert of the Diocese of Covington, Kentucky. Collins had ran afoul of Iffert after pointing out in a sermon that "not only was the Mass changed [at Vatican ii] but every single sacramental ritual was changed."[16]

"Cardinal Müller, your thoughts on the speed, the intensity, and the heavy-handed tactics being deployed against priests who celebrate the Old Rite or voice their opinions about the New or the Old Rite?" Arroyo asked.

"The Holy Mass is dogmatically instituted by Jesus Christ," Müller replied. "The Rites are different in the Catholic Church, and every Rite has a certain history and a certain variation."

Müller further argued that some bishops "look to Rome and then say to the Holy Father, 'I suppressed these people, and therefore I look for the reward of being promoted, being named archbishop, or cardinal.' This [is the] childish behavior of some bishops."

After the Vatican's release of *Fiducia Supplicans*, Müller, who previously served as Bishop of Regensburg, said it is "self-contradictory" to claim the Church can bless homosexual couples.[17] He also called for it to be "rewritten in the clear, Catholic theological understanding."[18]

Müller further explained to Arroyo that there is a sort of virtue signaling taking place among members in the hierarchy who try to appear "open" and

---

watch?v=gUmgtlaD O K I

15 Andreas Wailzer and Maike Hickson, "Cardinal Müller: Some statements by Pope Francis could be understood as material heresy," LifeSiteNews, November 9, 2023, https://www.lifesitenews.com/news/cardinal-muller-some-statements-by-pope-francis-could-be-understood-as-material-heresy/

16 LifeSiteNews Staff, "U P D A T E: Kentucky bishop removes two Latin Mass priests from public ministry," LifeSiteNews, January 17, 2024, https://www.lifesitenews.com/news/kentucky-bishop-removes-two-latin-mass-priests-from-public-ministry/

17 Andreas Wailzer, "Cardinal Müller tells Pope Francis: Blessing homosexual couples is 'impossible' and 'blasphemy," LifeSiteNews, December 21, 2023, https://www.lifesitenews.com/news/cardinal-muller-tells-pope-francis-blessing-homosexual-couples-is-impossible-and-blasphemy/

18 Andreas Wailzer, "Cardinal Müller calls Fiducia Supplicans a 'failed document' that needs to be 'rewritten," LifeSiteNews, January 26, 2024, https://www.lifesitenews.com/news/cardinal-muller-calls-fiducia-supplicans-a-failed-document-that-needs-to-be-rewritten/

"liberal" while simultaneously scrutinizing Traditional-minded clergy. If pastors come down too hard on laity who attend the Traditional Mass, they act as if they do "not care" for them and then "the people (will be) angry with the Church and they will leave the Church," he said.

LifeSiteNews • January 31, 2024

A CHURCH RISES FROM THE ASHES: LATIN MASS RETURNS TO MICHIGAN PARISH ABANDONED IN THE 1980S

In the 17th century, French Jesuit priests like Fr Jacques Marquette arrived in Northern Michigan and converted thousands of Native Americans to the Catholic faith. Today, several towns across the area have historical markers and monuments erected in his honor.

Much like the wider Church, a crisis of faith shook the Catholic community in Northern Michigan following the Second Vatican Council. Eventually, the Diocese of Gaylord was forced to close several churches in the 1980s, including St Charles Borromeo, one of the largest in the area.

St Charles was originally built in the early 1900s. It was later sold to a group of Protestants. Decades of neglect finally caught up with the building and by the mid-2000s it was practically unusable due to water damage and structural issues.

Bill Price, a former Marine, saw the church listed for sale in the 2010s after he and his wife, who grew up in Cheboygan, were visiting the area. In 2019, Price purchased the dilapidated church by taking out a mortgage on it. Since then, he's essentially single-handedly restored it to its former glory. A small group of volunteers have helped install air conditioning and other amenities.

In recent years, Price has done extensive work patching up holes in the roof to prevent further rain damage. He's also built the base of the altar and fixed the windows. He's installed donated altar rails as well. While financial support has generally been sparse, Price told LifeSite he's received several donations north of a thousand dollars.

Although work still needs being done, including the installation of new floors and bell towers, Price announced St Charles' grand re-opening on Sunday, July 11.

Traditional Catholics from across the state, including some from Cheboygan who attended and were married at St Charles before it closed, responded to the announcement with much celebration.

A 30-person choir composed of laity from more than five Latin Mass

NAVIGATING THE CRISIS IN THE CHURCH

churches in Michigan, along with approximately 300+ laypersons, attended the liturgy, which was offered by a priest of the Society of St Pius x (SSPX). It was the first Latin Mass celebrated at St Charles in over five decades.

Price said he initially approached the Gaylord Diocese about helping St Charles but that they said they were not interested.

Fr William Kimball of the SSPX told LifeSite that the restoration of St Charles is similar to the restoration to the Church as a whole. He explained that while the building is still marred by decades of poor treatment and neglect it is still the Bride of Christ and that God will restore it in time.

Price said he's excited about the possibility of other priests who want to say the Latin Mass coming to St Charles. He had special praise for Fr James Altman, who he said is more than welcome to visit St Charles any time.

LifeSiteNews • July 30, 2021

LATIN MASS CHURCH OWNER VOWS TO CONTINUE RESTORATION DESPITE DIOCESAN DISAPPROVAL

A layman restoring a Catholic church that was sold by the Diocese of Gaylord to Protestants in the 1980s says it is not telling the truth about their interactions. The man has also vowed to continue restoring the church despite the diocese's apostolic administrator wishing he wouldn't.

Bill Price is a former marine who bought St Charles Borromeo in 2019 for $25,000. The building is located in the sleepy vacation town of Cheboygan, Michigan, just 15 miles southeast of Mackinac Island. Jesuit missionary priest Fr Jacques Marquette converted thousands of Native Americans in the area to the Catholic faith in the 17th century.

Currently in his early 70s, Price has spent the majority of the last two years raising money to single-handedly fix up St Charles, which was built in the early 1900s and can hold up to 500 people. Many Catholics in the area who attended St Charles before it was sold have privately told Price that they support his efforts. Thus far, he has raised more than $8,000 on his GoFundMe page.

Price's hard work paid off when on Sunday, July 11, a Solemn High Mass was offered by a priest of the traditional Society of St Pius x. Over 300 Catholics from across the state attended the liturgy. A 30-person choir was on hand as well.

Since July, St Charles has hosted several Masses offered by various priests of the SSPX but it is currently without a regular Mass schedule. Price is the sole owner of the building and welcomes priests who want to say the traditional liturgy. St Charles is not owned or operated by the s s p x, he explained. In a statement released on August 9, the Diocese of Gaylord condemned Price's heroic efforts. The diocese currently does not have an installed bishop but is run by Bishop Emeritus Walter Hurley, who is serving as apostolic administrator.

Hurley is 84 and was previously the bishop of the Diocese of Grand Rapids, which is about 3 and 1/2 hours southwest. Hurley has a reputation for being a liberal and had been accused of covering up priestly abuse in the Dioceses of Detroit and Saginaw.[19][20]

In his statement, Hurley remarked that St Charles is being restored "with no authorization from the Bishop." He also said that Price never asked the Diocese to re-open St Charles as a Catholic church and that "no permission was sought or granted."

"Masses celebrated by the Society of St Pius x or others at the St Charles church site are valid but illicit," his statement reads. Masses at the church "should be avoided."[21]

Price told LifeSite that he adamantly rejects the claim that he never spoke with representatives of the diocese. He says he tried to work things out with them over a period of many months.

"In 2020, Fr Matthew Wigton contacted me via telephone on behalf of the bishop at the time, Bishop Steven Raica, in order to discover what my intentions were for this beautiful but severely neglected structure," Price said via telephone.

"I stated my intention was to restore St Charles in order to accommodate the beautiful ancient liturgy it was originally designed for. Fr Wigton conveyed to me Bishop Raica's very negative thoughts on that, alleging divisiveness, trauma, and emotional pain connected with our endeavor."

Raica is no longer the Bishop of Gaylord. He was re-assigned in 2020 to the Diocese of Birmingham, Alabama, where Mother Angelica's Poor Clare nuns reside.

Price additionally told LifeSite that he personally reached out to other diocesan priests to obtain a blessing of the church after he discovered satanic graffiti painted on its interior bell tower walls. Price says he spoke with several

19 Bradley Eli, "Detroit Cover-Up," Church Militant, October 26, 2018, https://web.archive.org/web/20230923102404/https://www.churchmilitant.com/news/article/detroit-cover-up

20 "Predator Protector Named to Oversee Saginaw Diocese," Church Militant, October 18, 2018, https://web.archive.org/web/20210512185316/https://www.churchmilitant.com/news/article/predator-protector-saginaw

21 Diocese of Gaylord, "Information on St Charles Church, Cheboygan," August 9, 2021, https://dioceseofgaylord.org/news/information-st-charles-church-cheboygan

priests but none of them came—potentially, he theorized, out of fear that the diocese would punish them. Some of the priests, he said, offered words of encouragement.

Price also said that Fr Duane Wachowiak of nearby St Mary's/St Charles church was telling Catholics on social media to not attend the re-opening on July 11 despite never personally contacting Price to learn about the details of the ceremony. LifeSite called Wachowiak's office but was told he is currently traveling.

Price said that he spent at least eight months trying to hash things out with the diocese to no avail.

LifeSite contacted several of the priests Price said he spoke to, including Fr Wigton, who was Vicar General of the Diocese under Raica.

"When I heard about [Bill Price's efforts], I informed Bishop Raica that I was going to just look into it and ask about it," Wigton said via a phone interview. "I don't remember if I was actually, exactly asked by Bishop Raica or just talking about it [with him]. It seemed like the right thing to do though, [to reach out to Mr Price]."

"At the time," Wigton added, "we had three to four churches that were designated for the celebration of the Extraordinary Form. Because those spots were designated, there was no idea of trying to start a new spot at that time. I reached out to speak with Mr Price. He had never reached out to speak with the Bishop for anything that I know of."

Price told LifeSite he flatly rejects those claims.

"Father told me directly that the bishop thought that restoring St Charles would be 'divisive.' He came out and spoke on behalf of the Bishop."

"I think the diocese is trying to do damage control," he added. "Fr Wigton contacted me and conveyed to me that Bishop Raica saw this whole thing as 'divisive' and that it could be emotionally 'disturbing' to the people living up here."

"How can the beautiful, life-giving Traditional Latin Mass be the cause of such things?" he wondered.

LifeSite contacted the Gaylord Diocese for additional comment. Diocesan spokeswoman Mackenzie Ritchie replied via email, saying, "Thank you for connecting with us ... the statement [that we already issued] on our website should provide clarity to many of your questions."

Price told LifeSite there will be more Traditional Latin Masses held at the church, which is located at 221 N. Bailey Street, and that his restoration efforts will continue. He has issued the following statement to LifeSite.

As the private owner of Old St Charles Church in Cheboygan, Michigan, this is my personal response to the Gaylord Diocese notice of August 9, 2021. Also, I am in no way representing or trying to speak on behalf of the s s p x in my following statement.

On July 11, 2021, we had over three hundred people witness a beautiful Solemn High Mass at St Charles in Cheboygan. This was the first celebration of that kind in almost sixty years.

Fr Matthew Wigton told me the bishop at the time thought the celebration of the traditional Latin liturgy would be divisive. How could so many receiving Our Lord be divisive? Salvation is obtained through the sacraments, yet 300 in attendance for a traditional Solemn High Mass is a negative? Why isn't our bishop happy that so many Catholics want to worship Our Lord the way billions have done for well over a thousand years?

There appears to be no logical explanation for Bishop Hurley's displeasure. Pope St Pius v, in *Quo Primum*, guaranteed our right of worship in the Traditional Latin liturgy forever.

The Catholic Church's primary mission is the salvation of souls. It is commonly known that the Church supplies jurisdiction for the sacraments instituted by Christ through its bishops, but if the local ordinary (bishop) fails through error or deliberately chooses not to treat serious problems or doubt expressed by the faithful, the Church itself for the good of those souls supplies the needed jurisdiction through its "executive power of governance" (1983 Code of Canon Law #144).

A condition of serious doubt continues in the Gaylord Diocese with the suppression of Church history regarding the traditional liturgy. Concerned souls are reaching out to priests that understand the nature and seriousness of their concerns regarding liturgy.

Several of the faithful here in Cheboygan have asked for priests to offer the Holy Sacrifice of the Mass in our ancient traditional Catholic liturgy, and also to hear our confessions. We are in very serious doubt by what is currently not being allowed, yet could be locally provided for in this Diocese.

There are Catholics in their 80s and 90s wanting to worship in the Traditional Latin liturgy. These souls have been and are being denied simply because Gaylord's bishops refuse to consider their infirmity, inability to travel great distances, or allow other priests willing to accommodate.

St Charles is currently privately owned for the purpose of restoration. The new owner along with several families in Cheboygan have reached out to priests trained in the Latin liturgy. The Latin Mass missals we use also have the English translation for those that wish to follow the priest through this liturgical worship.

It's exciting to once again have the opportunity to experience what our grandparents, great grandparents and literally tens of billions of Catholics for well over a thousand years, witnessed at least once a week. Thankfully, there are good priests ready to help the families and grandparents here in Cheboygan, assuring us that the Church is here to generously minister not simply dictate through austere measures regarding the sacraments.

In 2020, Fr Matthew Wigton contacted me, the new owner of St Charles, on behalf of Bishop Hurley in order to discover what my intentions are for this beautiful but severely neglected structure. I stated my intention to restore St Charles in order to accommodate the beautiful ancient liturgy it was originally designed for. Father conveyed the bishop's very negative sentiments alleging divisiveness, trauma, and emotional pain connected with our endeavor to restore Cheboygan's architectural gem, St Charles Borromeo.

Finally, due to some satanic graffiti painted on the interior tower walls at St Charles, I personally reached out to five diocesan priests requesting a mere blessing of my building. I informed at least two of those priests of the disturbing graffiti. This happened months before I contacted the SSPX, who thankfully immediately responded, unlike the diocesan clergy. The chancery now acts hurt, snubbed and violated.

Again, many of us are still attached to our traditional Mass, guaranteed to us in perpetuity by Pope St Pius V in *Quo Primum*.

LifeSiteNews • October 15, 2021

US APOSTOLIC NUNCIO RECEIVES BLOWBACK FOR RIDICULING THE CASSOCK, LATIN MASS

Pope Francis' Apostolic Nuncio to the United States, Cardinal Christophe Pierre, is being criticized for remarks about traditional vocations.

During an interview with left-wing *America* magazine this week, Pierre said that it is not good that young men are wanting to become priests who offer the Latin Mass.

"We are in the church at a change of epoch," the 77-year-old claimed. "People don't understand it. And this may be the reason why most of the young priests today dream about wearing the cassock and celebrating Mass in the traditional way."

"In some ways, they are lost in a society which has no security, and all of us when we feel lost look for some security," he continued. "But which kind of security?"

While confessing that young people today enjoy attending the Latin Mass, Pierre condescendingly asked, "is the liturgy [only] something you like? Is it a refuge? Is the church a refuge? If you look at it as a refuge, you isolate yourselves."

"The church is missionary," he further maintained. "It's not a reserve of people who feel well together." It is "not the church that will protect me. It's not the habit."[22]

Woefully Out of Touch

Pierre's remarks come one week after Francis himself made disparaging comments about Tradition-minded clergy. Speaking to hundreds of attendees at the Synod on Synodality in Rome on October 25, Francis belittled "young priests" who are going to shops in Rome and "trying on cassocks and hats, or albs and lace robes."[23]

Those remarks were simply an echo of previous comments he made in 2019 when he accused young men who wear traditional priestly attire of harboring "moral problems" and "imbalances."[24]

Fr Dave Nix, who lives in the United States, provided LifeSite with the following statement about Pierre's accusations:

It's dishonest to pit the missionary spirit against the cassock. Even the modern day, baby-boomer Jesuit in his Hawaiian shirt will admit the greatest missionary saints of his congregation all wore the cassock: St Francis Xavier, St Peter Claver, St Isaac Jogues and St John Brebeuf.

22 Gerard O'Connell, "Cardinal Pierre On Why The US Bishops are Struggling To Connect With Pope Francis," America Magazine, November 2, 2023, https://www.americamagazine.org/faith/2023/11/02/cardinal-christoph-pierre-interview-246416
23 Courtney Mares, "Pope Francis Speaks At Synod on Synodality: 'Clericalism' Defiles The Church," Catholic News Agency, October 26, 2023, https://www.catholicnewsagency.com/news/255817/pope-francis-speaks-at-synod-on-synodality-clericalism-defiles-the-church
24 Dorothy Cummings McLean, "Pope criticizes young Traditional priests' clothes: cassock suggests 'moral problems," LifeSiteNews, September 27, 2019, https://www.lifesitenews.com/news/pope-criticizes-young-traditional-priests-clothes-cassock-means-moral-problems/

You have to remember that the old lefty clergy in the Church are truly activists who try to close down the contemplative orders. But they don't know what to do with the greatest missionaries of their own congregations who had the richest contemplative lives possible.

One of the hallmarks of Francis' reign has been his relentless attacks on both men and women religious. Carmelites in Texas and Pennsylvania — as well as a Benedictine order in Pienza, Italy—are just a few women contemplative orders that have drawn his ire.[25] The Franciscan Friars of the Immaculate were also infamously targeted by the Vatican several years ago.[26] In the interview, Pierre also discussed the drop off of vocations in the United States. While failing to place blame for that on the modernist reforms of Vatican II, or on Francis' assaults on traditional priests, he simply stated that the Church today faces "new questions."

"The sisters have disappeared. You once had vocations and seminaries in 200 places, but the seminaries are now empty. So the church faces...challenges today."

An anonymous priest of the Society of St Pius x told LifeSite that Pierre's remarks exhibit an off-the-charts level of cognitive dissonance.

Mainstream seminaries are closing because they are wishy-washy. There is no doctoral punch. It's 'Mickey Mouse' Catholicism. The modern church and its updated liturgy effectively castrates men. Rome today encourages endless 'dialogue' instead of winning souls to Catholicism.

Archbishop Lefebvre went to Africa as a missionary and offered the Latin Mass, and everyone started converting. It's the *Novus Ordo* Church that isn't missionary. It wants to join with heretics.

As far as the cassock goes: it is a walking sermon. As a young man who was raised without direction in the *Novus Ordo*, it was Catholic

---

25 Michael Haynes, "Texas Bishop Ousts Carmelite Mother After Getting Vatican Backing in Ongoing Conflict," LifeSiteNews, June 1, 2023, https://www.lifesitenews.com/analysis/breaking-texas-bishop-ousts-carmelite-mother-after-getting-vatican-backing-in-ongoing-conflict/. Maike Hickson, "Traditional Nuns in Pennsylvania Will 'Stand Up And Fight' Vatican's Attack On Contemplative Life," LifeSiteNews, November 23, 2021, https://www.lifesitenews.com/blogs/contemplative-nuns-in-pennsylvania-have-chosen-to-stand-up-and-fight-vaticans-attack-on-the-cloister/. Archbishop Carlo Maria Viganò, "Abp Viganò: The Traditional Benedictine Nuns Are The Victims of Pope Francis' Mercenaries," LifeSiteNews, April 24, 2023, https://www.lifesitenews.com/opinion/abp-vigano-the-traditional-benedictine-nuns-are-the-victims-of-pope-francis-mercenaries/

26 Maike Hickson, "Hermit priest doubles down on claim that pope's plans will 'destroy' contemplative orders," LifeSiteNews, October 11, 2021, https://www.lifesitenews.com/blogs/744092/

Tradition that gave me the certitude to sacrifice my life to preach the Gospel to others. Tradition is the future.

Pierre succeeded Archbishop Carlo Maria Viganò as the pope's ambassador to the United States in April 2016. Since vacating that post, Viganò has repeatedly placed the blame for the crisis in the Church on Vatican II and has called for its complete and total repeal.

LifeSiteNews • November 3, 2023

WHY IS WHOOPI GOLDBERG PRAISING JOHN XXIII AND BASHING THE LATIN MASS?

Actress and noted left-wing feminist Whoopi Goldberg effusively praised Pope Francis during her visit to the Vatican earlier this month. She is in the beginning stages of producing "Sister Act 3" and a trip to Rome was apparently needed to gin up interest

"I wanted to thank him for all of my gay friends, and for all of my divorced friends, because he said 'Listen, God loves you no matter what,'" she remarked.

Oddly enough, Goldberg thanked the late John XXIII, who died in 1963, as well.

"For me as a little kid, [John XXIII] allowed the sisters to come out of the very heavy, big habits that they were wearing so that they looked like people—so you could talk to them," she told Vatican News. "And he loved music that different people in different parts of the world were making...but were not sung in Latin. And for kids like me, he allowed us to do the Mass in English, which was great!"[27]

Who Was John XXIII?

John XXIII's birth name was Giuseppe Roncalli. He was pope from 1958 until his death in 1963. He was elected under a cloud of suspicion.

Literally.

At the 1958 conclave following the death of Pius XII, white smoke billowed from the Sistine Chapel on the first day of balloting to indicate a new pontiff

---

27 Francesca Merlo and Sr. Nina Benedikta Krapić, VMZ, "Whoopi Goldberg: 'I've Waited Years To Thank Pope Francis For His Message!'," Vatican News, October 12, 2023, https://www.vaticannews.va/en/world/news/2023-10/pope-francis-meeting-whoopi-goldberg-interview-vatican.html

had been chosen. But no one emerged on the balcony. The Vatican later told the press that there was a mixup in the smoke's color and that no candidate had been chosen.

Some think that Genoa Cardinal Giuseppe Siri was elected and took the name Gregory XVII. A noted anti-communist, Siri was well know to, and feared by, intelligence agencies across the Western world.

This "Siri Theory" holds that a message was possibly relayed to the Cardinal that basically said if he accepted the papacy, either Catholics behind the Iron Curtain would be slaughtered or that the Vatican itself might be threatened. Either way, Siri refused his election under obvious duress, and the more liberal Roncalli was who exited the conclave wearing the papal vestments.

Months later, John announced his intention to convoke Vatican II. According to his own words, he received inspiration for that event "like a flash of heavenly light."[28] Whether or not that illumination was from above or from somewhere else, you decide.

Paul VI Approved The New Mass, Not John

I mention all this because Goldberg was born in November of 1955, which made her 9-years-old when Vatican II finished. She would have been seven when John died in June 1963, when changes to the Latin Mass had hardly taken place yet.

I don't share Goldberg's view of Papa Roncalli. If he had listened to the advice of the Curia and kept the original anti-modernist schema that were compiled over the previous two years, Vatican II could have been a great work of the Holy Spirit. Instead, he caved to liberal pressure and discarded all the preparatory documents—except the one on the liturgy—thereby paving the way for the crisis we have been living through ever since.

While it is true that John enabled suspected Freemason Fr Annibale Bugnini, the architect of what became the *Novus Ordo* Mass, to rise through the Church's ranks, *Sacrosanctum Concilium*, the Council's document on the new Mass, was ultimately approved by Paul VI. She should be thanking *him* if she wants to give due credit for the liturgy being in the vernacular.

Goldberg Has Had Multiple Abortions

Despite her laudatory remarks about the change from Latin to English, Goldberg—like many Catholics after the Council—didn't want anything to do

---

28 Richard McBrien, "John XXIII Calls The Council," National Catholic Reporter, January 20, 2009, https://www.ncronline.org/blogs/essays-theology/john-xxiii-calls-council

with the new Mass. In the book *The Choices We Made*, Goldberg admitted that she became pregnant at just 14-years-old in the late 1960s, right when the *Novus Ordo* Mass was being rolled out. And what did she do when she discovered she was with child? Sadly, she performed a "back alley" abortion.

Goldberg has also revealed that she got pregnant when she was 15 as well. Instead of going to one of those habit-less nuns to seek out the Church's wisdom, she went to Planned Parenthood. In total, Goldberg had more than five abortions before age 25.

"God gives you freedom of choice," she once said.

Is this really the person Vatican News wants to prop up as a spokesperson for the "great" *Novus Ordo* liturgy?

John XXIII Praised Latin

Complicating things for Goldberg, as well as for the Vatican's media team, is the oft-forgotten fact that in his 1962 Apostolic Constitution *Veterum Sapientia*, John XXIII not only defended the Church's use of Latin but called for its continued use in the future.

"Of its very nature Latin is most suitable for promoting every form of culture among peoples. It gives rise to no jealousies," he taught. "It does not favor any one nation, but presents itself with equal impartiality to all and is equally acceptable to all."

"The Catholic Church has a dignity far surpassing that of every merely human society," he added. "It is altogether fitting, therefore, that the language it uses should be noble, majestic, and non-vernacular."

Even *Sacrosanctum Concilium* says that Latin is supposed to be "preserved in the Latin Rites."

On top of that, Paul VI himself said in 1966 that he was "somewhat disturbed and saddened" to receive requests from clergy who "wish to use the vernacular within the choral office" during the Divine Office.[29]

By Their Fruits You Shall Know Them

Goldberg's praise for the Vatican's decision to let nuns "come out of the very heavy, big habits" so that they could look like people "you could talk to" also makes little sense.

Indeed, one wonders how much "talking" Goldberg ever did with them. Aside from her multiple abortions, she has been divorced three times. In her

---

29 Paul VI, Apostolic Letter, *Sacrificium Laudis,* August 15, 1966, https://www.ccwatershed.org/2013/08/05/paul-vi-disturbed-and-saddened-purge-latin/

many public appearances over the past forty years, she has viciously attacked the Church's teachings on abortion and same-sex "marriage," among other topics. While on *The View* this past week, she spoke about her meeting with Francis. Predictably, she said that it didn't change her mind.

"I don't know that it's going to jump me back into Church," she quipped. "But what it did was ... I feel better because I feel like somebody up there likes me. That's the best way I can put it."[30]

In other words, her time at the Vatican made her warm and fuzzy on the inside but did little to cause her to go to confession, repent of her ways, and live a Christian life. This sort of reaction shouldn't be that surprising. Francis has repeatedly said that he approaches all of his meetings with non-Catholics in this way. Seeking their conversion is not something that enters his mind.

Traditional Nuns are Making a Comeback

Goldberg told Vatican News that she is sad that "recruitment" with women religious is difficult these days. She hopes Sister Act 3 will be of some assistance to that.

Well, she needn't look far to see where and why this has happened. In religious communities where Hillary Clinton-style pants suits and social justice activism are the norm, there is barely any interest from young women. In traditional communities where prayer, sacrifice, and, yes, habits, are the norm, far more attention is given.

In 2019, *The Catholic Herald* published an article titled "The new Sisterhood: traditional orders are booming." The essay highlighted several women religious communities in the United Kingdom that are seeing a massive increase in new entrants.[31]

The growth of the Dominican Sisters in Nashville, the Traditional-minded Consoling Sisters in Italy, and the s s p x-affiliated Dominican Sisters of Fanjeaux, France are also a sure sign that God is slowly restoring what Goldberg and liberal clergy in the 1960s sought to eradicate. And that should give Catholics a reason to hope for the future.

LifeSiteNews • October 18, 2023

30 Nicholas Fondacaro, "Whoopi: Pope Francis Is a 'Progressive' Because 'He's a Human Being," NewsBusters, October 16, 2023, https://www.newsbusters.org/blogs/nb/nicholas-fondacaro/2023/10/16/whoopi-pope-francis-progressive-because-hes-human-being?utm_source=dlvr.it&utm_medium=twitter

31 Joanna Bogle, "The New Sisterhood: Traditional Orders Are Booming," Catholic Herald, January 17, 2019, https://catholicherald.co.uk/the-new-sisterhood-traditional-orders-are-booming/

CHAPTER IV: THE SECOND VATICAN COUNCIL

THE COUNCIL FATHERS SPEAK

The more Catholics familiarize themselves with the Second Vatican Council, the likelier it is they will see it not only as a revolutionary event but also a diabolical one.

To make such a claim will surely be viewed as heresy. "Vatican II was an opening of the Church to the Holy Spirit," many people today think. "Who are you to suggest that the clergy God gave us are leading souls to hell? You are acting like a Protestant and a schismatic!"

In an effort to illuminate the minds of those who have been spoon-fed the history of Vatican II by mainstream Catholic media outlets and churchmen, I want to present several quotes from the Council Fathers themselves. These will expose the real motives of the men who deemed it necessary to "update" the Church.

All but one of the following quotations is taken from the 1963 propaganda book *Twelve Council Fathers.* As you're scanning these, have in the back of your mind 2 Thessalonians 2:15: "Therefore, brethren, stand fast; and hold the traditions which you have learned, whether by word, or by our epistle." Ask yourself: Are these princes of the Church holding fast to what was handed down to them? Or do they seem more concerned with human respect and relying on their own novel ideas instead?

Cardinal Paul-Émile Léger, Archbishop of Montreal:

- "I am delighted that Catholic priests and Protestant clergymen meet more often now to engage in fraternal dialogue."[1]

- "We had to do something to break down the barriers that separate the various Christian confessions. The presence of the delegate-observers … was an inspiration for us … Their presence reminded us to be sure we rid ourselves of historical and psychological prejudices."[2]

- "If we do not take steps to do more about achieving rapprochement

---

1 Rev. Walter M. Abbott, *Twelve Council Fathers,* The Macmillan Company, First Edition, New York, New York, January 1, 1963, p. 3
2 Ibid, p.20

between the Church and the modern world, we are in danger of finding ourselves considered unrealistic and irrelevant."[3]

Cardinal Richard Cushing, Archbishop of Boston:

• "Protestant clergymen and Orthodox leaders have been engaged in serious theological conversations with priests in my archdiocese.... Our understanding them better reduces friction to a minimum. We keep our convictions, but we get rid of the prejudices which make the idea of Christian unity impossible."[4]

• "I was so impressed by the fervor of the Protestant ecumenical group known as the Brothers of Taize that I approved establishment of one of their centers here in my archdiocese."[5]

• "We are not trying to make converts. We are not yet at the state of discussing practical means of union. We are just trying to understand each other...we are not attacking the assertions of other faiths...The unity willed by Christ and sought by the Church is not an absorption, not a Latinization, not a diminution."[6]

Cardinal Franz König, Archbishop of Vienna:

• "Whatever may have been the thinking of Church authorities in the past on the subject, we have entered into a new era now. In the past, relations between the Church and State...were largely the product of the local situations. In our era, we can and should work out a mode of operation that corresponds to the realities of the times. These are days of separation of Church and State...Our relationships with people around us of other religious beliefs must certainly express a spirit of tolerance...We have emerged into a period of clearer understanding about freedom of conscience."[7]

• "A common translation of the Bible could give the ecumenical movement a great psychological boost."[8]

3 Ibid, p.48
4 Ibid, p.153
5 Ibid, p.153
6 Ibid, p.154
7 Ibid, pp. 67–68
8 Ibid, p.69

Cardinal Achille Liénart, Bishop of Lille, France:

- "It was important from an ecumenical point of view...that the Council should define something about the collegiality of bishops, as well as from the bishops' own point of view, because the role and powers of bishops meant so much to the Orthodox."[9]

Bishop G. Emmett Carter, Bishop of London, Ontario:

- "The big objection about the document *De Ecclesia* was that it presented to the world a juridical notion of the Church....Why exacerbate other believers in Christ by insisting upon their removal from us? Why not try and to find ground in which we could share a common identity and...to some form of common brotherhood?"[10]

Cardinal Albert Meyer, Archbishop of Chicago:

- "[Dignitatis Humanae] is very necessary, and men of our time expect this declaration. Let us demonstrate that which is essential is a free and sincere conscience. The *schema* will make ecumenical dialogue possible. We must take our stand on this platform of the rights of the human person. Without this declaration, our separated brethren would doubt our sincerity, and with good reason. Without this declaration, whatever she the Council might say would not be accepted by the world."[11]

A Rupture with the Past

It should be clear that the leading voices at the Second Vatican Council did not intend to hand down what was given to them. They preferred to significantly alter, under the guise of making the Catholic faith more "understandable" to modern man, the "pastoral" approaches of the Church. Of course, changing "pastoral" practices necessarily means a practical change in doctrine (this fact

9 Ibid, p.46
10 Ibid, p.115
11 These are remarks His Eminence delivered during the third session of the Council in 1964 during a debate on the Declaration on Religious Freedom. Quoted in Kenneth Whitehead's *Affirming Religious Freedom: How Vatican Council II Developed the Church's Teachings to Meet Today's Needs,* Society of St Paul/Alba House, New York, 2010, p.24

was admitted by some attendees of the most recent Synod on the Family in Rome).[12]

How, then, did these men implement their drastic changes? Did the Holy Ghost simply guide the discussions that took place at the Council? Was God just filling the hearts of the Cardinals and Bishops so they could understand that the Church before the 1960s was radically deficient and in need of a massive overhaul? The answer to those questions partially lies in understanding the influence non-Catholics had on the event.

Apologists for the Council are quick to point out that just because some non-Catholics attended Vatican II as "delegate observers" doesn't mean they influenced the documents in any meaningful way. They also say Catholics should not worry about their input anyway because the Holy Spirit protects an Ecumenical Council from teaching error. But basic research shows that these "observers" had more than a passing influence on the Council's documents.

Paul Blanshard was perhaps the most well-known American critic of Roman Catholicism in the 1950s and 60s. He once noted that Methodist observer bishop Fred Pierce Corson was "given the exceptional distinction of several private papal audiences." He also admitted that "the private remarks of some Protestant observers undoubtedly had some effect in shaping Council policy." [13]

In Michael Davies' book *Liturgical Time Bombs in Vatican II*, he relates that an Anglican archdeacon reported that "in the course of the Council itself, the fullest courtesies and opportunities for communication and exchange were allowed to the observers at every stage, and traces of the process can be recognized in the documents themselves." [14]

Davies also recounts the testimony of Robert McAfee Brown, a Presbyterian observer who said that "although we had no direct 'voice' on the council floor, we did indeed have an indirect voice through the many contacts that were possible with the Fathers and their indispensable strong arms, the periti," or theological experts. [15]

Cardinal Richard Cushing, the Archbishop of Boston, admits in the book *Twelve Council Fathers* that this sort of sneaky behavior took place quite regularly. "I envied the help in translation that [the delegate observers] were

12 Hilary White, "Detaching 'pastoral practice' from Catholic doctrine is a 'dangerous schizophrenic pathology': Vatican cardinal," LifeSiteNews, February 23, 2015, https://www.lifesitenews.com/news/detaching-pastoral-practice-from-catholic-doctrine-is-a-dangerous-schizophr/

13 Paul Blanshard, *Paul Blanshard on Vatican II*, Beacon Press, First Edition, Boston, 1966, pp.160–161

14 Michael Davis, *Liturgical Time Bombs of Vatican II*, TAN Books and Publishers, Rockford, Illinois, 2003, p.78

15 Ibid, p.78

getting from Father Gustave Weigel ... I met many of the delegate observers, and on one occasion I invited twenty of them to dinner."[16]

Question: are these sorts of antics what Catholic Bishops and Cardinals are supposed to engage in? Fraternizing with the enemies of Christ? Is this behavior what St Peter and St Paul would have done had they attended Vatican II? Surely not. They and countless other saints would have denounced such shocking conduct.

I don't know about you, but the fact that 1) Methodist "bishops" were meeting with the pope 2) that Anglicans were given "the fullest courtesies" and 3) that Presbyterians had "an indirect voice" on the Council's documents is enough to taint the entire enterprise. Come to think of it, I'm convinced had John XXIII banned "delegate observers" of any kind from attending the Council, we would all be better off today.

Magnificat Media • June 15, 2016

WHY WERE NON-CATHOLIC 'OBSERVERS' INFLUENCING VATICAN II'S DOCUMENTS?

Far too many Catholics today think the Church before Vatican II was desperately in need of an update, and that a "deep" recovery of "the early Church" was sorely needed. If the Church didn't do this, she would've become obsolete and irrelevant in the modern world.

This is flat out wrong. And un-Catholic.

First, the Council of Trent teaches that the Church "was instructed by Jesus Christ and His Apostles and that *all truth was daily taught it* by the inspiration of the Holy Spirit."

Pope Gregory XVI in his 1832 encyclical *Mirari Vos* likewise said that it is "absurd and injurious to propose a certain 'restoration and regeneration' for [the Church] as though necessary for her safety and growth, as if she could be considered subject to defect or obscuration or other misfortune."

No updating, in other words, was needed, at least not the *aggiornamento* sort the liberal clergy at the Council had in mind.

Second, the duty of the Church is to please God first and to preach the truth in season and out, not to be paranoid about making itself fashionable to the world and worrying what its anti-Christian leaders think might of it. Sadly, this is exactly what happened.

16 Rev. Walter M. Abbott, *Twelve Council Fathers*, The Macmillan Company, First Edition, New York, New York, January 1, 1963, p.145

Third, according to the late Ralph McInerney, a long-time professor at Notre Dame during the 20th century, the pre-conciliar Church wasn't in need of a drastic fixing. "It would be very wrong to imagine that it was something broken and in need of repair," he wrote in his 1998 book *What Went Wrong With Vatican II*.[17]

Fr John W. O'Malley sj echoed those remarks in a 2007 book on the Council. "In 1959, no obvious crisis was troubling the Catholic Church."[18]

Being Afraid About What the World Thinks

Despite the clear wisdom of pre-conciliar popes (and the good fruits in the Church before Vatican II) the progressive theologians who attended the Council successfully imposed their previously censored ideas on their brother bishops, ideas which they naively claimed would prevent the Church from becoming irrelevant but have now been shown to have that precise effect.[19]

In the 1963 propaganda book *Twelve Council Fathers*, Cardinal Paul-Émile Léger, Archbishop of Montreal, worried that, "If we do not take steps to do more about achieving rapprochement between the Church and the modern world, we are in danger of finding ourselves considered unrealistic."[20]

His paranoia was shared by Canadian Bishop G. Emmett Carter, who, in the same book, said: "Why exacerbate other believers in Christ by insisting upon their removal from us? Why not try and find ground in which we could share a common identity and thereby move a step closer to Christ and to some form of common brotherhood."

Maybe because Christ instructed His disciples to teach all nations the Catholic faith and to be united in the same Church under the same pope?

One has to wonder if either of these princes of the Church believed the Gospel they were entrusted to guard and transmit!

Rolling Out the Red Carpet for Heretics

Paul Blanshard (1892–1980) was perhaps the most well-known American critic of Roman Catholicism in the mid-20th century. In his 1966 book on

17 Ralph M. McInerny, *What Went Wrong with Vatican II: The Catholic Crisis Explained*, Sophia Institute Press, Manchester, New Hampshire, 1998, pp.7–8

18 Fr John O'Malley, Fr Joseph Komonchak, et al., *Vatican II: Did Anything Happen?*, Continuum, New York, 2007, p.3

19 See Robert Nugent, *Silence Speaks: Teilhard de Chardin, Yves Congar, John Courtney Murray and Thomas Merton*, Paulist Press, New York/Mahwah, New Jersey, 2011

20 Rev. Walter M. Abbott, *Twelve Council Fathers*, The Macmillan Company, First Edition, New York, New York, January 1, 1963, p.48

the Council, he stated that Methodist observer "bishop" Fred Pierce Corson was given "the exceptional distinction of several private papal audiences."[21]

In Michael Davies' book *Liturgical Time Bombs in Vatican II*, it is related that an Anglican archdeacon said that, "the fullest courtesies and opportunities for communication and exchange were allowed to the observers at every stage, and traces of the process can be recognized in the documents themselves."[22]

Cardinal Paul-Émile Léger confessed in the book *Twelve Council Fathers* that, "The presence of the delegate-observers...was an inspiration for us." Their "presence reminded us to be sure we rid ourselves of historical and psychological prejudices."[23]

Are these the sort of antics which Bishops and Cardinals are supposed to engage in? When has this sort of fraternizing with representatives of anathematized sects ever taken place in Church history? Can it not be said that the entire Council was marred by syncretism and heresy as a result of this?

The 'Observers' and Their Influence

One "observer" in particular stands out more than others: George Lindbeck, a prominent Lutheran minister who died just this past year.

In the 2012 book *Postliberal Theology and the Church Catholic*, Lindbeck spills the beans about the influence he and other non-Catholics had on the Council:

> We would be invited to the most extravagant, exalted kinds of receptions, all the observers...one time an eminent Catholic bishop was asking a young Protestant observer for advice on what he should do for his priests....That kind of thing took place all the time. A Connecticut bishop and I had lunch together once...on what Hans Küng had written.
>
> The high peak of the ecumenical movement took place at the Second Vatican Council. I say the high peak because, just think of it, invited observers, chosen and sent by other churches, were given entrance into the inner circles of the Roman Catholic Church. Their advice was listened to.[24]

21 Paul Blanshard, *Paul Blanshard on Vatican II*, Beacon Press, First Edition, Boston, 1966, p.160

22 Michael Davis, *Liturgical Time Bombs of Vatican II*, TAN Books and Publishers, Rockford, Illinois, 2003, p.78

23 Rev. Walter M. Abbott, *Twelve Council Fathers*, The Macmillan Company, First Edition, New York, New York, January 1, 1963, p.120

24 John Wright, Editor, *Postliberal Theology and the Church Catholic*, Baker Academic,

In a 1994 softball interview with neoconservative luminary George Weigel, Lindbeck spoke about Pope Pius XII's condemnation in his 1950 encyclical *Humani Generis* of the progressive, "new" theology that he helped promote at the Council:

> The Catholic anti-Modernist campaign of the early twentieth century had created a situation in which a very rigid and biased interpretation of Thomas emerged...*Humani Generis* was intended to say "No" to the sorts of approaches represented by the *nouvelle theologie*...the real problem with *Humani Generis* was the way it reinforced the position of the regnant powers in the congregations and the academy, who used the encyclical to make the *nouvelle theologie* people personae non gratae. Which meant that the encyclical reinforced the anti-Modernist style of dealing with exploratory theology.[25]

Weigel himself admits in the interview's introduction to the enormous influence non-Catholics had on the documents.

"As Lindbeck has noted on previous occasions, the ecumenical observers...had special access to the Council aula...and were frequently consulted, formally and informally, about the drafts of conciliar texts," he wrote.

Assessing the Rotten Fruits of the Council

It's high time Catholics stopped thinking Vatican II was a glorious unleashing of the Holy Spirit. A Council that consecrated Russia and condemned Communism and Modernism would have accomplished a great deal of good for the Mystical Body of Christ and the post-war world.

At the end of the day, dissident clergy and non-Catholics were invited to Vatican II, were given the fullest courtesies, and directly and indirectly shaped the text of the Council's documents, a fact that cannot be said about the non-Catholic observers who attended previous Councils.[26]

It has now been a half-century since the close of Vatican II. Since then, the Church has been suffering from what Bishop Athanasius Schneider calls "the

Grand Rapids, Michigan, 2012, pp. 64, 127

25 George Weigel, "Reviewing Vatican II," First Things, December 1994, https://www.firstthings.com/article/1994/12/re-viewing-vatican-ii

26 Pius IX's invitation of non-Catholics to Vatican I was out of a spirit of true charity, one that desired their conversion by way of authentic ecumenism. Vatican II welcomed non-Catholics in the name of human respect and dialogue so to establish a false sense of "unity" while not calling on them to leave their respective sects behind. See Pope Pius IX, Apostolic Letter, *Iam Vos Omnes*, 1868, https://novusordowatch.org/pius9-iam-vos-omnes/

fourth great crisis" in Church history.[27] The one Bible passage that perfectly describes the Church in these times is Isaiah 5:5–6: "And now I will show you what I will do to My vineyard. I will take away the hedge thereof, and it shall be wasted: I will break down the wall, and it shall be trodden down. I will make it a wasteland, neither pruned nor cultivated, and briers and thorns will grow there. I will command the clouds not to rain on it."

Catholic Family News • March 22, 2019

DEBUNKING THE MOST POPULAR MYTHS OF VATICAN II

One of the more well-known arguments so-called "conservative Catholics" rely on to divert attention away from Vatican II's blatant contradictions with the Church's pre-conciliar magisterium is to claim that the "historical context" of past papal pronouncements renders them obsolete.[28] Not only that, but the popes who issued them—as well as the clergy who defended their teachings—were "impulsive" and "reactionary."[29][30] As such, Catholics can rest easy in rejecting what they taught.

One churchman guilty of repeatedly doing this is former Philadelphia Archbishop Charles Chaput. In his book *Render unto Caesar*, Chaput claims that part of the reason Pope Pius IX wrote his *Syllabus of Errors* in 1864 was because he "had to be smuggled out of Rome to escape being killed. That event marked him deeply."[31] Chaput has also said that "all people are shaped by their time"[32] and that "Catholic resistance to modern thought was caused by the persecution of the church after the French Revolution and fears that popular governments might elsewhere do the same."[33]

Whether he knows it or not, Chaput's remarks, which are clearly intended to throw the entire pre-Vatican II Church under the bus, tricks Catholics

27 Sarah Atkinson, "Bishop Athanasius Schneider: 'We Are In The Fourth Great Crisis Of The Church," Catholic Herald, June 6, 2014, https://web.archive.org/web/20150107064055/https://catholicherald.co.uk/features/2014/06/06/bishop-athanasius-schneider-we-are-in-the-fourth-great-crisis-of-the-church/

28 John Pinheiro, PhD, "Liberalism and Leo XIII," Public Discourse, January 25, 2023, https://www.thepublicdiscourse.com/2023/01/86614/

29 Russell Hittinger, *The Teachings of Modern Roman Catholicism: On Law, Politics, & Human Nature*, Columbia University Press, August 7, 2007, p.9

30 Avery Cardinal Dulles, "Development or Reversal?" First Things, October 2005, https://www.firstthings.com/article/2005/10/development-or-reversal

31 Archbishop Charles Chaput, *Render Unto Caesar*, Doubleday, New York, 2008, p.131

32 Ibid, p.97

33 Ibid, p.130

into embracing a subjectivist outlook. Consider that one can easily turn his arguments around on him by saying that the "historical context" of the post-World War II political and cultural landscape that the Council was held in was nothing but a fleeting and transitory moment that deceived those who attended it into naively adopting changes for a world that no longer exists. French Archbishop Marcel Lefebvre, the founder of the Society of St Pius X, understood the absurdity of Chaput's claims. He once said of the liberals who attended the Council that they "systematically relativize the statements of the Magisterium of the Popes of the nineteenth century" and in so doing embrace "relativism and ... doctrinal evolutionism." This eventually leads to undermining "the stability of the rock of Peter in the midst of human fluctuations."[34]

The Myths of Vatican II

Other commonly-accepted tall tales Catholics today have been deceived into believing is that the Council was a return to the "sources" of our religion—especially "the Early Church"—so that it could delve "deeper" into the faith. Marcellino D'Ambrosio, a popular defender of Vatican II, has made this argument many times.

The "theological syntheses of the past" were "hopelessly outdated," he has claimed. The "revolution" that the Church "so desperately needed" in the 1960s was aimed at a "creative recovery of its past" so that it could "break the 'fortress mentality'" that it had adopted. [35]

Another widely-regurgitated falsehood has been shared by former Traditionalist Michael Lofton. In remarks made on Catholic Answers radio several years ago, Lofton argued that the Council's original documents—which took officials in Rome over two painstaking years to complete ahead of its first session in the fall of 1962—were "very technical in their language" and "not very accessible to the average person." This caused the Council Fathers to "write up new documents that would express the teachings of the church, but in a way that's more accessible to the average person."[36]

Aside from the fact that those "more accessible" documents are still not

34 Archbishop Marcel Lefebvre, *They Have Uncrowned Him*, Angelus Press, Kansas City, Missouri, 2003, p.77

35 Dr Marcellino D'Ambrosio, "Ressourcement Theology, Aggiornamento, and The Hermeneutics of Tradition," October 1, 2019, Crossroads Initiatives, https://www.crossroadsinitiative.com/media/articles/ressourcement-theology-aggiornamentoand-the-hermeneutics-of-tradition/

36 Michael Lofton, "Was Vatican II Merely Pastoral," December 21, 2022, Catholic Answers, https://www.catholic.com/audio/caf/was-vatican-ii-merely-pastoral

understood—or even known by the "average" Catholic today—the Council's original schemas, which can easily be found online and read by anyone in possession of basic comprehension skills, were crystal clear in their reaffirmation of the Church's Thomistic, anti-modernist theology. *That* is what infuriated the liberals and drove them to replace them with new ones, not the so-called "very technical" language they contained, which is a completely bogus claim that progressives made up on the spot.

The truth is that liberal foot soldiers circumvented the Council Fathers by making backroom deals to get what they wanted. "In the rules governing the Council it had been laid down that there must be a two-thirds majority vote 'against' if a preparatory schema was to be rejected," French Archbishop Marcel Lefebvre, the founder of the Priestly Society of St Pius x (1905–1991) has recalled. "In the sixth or seventh sitting of the Council, a vote was taken as to whether the preparatory schemas should be accepted for discussion or not. In fact, only 60% voted 'against' and 40% 'for' ... [so the liberals] brought pressure to bear upon Pope John ... [who] let it be known that since these schemas were not acceptable to even half the members of the Assembly, they must be withdrawn." [37]

On this subject, Archbishop Carlo Maria Viganò has rightly noted that "hostile forces" succeeded in "rejecting the perfectly orthodox preparatory schemas that had been prepared by Cardinals and Prelates with a reliable fidelity to the Church" and replaced them with "a bundle of cleverly disguised errors behind long-winded and deliberately equivocal speeches." [38]

We have been living with the disastrous consequences ever since.

Disrespecting Our Ancestors

While many of the arguments used to defend the Council today may sound entirely plausible on the surface, they are nothing more than empty talking points handed down from a dusty, 60-year-old sinister playbook designed to belittle the courageous, anti-modernist popes who reigned in the decades and centuries beforehand. Their ultimate goal is to depict dissident liberal clergy as beleaguered crusaders who fought a justified Holy War against an encrusted Vatican bureaucracy run by irrational, emotionally unstable, and worldly and narrow-minded men.

I myself bought into this nonsense for several years in my 20s. All of the

37 Quoted in Michael Davies, *Pope John's Council: Liturgical Revolution—Part II*, The Angelus Press, Dickinson, Texas, 1977, p.39

38 Archbishop Carlo Maria Viganò, "Interview with Phil Lawler," Catholic Culture, June 2020, https://www.catholicculture.org/culture/library/view.cfm?recnum=12379

Catholic writers and books I was reading alleged that the Council was a great and grand event that pulled the Church out of the past and into the present age. Below are just a few of the many quotations I encountered back then.

"In the eighteenth and nineteenth centuries .... the Catholic Church became, in the main, a defensive bastion,"[39] John Paul II biographer George Weigel once snidely remarked. The 1958 papal conclave "let in some fresh air" when it elected John XXIII."[40]

"Pius XII came from an established, aristocratic family. John XXIII, elected in October 1958 at the age of seventy-seven, came from Italian peasant stock," the aforementioned Charles Chaput has purposefully emphasized in his writings.[41] "Catholic life in the 1950s appeared solid, but the Church also suffered from brittleness," he has also asserted, without proof."[42]

"For many Catholics [who lived before Vatican II], practicing the faith was largely a matter of external observance," author Russell Shaw has similarly claimed."[43]

The obvious implication here is that Pius XII was an elitist who was out of touch with his flock and irresponsibly overseeing a fragile Church desperately in need of being rescued from a backwards-thinking hierarchy that was failing to adequately pass on the faith.

The world-wide echo chamber that repeats these defamatory attacks against our grandparents and great-grandparents is how the Vatican II hierarchy has succeeded for six decades in preventing ordinary Catholics from not only knowing what was taught before the Council but how they smuggled their left-wing ideology into the Church. In essence, gaslighting and brainwashing tactics have been used to program the faithful so they will dismiss out of hand the plain as day denunciations of the Council's key teachings that are made in purposefully-not-talked-about magisterial documents of pre-Vatican II popes.

The Church Cannot Err

Even some of the more moderate voices who defend the Council have pointed out that the reasons that are given to justify its reforms aren't entirely honest.

39 George Weigel, "This Catholic Moment," First Things, October 2019, https://www.first-things.com/article/2019/10/this-catholic-moment

40 George Weigel, "The Unique Conclave Microculture," National Review, March 12, 2013, https://www.nationalreview.com/2013/03/unique-conclave-microculture-george-weigel/

41 Charles Chaput, *Render Unto Caesar,* Doubleday, New York, 2008, p.104

42 Ibid, p.103–104

43 Russell Shaw, *American Church: The Remarkable Rise, Meteoric Fall, and Uncertain Future of Catholicism in America,* Ignatius Press, March 31, 2013, p.93

"In 1959, no obvious crisis was troubling the Catholic Church," Fr John W. O'Malley SJ has observed.[44] The late Ralph McInerney, a 20th century professor at the University of Notre Dame, said in his 1998 book *What Went Wrong With Vatican II* that "it would be very wrong to imagine that [the Church before Vatican II] was something broken and in need of repair."[45]

Fortunately for us, God was not unaware of—nor did He fail to foresee—the schemes hatched by the spiritual fornicators who hijacked what can only be called the Church's one and only Judas Council. He preemptively raised up multiple popes before the 1960s to rebuke their hollow arguments ahead of time so we could see through their many falsehoods today.

It is "absurd and injurious to propose a certain 'restoration and regeneration' for [the Church] as though necessary for her safety and growth, as if she could be considered subject to defect or obscuration," Pope Gregory XVI taught in 1832.[46] It is a "grievous and pernicious error" to believe the Church could ever be "without the perennial communication of the gifts of [God's] divine grace," Leo XIII reiterated in 1896.[47] "The doctrine of Faith that God has revealed, was not proposed to the minds of men as a philosophical discovery to be perfected, but as the divine deposit...never is it permissible to depart from this in the name of a *deeper* understanding," Vatican Council I likewise affirmed.

In brief, the Church could never—as D'Ambrosio, Lofton ,Weigel, Chaput, and others claim—fall into a state of "defensive" squalor that would make it "hopelessly outdated" or in need of a "charismatic expansion" and "creative recovery" from a previous "brittleness." Catholics should pray to God that He will help them understand these false claims made by the Council's defenders so they can fully grasp the true nature of the crisis afflicting the Church.

Unpublished • July, 2024

---

44 Fr John O'Malley, Fr Joseph Komonchak, et al., *Vatican II: Did Anything Happen?*, Continuum, New York, 2007, p.3

45 Ralph M. McInerny, *What Went Wrong with Vatican II: The Catholic Crisis Explained*, Sophia Institute Press, Manchester, New Hampshire, 1998, pp. 7–8

46 Gregory XVI, *Mirari Vos*, 10, Quoted in Papal Encyclicals, https://www.papalencyclicals.net/greg16/g16mirar.htm

47 Leo XIII, *Satis Cognitum*, 3, Vatican website, https://www.vatican.va/content/leo-xiii/en/encyclicals/documents/hf_l-xiii_enc_29061896_satis-cognitum.html

ESTABLISHMENT CHURCHMEN RUSH TO DEFEND
VATICAN II AFTER ARCHBISHOP VIGANÒ'S CRITICISMS

The *Empire Strikes Back* (1980) is generally regarded as one of the better, if not the best, *Star Wars* films. If you haven't seen it, Darth Vader and Emperor Palpatine (the "bad guys") throw down the hammer against the "rebel alliance," a ragtag group of freedom fighters trying to bring peace to the galaxy, against all odds.

The various responses made by establishment Catholics in recent days to the blunt though undoubtedly true remarks about Vatican II made by Archbishop Carlo Maria Viganò, the former Apostolic Nuncio to the United States, mirror what played out in that movie.

Up until now, Archbishop Viganò has largely been ignored by the power players who run what Archbishop Marcel Lefebvre once called the "Conciliar Church." Catholic writers and media outlets have largely been content to dismiss him as a "conspiracy theorist" who touts absurd claims about rampant homosexuality in the Vatican.

In recent days, however, His Excellency has received more attention than usual, undoubtedly because President Trump thanked him on Twitter for the letter he wrote to him about the need to fight the Deep State. He's also earning their ire because of his increasingly stringent, nerve-striking assaults on the Second Vatican Council.[48]

Predictably, conciliar authorities have leapt into action in order to prevent Catholics from thinking the Council was, as Viganò suggests it is, discontinuous with the past.

Neoconservatives Attack

Among the dutiful soldiers following the Deep Church's marching orders is Americanist commentator George Weigel and Bishop Robert Barron of the Archdiocese of Los Angeles.

In a recent article for *First Things*, Weigel argues that both "ultra-traditionalist" and "progressive" Catholics are wrong about their view of the Council.

"To claim that Vatican II was a Council of rupture and reinvention is to say, in effect, that [John XXIII, Paul VI, and John Paul II] were either duplicitous, anti-conciliar reactionaries … or material heretics." "Neither indictment has

---

48 Matt Gaspers, "Abp Viganò to Sandro Magister: 'I Do Not Find Anything Reprehensible in Suggesting We Should Forget Vatican II," Catholic Family News, July 6, 2020, https://catholicfamilynews.com/blog/2020/07/06/abp-vigano-to-sandro-magister-i-do-not-find-anything-reprehensible-in-suggesting-we-should-forget-vatican-ii/

any merit, although the latter has recently gotten undeserved attention, thanks to … the ultra-traditionalist blogosphere."[49]

Presumably, he's speaking about Archbishop Viganò.

Interestingly enough, Bishop Barron has taken up almost the exact same line of argumentation. In a recent YouTube video, Barron marshals non sequitur after non sequitur in an embarrassing attempt to paint himself (and the liberals who guided the Council) as being on "firm middle ground" between those who have fallen too far to the right and too far to the left.[50]

"Others believe that the Church should turn backward and inward on itself," he tweeted, without naming names. "But Vatican II avoids both extremes by emphasizing both doctrinal stability and a robust missionary zeal."[51]

Say what? Was the Church before the 1960s doctrinally "unstable" and lazy? Did the Church of our grandparents not want a "Christ-centric" world? It's patently absurd to insinuate such things. Missionary activity as well as Catholic Action was alive and well across the world during the first half of the 20th century. Multiple pre-conciliar popes repeatedly urged laity to convert non-Catholics to Christ. St Pius X spoke about this in *Il Fermo Proposito* and *Fin Dalla Prima Nostra*. Pope Pius XI affirmed his teachings in *Non Abbiamo Bisogno*.

Ultimately, the post-war world order greatly feared the Catholic Church as it existed before the Council. "It would be very wrong to imagine that [the pre-conciliar church] was something broken and in need of repair," the late University of Notre Dame Professor Ralph McInerny once remarked.[52]

Empty Catch Phrases Won't Cut It Anymore

Catholics today, especially those under 35 years of age, aren't buying what Barron and Weigel are selling. The Vatican II Church is a dying Church. Not only has it been hemorrhaging vocations for decades, the so-called "New Evangelization" (how long are we going to hear that term for anyway?

---

49 George Weigel, "The Next Pope and Vatican II," First Things, July 15, 2020, https://www.firstthings.com/web-exclusives/2020/07/the-next-pope-and-vatican-ii

50 Bishop Robert Barron, "How Have Catholic Extremists Missed the Point of Vatican II?—Bishop Barron on Vatican II," YouTube, https://www.youtube.com/watch?v=swv5HoikE3g

51 Bishop Robert Barron, "Others believe that the Church should turn backward and inward on itself," Twitter, July 15, 2020, https://twitter.com/BishopBarron/status/1283424963970699266

52 Ralph M. McInerny, *What Went Wrong with Vatican II: The Catholic Crisis Explained*, Sophia Institute Press, Manchester, New Hampshire, 1998, pp. 7–8

NAVIGATING THE CRISIS IN THE CHURCH

Another three decades?) has been an unmitigated disaster.[53] A tree is known by its fruits!

Fr Joseph Clifford Fenton (1906–1969), an American priest who attended the Council, wrote in his diary in 1962 that, "from surface appearance it would seem that the Lord Christ is abandoning His Church … as far as I can see the Church is going to be very badly hurt by this council."[54] He was undoubtedly right.

Anyone who studies Vatican II from an objective point of view will realize that no matter what this bishop or that pope says about it (even if they are considered a "saint"), the Council represents a profound break with what came before.

The Council's original preparatory schemas, which drew from thousands of insights provided to the Vatican by bishops and learned clergy, took several years to compile. All were written in crystal clear, unambiguous, and wholly Catholic language. One of them discussed in great detail the subject of Mary being the "Mother of the Church." Another condemned Communism.[55]

Yet all were thrown out (or watered down and incorporated into the Council elsewhere) within days of the Council's opening. Why did that happen? Not because the Holy Ghost wanted them to be. Rather, because they weren't ecumenical enough for the liberal Council Fathers, who used parliamentary maneuvers and complaints to John XXIII to get rid of them and start from scratch.

The schema that were supposed to be used by the Council were disdained by progressive clergy because, among other things, they affirmed Scholastic, anti-modernist theology. "When we began our work, we found ourselves confronted with schemata that were very juridical in content and in tone," Cardinal Leo Joseph Suenens of Belgium complained at the time.[56] Suenens later described Vatican II as the "1789 of the Church."

"Much of what was in the schemata proposed for the considerations of the Fathers of the Council was juridical and academic in tone," Cardinal

53 Steve Skojec, "New Survey Shows Disparity of Beliefs Between Latin Mass, Novus Ordo Catholics," One Peter Five, February 25, 2019, https://onepeterfive.com/new-survey-shows-disparity-of-beliefs-between-latin-mass-novus-ordo-catholics/
54 "The Vatican II Diaries of Msgr. Joseph Clifford Fenton," Novus Ordo Watch, July 7, 2017, https://novusordowatch.org/2017/07/vatican2-diaries-fenton/
55 Matthew Cullinan Hoffman, "Vatican II's lost condemnations of communism revealed to public for first time," LifeSiteNews, October 25, 2017, https://www.lifesitenews.com/news/vatican-iis-lost-condemnations-of-communism-revealed-to-public-for-first-ti/
56 Rev. Walter M. Abbott, Twelve Council Fathers, The Macmillan Company, First Edition, New York, New York, January 1, 1963, p. 3

Paul-Émile Léger of Canada likewise remarked. "We could see that the schemata were not pastoral enough."[57]

What His Eminence meant to say was that they weren't sufficiently liberal enough.

The new texts conjured up by the neo-modernist theologians who attended the Council (some of whom had been censured by Rome just years before)[58] included hidden "time bombs" so that in the years following the Council they could be used by liberal-minded clergy to implement novel practices. The documents were simply never meant to be interpreted in a "traditional" manner.

I once read that where is no hatred of heresy, there is no holiness. Well, did the documents produced by Vatican II express hatred of heresy? Did they clearly and unambiguously uphold Church doctrine? Not at all. In fact, not only did the Council not issue one anathema, Paul VI declared in his closing speech in 1965 that it "insisted very much more upon this pleasant side of man, rather than on his unpleasant one."[59]

During a recent interview with journalist Phillip Lawler, Archbishop Viganò said that at Vatican II the "perfectly orthodox preparatory schemas" were replaced with "a bundle of cleverly disguised errors behind long-winded and deliberately equivocal speeches." Vatican II was thus "a subversive and revolutionary act" marked by "the infiltration of the enemy into the heart of the Church."[60] He's absolutely right.

Vatican II Founded a New Religion

Again, what the Council produced was not remotely in continuity with the past. What Catholics were given in the years after was a new Mass, a new liturgical calendar, new rules on fasting, new rules on marriages, a new catechism, a new Code of Canon Law, a new translation of the Bible, a new understanding of who actually comprises "the Church of Christ," and new teachings on Jews, Protestants, and non-Catholics.

There isn't the faintest desire to carry on the Catholic religion as it existed before. Even Bishop Barron has admitted that John Paul II had "zero interest

---

57 Ibid, pp. 16–17

58 Michael Swan, "The bishops and the 'periti': Key church leaders at Vatican II," *Angelus News*, October 11, 2012, https://angelusnews.com/news/us-world/the-bishops-and-the-periti-key-church-leaders-at-vatican-ii/

59 Paul VI, Closing Address of Vatican II, December 7, 1965, https://www.vatican.va/content/paul-vi/en/speeches/1965/documents/hf_p-vi_spe_19651207_epilogo-concilio.html

60 Archbishop Carlo Maria Viganò, "Interview with Phil Lawler," *Catholic Culture*, June 2020, https://www.catholicculture.org/culture/library/view.cfm?recnum=12379

in reviving pre-conciliar conservatism."[61] Trying to apply a "hermeneutic of continuity" to such a situation is simply not possible.

Today's 'Conservatives' Are Actually Liberals

Weigel, Barron, and others like to paint themselves as the moderate middle between the "the progressive left" and "the ultra-traditionalist right." This is a totally bogus comparison.

One way to think about what happened at the Council is to imagine the Church as if it were a train. Since the "Enlightenment" and the French Revolution, the Church was barreling full steam ahead, condemning liberalism and modernism in the 19th and 20th centuries while calling on men to repent of their errors and come back to Christ during and after the Second World War.

Vatican II changed all that. The railroad switch was pulled in the opposite direction and the train veered to the left, deviating onto a new set of poorly constructed tracks. What used to be "liberal" before the Council became "conservative" and what used to be "conservative" became "traditional."

What Weigel and Barron fail to mention amid all their flowery language about "continuity" is the simple fact that the Council was a total victory for the neo-modernist, liberal faction. As Cardinal Joseph Ratzinger remarked in 1984, "The problem of the Council was to acquire the best expressed values of two centuries of 'liberal' culture...and purify them."

Church historian Professor Roberto de Mattei has likewise pointed out that, "Liberal Catholics were defeated by the First Vatican Council but after a century, they became the protagonists and winners of Vatican II."[62]

The Need to Embrace Tradition

By the grace of God, Archbishop Viganò has been blessed to realize that returning to the Council is not the answer. He's even waking up some mainstream Catholics to the fact that embracing tradition, *tout court*, is the only way forward.

"The Council was in fact a dishonest operation, a scam carried out against the faithful and the clergy," His Excellency recently said. "I do not find anything

---

61 Timothy Flanders, "Bishop Barron and the 'Unhappy' Renewal of the 'Trad' Movement," One Peter Five, October 24, 2019, https://onepeterfive.com/bishop-barron-unhappy-trad/

62 Roberto de Mattei, "Tu es Petrus: True Devotion to the Chair of Saint Peter," Transcript of speech delivered at the "Weapons of Our Warfare" conference hosted by Catholic Family News, Deerfield, Illinois, April 7, 2018, https://catholicfamilynews.com/blog/2018/04/10/tu-es-petrus-true-devotion-to-the-chair-of-saint-peter/

reprehensible in suggesting that we should forget Vatican II."[63]

Only when the Vicar of Christ thinks like Archbishop Viganò does and confirms his brethren in the traditional teachings of the faith will the six-decades-long crisis afflicting the Mystical Body of Christ come to an end. Until that happens, the mainstream Church will continue to lumber on, stumbling and staggering along the way while men like George Weigel and Bishop Barron try to convince souls that an event as radical and revolutionary as Vatican II was actually an instance of the Holy Ghost leading them into a New Pentecost. May God in His infinite mercy spare us from such blind guides.

Catholic Family News • July 23, 2020

CARDINAL MANNING REFUTES VATICAN II'S TEACHINGS ON ECUMENISM

It is difficult to see how there is continuity with the Church's teaching on "Christian unity" and non-Catholic religions before Vatican II and after Vatican II.

Unitatis Redintegratio, the Second Vatican Council's document on ecumenism, claims that non-Catholic "ecclesial communities" can "enrich" the "Church of Jesus Christ." Baptized members of these communities, it further alleges, are "in communion with the Catholic Church even though this communion is imperfect."

The Council's document *Lumen Gentium* re-iterates this novel outlook. Christ's Church "subsists in the Catholic Church," it states. "Many elements of sanctification and truth can be found outside her structure." These "elements" are "gifts belonging to the Church of Christ" and "impel towards catholic unity."[64]

Taken collectively, the Council teaches that Catholics should not act "polemically" towards non-Catholic cults, but "must gladly acknowledge and esteem the truly Christian endowments from our common heritage which are to be found among our separated brethren." Catholics must thus work for visible unity with "all Christians" so the "Church of Christ" can be restored.[65]

---

63 Quoted in Matt Gaspers, "Abp Viganò to Sandro Magister: 'I Do Not Find Anything Reprehensible in Suggesting We Should Forget Vatican II,'" Catholic Family News, July 6, 2020, https://catholicfamilynews.com/blog/2020/07/06/abp-vigano-to-sandro-magister-i-do-not-find-anything-reprehensible-in-suggesting-we-should-forget-vatican-ii/

64 *Lumen Gentium*, 8

65 *Unitatis Redintegratio*, 4, 9

Henry Cardinal Manning, who served as the Archbishop of Westminster from 1865 until his death in 1892, would have looked upon these words with abject horror, as they represent a clear break with traditional ecclesiology. In accordance with Church practice and teaching before the 1960s, Manning understood that those who are separated from the Catholic Church's sacraments, doctrines, and hierarchy cannot, objectively speaking, be said to belong to the "Church of Christ," which he would have understood simply to be "the Catholic Church."

Knowing that "Christian unity" can only brought about by non-Catholics embracing the Catholic faith, Manning once wrote, "I believe there is no surer instrument of their return to the unity of grace and truth than the manifestation of the love of Jesus in the Holy Eucharist."[66]

The following excerpt is taken from one of Manning's sermons titled *The Blessed Sacrament: The Center of Immutable Truth*, which was published in booklet form by Neumann Press in 1992. It refutes in every way Vatican II's claims on non-Catholic "ecclesial communities" as means of salvation and as tools for "Christian unity."

Separation from the visible Body of Christ is separation from the presence and assistance of the Holy Ghost Who inhabits it. There is no influx of His divine and infallible light into the intelligence of a body which breaks from the unity of the Church. There is no divine voice speaking through it as His organ of immutable truth. Straightaway all began to dissolve and go to pieces… For three hundred years it has been returning to dust. In the day when the Blessed Sacrament was carried out of the churches of England, the whole population was contained within the unity of the one Body. Now, hardly one-half remains to the Church which taught the fatal lesion of separation. From generation to generation, by a succession of crumbling secessions, divisions, and subdivisions, the flock it could not retain when the Blessed Sacrament is no longer upon the altar…

If dogma be the intellectual conception of divine realities, what dogma is to be found where the divine realities of the Sacramental Body and mystical Body of Jesus, His Presence, His Sacrifice, His Seven Sacraments, His infallible and perpetual Voice, are denied?[67]

Magnificat Media • July 4, 2016

66 Cardinal Henry Edward Manning, *The Blessed Sacrament,* The Neumann Press, Long Prairie, Minnesota, 1992, p. 31
67 Ibid, p.30

FULTON SHEEN AGAINST THE COUNCIL

Earlier this week, the relatives of Bishop Fulton Sheen asked for his remains to be moved from St Patrick's Cathedral in New York to Peoria, Illinois, the diocese in which he was ordained. The Archdiocese of New York, according to reports, is expected to comply with the request. This matters because once Sheen's body arrives in Illinois, his cause for canonization is expected to proceed.

To be honest, Bishop Sheen has always struck me as a puzzling figure. I know some Catholics who attribute their entire conversion to him. Good for them. For me, he played next to no role in my return from the road to perdition.

Admittedly, I have read, and do own, several of his books. I have watched his videos on YouTube as well. Beyond a doubt he was a gifted and holy priest. But what happened to him after Vatican II? In the 1930s and 40s, he was a lion of doctrine. In the 50s, he had a hit television program. But in the late 60s and 1970s? Most Catholics probably couldn't tell you.

My guess is that like many other princes of the Church, he was punched in the nose by the progressive movement at Vatican II and afterwards wasn't sure if he should stick to what he always taught or simply go with the flow.

I have always wondered if any of his biggest apologists today have ever read his earlier writings. Indeed, much of what Sheen wrote—at least before 1962—is anti-modernist, anti-ecumenical and directly opposed to what was promulgated at the Council. Here are just a few of his best insights before Vatican II:

* "If I were not a Catholic, and were looking for the true Church in the world today, I would look for the one Church which did not get along well with the world; in other words, I would look for the Church which the world hates. My reason for doing this would be, that if Christ is in any one of the churches of the world today, He must still be hated as He was when He was on earth in the flesh. If you want to find Christ today, then find the Church that does not get along with the world. Look for the Church that is hated by the world as Christ was hated by the world. Look for the Church which is accused of being behind the times, as Our Lord was accused of being ignorant and never having learned."[68]

---

68 Fr Leslie Rumble and Fr Charles Carty, *Radio Replies, First Volume*, TAN Books and Publishers, Rockford, Illinois, 1938, Reprinted 1979, p.ix

- "Modern religion has enunciated one great and fundamental dogma that is at the basis of all other dogmas, and that is, that religion must be freed from dogmas. Creeds and confessions of faith are no longer the fashion; religious leaders have agreed not to disagree over those beliefs for which some of our ancestors would have died. They have melted into a spineless Humanism. Like other Pilates they have turned their backs on the uniqueness of truth and have opened their arms wide to all the moods and fancies the hour might dictate. The passing of creeds and dogmas means the passing of controversies."[69]

- "That Church or that Mystical Person which has been living all these centuries is the basis of our faith and to us Catholics it speaks this way.... 'It is true I have not changed my doctrine, but that is because the 'doctrine is not mine but His who sent me.' I know I shall live to chant a requiem over the modern ideas of this day, as I chanted it over the modern ideas of the last century.'"[70]

These comments would likely qualify Sheen as a "neo-Pelagian" Radical Traditionalist were he around today![71]

I'll leave you with this quote from one of his 1955 television programs titled *How to Think*: "It's always a good thing to remember that if you marry the mood or the spirit of an age you will be a widow in the next one."

If only the Council Fathers, and Sheen himself, had taken his advice, the Church would be much better off today.

Magnificat Media • June 18, 2016

THE 'PROPHETS OF DOOM' WERE RIGHT ALL ALONG

Rod Dreher's long-awaited book *The Benedict Option* has been released. A common theme among reviewers is that Dreher is overly dramatic in his critique of contemporary culture, that he is too dark, too pessimistic.

One of Dreher's defenders is Philadelphia Archbishop Charles Chaput.

69 Fr Leslie Rumble and Fr Charles Carty, *Radio Replies, Third Volume*, TAN Books and Publishers, Rockford, Illinois, 1942, Reprinted 1979, p.vii
70 Fr Leslie Rumble and Fr Charles Carty, *Radio Replies, First Volume*, TAN Books and Publishers, Rockford, Illinois, 1938, Reprinted 1979, pp. x-xi
71 Diane Montagna, "Is new Vatican doc on neo-Pelagianism at odds with pope's preferred pejorative?" LifeSiteNews, March 1, 2018, https://www.lifesitenews.com/news/vatican-doctrinal-office-issues-letter-on-modern-obstacles-to-salvation/

Writing for *First Things*, Chaput pushed back against critics of Dreher's book, Calvin College professor James Smith in particular, who had said *The Benedict Option* is "tinged with a bitterness and resentment and sense of loss that carries the whiff of privilege."[72]

Chaput argues that Smith's column, aptly titled, "The new alarmism: How some Christians are stoking fear rather than hope," reflects a "contempt for discomforting ideas rather than real criticism of the actual content" of Dreher's book. Chaput continues:

> The Word of God has a generous collection of alarmisms: 'I have set before you life and death, the blessing and the curse'; 'repent and believe in the Gospel'; you 'brood of vipers'; you 'whitened sepulchres'; the parable of the sheep and goats, among many others … Jesus had the awkward habit of talking about hell—far more often, in fact, than St Paul ever did…
>
> Irenaeus was an alarmist. Augustine was an alarmist. Basil was an alarmist. John Calvin and the Reformers, both Protestant and Catholic, were alarmists…

Chaput goes on:

> Pessimism is the selfish refusal to hope; a surrender to the world as it is; a repudiation of trust in the goodness of God, his love for us, and his desire for our joy, no matter how challenging our circumstances. This pessimism is precisely what the books by Dreher, Esolen, and others (including, I hope, my own) seek to work against. Naming the problems in a culture truthfully, and pointing a way forward for those awake enough to notice, is neither bleak nor negative. It's called Christian realism, and it's a virus that's going around.
>
> If that's also a 'new alarmism,' then we need more of it, not less.[73]

The archbishop is no doubt correct. To identify the problems in modern society and to prescribe the proper course of action in response to them is neither bleak, pessimistic, or "negative." Indeed, it is what the Church has

---

72 James Smith, "The new alarmism: How some Christians are stoking fear rather than hope," The Washington Post, March 10, 2017, https://www.washingtonpost.com/news/acts-of-faith/wp/2017/03/10/the-new-alarmism-how-some-christians-are-stoking-fear-rather-than-hope/

73 Archbishop Charles Chaput, "In Praise of the 'New Alarmism," First Things, March 17, 2017, https://www.firstthings.com/web-exclusives/2017/03/in-praise-of-the-new-alarmism

done throughout the ages by issuing anathemas and condemning errors.

That being said, one can't help but notice that when the princes of the Church gathered together at Vatican II in the 1960s, that time-tested method of defending the faith was abandoned in favor of a new "pastoral" approach.

During his closing speech at the Council, Paul VI declared that Vatican II "insisted very much more upon this pleasant side of man, rather than on his unpleasant one. Its attitude was very much and deliberately optimistic."

Similarly, in his opening address in 1962, John XXIII chastised those whom he called the "prophets of doom." These men, he argued, were "always forecasting worse disasters, as though the end of the world were at hand."

Intellectual honesty demands that Archbishop Chaput admit that just like how he thinks Dreher is not overreacting to what he is seeing, those wrongly-maligned "prophets of doom" at the Second Vatican Council were also not overreacting to what they were seeing. Rather, they were reading the signs of the times and predicting what would happen if the Church did not act swiftly and forcefully in response.

Chaput should also acknowledge that French Archbishop Marcel Lefebvre, Brazilian Bishop Antonio de Castro Mayer, and the other members of the *Coetus Internationalis Patrum*—the best organized group of "conservative" clergy at Vatican II—were neither bitter nor paranoid. Instead, they were, to borrow Chaput's own terms, "Christian realists."

In layman's terms, the conservatives at Vatican II who were fighting to defend Catholic Tradition were the original "alarmists" who quite rightly recognized the evils of the 20th century for what they were by urging the Council to condemn communism, affirm Thomistic theology, re-iterate the Social Kingship of Christ, and defend the Church's teachings on the Blessed Virgin Mary.

Sadly, they were not victorious in their efforts.

While Chaput's defense of "the new alarmism" is no doubt welcome news, if His Excellency wants to be consistent, he should admit two things. First, that Professor Smith's belittling of the "new alarmists" is the same sort of uncharitable smearing John XXIII and his successors carried out against the conservatives at the Council. Second, he should confess that Smith's naive dismissal of Dreher's concerns is the same tactic mainstream churchmen—himself included—have used against Traditionalists since the 1960s. God knows if the Council Fathers had listened to them instead of the neo-modernists who hijacked that event the Church wouldn't be in the mess it is today.

Magnificat Media • March 21, 2017

A POPE WHO PROMOTES INDIFFERENTISM?

In a surprising moment of candor and courage, Fr Dwight Longenecker has called out the Church's teaching on ecumenism. Although he claims he is arguing against "indifferentism," he is really exposing the rotten fruit the Church's approach toward "Christian unity" has had since being changed at Vatican II. Interestingly enough, Longenecker's spot-on commentary came just one day before Pope Francis said Christians and atheists can meet on "common ground" by doing good together.

The following is an excerpt from Father's column, which is available at *Patheos.com*. It is worth quoting at length. Keep in mind that he is writing to parents whose children were raised Catholic but are now leaving the Church:

> One of the reasons why Catholic kids leave the church is that our catechism and worship styles and preaching for the past fifty years did not prepare them for the rigors and demands of a fully Catholic life.
>
> There is another huge contributing factor to the hemorrhage from the Catholic Church. It is indifferentism, and the indifferentism has three aspects.
>
> First is the aspect that it doesn't really matter what church you go to. You wouldn't believe the number of potential convert clergy who are told by a Catholic priest to stay where they are in the Protestant denomination and "work for church unity."
>
> The unique claims to Catholic truth have been watered down or denied completely.
>
> Faithful parents will protest, 'But we never taught our kids that! We sent them to Catholic school.' You don't get it. They were taught indifferentism in their Catholic school. They picked it up at that CCD class you thought was okay. They were fed it at that Catholic high school you thought was just fine. The bishop thought that was the way forward. They heard it at their confirmation class. The priests learned it at seminary from modernist professors. To say that other Christians were in error was 'judgmental' and 'unloving,' 'narrow minded,' 'rigid,' etc.
>
> Indifferentism also applies in a second way: we became indifferent to the importance of doctrine.
>
> We were taught to be indifferent about doctrine ... that doctrine doesn't matter ... All Christians were coming together, and this wonderful unity would be accelerated as we left all those dull, old arguments about doctrine behind us.

The third aspect of indifferentism is simply being indifferent. Careless. Complacent. Worldly. Lacking in passion ... It waters down the wine.

[Parents] asked their kids why they didn't believe the Catholic faith and the answer was stark and simple: 'If it really is the body and blood of Christ and he is really present—why don't Catholics—priests included (or should I say priests especially) behave as if it is so? They have shopped elsewhere and found other Christians who seem to love Jesus Christ more and wish to serve him with their whole lives.'[74]

This brutally honest appraisal of where the Church has gone wrong was met with unexpected support in the comment section. I say unexpected because this is what traditionalists have been preaching since the end of the Second Vatican Council. Yet, when they condemn indifferentism they are labeled heretical.

Converting Non-Catholics is 'Not Allowed'

Longenecker's arguments should remind us of Pope Pius XI's 1928 encyclical *Mortalium Animos*. In that document, he teaches that "there is but one way in which the unity of Christians may be fostered, and that is by furthering the return to the one true Church of Christ of those who are separated from it."

Unfortunately, the words of Fr Longenecker—as well as those of Pius XI—are ignored by the Church's hierarchy. A September 18, 2009 press release issued by the United States Conference of Catholic Bishops (USCCB) warned Catholics that "proselytism, or the deliberate targeting of another Christian or group of Christians for the sole purpose of getting them to reject their church to join another, is not allowed."[75]

I don't know how the USCCB's guidelines on ecumenism comport with Jesus' instruction to "Go make disciples of all nations,"[76] but indifference to converting non-Catholics, especially the Jews, is something Pope Francis himself agrees with.

In his 2010 book *On Heaven and Earth*, then-Cardinal Jorge Bergoglio told Rabbi Abraham Skorka, the co-author of the book, that "when I speak with

74 Fr Dwight Longenecker, "Help My Kids Still Aren't Catholic!" Patheos, May 22, 2013, https://www.patheos.com/blogs/standingonmyhead/2013/05/help-my-kids-still-arent-catholic.html
75 "Christian Unity A Goal, But Won't Happen Overnight, Says USCCB Official In Ecumenism, Interreligious Affairs," United States Conference of Catholic Bishops, September 18, 2009, http://web.archive.org/web/20100109094244/https://www.usccb.org/comm/archives/2009/09-182.shtml
76 Matthew 28:19

atheists, I will sometimes discuss social concerns, but I do not propose the problem of God as a starting point, except in the case that they propose it to me." He added that, "I do not approach the relationship in order to proselytize, or convert the atheist." I "do not have any type of reluctance, nor would I say that his life is condemned."[77]

After Skorka agrees with him and shares a snide remark about Pope Pius XII, Bergoglio comments that "evangelization is essential, but not proselytism; that [word] today—thanks be to God—is crossed out of the pastoral dictionary."[78] He then references French Lutheran theologian Oscar Cullman (1902–1999), an observer at Vatican II, to substantiate his views:

Cullman ... says we should not seek that everyone, from the outset, affirm the same thing, but instead he proposes that we walk together in a reconciled diversity; he resolves the religious conflict of the many Christian denominations by walking together, by doing things together, by praying together. He asks that we not throw rocks at each other, but rather that we continue walking together.[79]

This is astonishing. Bergolgio is citing a heretic to justify his belief that instead of seeking to bring others to the one true faith established by Jesus Christ, Catholics should put aside their differences with non-Catholics and instead erect a global confederation with false religions. This is pure Freemasonry and totally against the Gospel!

As Fr Longenecker so lucidly pointed out in his blog post, indifferentism has lead to the loss of faith for many Catholics in the United States over the past 50 years. Until it is rebuked by the Vatican, it will continue to lead souls astray. It is frightening to know that the leaders in the Church at the highest level cannot see this after all these years.

Unpublished • May 25, 2013

VATICAN II, PROPERLY UNDERSTOOD

There is a quote that is often attributed to Winston Churchill, the Prime Minister of the United Kingdom during World War II, that I often reference.

77 Jorge Mario Bergoglio and Abraham Skorka, *On Heaven and Earth: Pope Francis on Faith, Family, and the Church in the Twenty-First Century,* Image Books, New York, 2015, Originally published in Spanish in 2010, p.12
78 Ibid, p.234
79 Ibid, p.217

NAVIGATING THE CRISIS IN THE CHURCH

I don't know if he said it for certain but the comment, much like he was, is short and to the point: "History is written by the victors." I like that. I don't see how you can't. After all, it's factually true. Fr Brian Harrison, an Australian Catholic priest who I have written about before on, explained back in 2002 the meaning of that remark:

> The idea is that after a war has been fought, those, who, by emerging as the winners, succeed in controlling the present, can, in a certain sense, control the past as well. They can ensure that the dominant communications media will present the history of the recent conflict from their own viewpoint, depicting themselves, naturally, as the heroes, and the vanquished opposition as the villains. Indeed, it often turns out to be deliciously easy for the all-powerful victors to rewrite that history in such a way as to make it appear that their triumph was not only just and right, but also inevitable: they can depict themselves as simply having moved along on the crest of those great ocean waves of destiny which are supposed to be constantly sweeping human history forward in its inexorable progress toward ever higher levels of maturity, freedom, prosperity, and scientific enlightenment. Such rewriting of history, in short, can often be a powerful weapon in that 'culture war' against rationalist secularism in which Catholics have increasingly found themselves immersed over the last century.[80]

If this is accurate, and undoubtedly it is, the following question needs to be asked: What are Catholics today taught about Church history? How, in other words, do the majority of Catholics understand their own religion for the past 2,000 years? The answer, at least it seems to me, goes something like this:

> Following the Protestant Reformation, the Catholic Church turned inward on itself. Issuing anathemas and condemnations, the Vatican embraced legalism and rigidity. The Church grew ever more intransigent after the French Revolution, lashing out at the modern world at every turn. This was most evident in Pius IX's *Syllabus of Errors*, a narrow-minded, terse document that failed to take into account the nuances of the modern world. What the *Syllabus* really amounted to is nothing more than a crotchety old man's bitter anguish over losing the papal states. This pessimistic attitude began to shift ever so slightly

80 Fr Brian Harrison, *Culture Wars Magazine*, January 1999, Taken from "On Rewriting the Bible," Christian Order, March 2002, https://www.christianorder.com/features/feature_2002-03.html

with Pope Leo XIII. It eventually culminated in the optimistic papacy of the humble John XXIII. Good Pope John's simplicity and openness to the world helped unleashed the Holy Spirit. The Church in the 1960s re-discovered the wisdom of the Early Church, especially Her ancient liturgical practices. 1,600 years of misapplied teachings on Church-State relations had also finally been thrown out. The Church likewise freed itself from the chains of the pre-Vatican II mindset by updating its theological outlook and its approach towards non-Catholics by adopting a much needed pastoral attitude that could address contemporary problems and speak to men of today. Catholics simply need to focus on what unites them with fellow Christians as well as their elder brothers in the faith, the Jews, instead of clinging to what divides them. We are all children of God, as John Paul II and Pope Benedict have shown us.

For years I believed this narrative. Many "conservative" Catholics still buy into it without even knowing it is in actuality an ideologically-driven whitewashing of historical events by the "victors" of the Second Vatican Council: Modernists, Liberals, Freemasons, and others.

Before putting forward a more accurate version of history—the "Traditional Catholic" understanding of history—I'd like to rely on a number of Catholics who have gone before me to get a fuller picture of how we should understand the past.

History is Ordered to Jesus Christ

French Archbishop Marcel Lefebvre (1905–1991), the founder of the Society of St Pius X, shared the following in his book *Spiritual Journey:* "We will never fully understand the struggle between the good and the wicked throughout history, as long as we do not see it as the personal and unyielding battle for all time between Satan and Jesus Christ."[81]

His Excellency also said in *They Have Uncrowned Him* that "history is all ordered to a person, who is the center of history, and who is our Lord Jesus Christ."[82]

Fr Denis Fahey, an Irish priest who died in 1954, wrote something similar in his book *The Kingship of Christ:*

81 Archbishop Marcel Lefebvre, *Spiritual Journey,* Angelus Press, Kansas City, Missouri, 2011, p.40
82 Archbishop Marcel Lefebvre, *They Have Uncrowned Him,* Angelus Press, Kansas City, Missouri, 2003, p.139

The real history of the world is the acceptance or rejection by the world of God's plan for the restoration of Divine Life. History is concerned with individual and contingent facts. In order to discern the supreme causes and laws of the event which historians narrate, we must stand out from, and place ourselves above these event. To do this with certainty one should, of course, be enlightened by Him who holds all things in the hollow of His hand. Unaided human reason cannot even attempt to give an account of the supreme interest at stake in the world, for in the world, as it is historically, these interests are supernatural.

Human reason strengthened by faith, that is, by the acceptance of the information God has given us about the world through His Son and through the Society founded by Him, can attempt to give this account.[83]

Fr Juan Carlos Iscara of the Society of St Pius x likewise remarked:

There is a Christian view of History that has nothing to do with the historical rot we are routinely taught. It is a 'theology of history'. … an interpretation of time in terms of eternity, and of human events in the light of divine Revelation.

The Church 'reads' the succession of events in the light of Faith, and discerns in that bewildering multiplicity the pattern of the providential design of God, ineluctably moving towards the end intended by the Creator from all eternity: our beatitude.[84]

But how, one might wonder, can a Catholic truly discern the "multiplicity of the pattern of the providential design of God"? Is this even possible?

Carol Robinson, a prolific American writer for *Integrity* magazine in the 1940s and 50s, provides an answer:

We must first of all see the meaning of history. Time unrolls. It begins with the creation of the world out of nothing. Then there is the beginning of man, the fall, the selection of the Jews as the chosen race, and their history in preparation for the coming of Christ. The Incarnation

83 Rev. Denis Fahey, *The Kingship of Christ: According to the Principles of St Thomas Aquinas*, Christian Book Club of America, Palmdale, California, First published 1931, Reprinted 2004

84 Fr Juan Carlos Iscara, "Preface For A Catholic Understanding Of History," *The Angelus: Christendom and Revolution*, September 2003, http://www.angelusonline.org/index.php?section=articles&subsection=show_article&article_id=2225

and the Redemption are the center of history, not the middle-point in years, but the focal point in meaning. After them comes the application of the fruits of the Redemption to successive generations and to all nations until the number of the elect is filled. Then time comes to an end.[85]

But the vast majority of countries today reject that the Incarnation has any role to play in social life. Francis Conklin, in his introduction to a 1992 Neumann Press book titled *The Blessed Sacrament: The Center of Immutable Truth* by Henry Cardinal Manning (1808–1892), recognized that sad reality. He said the following:

> The Western world, the world formerly denominated Christian, has forsworn Christianity in the Person of the Incarnate Word, and has attempted to implement a culture without a spiritual or moral Foundation. The informing Principle of Christianity was, and will ever be, the abiding Reality of our Lord wholly and substantially present in the Blessed Sacrament.
>
> In the sixteenth century, Protestantism arose and attempted to reconstruct Christianity without the Papacy and the Holy Sacrifice of the Mass: thus religion changed instantly and internally, in all of its aspects, in its very substance and its constituent parts. In that instant of denial, change, distortion and reform, religion became a new thing, a complete departure from the Word Made Flesh, wholly divorced from the Fount of grace and His vicar upon earth.

Conklin concludes:

> The denial of the Incarnation, of the Incarnate Word, the True Presence of our Lord in the Sacrament and Sacrifice of the Mass, is the dissolution of the Word made Flesh, the dissolution of the mystical order, and the complete ruin of the order of reality; of such is the work of the Antichrist.[86]

The aforementioned Fr Fahey would agree with him. In *The Kingship of Christ and the Conversion of the Jewish Nation*, he writes that:

---

85 Carol Robinson, "My Life With Thomas Aquinas," The Angelus Press, 1992, United States, p.178

86 Cardinal Henry Edward Manning, *The Blessed Sacrament,* The Neumann Press, Long Prairie, Minnesota, 1992, p.5–8

The decay in the social acceptance of the Divine plan for ordered life, since the 13th century, has had for inevitable consequence the gradual disappearance of supernatural influences and ideals from the political and economic life of nations. This is the first result. There is a second. The elimination of the supernatural from public life is making smooth the path for the coming of the Natural Messiah.[87]

The Traditional Catholic Understanding of History

If one takes all of this into account you can tear away the myths 'conservative' Catholics have been told about the Church since Vatican II and recognize that the true understanding of Church history is as follows:

Christendom was not perfect but that is because man is not perfect. The Middle Ages was the closest mankind ever got to fulfilling the mandate Christ gave to His followers to go forth and teach all nations the Gospel. Luther's heretical ideas and his schismatic rebellion led countless souls into hell, destroying nation after nation along the way. His erroneous claims infected the hearts and minds of untold persons. Many of the "accomplishments" of "the modern world" are merely a result of man's unchecked passions—vain curiosity, intellectual pride, materialism, and the like. Like any good mother, the Church was right to protect its children by condemning and anathematizing the errors of the modern age. Liberalism, which is merely the political manifestation of Luther's faulty theology, substitutes man for the place of God in public life. As such, it plants the seeds for the coming of the anti-Christ. It deserves only rebuke. Holy Mother Church is the only institution on earth capable of defeating the prince of this world. Non-Catholics can join Catholics in their battle against evil but this can never be done in such a way as to dilute the Catholic faith, or to imply false religions are equal to Catholicism. The popes of the 19th and early 20th century were not naive or bitter. They understood the battle the children of darkness were waging against them. They were acutely aware of the need to defend the Church's perennial teachings, especially the truth that error has no rights and that Thomistic theology must be upheld in opposition to Modernism. The grave fault of the Church during the

87 Fr Denis Fahey, *The Kingship of Christ and the Conversion of the Jewish Nation*, Holy Ghost Missionary College and Regina Publications, Dublin, Printed in Ireland by John English and Co. Ltd., Wexford, January 1953, p.48, https://traditionalcatholicsemerge.com/wp-content/uploads/2019/06/Kingship-of-Christ-Fahey-Fr.-Denis-1.pdf

1960s was its false optimism of the world as well as its high appraisal of non-Catholic religions and its admiration for Western democracy. Far from unleashing a new springtime, John XXIII, along with the cowardly Council Fathers and liberal theologians, lobotomized the Catholic faith, resulting in an effeminate Church that was stripped of its virility. Not only has the Mass but everything that has been updated since the Council brought forth rotten fruit. God is now punishing it for its disobedience by giving it weak priests, heterodox bishops, and Masonic cardinals and popes. The Church is living through its passion, the one predicted by so many Marian apparitions down through the ages.

Magnificat Media • June 1, 2016

CHAPTER V: TRADITIONAL CATHOLICISM

BOMBSHELL FBI MEMO REVEALS AGENCY USED MULTIPLE OFFICES TO SPY ON TRADITIONAL CATHOLICS

FBI Director Christopher Wray has seemingly been caught lying to Congress about the extent of his agency's surveillance of Traditional Catholics in the United States, particularly the Priestly Society of St Pius X (SSPX).

House Judiciary Committee Chairman Jim Jordan (R-Ohio) released a letter addressed to Wray earlier today announcing that documents he obtained from the FBI last month indicate that its field office in Richmond, Virginia coordinated with two other offices across the country to spy on Traditional Catholics.

The finding stands in contrast to Wray's previous testimony that an FBI memo describing Traditional Catholics as potential domestic terrorists was only utilized at the one location in Richmond.

In his letter, Jordan noted that the newly obtained document reveals that "an FBI undercover employee with 'direct access' reported on a subject who 'attended the SSPX-affiliated [redacted] Church in [redacted] California, for over a year prior to his relocation.'"

It is "most concerning," Jordan exclaimed, that it "appears that both FBI Portland and FBI Los Angeles field offices were involved in or contributed to the creation of the FBI's assessment of traditional Catholics as potential domestic terrorists."

Relying on the Anti-Catholic SPLC

FBI whistleblower Kyle Seraphin first leaked the agency's memo to the public in February. Among other things, it indicated the agency was planned to intensify its "assessment" and "mitigation" of "Radical Traditionalist Catholic" (RTC) ideology over the next 12 to 24 months due to alleged concerns that Latin Mass attendees are adopting "white nationalist" attitudes.

One of the more controversial aspects of the document is that it directly cites a defamatory study conducted by the Southern Poverty Law Center (SPLC) on "Radical Traditional Catholicism" to substantiate the monitoring.

The SPLC has long been rejected as a legitimate resource for the FBI but in this instance it was relied on as a primary reference to validate its efforts.

The document also cited three anti-Catholic articles published by left-wing websites *Salon* and *The Atlantic* to defend the surveillance.

Jordan rightly urged Wray to "amend" his testimony and to more fully "explain the nature and scope of the FBI's assessment of traditional Catholics as potential domestic terrorists."

The Anti-Defamation League is Directing the Deep State

As reported by LifeSite, the FBI, which enlists the pro-Jewish Anti-Defamation League to help train its staff on "hate" groups,[1] was purportedly concerned with Traditional Catholics holding "anti-Semitic, anti-immigrant, anti-LGBT, and white supremacy" beliefs. It's memo contrasts adherents of RTC extremist "ideology" with ordinary "Traditional Catholics" who simply "prefer the Latin Mass and pre-Vatican II teachings and traditions, but without the more extremist ideological beliefs and violent rhetoric."

The memo identifies nine organizations that promote RTC ideology, including *Catholic Family News*, *The Remnant*, The Fatima Center, Tradition in Action, In the Spirit of Chartres, and Christ or Chaos. *Catholic Family News* Editor-in-Chief Brian McCall shared the following remarks with LifeSite regarding the document:

> The release by a courageous whistleblower of this internal FBI memorandum confirms the dystopian state of the country in which we sadly live.
>
> This memo, combined with the targeting and persecution of those working to protect the lives of unborn children, proves beyond any doubt the evil people who control the levers of power in the US government are using that power to persecute any who dissent from their godless ideology.
>
> The FBI is spying on and infiltrating traditional Roman Catholic groups and even parishes for simply exercising their First Amendment Rights. The absurdity of the outrageous allegations of the FBI memo are blatant.
>
> Although the author acknowledges that white supremacists are and have always been violently anti-Catholic (the KKK burn crosses

---

1 Speech of FBI Director James Comey to Anti-Defamation League National Leadership Summit, Washington DC, May 8, 2017, https://www.fbi.gov/news/speeches/the-fbi-and-the-adl-working-together-to-fight-hate. "ADL Trains Law Enforcement Commanders from Across the Country on the Latest Extremist and Terrorist Threats, " ADL, June 11, 2014, https://dc.adl.org/adl-trains-law-enforcement-commanders-from-across-the-country-on-the-latest-extremist-and-terrorist-threats/

specifically to show their hostility to Catholics),the author believes these white supremacist groups are now deeply attracted to strongly Catholic parishes and groups that they despise.

Traditional Catholicism has never had anything to do with racial bigotry or hatred. In fact the White Supremacist groups that have been active throughout US history (such as the Know Nothing Party) have targeted Catholics because Catholics have always sought the salvation and improvement in this world of the lot of those races and ethnicities despised by the white Protestant elitists.

Ironically every traditional Latin Mass parish I have ever attended is more ethnically diverse than liberal Catholic parishes that segregate attendees by linguistic, and hence ethnic, lines (i.e., Spanish Masses, Vietnamese Masses, etc.).

Traditional Catholics seek the conversion of everyone regardless of race, color, ethnicity, or any other attribute, to the Kingship of Christ. They seek to bring the love of Christ and His Church to all races and ethnicities.

The memo's prominent reliance on the utterly discredited and bigoted Southern Poverty Law Center, which is not a law center at all but merely a radical political leftist front, further discredits this memo and its author.

The Department of Justice in its continued persecution of pro-life advocates and now simple Traditional Catholics should be renamed from its Orwellian title to the more accurate Department of Injustice.

LifeSiteNews • August 9, 2023

CATHOLIC PRIEST DEFENDS CHURCH'S BAN ON FREEMASONRY

The vicar general of the Diocese of Evansville, Indiana has reminded Catholics that the Church does not allow its members to join Freemasonic Lodges.

"We cannot support organizations … that stand against the Catholic Church and have its downfall as one of their objectives," Father Alex Zenthoefer explained in *The Message*, the diocese's newspaper, earlier this month.[2]

Freemasonry has been condemned by more than seven popes throughout Church history, beginning with Clement XII in 1738. However, the revised 1983 Code of Canon Law made no explicit mention of it. The previous 1917 Code,

---

2 Fr Alex Zenthoefer, "Masons and the Catholic Church," The Message, May 4, 2023, https://evdiomessage.org/masons-and-the-catholic-church/

on the other hand, punished Catholics with automatic excommunication if they were found guilty of associating with Masonry.

In November of 1983, Cardinal Joseph Ratzinger, the Prefect of the Congregation for the Doctrine of the Faith at the time, issued a "Declaration on Masonic Associations" that sought to clarify the omission. The "negative judgment" of the Church toward Masonry "remains unchanged," he said. Any Catholic who becomes a Mason is "in a state of grave sin and may not receive Holy Communion."[3]

Zenthoefer told LifeSite via email that an increasing number of laity have been approaching him in recent months informing him they are Masons.

"At the request of some of the faithful ... I wrote this article, firstly, with the intention of helping people to become aware of the tenets of Freemasonry."

Evansville, Indiana was home to several influential members of the Ku Klux Klan in the early part of the 20th century. Freemasonry has also enjoyed a long history in the state, having first established a lodge there in the early 1800s. Presently, there are approximately 50,000 Masons in nearly 400 lodges across Indiana.

Three Reasons Catholics Cannot Be Masons

In his article, Zenthoefer recalls that there is an "explicit hostility in the Masonic tradition towards the Catholic Church." He also points to what he believes are three main problems with Freemasonry, the first being that it "diminishes the role of faith and proposes an alternative foundation for living one's life."

"During the initiation rite the candidate expresses a desire to seek 'light,' and he is assured he will receive the light of spiritual instruction that he could not receive in another Church, and that he will gain eternal rest in the 'celestial lodge' if he lives and dies according to masonic principles," he writes. "Such secularism puts the members at risk of losing sight of Jesus Christ as the Lord of life and salvation."

His second point is that Masonic rituals put Catholics at odds with their faith.

Since masonry involves non-Christians, the use of the name of Jesus is forbidden within the lodge. When one reaches the 30th degree in

---

3 Joseph Cardinal Ratzinger, "Declaration on Masonic Associations," Congregation for the Doctrine of the Faith, Vatican website, November 26, 1983, https://www.vatican.va/roman_curia/congregations/cfaith/documents/rc_con_cfaith_doc_19831126_declaration-masonic_en.html

the masonic hierarchy, called the Kadosh, the person crushes with his foot the papal tiara and the royal crown, and swears to free mankind 'from the bondage of despotism and the thraldom of spiritual tyranny.'

The last problem Zenthoefer mentions is the hatred Masonic leaders have for the Church.

There is an explicit hostility in the masonic tradition towards the Catholic Church. In the United States, one of the leaders of freemasonry, General Albert Pike (1809–1891) referred to the papacy as 'a deadly, treacherous enemy,' and wrote, 'The papacy has been for a thousand years the torturer and curse of humanity, the most shameless imposture, in its pretense to spiritual power of all ages.' Such words, along with masonic rituals, illustrate a real and irreconcilable division between Catholicism and masonry.

Has Freemasonry 'Infiltrated' the Church?

Papal denunciations of Freemasonry were a common occurrence in the Church before the Second Vatican Council. Pope Leo XIII's 1884 encyclical *Humanum Genus* is perhaps the most well-known. In it, he calls Masonry a "fatal plague" whose "ultimate purpose" is "the utter overthrow of that whole religious and political order of the world which the Christian teaching has produced."

When asked if he believes Freemasonry has infiltrated the Church, Zenthoefer, who also serves as the rector of the St Benedict Cathedral, gave a mixed answer.

I would not go so far as to say that Masonry has explicitly or intentionally infiltrated the Church. However, I do think the secular mentality employed by Masonry has shifted our focus from the person of Jesus Christ to the will and 'personal truth' of the individual. As a result, we have lost some sense of our obedience to the Church, dismissing even the possibility that authentic freedom can be found there.

Many conservative and Traditional Catholics maintain that the Church has, in fact, been infiltrated, both by Masonic thinking and by Masonic clergy.

French Archbishop Marcel Lefebvre, the founder of the Priestly Society of St Pius X, argued in the decades after Vatican II that the Council's embrace of religious freedom, ecumenism, and collegiality was the Church's acceptance of the Masonic principles of liberty, equality, and fraternity. Some also allege that Pope John Paul I was assassinated by Masonic forces in 1978 and that Annibale Bugnini, the main architect of the *Novus Ordo* Mass in the 1960s, belonged to the lodge. Still others point to the testimony of Bella Dodd, a 20th century labor activist, who admitted that communists were sent to infiltrate Catholic seminarians as evidence of ecclesial corruption. *AA-1025*, the diary of one such individual, appears to confirm her claims. So too does the 19th century document "The Permanent Instruction of the Alta Vendita," which lays out how Masons planned to install a "pope" who shares their views.[4]

Freemasons Praise Francis

In 2021, the Grand Masonic Lodge of Spain heaped praise on Pope Francis for remarks he made on the "International Day of Human Fraternity."[5] The group also thanked him for his 2020 encyclical *Fratelli Tutti*.[6] "Pope Francis' last encyclical shows how far the current Catholic Church is from its former positions," they wrote.[7]

In 2022, Francis appointed Cardinal Matteo Zuppi as president of the Italian Bishops Conference. Zuppi had received high praise from Gioele Magaldi, a former Master of the Roman Masonic Lodge, just two years prior. "I know the Vatican world and among the cardinals the one I respect most is Matteo Zuppi, who by the way married me," Magaldi said. "He would be a very good pope."[8]

In 2016, Gianfranco Cardinal Ravasi, then-president of the Vatican's Pontifical Council for Culture, wrote a letter addressed to "Brother Masons,"

4 Raymund Maria, "Is Masonic infiltration responsible for the widespread apostasy among Catholic clergy?" LifeSiteNews, October 20, 2022, https://www.lifesitenews.com/opinion/is-masonic-infiltration-responsible-for-the-widespread-apostasy-among-catholic-clergy/

5 Jeanne Smits, "Spanish Freemasons praise Pope Francis, laud 'International Fraternity Day," LifeSiteNews, February 10, 2021, https://www.lifesitenews.com/blogs/spanish-freemasons-praise-pope-francis-laud-international-fraternity-day/

6 Dorothy Cummings McLean, "Faithful Catholics as well as dissidents react to Pope Francis' new 'brotherhood' encyclical 'Fratelli tutti," LifeSiteNews, October 7, 2020, https://www.lifesitenews.com/news/faithful-catholics-as-well-as-dissidents-react-to-pope-francis-new-brotherhood-encyclical-fratelli-tutti/

7 Michael Haynes, "Freemasons appeal to Pope for support after bishop repeats Church's condemnation," LifeSiteNews, February 15, 2023, https://www.lifesitenews.com/news/freemasons-appeal-to-pope-for-support-after-bishop-repeats-churchs-condemnation/

8 Michael Haynes, "Pope Francis appoints pro-LGBT cardinal praised by top Freemason as president of Italian bishops' conference," May 24, 2022, https://www.lifesitenews.com/news/pope-francis-appoints-pro-lgbt-cardinal-praised-by-top-freemason-as-president-of-italian-bishops-conference/

informing them that despite past hostilities between the Church and Free-masonry, the "various declarations on the incompatibility of the two...do not impede...dialogue."[9]

These developments, as well as others, have caused former Apostolic Nuncio to the United States, Archbishop Carlo Maria Viganò, to conclude that the Vatican is a witting collaborator in the global Masonic power structure that has for its aim the ushering in of the reign of the Antichrist.[10] *Fratelli Tutti* is "the ideological manifesto of Bergoglio, his profession of the Masonic faith, and his candidacy for the presidency of the Universal Religion, handmaid of the New World Order," His Excellency argued in 2020.[11]

Founded in London in 1717, Freemasonry promotes a naturalistic, man-centered ideology that, among other things, rejects original sin, denies sanctifying grace, and promotes a generic belief in the "Grand Architect of the Universe" as opposed to the Trinitarian God of Christianity.[12] Freemasons have been involved in a number of political upheavals through history, most notably the French Revolution in 1789.

LifeSiteNews • May 30, 2023

TRADITIONAL CATHOLIC REPORTER EXPLAINS WHY HE'S EXPOSING FREEMASONRY, THE BOHEMIAN GROVE

Kyle Clifton has released multiple explosive videos uncovering Freemasonic rituals over the last several months. He says he has received threatening messages for doing so.

"My inspiration will always be Jesus Christ. I watch my back and have God protecting me. I have Saint Michael the Archangel on my side," he told LifeSite this week.

9 Steve Skojec, "Vatican Sees No Impediment to Dialogue With Freemasonry," One Peter Five, February 16, 2016, https://onepeterfive.com/vatican-sees-no-impediment-to-dialogue-with-freemasonry/

10 See "Abp Viganò: Freemasonry is using the WHO and the 'Bergoglian church' to advance its global coup," LifeSiteNews, June 17, 2022, https://www.lifesitenews.com/opinion/abp-vigano-freemasonry-is-using-the-who-and-the-bergoglian-church-to-advance-its-global-coup/

11 Quoted in Dorothy Cummings McLean, "Faithful Catholics as well as dissidents react to Pope Francis' new 'brotherhood' encyclical 'Fratelli tutti'," LifeSiteNews, October 7, 2020, https://www.lifesitenews.com/news/faithful-catholics-as-well-as-dissidents-react-to-pope-francis-new-brotherhood-encyclical-fratelli-tutti/

12 Raymund Maria, "Everything you need to know about Freemasonry's core teachings," LifeSiteNews, July 18, 2022, https://www.lifesitenews.com/opinion/is-freemasonry-a-religion/

Clifton, who goes by "Kyle Undercover," has built a reputation as a truth-telling zealot willing to risk his safety to expose evil. A devout Traditional Catholic who admits he is likely on the FBI's radar, his new target is the shadowy Bohemian Grove group in northern California. "I would like for this club to be ended once and for all," he explained via email. "I would encourage other members, especially those that are Catholic and are part of this club, to come clean and admit that it is wrong and release more footage or information about it."

Undercover announced on March 15 that he obtained a leaked Bohemian Grove "top-secret official document" that includes a list of "all persons in attendance to their most recent secret society meeting." Among those on the list, he says, includes the husband and son of Democrat Congresswoman Nancy Pelosi. David Gergen, a former CNN political analyst, is also named.

Gergen, who is now 81, spent decades in Washington, DC as an adviser to multiple presidents, including Richard Nixon, Ronald Reagan, and Bill Clinton. The ultimate insider, Gergen was caught on camera scolding Alex Jones several years ago when Jones ambushed him about the group's "Cremation of Care" ritual, which Undercover says has roots in Jewish Kabbala practices.

"It is funny to watch these people get confronted over their Satanic Rituals in the middle of the forest. They think they are safe from prying eyes under the canopy of all those Redwood trees, but they are not. It is comparable to shining a light on cockroaches in the dark."

The all-male Bohemian Grove club was started by San Francisco businessmen and others in 1878. After World War II, it expanded to include people from around the world. Former president Richard Nixon once remarked privately that the gathering is "the most faggy" thing there is, a reference to alleged homosexual behavior that occurs there.[13] Undercover explains that to be a member of the Grove you have to be invited. "It is rumored that the upcoming President of the United States is 'chosen' in advance at the Bohemian Grove. It is also common knowledge that the Manhattan Project was born at the Grove," he says. "Foreign policy is discussed and many backdoor deals happen there as many members were in similar fraternities in college and are connected by their career paths."

Undercover released a video earlier this month of Daniel Donahoe III, a man he says is a former member of the Grove. Undercover located him in Arizona and filmed him discreetly without his knowledge, as the state has one-party consent laws. Undercover says Donahoe admits members will go into

13 Marty Miller, "Nixon Tape Discusses Homosexuals at Bohemian Grove," YouTube, July 19, 2006, https://www.youtube.com/watch?v=dPb-PN9F2Pc

the nearby town and visit prostitutes. Asked by LifeSite if members engage in pedophilia and homosexual activity on the club's grounds, Undercover said there are "only rumors" of such behavior.

Undercover further explained that the documents he obtained came from an employee of an invited guest to the Grove. He said they reveal how the campground is broken up into more than two dozen camps:

> Some camps only house two members whereas other camps house 50. 'The Hillbilly's' was known as the Bush's group in the 1980s or 90s and is how Alex Jones, who is from Texas, was able to remain under the radar [when he infiltrated] because they were known for their thick Texas accent. After reviewing most of the members on this list and seeing a ton of Yale graduates, I would bet that there are many Skull & Bones connections as well.

Undercover says the group is far from benign. Its main ritual, also known as the Cremation of Care, is rooted in the occult:

> The Cremation of Care ceremony is at the very least a mocking of Catholicism and is said to make fun of the story of Saint John, who is considered to be the High Priest. According to the documents that I leaked to the public, the High Priest puts all of the member's sins upon this effigy called Dull Care, but he is unable to 'kill' the Dull Care effigy with the earthly fire they use so Dull Care mocks him when he fails. Dull Care laughs and says that priestly fires cannot kill Dull Care and they must use the only fire that can overcome the great enemy—the fire of the bird. They refer to it as the flame which burns in the Lamp of Fellowship on the Altar of Bohemia. They then scream, 'Hail, Fellowship,' and 'Dull Care, begone!'

"Most people wrongly equate The Owl as Moloch worship," he continued, "which does not quite make sense as Moloch has often been portrayed as a bull-headed idol with outstretched hands over a fire. The Owl is regarded by Grove members as a symbol for Lilith, a demon known to be Adam's first wife in Jewish tradition and is said to have taken the form of an owl after she left Adam on Earth. Lilit and Lilith are used interchangeably in the Jewish Talmud and the Hebrew word for Lilit is a Night Owl."

Undercover is currently raising money to support his efforts. He is also looking for like-minded reporters, both men and women, who want to expose evil and corruption. Those who are interested can reach him on his website: https://taplink.cc/kyleaz.

LifeSiteNews • February 23, 2024

SEVEN SIMILARITIES BETWEEN ST ALPHONSUS LIGUORI AND ARCHBISHOP MARCEL LEFEBVRE

During the last weekend in January this years, I was invited to give a talk to a group of Traditional Catholics in Cleveland, Ohio. I was there to promote my book *St Alphonsus for the 21st Century: A Handbook for Holiness* (St Peter's Press, 2023).

Aside from providing insights on who St Alphonsus was, and sharing with them his most well-known teachings, I discussed areas of overlap between him and Archbishop Marcel Lefebvre, the founder of the Society of St Pius x.

I can't recall which of these two holy men I encountered first on my journey out of the Novus Ordo sect and into Traditional Catholicism during the early 2010s. I think it was St Alphonsus' book *Dignities and Duties of the Priest* that first got me interested in the Latin Mass, at which point Archbishop Lefebvre's *They Have Uncrowned Him* found its way across my desk soon after. Whichever was first, both men have had an outsized influence on me.

In this article, I'd like to present seven similarities between St Alphonsus and Archbishop Lefebvre. By no means is this an exhaustive list of the commonalities these two giants of our faith, one of whom is a Doctor of the Church, share But it can serve as a simple reminder of how God raised up both of them to address similar needs in His Church at different times in history.

1. Both St Alphonsus and Archbishop Lefebvre founded priestly orders to help those who were left behind by the mainstream Church. In fact, the motto of the Redemptorists is to serve "the most abandoned souls." Founded in the Kingdom of Naples in 1732, the Redemptorists focused their efforts on laity who lived in remote areas that the dioceses refused or didn't have the ability to help. Alphonsus and his companions believed that every soul, especially the most uneducated and poor, deserved spiritual assistance. In like manner, Archbishop Lefebvre established the sspx to help Catholics who were neglected by the Conciliar authorities following Vatican ii. He wanted to ensure they had access to the Church's traditional sacraments. In the early days of the sspx, priests would often say Masses in houses, hotel rooms, and basements. Such spartan environments were probably not that

dissimilar from the places the first Redemptorists would have offered their own Masses in.

2. Both understood the crisis afflicting the Church in their time. In a private letter, St Alphonsus lamented that the Church in the 1700s was in a "state of relaxation and confusion." He also said that "all the human science and prudence there is cannot extricate the Church from [this] present state." He remarked that "very few" bishops "possess genuine zeal for souls" and that "almost all religious communities are relaxed." These words could very well be applied to the Church in our own time. Archbishop Lefebvre was blessed to understand the crisis following Vatican II far better than others. He too understood that "very few" bishops after the Council were going to stand up for Tradition and that he needed to do what was necessary to defend the Faith. The parallels on this topic are all too obvious.

3. Both defended the Faith with their writings. St Alphonsus didn't publish his first work until he was 47 years old. Before his death at the age of 90, he had written more than 110 books, pamphlets, and treatises on moral, doctrinal, and spiritual topics. There is hardly a single subject he did not touch on. His *Glories of Mary, Visits to the Blessed Sacrament,* and *Preparation for Death* are among his most popular writings. In a similar way, Archbishop Lefebvre's essays left very few stones unturned. While serving as papal ambassador to French-speaking Africa, he wrote scores of pastoral letters on politics, spirituality, and more. His masterful *Open Letter to Confused Catholics* as well as *They Have Uncrowned Him* explains in great detail the crisis in the Church and the traditional teaching on the Social Kingship of Christ, respectively. His *Priestly Holiness* (compiled by an SSPX priest using thousands of his past remarks) serves as the gold standard on the priesthood in the aftermath of the Council.

4. Both were spiritual masters. St Alphonsus was renowned for his simple yet profound preaching style. He said he never gave a sermon that the little old lady in the back of the church could not understand. Redemptorists specialize in giving missions that focus on the four last things—death, judgment, heaven, and hell. Their deep awareness of all facets of the spiritual life came directly from their founder, who frequently gave retreats himself. Archbishop Lefebvre was also deeply in tune with the Holy Spirit. Indeed, the Church may have lost the traditional Spiritual Exercises of St Ignatius of Loyola if it wasn't for him. The story goes that in the 1970s Fr Ludovic Marie Barrielle was informed about the Archbishop's seminary in Ecône. Fr Barrielle arrived and soon became a spiritual director to many seminarians. He would often preach five-day Ignatian retreats. To this day, the Society of St Pius X offers retreats to laity and priests. God clearly chose to work through Archbishop

Lefebvre to keep this great treasure alive so souls could grow closer to Him. 5. Both had a special charism for helping women religious. Most Catholics are unaware that it was actually a woman who was indirectly responsible for the founding of the Redemptorist Order. Sister Maria Celeste Crostorosa was a nun who lived at the time of St Alphonsus. She had received visions from Our Lord about founding the Redemptoristine Nuns in the 1720s. It was St Alphonsus who investigated those visions and ultimately established the rule for the order. Not long after, Sr. Celeste experienced yet more visions, but this time they were of St Alphonsus conversing with Our Lord Himself. This ultimately led to the founding of the Redemptorists in 1732. Throughout his life, St Alphonsus gave retreats to the Redemptoristine Nuns and made sure to encourage young women to enter the convent. Archbishop Lefebvre's own sister, Mother Marie-Gabriel Lefebvre, co-founded with him the Sisters of the SSPX in 1974. Having both been missionaries of the Congregation of the Holy Ghost, they knew the great need for traditional women orders, of which there are many associated with the SSPX, including the Dominicans Teaching Sisters and the Consoling Sisters in Italy.

6. Both had set-backs early on and throughout their ministry. There was much enthusiasm surrounding the foundation of the Redemptorists. A half-dozen young men went to live with St Alphonsus at the time. But only six months after their first ceremony the only one who remained with him was a lay brother. It took many more years and wisdom before St Alphonsus grew the order in the decades that followed. Moreover, he was almost always at odds with the secular authorities in the Kingdom of Naples. There have been many times in the history of the SSPX that Archbishop Lefebvre felt the sting of allies turning their backs on him. In the 1970s, following his suspension from Paul VI, he saw several professors leave his seminary. In 1983, nine American priests departed the Society. In 1988, priests who did not agree with the Archbishop's decision to consecrate four bishops made a deal with the Vatican to establish the Priestly Fraternity of St Peter. In the 1990s and even in the 2000s, others departed his path as well, including Dom Gérard Calvet (Le Barroux, France), Fr Paul Aulagnier (Institute of the Good Shepherd), and the Diocese of Campos (Brazil), which was overseen by Bishop de Castro Mayer until his death in 1991.

7. Both were persecuted by the authorities and died a white martyrdom. Near the end of his life, St Alphonsus sought approval from the government of the Kingdom of Naples for official recognition of his order. The Redemptorists had already been approved in the Papal States to the north. The authorities were willing to grant recognition, but they sought changes to the Redemptorist rule. Alphonsus, then in his 80s and severely ill with a curved spine

and poor eyesight, delegated the matter to younger clergy. He eventually added his signature to the document that was returned to him. The changes were so significant that it essentially created a new order, infuriating many priests, as well as the pope. Alphonsus was eventually expelled as a result. Although he took responsibility for the matter, he was more or less deceived. It wasn't until after his death that he was rehabilitated and later declared innocent of wrongdoing. As was just mentioned, Archbishop Lefebvre was suspended *a divinis* by Paul VI in 1976. After the 1988 consecrations, the Vatican announced that he incurred the penalty of "excommunication," which he considered a badge of honor. Like St Alphonsus, he too will one day be recognized for having done nothing wrong. May we pray that that day comes sooner rather than later.

Catholic Family News • March 2024

MY OPEN LETTER TO ARCHBISHOP CARLO MARIA VIGANÒ

Archbishop Viganò has spurred a long-overdue, Church-wide debate about Vatican II. If nothing else, ordinary Catholics are now able to see for themselves what some of the most well-known clergy and theologians in the world truly think about the Council. All cards are on the table.

It seems to me every Catholic is being given the chance by God to know the truth, and that He doesn't want us to go to our judgement ignorant of what has been happening these past 60 years. He wants us to think, pick a side, and "test all things" (1 Thessalonians 5:21) and not just be blind followers.

Speaking for myself, I find a lot of the claims made by mainstream churchmen who claim Vatican II was pretty much like every other Council (and that it in no way "ruptured" with the past) to be wholly unconvincing. But I'm also starting to wonder if Archbishop Viganò needs to give more advice to laity and priests on what they should be doing. He's certainly diagnosed the problem, but what are his solutions? What, in other words, is it he believes Catholics in the 21st century should do in response to this crisis?

How are Catholics Supposed to Survive This Crisis?

In his many remarks, His Excellency has frequently borrowed terminology from the late Archbishop Marcel Lefebvre (1905–1991). On multiple occasions, he's spoken of "the Conciliar Church," a term Archbishop Lefebvre often used when describing the post-Vatican II religion. In his response to

Fr Thomas Weinandy, Archbishop Viganò called Vatican II "the *de facto* first council, for all practical purposes, of a schismatic church," another phrase employed by Lefebvre.[14]

As far as I can tell, His Excellency is in lockstep with the Archbishop on the root cause of the crisis. And he has proposed a possible solution for the Church at the macro level—the Church should simply "forget" the Council. Yet, he has not yet necessarily addressed what ordinary Catholics should do until that happens.

Would he, I wonder, start his own priestly institute if it came down to it? Which religious communities does he think are holding firm to the Church's traditions today? Also, does he believe it's good for the laity to attend diocesan-approved Latin Masses and to stay within the confines of the "Conciliar Church"? Does he think it's admissible to assist at the *Novus Ordo* Mass? Or perhaps His Excellency wishes Catholics to attended the FSSP, SSPX, or even SSPX "Resistance" chapels? Does he, moreover, think "supplied jurisdiction" allows for most traditional priests to disobey ordinary diocesan bishops? Which seminaries or convents does he think young men and women who want to try a vocation should enter?

Some Catholics may speculate that His Excellency's constant use of "Bergoglio" is a sign that either he believes Francis is not the pope and that Benedict still is, or that Francis, by his words and deeds, has automatically deposed himself from the papal throne. It would be interesting to see His Excellency to respond to that speculation.

A Duty to 'Separate' From the Conciliar Church?

One theory presented in 2013 by SSPX Bishop Bernard Tissier de Mallerais is that the crisis in the Church has reached such a crescendo that there now exists two distinct churches that have the same pope as their shared head.

"The Catholic Church is the society of the baptized who want to save their souls in professing the Catholic faith, in practicing the same Catholic worship and in following the same pastors, successors of the Apostles," Tissier wrote. He continued:

> The conciliar church is the society of the baptized who follow the directives of the current Popes and bishops, in espousing more or less

14 Maike Hickson, Ph.D., "Abp Viganò: When We Can Criticize Pope Francis, Can We Not Also Criticize Vatican II?" Catholic Family News, August 11, 2020, https://catholicfamilynews.com/blog/2020/08/11/abp-vigano-when-we-can-criticize-pope-francis-can-we-not-also-criticize-vatican-ii/

consciously the intention to bring about the unity of the human race, and in practice accepting the decisions of the Council, following the new liturgy and submitting to the new Code of Canon law.

"We have two churches who have the same heads and most of the same members, but who have different forms and ends diametrically incongruous," he argues. He then adds:

On the one hand eternal salvation seconded by the social reign of Christ, King of Nations, on the other hand the unity of the human race by liberal ecumenism, that is to say broadened to all religions … formally considered the conciliar church is a sect which occupies the Catholic Church.[15]

The statements of Archbishop Viganò the past few months seem to coincide with those of Bishop Tissier's views. It would be beneficial if Archbishop Viganò addressed the argument he presents.

I also wonder if His Excellency agrees with Archbishop Lefebvre's 1991 remarks about having "a strict duty for every priest wanting to remain Catholic to separate himself from this Conciliar Church for as long as it does not rediscover the Tradition of the Church and of the Catholic Faith"?[16]

What, one also has to wonder, would "separating" from the Conciliar Church look like in Archbishop Viganò's opinion? Should priest's leave their dioceses for traditional orders? Should they work "from within" to bring the Church back to Tradition? Does he think the SSPX should be "regularized" or wait for the conversion of Rome back to the faith? Does he believe we are at a point where consecrating more traditional bishops, even without the pope's approval, is a necessity?

What to Do When Surrounded by Modernists?

Lastly, I wonder if Archbishop Viganò believes the true Church is no longer in Rome but instead in small pockets of Traditional communities of priests and laity scattered about the world? Does His Excellency think the Church has been so overrun by her enemies that there's hardly any faith left on earth? To which clergy are lay Catholics supposed to submit themselves, given the

15 Bishop Tissier de Mallerais, "Is There A Conciliar Church?" Dominicans of Avrille, Originally published in *Le Sel de la Terre*, Number 85, Summer 2013, https://dominican-savrille.us/is-there-a-conciliar-church/

16 Archbishop Marcel Lefebvre, *Spiritual Journey*, Angelus Press, Kansas City, Missouri, 2011, p.17

proliferation of neo-Modernism in the Church? Are we, for example, to simply cling to a priest who is faithful to tradition, no matter what order he belongs to, and hold on for dear life? Since Canon Law states that the supreme law of the Church is the salvation of souls, what is off-limits at this point? Anything? One has to wonder how much God will hold lay people accountable on Judgment Day given that there are so many priests and bishops who have conflicting answers about these questions.

It is my sincerest hope that Archbishop Viganò will address these and other pressing issues in the days, weeks, and months ahead. Catholics have been praying for decades that God would give them leaders who possess the wisdom needed to provide answers so they can obtain eternal happiness. True spiritual guidance is needed now more than ever.

Catholic Family News • August 22, 2020

ARCHBISHOP VIGANÒ'S RESPONSE TO MY OPEN LETTER

Dear Mr Kokx,

I read with lively interest your article "*Questions for Viganò: His Excellency is Right about Vatican II, But What Does He Think Catholic Should Do Now?*" which was published by *Catholic Family News* on August 22. I am happy to respond to your questions, which address matters that are very important for the faithful.

You ask: "*What would 'separating' from the Conciliar Church look like in Archbishop Viganò's opinion?*" I respond to you with another question: "*What does it mean to separate from the Catholic Church according to the supporters of the Council?*" While it is clear that no admixture is possible with those who propose adulterated doctrines of the *conciliar ideological manifesto*, it should be noted that the simple fact of being baptized and of being living members of the Church of Christ does not imply adherence to the *conciliar team*; this is true above all for the simple faithful and also for secular and regular clerics who, for various reasons, sincerely consider themselves Catholics and recognize the Hierarchy

Instead, what needs to be clarified is the position of those who, declaring themselves Catholic, embrace the heterodox doctrines that have spread over these decades, with the awareness that these represent a rupture with the preceding Magisterium. In this case it is licit to doubt their real adherence to the Catholic Church, in which however they hold official roles that confer authority on them. It is an illicitly exercised authority, if its purpose is to force the faithful to accept the revolution imposed since the Council.

Once this point has been clarified, it is evident that it is not the traditional faithful—that is, true Catholics, in the words of Saint Pius X—that must abandon the Church in which they have the full right to remain and from which it would be unfortunate to separate; but rather the Modernists who usurp the Catholic name, precisely because it is only the *bureaucratic* element that permits them not to be considered on a par with any heretical sect. This claim of theirs serves in fact to prevent them from ending up among the hundreds of heretical movements that over the course of the centuries have believed to be able to reform the Church at their own pleasure, placing their pride ahead of humbly guarding the teaching of Our Lord. But just as it is not possible to claim citizenship in a homeland in which one does not know its language, law, faith and tradition; so it is impossible that those who do not share the faith, morals, liturgy, and discipline of the Catholic Church can arrogate to themselves the right to remain within her and even to ascend the levels of the hierarchy.

Therefore let us not give in to the temptation to abandon—albeit with justified indignation—the Catholic Church, on the pretext that it has been invaded by heretics and fornicators: it is they who must be expelled from the sacred enclosure, in a work of purification and penance that must begin with each one of us.

It is also evident that there are widespread cases in which the faithful encounter serious problems in frequenting their parish church, just as there are ever fewer churches where the Holy Mass is celebrated in the Catholic Rite. The horrors that have been rampant for decades in many our parishes and shrines make it impossible even to assist at a "Eucharist" without being disturbed and putting one's faith at risk, just as it is very difficult to ensure a Catholic education, Sacraments being worthily celebrated, and solid spiritual guidance for oneself and one's children. In these cases faithful laity have the right and the duty to find priests, communities, and institutes that are faithful to the perennial Magisterium. And may they know how to accompany the laudable celebration of the liturgy in the Ancient Rite with adherence to sound doctrine and morals, without any subsidence on the front of the Council.

The situation is certainly more complex for clerics, who depend hierarchically on their bishop or religious superior, but who at the same time have the right to remain Catholic and be able to celebrate according to the Catholic Rite. On the one hand laity have more freedom of movement in choosing the community to which they turn for Mass, the Sacraments, and religious instruction, but less autonomy because of the fact that they still have to depend on a priest; on the other hand, clerics have less freedom of movement, since they are incardinated in a diocese or order and are subject to ecclesiastical authority, but they have more autonomy because of the fact that they can legitimately decide to celebrate the Mass and administer the Sacraments in the Tridentine Rite and to preach in conformity with sound doctrine. The Motu Proprio *Summorum Pontificum* reaffirmed that faithful and priests have the inalienable right—which cannot be denied—to avail themselves of the liturgy that more perfectly expresses their Catholic Faith. But this right must be used today not only and not so much to preserve the *extraordinary form* of the rite, but to testify to adherence to the *depositum fidei* that finds perfect correspondence only in the Ancient Rite.

I daily receive heartfelt letters from priests and religious who are marginalized or transferred or ostracized because of their fidelity to the Church: the temptation to find an *ubi consistam* [a place to stand] far from the clamor of the Innovators is strong, but we ought to take an example from the persecutions that many saints have undergone, including Saint Athanasius, who offers us a model of how to behave in the face of widespread heresy and persecuting fury. As my venerable brother Bishop Athanasius Schneider has many times recalled, the Arianism that afflicted the Church at the time of the Holy Doctor of Alexandria in Egypt was so widespread among the bishops that it leaves one almost to believe that Catholic orthodoxy had completely disappeared. But it was thanks to the fidelity and heroic testimony of the few bishops who remained faithful that the Church knew how to get back up again. Without this testimony, Arianism would not have been defeated; without our testimony today, Modernism and the globalist apostasy of this pontificate will not be defeated.

It is therefore not a question of working from within the Church or outside it: the winemakers are called to work in the Lord's Vineyard, and it is there that they must remain even at the cost of their lives; the pastors are called to pastor the Lord's Flock, to keep the ravenous wolves at bay and to drive away the mercenaries who are not concerned with the salvation of the sheep and lambs.

This hidden and often silent work has been carried out by the Society of Saint Pius X, which deserves recognition for not having allowed the flame of Tradition to be extinguished at a moment in which celebrating the ancient Mass was considered subversive and a reason for excommunication. Its priests have been a healthy thorn in the side for a hierarchy that has seen in them an unacceptable point of comparison for the faithful, a constant reproach for the betrayal committed against the people of God, an inadmissible alternative to the *new conciliar path*. And if their fidelity made *disobedience* to the pope inevitable with the episcopal consecrations, thanks to them the Society was able to protect herself from the furious attack of the *innovators* and by its very existence it allowed the possibility of the liberalization of the Ancient Rite, which until then was prohibited. Its presence also allowed the contradictions and errors of the *conciliar sect* to emerge, always winking at heretics and idolaters but implacably rigid and intolerant towards Catholic Truth.

I consider Archbishop Lefebvre an exemplary confessor of the Faith, and I think that by now it is obvious that his denunciation of the Council and the modernist apostasy is more relevant than ever. It should not be forgotten that the persecution to which Archbishop Lefebvre was subjected by the Holy See and the world episcopate served above all as a deterrent for Catholics who were refractory toward the *conciliar revolution.*

I also agree with the observation of His Excellency Bishop Bernard Tissier de Mallerais about the co-presence of two entities in Rome: the Church of Christ has been occupied and eclipsed by the modernist conciliar structure, which has established itself in the same hierarchy and uses the authority of its ministers to prevail over the Spouse of Christ and our Mother.

The Church of Christ—which not only *subsists* in the Catholic Church, but *is exclusively* the Catholic Church—is only obscured and eclipsed by *a strange extravagant Church* established in Rome, according to the vision of Blessed Anne Catherine Emmerich. It coexists, like wheat with the tare, in the Roman Curia, in dioceses, in parishes. We cannot judge our pastors for their intentions, nor suppose that all of them are corrupt in faith and morals; on the contrary, we can hope that many of them, hitherto intimidated and silent, will understand, as confusion and apostasy continue to spread, the deception to which they have been subjected and will finally shake off their slumber. There are many laity who are raising their voice; others will necessarily follow, together with good priests, certainly present in every diocese. This *awakening* of the Church militant—I would dare to call it almost a *resurrection*—is necessary, urgent and inevitable: no son tolerates his mother being outraged by the servants, or his father being tyrannized by the administrators of his goods. The Lord offers us, in these painful situations, the possibility of being His allies in fighting this holy battle under His banner: the King Who is victorious over error and death permits us to share the honor of triumphal victory and the eternal reward that derives from it, after having endured and suffered with Him.

But in order to deserve the immortal glory of Heaven we are called to rediscover—in an emasculated age devoid of values such as honor, faithfulness to one's word, and heroism—a fundamental aspect of the faith of every baptized person: the Christian life is a *militia*, and with the Sacrament of Confirmation we are called to be *soldiers of Christ*, under whose insignia we must fight. Of course, in most cases it is essentially a spiritual battle, but over the course of history we have seen how often, faced with the violation of the sovereign rights of God and the liberty of the Church, it was also necessary to take up arms: we are taught this by the strenuous resistance to repel the Islamic invasions in Lepanto and on the outskirts of Vienna, the persecution of the *Cristeros* in Mexico, of the Catholics in Spain, and even today by the cruel war against Christians throughout the world. Never as today can we understand the theological hatred coming from the enemies of God, inspired by Satan. The attack on everything that recalls the Cross of Christ—on Virtue, on the Good and the Beautiful, on purity—must spur us to get up, in a leap of pride, in order to claim our right not only not to be persecuted by our external enemies but also and above all to have strong and courageous pastors, holy and God-fearing, who will do exactly what their predecessors have done for centuries: preach the Gospel of Christ, convert individuals and nations, and expand the Kingdom of the living and true God throughout the world.

We are all called to make an act of Fortitude—a forgotten cardinal virtue, which not by chance in Greek recalls virile strength, ἀνδρεία—in knowing how to resist the Modernists: a resistance that is rooted in Charity and Truth, which are attributes of God.

If you only celebrate the Tridentine Mass and preach sound doctrine without ever mentioning the Council, what can they ever do to you? Throw you out of your churches, perhaps, and then what? No one can ever prevent you from renewing the Holy Sacrifice, even if it is on a makeshift altar in a cellar or an attic, as the *refractory priests* did during the French Revolution, or as happens still today in China. And if they try to distance you, resist: canon law serves to guarantee the government of the Church in the pursuit of its primary purposes, not to demolish it. Let's stop fearing that the fault of the schism lies with those who denounce it, and not, instead, with those who carry it out: the ones who are schismatics and heretics are those who wound and crucify the Mystical Body of Christ, not those who defend it by denouncing the executioners!

The laity can expect their ministers to behave as such, preferring those who prove that they are not contaminated by present errors. If a Mass becomes an occasion of torture for the faithful, if they are forced to assist at sacrileges or to support heresies and ramblings unworthy of the House of the Lord, it is a thousand times preferable to go to a church where the priest celebrates the Holy Sacrifice worthily, in the rite given to us by Tradition, with preaching in conformity with sound doctrine. When parish priests and bishops realize that the Christian people demand the Bread of Faith, and not the stones and scorpions of the neochurch, they will lay aside their fears and comply with the legitimate requests of the faithful. The others, true mercenaries, will show themselves for what they are and will be able to gather around them only those who share their errors and perversions. They will be extinguished by themselves: the Lord dries up the swamp and makes the land on which brambles grow arid; he extinguishes vocations in corrupt seminaries and in convents rebellious to the Rule.

The lay faithful today have a sacred task: to comfort good priests and good bishops, gathering like sheep around their shepherds. Give them hospitality, help them, console them in their trials. Create community in which murmuring and division do not predominate, but rather fraternal charity in the bond of Faith. And since in the order established by God—κόσμος—subjects owe obedience to authority and cannot do otherwise than resist it when it abuses its power, no fault will be attributed to them for the infidelity of their leaders, on whom rests the very serious responsibility for the way in which they exercise the vicarious power which has been given to them. We must not rebel, but oppose; we must not be pleased with the errors of our pastors, but pray for them and admonish them respectfully; we must not question their authority but the way in which they use it.

I am certain, with a certainty that comes to me from Faith, that the Lord will not fail to reward our fidelity, after having punished us for the faults of the men of the Church, granting us holy priests, holy bishops, holy cardinals, and above all a holy Pope. But these saints will arise from our families, from our communities, from our churches: families, communities, and churches in which the grace of God must be cultivated with constant prayer, with the frequenting of Holy Mass and the Sacraments, with the offering of sacrifices and penances that the Communion of Saints permits us to offer to the Divine Majesty in order to expiate our sins and those of our brethren, including those who exercise authority. The laity have a fundamental role in this, guarding the Faith within their families, in such a way that our young people who are educated in love and in the fear of God may one day be responsible fathers and mothers, but also worthy ministers of the Lord, His heralds in the male and female religious orders, and His apostles in civil society.

The cure for rebellion is obedience. The cure for heresy is faithfulness to the teaching of Tradition. The cure for schism is filial devotion for the Sacred Pastors. The cure for apostasy is love for God and His Most Holy Mother. The cure for vice is the humble practice of virtue. The cure for the corruption of morals is to live constantly in the presence of God. But obedience cannot be perverted into stolid servility; respect for authority cannot be perverted into the obeisance of the court. And let's not forget that if it is the duty of the laity to obey their Pastors, it is even a more grave duty of the Pastors to obey God, *usque ad effusionem sanguinis.*

Archbishop Carlo Maria Viganò, Catholic Family News • September 1, 2020

ROME TELLS THE SOCIETY OF ST PIUS X THAT VATICAN II 'HAS ITS VALUE'

Cardinal Gerhard Müller is the head of the Congregation for the Doctrine of the Faith. Not long ago, he granted an interview to a German newspaper wherein he provided some rather candid remarks regarding the Society of St Pius X. Here is how Edward Pentin of the *National Catholic Register* reported on it:

> Cardinal Gerhard Müller has said he expects the Society of St Pius X, which has always opposed the Second Vatican Council's declarations on religious freedom and ecumenism, to 'unreservedly recognize' freedom of religion as a human right, and an obligation to ecumenism.
>
> The recognition of the Second Vatican Council is 'not an unreasonably high hurdle' to overcome, he said, adding that it was rather 'the adequate remedy to enter into full communion with the Pope and the bishops in communion with him.'
>
> 'Key statements, even if they are not proclaimed *ex cathedra* [and thus infallible], are, for us Catholics, still essential,' he said, adding that it is 'not acceptable to take one and reject the other.'[17]

Müller's comments are the complete opposite of what Archbishop Guido Pozzo, the Secretary of Ecclesia Dei, said back in April to the French paper *La Croix* regarding the Society:

> The acceptance of the texts on relations with other religions [*Nostra Aetate*] does not constitute a prerequisite for juridical recognition of the Lefebvrist society and certain questions will be able to remain objects of discussion and clarification.
>
> The affirmations of truths of faith and of sure Catholic doctrine contained in the Second Vatican Council documents must be welcomed

---

17 Edward Pentin, "Cardinal Müller Expects sspx to Recognize Disputed Council Teachings," National Catholic Register, Mat 24, 2016, http://www.ncregister.com/blog/edward-pentin/cardinal-mller-expects-sspx-to-recognize-disputed-council-declarations

according to the degree of required adherence.

[Doctrinal discussions] will constitute and be part of, after canonical recognition, a subject of discussion and further deepening, in view towards a greater precision, in order to avoid misunderstandings...[18]

Müller, in my view, has spilled the beans. Rome has to be none too pleased that he's made these comments, as they may torpedo any sort of deal between the Vatican and the Society. On the other hand, Müller's words seem to be nothing more than a less diplomatic way of saying what the Holy Father has always believed about a possible deal with the SSPX. Consider that when speaking with *La Croix* on May 9th, the pope said the following when asked if he would be willing to grant the Society a personal prelature:

It would be a possible solution, but, before, a fundamental agreement should be established with them. The Second Vatican Council has its value. We move forward slowly, with patience.

"The Second Vatican Council has its value." We "move forward slowly, with patience." That's essentially the same as what Cardinal Müller has said.

It seems to me that the end goal of all this "dialogue" between Rome and the Society has always been to get them to come over to the Council, and not to seriously entertain the criticisms the SSPX has of it.

Scripture tell us we can judge a tree by its fruits. Can it not be argued that despite the fact Francis may say he admires the Society, his actions indicate his intentions are full of guile? Chris Jackson over at *The Remnant* certainly thinks so. In an essay he recently wrote for that website, Jackson rightly notes that we cannot forget "the recent brutal oppression of Franciscan Friars of the Immaculate under Pope Francis." He also adds:

It seems that Pope Francis and Msgr. Pozzo are saying the same thing and taking the same approach that Cardinal Hoyos did years ago. The difference is that Cardinal Müller is firing a warning shot letting the Society know that sooner or later they must accept the Council. And once the SSPX is regularized and has a canonical structure under Rome, what position are they in to oppose a Roman authority insisting they accept contended novelties of the Council? At that point couldn't Francis, Pozzo, or Müller demand that the SSPX accept ecumenism

---

18 "New prerequisites for the SSPX: Abp Pozo," US District SSPX, April 12, 2016, https://sspx.org/en/news-events/news/new-prerequisites-sspx-abp-pozzo-15229

and religious liberty under obedience?[19]

Michael Matt, *The Remnant's* editor-in-chief, has also expressed doubt over a possible deal between Rome and the Society:

> One can speculate as to whether or not the Pope's bizarre no-strings-attached offer to regularize the Society of St Pius x isn't also connected in some way to the same old utopian dream of a 'one world religion,' in that everyone and anyone—even 'rad trad' traditionalists—must be brought into the circle if the religious component of the New World Order is ever to become a reality.[20]

Tough to disagree, is it not?

Magnificat Media • May 25, 2016

WOULD ARCHBISHOP LEFEBVRE BE A 'MAN OF DIALOGUE' WITH THE VATICAN TODAY?

Pope Francis gave a rather revealing interview to the French daily *La Croix* on May 9. In his remarks, he said the following regarding the Society of St Pius x:

> In Buenos Aires, I always spoke with them. They saluted me, they asked for [my] blessing on their knees. They consider themselves Catholic. They love the Church. Bishop Fellay is a man with whom we can dialogue. It is not the case of other somewhat strange elements, such as Bishop Williamson, or others who have radicalized. I think, as I had expressed in Argentina, that they are Catholics on the path to full communion. During this Year of Mercy, it seemed that I should authorize their confessors to pardon the sin of abortion [and others as well]. They thanked me for this gesture. Before that, Benedict xvi, whom they respect greatly, had liberalized the Mass according to the

---

19 Chris Jackson, "Cardinal Müller to sspx: Acceptance of Vatican ii is as essential as accepting Resurrection," The Remnant Newspaper, May 25, 2016, https://remnantnewspaper. com/web/index.php/fetzen-fliegen/item/2538-cardinal-muller-to-sspx-acceptance-of-vatican-ii-is-as-essential-as-accepting-resurrection

20 Michael Matt, "That All May Be One: The Utopian Dream of a One World Religion," The Remnant Newspaper, May 25, 2016, https://remnantnewspaper.com/web/index.php?option=com_k2&view=item&id=2536:that-all-may-be-one-the-utopian-dream-of-a-one-world-religion

Tridentine Rite. We dialogue well, we do a good work.[21]

The pope was then asked: "Would you be ready to grant them a status of personal prelature?" He responded: "It would be a possible solution, but, before, a fundamental agreement should be established with them. The Second Vatican Council has its value. We move forward slowly, with patience."[22] This is sure to get more than a few Society supporters riled up. After all, "dialogue" and "moving forward slowly" are terms Francis, a dyed in the wool modernist and master politician, uses when engaging with followers of false religions. It seems he is applying the same ecumenical principles to the Society.

A friend of mine emailed me some thoughts he had on Pope Francis and the SSPX. I'd like to share them here:

> A Catholic cannot praise an abortionist for following industry practices in his office. For instance, when an abortionist anesthetizes the woman whose child he is about to murder, you don't applaud him for following proper procedures. You don't say, "You know what, at least he discussed her options with her and got her consent. At least he has a nurse at his side to help the patient and a phone nearby to call 9-1-1 if something were to go wrong." No, what you do is call him out for murdering the unborn child!
>
> Everyone knows Pope Francis is destroying the Church. He is spiritual abortionist. He may want to engage in discussions with Traditionalists. He may even say some Traditionalists are Catholic and pious. Still, at the end of the day, he is a Modernist who is making the crisis in the Church worse. Where are the public condemnations of this man? Why is there such an interest in "dialoguing" with him? Why is there so much excitement over him thinking the SSPX is Catholic when he himself isn't Catholic?

SSPX leadership is (or so I've heard) going to gather soon to discuss Rome's proposal of "regularization." In my humble opinion, it would be wise to ask themselves the following questions. Of course, given the intellectual giants

---

21 Rorate Caeli, "Pope Francis speaks: 'The Society of St Pius X are Catholics on the path to full communion,'" May 16, 2016, https://rorate-caeli.blogspot.com/2016/05/pope-francis-speaks-society-of-st-pius.html

22 Guillaume Goubert and Sébastien Maillard, "Interview—Pope Francis," La Croix, May 17, 2016, https://www.la-croix.com/Religion/Pape/INTERVIEW-Pope-Francis-2016-05-17-1200760633

God has provided the Society with, I'm guessing that most of these are nothing new and that they've already been talked about.

• Would Archbishop Lefebvre be a "man of dialogue" with the deceivers currently occupying positions of power in Rome today?

• What does Scripture, the Saints, and Tradition say about dialoguing with those who obstinately refuse to hear the Truth and who repeatedly fail to embrace the Catholic faith? Is this a situation of casting pearls before swine?

• Would modernists ever strike a deal with a group of non-modernists that would ultimately bring to an end the power they have worked to acquire over the past 60 years?

• Can Pope Francis and Archbishop Pozzo, the Secretary of Ecclesia Dei, be trusted? In other words, how have they acted towards similar Traditional groups in the past?

• The Alta Vendita claimed Masonic infiltration of the Church would take centuries. We know there are Masons in the Church today and that Masons have praised Pope Francis in the past. Is his proposal for the SSPX a proposal from Masons in the Church?

• Do the prophesies of Our Lady of Good Success, Our Lady of Fatima, Our Lady of Akita and others point to Pope Francis being an end-times figure? How can we work with someone who is essentially laying the groundwork for the anti-Christ?

• Is the SSPX, which opposes ecumenism and dialogue with false religions, going to now be "regularized" with the enemies of Eternal Rome by way of "ecumenism" and "dialogue"? Won't this undermine their credibility?

• Is accepting a "personal prelature"—itself an innovation of Vatican II—a departure from Tradition and Archbishop Lefebvre's most mature thought on relations with Rome?

• What do we make of the following words of Archbishop Lefebvre: "We would have to re-enter this Conciliar Church in order, supposedly, to make it Catholic? That is a complete illusion! It is not the subjects that make the superiors, but the superiors who make the subjects."

• Do we still stand by Bishop Fellay's comments in 2003 when he said that to "foster illusions [of a practical accord with the Vatican] would be deadly for the SSPX."[23]

I could go on, as there are many more questions that need answering. In the meantime, pray for the Church and for the Society of St Pius X.

Magnificat Media • May 17, 2016

LESSONS FROM TRADITIONALISTS WHO RECONCILED WITH THE CONCILIAR CHURCH

On July 22nd, an anonymous blogger for *Rorate Caeli* who goes by the name "New Catholic" wrote a post titled "Thank God for Sainte-Madeleine du Barroux."

"New Catholic"—whoever he (or she) is—expressed praise for the work of the late Dom Gerard Calvet, the founder of the Abbey of St Mary Magdalene in Le Barroux, France.[24] Long-time supporters of the Society of St Pius X may remember the drama of Dom Gerard. Those under the age of 30 probably don't.

Some Historical Context

On July 6th, 1988, the Superiors of the Society of St Pius X's Districts, Seminaries and autonomous houses wrote an open letter to Cardinal Bernardin Gantin, the Prefect of the Congregation for Bishops.

Among other things, the letter declares that the SSPX is "in full communion with all the Popes and Bishops before the Second Vatican Council." Noting the "blindness of spirit" and the "hardening of heart" of the "Roman authorities," the Superiors proclaim that "we have never wished to belong to this system which calls itself the Conciliar Church."

They then say the following: "We ask for nothing better than to be declared out of communion with this adulterous spirit which has been blowing in the Church for the last 25 years; we ask for nothing better than to be declared outside of this impious communion of the ungodly.[25]

23 Super General's Letter to Friends and Benefactors, Number 63, January 6, 2003, Quoted in https://blessedvirginmary-priory.com/en/publications/january-2003-superior-generals-letter-63-36083
24 New Catholic, "Thank God for Sante-Madeleine du Barroux," Rorate Caeli, July 22, 2016, https://rorate-caeli.blogspot.com/2016/07/thank-god-for-sainte-madeleine-du.html
25 Open Letter to Cardinal Gantin, Prefect of the Congregation for Bishops, SSPX Asia, July 6, 1988, https://www.sspxasia.com/Documents/Archbishop-Lefebvre/Archbishop_Lefeb-

Not all friends of the Society agreed. One such friend was Dom Gerard Calvet, superior of the Benedictine Monastery of St Mary Magdalene.

Dom Gerard Favored Reconciliation

On August 18, 1988 Dom Gerard publicly declared he would seek out what Fr Lourenco Fleichman (a one-time monk at Le Barroux) later called "the siren song of legality" from the Conciliar Church.[26]

In his statement, Dom Gerard notes that in negotiating with Rome he was able to have his demands granted "without doctrinal counter-part" and "without concession." The Holy Father, Gerard said, was "offering us to be integrated into the Benedictine Confederation as we are," and "that no silence be imposed on our anti-Modernist preaching."

Gerard goes on to list several reasons why he put himself into the hands of the Romans.

One (1) reason was because he believed it would be better for Tradition to "enter into" the Roman Church. "That the tradition of the Church be pushed out of her official, visible perimeter brings prejudice to it," he claimed.

A second (2) reason why Dom Gerard agreed to an arrangement was because he believed that even though the Church was run by Modernists, it is "better to be in agreement with the laws of the Church rather than contravene them."

A third (3) reason was the belief that it would be better for Tradition if the Roman authorities viewed his apostolate not as a disobedient one but as a Catholic one. This way, the laity would be put at ease and eventually more souls would come to the Latin Mass:

> Lastly the reason, perhaps the determining one, which inclined us to accept that the *suspens a divinis* be lifted from our priests, is a missionary reason: should not the maximum number of faithful be enabled to assist at our Masses and liturgical celebrations without being hindered by their local priests or bishop? I think, especially, of some young college students, scouts and seminarians who have never seen a traditional Mass.[27]

vre_and_the_Vatican/Part_I/1988-07-06.htm

26 Fr Lourenco Fleischmann, OSB, Open Letter to the Priests of Campos, SSPX Asia, October 30, 2001, https://www.sspxasia.com/Documents/Society_of_Saint_Pius_X/Open_Letter_to_the_Priests_of_Campos.htm

27 Declaration on Dom Gerard, SSPX Asia, August 18, 1988, https://www.sspxasia.com/Documents/Archbishop-Lefebvre/Archbishop_Lefebvre_and_the_Vatican/Part_II/1988-08-18.htm

The SSPX *Opposed Dom Gerard's Deal with Rome*

Followers of Archbishop Lefebvre responded swiftly to Dom Gerard's declaration. Fr Franz Schmidberger, the Superior General of the Society from 1983–1994, refuted each point Gerard put forth. Responding to Gerard's first (1) claim, Fr Schmidberger said:

> It seems rather contrary to the plan of Divine Providence that the Catholic Tradition of the Church be re-integrated into the pluralism of the Conciliar Church, as long as the latter dishonors the Catholic Church and scandalizes its unity and visibility.

Responding to Gerard's second (2) claim, Fr Schmidberger said:

> It is an honor for Le Barroux to have been rejected by the other Benedictines for its integral fidelity to the Mass of All Times, and thus to have become a wonderful sign of contradict...when the laws of the Church are abused everywhere, in such a way as to desiccate the living sources of Faith and grace, it is better not to succumb to this scheme.

Responding to Gerard's third (3) claim, Fr Schmidberger said:

> If the priests of Le Barroux considered that they were validly suspended, they have been living for 15 years in mortal sin. If they think that the so-called *suspens a divinis* merely damages their apostolic influence, they are wrong. The hard way of the Cross is more fruitful than the easy way.[28]

Fr Schmidberger's three responses may well be summed up in the following manner:

> What does Truth have with Belial? The same that Tradition has with Modernism. Nothing. The Conciliar Church, so long as she clings to her errors, dishonors Christ. It seems contrary to God's plan that Tradition be integrated into this scandalous structure. Far from being a recognition of Tradition, the Modernists are placing you, Dom Gerard, into an ecumenical zoo in the name of pluralism. To be considered outside this scheme is an honor, and a wonderful sign of contradiction. It lets the faithful know that we practice different religions, and that there

---

28 Ibid.

can be no union with truth and error. Certainly it is a cross to be seen as "outside the Church" and "suspended a divinis" but we must hold together until Rome recovers her ways. It is in God's hands.

Other Traditionalists Opposed Reconciliation as Well

Dom Tomás Aquino, the Prior of the Monastery of Santa Cruz in Nova Friburgo, Brazil echoed Fr Schmidberger's remarks in a letter he sent to Dom Gerard on August 25th.

Dom Aquino said that Gerard's agreement signified an "insertion" into the "Conciliar Church." He believed the deal would have the long term goal of a "full reconciliation with the Apostolic See according to the terms of the motu proprio *Ecclesia Dei*, a document which has proclaimed the excommunication of Archbishop Lefebvre."

He then made the following comparison:

> We follow the Catholic Church, but at the present time Archbishop Lefebvre and Bishop de Castro Mayer have been the only two bishops to stand against the auto-demolition of the Church. It is not possible to separate ourselves from them. So, as in the fourth century at the time of Arianism, to be "in communion with Athanasius" (and not with Pope Liberius), was a sign of orthodoxy, so now to be united with Archbishop Lefebvre and Bishop de Castro Mayer is a sign of fidelity to the Church of all times.[29]

An Accord with Rome is a Liberal Illusion

In October of 2001, Fr Lourenco Fleichman wrote a letter wherein he voiced opposition to the agreement between Rome and the priests of the Diocese of Campos, Brazil. The name of Dom Gerard was invoked:

> Dom Gerard, placing the particular interests of his monastery above the Church's good, accepted a separation from Archbishop Lefebvre in order to "normalize" his juridical and canonical status, thereby letting fall the sword of combat.
> Dom Gerard gave me three reasons that he considered sufficient for going ahead and concluding the agreement…1) many new persons

---

29 Declaration of Dom Tomás Aquino, SSPX Asia, August 24, 1988, https://www.sspxasia. com/Documents/Archbishop-Lefebvre/Archbishop_Lefebvre_and_the_Vatican/Part_11/1988-08-24.htm

would rejoin Tradition; 2) we would have a foot in the door of modernist Rome for preaching Tradition; 3) we could still go back to our former position in case we were unduly pressured.

Fr Fleichman then explained to the priests of Campos why each of those claims are erroneous:

> 1) The new people that will join you will not desire to convert to true Tradition. They will come to you because the legal obstacles have been removed, and not for reasons of faith. They will be very sympathetic, but they will not be seeking the whole truth with the doctrinal conviction that leads souls to martyrdom.
>
> 2) Being in modernist Rome—and this is proven—invariably results in contamination by the guiding principles of Vatican II, administered in homeopathic doses until the fruit falls, as the St Peter's Fraternity fell.
>
> 3) As for going back: who among them has ever returned to his former position? They would rather concelebrate with the Pope than go back. And if they did go back, what would become of the faithful in their parishes? Would they all go back? How many would be entangled over the question of legality? I consider such an attitude reckless; it does not take into account the constancy of the souls that Providence has entrusted to you. You regularize on paper a phony problem of excommunication, and the faithful have only to follow and obey, and then, tomorrow, to about face and retreat with you. I cannot quite see in this the respect for souls the priestly life requires.[30]

Are There Lessons the SSPX Can Learn from Dom Gerard?

On the website *DICI*—the official communications agency of the Society of St Pus x—there appeared an obituary for Dom Gerard upon his passing in 2008:

> Archbishop Lefebvre was even invited once to preach the annual retreat to the monks at Le Barroux. But "with the passage of time the ghosts of union with the Church and the Benedictine order would wear down the monastery's ability to resist," and in 1988, after the bishops' conse-crations, Dom Gerard, in a declaration...deemed it 'prejudicial to the very Tradition of the Church' to be 'relegated outside of the official

---

30 Fr Lourenco Fleischmann, OSB, "Open Letter to the Priests of Campos," SSPX Asia, October 30, 2001, https://www.sspxasia.com/Documents/Society_of_Saint_Pius_X/Open_Letter_to_the_Priests_of_Campos.htm

visible perimeters of the Church.' As Bishop Tissier de Mallerais notes: 'Archbishop Lefebvre lamented the defection of one for whom he had done so much.' (quotes taken from *Marcel Lefebvre: The Biography*)[31]

How, then, did it all end for Dom Gerard and the Abbey of St Mary Magdalene in Le Barroux? Again, recall that Dom Gerard was promised 1) that he would be recognized "without doctrinal concessions" 2) that he would be "integrated" into the Benedictine Confederation "as we are" 3) that "no silence" would be imposed on his "anti-Modernist preaching" 4) that he would "have a foot in the door of modernist Rome for preaching Tradition" 5) that he believed he could resist contamination from the Conciliar Church and 6) that he thought "many new persons would rejoin Tradition."

In a six part essay titled, "A short history of the ss px," Fr Ramon Angles ss px informs us of Dom Gerard's fate:

> 1988: Another Benedictine with a different concept of loyalty, Dom Gerard Calvet, prior of Le Barroux, breaks with the Archbishop and condemns the episcopal consecrations at which he was present, turning himself into Rome's hands 'without any doctrinal or liturgical concession.' In 1995, Abbot Calvet concelebrates the New Mass with John Paul II in Rome.[32]

If only Dom Gerard had heeded the following words of Archbishop Lefebvre from his sermon during the 1988 consecrations could we actually say: "Thank God for Sainte-Madeleine du Barroux."

> Taking into account the strong will of the present Roman authorities to reduce Tradition to naught, to gather the world to the spirit of Vatican II and the spirit of Assisi, we have preferred to withdraw ourselves and to say that we could not continue. It was not possible. We would have evidently been…putting ourselves into the hands of those who wish to draw us into the spirit of the Council and the spirit of Assisi. This was simply not possible.
>   This is why I sent a letter to the Pope, saying to him very clearly: 'We simply cannot accept this spirit and proposals, despite all the desires which we have to be in full union with you. Given this new spirit which

31 "France: Dom Gerard Passed Away," FSSPX News, http://www.dici.org/en/news/france-dom-grard-passed-away/
32 Fr Ramon Angles, "25 years of the SS PX: Part 5," SS PX, http://sspx.org/en/25-years-of-the-sspx-fr-angles-talk-part-5

now rules in Rome and which you wish to communicate to us, we prefer to continue in Tradition; to keep Tradition while waiting for Tradition to regain its place at Rome, while waiting for Tradition to reassume its place in the Roman authorities, in their minds.' This will last for as long as the Good Lord has foreseen.

If I had made this deal with Rome, by continuing with the agreements we had signed, and by putting them into practice, I would have performed 'Operation Suicide.' There was no choice, we must live![33]

Magnificat Media • August 4, 2016

IS IT A 'MATTER OF JUSTICE' THAT THE SSPX BE GRANTED A PERSONAL PRELATURE?

Over the past several months, there has been a coalescence around the idea that the Society of St Pius x (SSPX) has, as a matter of justice, the "right" to be canonically "regularized" by the Conciliar Church.

Louie Verrechio, *First Things* editor Eliot Milco, and *Catholic Family News* editor John Vennari are all in agreement on this. Others are yet to express support for such a position.

Michael Matt from *The Remnant* has been one of the most skeptical Catholic voices regarding a possible deal (of any kind) between Rome and the SSPX. While commenting on Bishop De Galarreta's sermon from the 2016 ordinations in Winona, Minnesota, Matt wrote the following:

> The question many concerned friends of the SSPX are asking now is: What has changed since 1987 ... other than that the situation in Rome has become much worse? Was Archbishop Lefebvre hasty in 1988, perhaps lacking in due prudence and patience? Or was he right not to trust Rome farther than he could throw Rome?[3435]

While the Archbishop undoubtedly stayed in touch with Rome up until

---

33 Sermon of Archbishop Marcel Lefebvre, Episcopal Consecrations, SSPX Asia, June 30, 1988, https://www.sspxasia.com/Documents/Archbishop-Lefebvre/Episcopal-Consecration. htm

34 Michael Matt, "Bishop de Galarreta on the SSPX 'Recognition' of Vatican II," The Remnant Newspaper, June 8, 2016, https://remnantnewspaper.com/web/index.php?option=com_ k2&view=item&id=2569:bishop-de-galarreta-on-the-sspx-recognition-of-vatican-ii

35 Bishop de Galarreta's Sermon, CathInfo, June 3, 2016, https://www.cathinfo.com/index. php?pretty;board=19;topic=41122.o

the '88 consecrations, his most mature thought on the matter comes from his 1990 book *Spiritual Journey:* "It is a strict duty for every priest who wishes to remain Catholic to separate off from the conciliar church, as long as she does not recover the Tradition of the Magisterium of the Church and of the Catholic Faith!"

What, then, are we to make of the argument that this so-called "regularization" is a matter of "justice"?

It's a question that should be open to discussion, one where charity and ideas—not labels, accusations or vindictiveness—should take center stage. I make no claims to infallibility and am genuinely interested in the views of others. Getting this question right is of the highest importance. If I am wrong, I will recant my position. Countless souls are at stake and I only wish to humbly add my voice to the debate, even though there are some who have grappled with this issue longer than I have been alive!

The first thing that comes to my mind is Louis Vueillot's book *The Liberal Illusion.* Vueillot was a 19th century French anti-liberal. Among the many excellent points raised in his book, the ones most pertinent to the "regularization" of the Society of St Pius x are his comments on Liberal Catholicism.

Liberal Catholics, Vueillot writes, "glorify prudence to the point of madness." They also clamor for "a free Church" in "a free State." Additionally, they speak of "independence for the Church from the state" but, in reality, they wish to make Catholicism reliant upon "the goodwill of her enemies."

As I reflect upon these points, what comes to mind is the following analogy, taken directly from Vueillot's book:

> Imagine a King deposed from his throne, the last, best hope of his conquered fatherland, who was suddenly to declare that he considered himself justly deposed and that he only aspired to enjoy his personal possessions according to the laws governing all citizens, beneath the protection of the very men who were plundering his subjects.
>
> The King, we would imagine, would disgrace himself in vain. No one would believe him. Those to whom he offered to sell his rights and his honor would tell him: 'Are you mad, you are King!'

How does this example apply to the Society of St Pius x? Well, if you believe that the Society is Tradition, if you believe that Tradition is Catholicism, and if you believe Modernists are the enemies of Tradition, then you can say that in the analogy above, the Society of St Pius x is "the King" and the modernist progressives now occupying Rome are "the revolutionaries" who at Vatican II unjustly deposed the King from his palace. If this is accurate, then true justice can only be served when the occupiers reject their doctrinal errors, embrace Catholicism (Tradition) and restore the King to his throne. Such an act would fulfill the right all Catholics have to a modernist-free Church. It would not, as far as I can tell, be an act of justice for a King (SSPX) to be granted the status and rights (a practical, non-doctrinal deal) that come with life as a commoner under revolutionaries still convinced of their errors.

From what I can gather, and I may be wrong, Louis Vueillot would have also considered the desire to "regularize" the SSPX with the revolutionaries in Rome as an instance of Liberal Catholicism, as he may well have viewed it as nothing more than a wish for "a free Society of St Pius X" in "a free Conciliar Church," which is simply an updating of the Liberal Catholic mantra "a free Church" in "a free State."

It should be noted that Archbishop Lefebvre's focus was not so much on getting the modernist progressives to recognize he himself as Catholic, but rather, on getting them to re-instate "the King" to his rightful place. Here are his thoughts while speaking with *Fideliter* in late 1988:

> Supposing that Rome calls for a renewed dialogue, then, I will put conditions. I shall not accept being in the position where I was put during the dialogue. No more. I will place the discussion at the doctrinal level: Do you agree with the great encyclicals of all the popes who preceded you? If you do not accept the doctrine of your predecessors, it is useless to talk! As long as you do not accept the correction of the Council, in consideration of the doctrine of these popes, your predecessors, no dialogue is possible. It is useless.[36]

Lefebvre believed that anything less than a full conversion by the Romans would spell doom for Tradition, as it would be akin to placing Catholicism into the hands of the revolutionaries. Or, as Veuillot would say, it would be akin to making Catholicism dependent upon "the goodwill of her enemies."

Archbishop Lefebvre also seems to have been given the great blessing to understand that his fight was precisely the one Veuillot was engaged in in the 1800s. In 1990, His Excellency acknowledged that reality when he said the following:

> In the last few weeks (since I am now unemployed!) I have been spending a little time re-reading the book by Emmanuel Barbier on liberal

---

36 Interview of Archbishop Lefebvre given to *Fideliter* magazine, November-December 1988, SSPX Asia, https://www.sspxasia.com/Documents/Archbishop-Lefebvre/Archbishop_Lefebvre_and_the_Vatican/Part_11/1988-11.htm

Catholicism. And it is striking to see how our fight now is exactly the same fight as was being fought then by the great Catholics of the 19th century... Well, we find ourselves in the same situation. We must not be under any illusions. Hence, we should have no hesitation or fear, hesitation such as, "Why should we be going on our own? After all, why not join Rome, why not join the pope?" Yes, if Rome and the pope were in line with Tradition, if they were carrying on the work of all the popes of the 19th and the first half of the 20th century, of course. So we do not have to worry. We must after all trust in the grace of God. "What is going to happen? How is it all going to end?" That is God's secret. Mystery. But that we must fight the ideas presently fashionable in Rome.[37]

Now, it may be said that Archbishop Lefebvre was never promised what the Society is (allegedly) promised today—a unilateral, one-sided "recognition" with no strings attached. That proposal may be offered to the Society at some point in the future, but to the best of my knowledge that is not what is on the table at present.

Moreover, the past several months suggest that Rome has no intention of simply "recognizing" the Society as they are. As Cardinal Muller's remarks as well as Pope Francis' words indicate, "the revolutionaries" have no desire to let "the King" be recognized *as King.* "Vatican 11," the pope believes, "has its value." It is obvious that the occupying powers have always had for their end game the aim of bringing "the King" over to their revolutionary ideas.

As a closing comment, allow me to suppose that some sort of deal will be struck between the Society and the revolutionaries in the near future. What will be said then? Will it be an instance of Rome "recognizing" Tradition?

I want to provide you a quote from Bishop Bernard Fellay from March 2002 regarding the Campos-Rome deal. Granted, the Campos-Rome deal will likely be different from anything the current sspx leadership would ever agree to with Rome, but still, the good Bishop's words do provide us with some insight:

> What kind of Rome do we have when it can sign an agreement with *Campos* and in the same week can do something like *Assisi 11?* They definitely will not say "We recognize Tradition" in any universal sense. But *Campos* is contented because Rome has recognized Tradition in *Campos.* But has it, really? If Rome truly recognized Tradition anywhere

37 Archbishop Lefebvre, "Two Years after the Consecrations," sspx, September 6, 1990, https://sspx.org/en/two-years-after-consecrations

it wouldn't be able to have an Assisi II, the very contrary of Tradition. It is impossible to see in the recognition of *Campos* a recognition of Tradition.[38]

Let's update that with what could be written if Rome and the Society come to some sort of an arrangement in 2016:

What kind of Rome do we have when it can sign an agreement with *the Society of St Pius X* and in the same year can do something like *celebrate the 500th anniversary of the Protestant Reformation?* They definitely will not say "We recognize Tradition" in any universal sense. But the sspx is contented because Rome has recognized Tradition in *the Society.* But has it, really? If Rome truly recognized Tradition anywhere *it wouldn't celebrate the 500th anniversary of the Protestant Reformation,* the very contrary of Tradition. It is impossible to see in the recognition of *the Society* a recognition of Tradition.

Does that sound like "justice" has been served?

Magnificat Media • June 11, 2016

FRENCH SSPX DISTRICT SUPERIOR SAYS IT IS 'NECESSARY TO CONSIDER' CONSECRATING NEW BISHOPS

The district superior of the Society of St Pius X (sspx) in France has published a letter to friends and benefactors laying out arguments for why the time has possibly arrived to consecrate more bishops.

Fr Benoît de Jorna was tapped to lead the French district in 2018 by sspx Superior General Fr Davide Pagliarani. De Jorna previously served as rector of the Society's flagship seminary in Ecône, Switzerland for many years.

On Wednesday, June 19, de Jorna, who was also the superior of France from 1994 until 1996, issued a statement titled "Let's be strong!" on the Society's *La Porte Latine* website.[39] In his remarks, de Jorna recalled that sspx

---

38 Bishop Bernard Fellay, "Rome, the sspx, Campos, Assisi, etc." Angelus Online, May, 2002, www.angelusonline.org/index.php?section=articles&subsection=show_article&article_id=2140

39 Fr Benoît de Jorna, "Let's be Strong! Letter to Friends and Benefactors," La Porte Latine, June 19, 2024, https://laportelatine.org/actualite/lettre-aux-amis-et-bienfaiteurs-n95-soyons-forts

founder Archbishop Marcel Lefebvre attempted to avoid consecrating bishops without Rome's permission but that he ultimately had to do so for "the Church" to "continue."

Fr de Jorna further observed that the SSPX has grown to over 700 priests from the 200 it had in the 1980s. Schools, priories, and the overall missionary work of the SSPX has also increased. This has made life "easier" for Traditional Catholics, he said, but it is also "a danger, because it can lead us to fall asleep in comfort, and lose the vigor, dynamism and impetus of our spiritual life."

De Jorna proceeded to argue that Catholics young and old need to be "strong" and not compromise the faith in the years ahead. He then noted that "we're also going to need [the virtue of strength] in the near future to face up to the ecclesial event that's beginning to take shape."

That "ecclesial event," he said, is the consecration of new bishops.

"Since the ecclesiastical situation has not improved since 1988, it has become necessary to consider giving them assistants, who will one day become their replacements," de Jorna explained, referencing the Society's three bishops. "When such a decision is announced by the Superior General, we can expect a media frenzy against the 'fundamentalists', the 'rebels', the 'schismatics', the 'disobedient', to name but a few. At that point, we'll have to face contradictions, insults, scorn, rejection, perhaps even break-ups with people close to us."

De Jorna concluded by recalling that "the virtue of strength will be very necessary for us on this crucial occasion, and through it we must all demonstrate our absolute fidelity to the Catholic faith."

A Much Needed Event

De Jorna's letter is not the first time the consecration of bishops has been addressed by the Society. The matter was raised in June 2023 after Traditionalists on social media speculated that an announcement on the subject was imminent. Fr Jean-Michel Gleize, a professor at the SSPX's Ecône seminary, published a rebuttal on the Society's website on June 5 dismissing the allegations as "tall tales" and "rumors."[40]

At present, the SSPX has three bishops who act as "auxiliary bishops" without jurisdiction: Bishop Bernard Tissier de Mallerais, who is 78 and was born in France; Bishop Alfonso de Galarreta, who is 67 and was born in Spain; and Bishop Bernard Fellay, 66, who hails from Switzerland. Bishop Richard Williamson of England, 84, was also a bishop of the Society until his expulsion in 2012.

---

40 Fr Jean-Michel Gleize, "Bishops for the SSPX to be Consecrated on June 30, 2023?" SSPX, June 5, 2023, https://sspx.org/en/news/bishops-sspx-be-consecrated-june-30-2023-29423

Williamson's dismissal came after discussions between the SSPX and Rome were taking place in the early 2010s about a possible prelature. De Jorna, Gleize, de Gallareta, and several other priests of the Society had been meeting with members of the Ecclesia Dei community in Rome, as well as with the Congregation of the Doctrine of the Faith. Their reconciliation efforts ended primarily due to pushback within the Society from clergy like Williamson, who maintain that the SSPX's founder Archbishop Marcel Lefebvre laid down a policy of no practical negotiations with "the Conciliar Church" until it came back doctrinally to Tradition.

The topic of bishops for the SSPX has been a particular point of conversation for both priests and laity associated with the SSPX in recent years as its current bishops continue to age. When Williamson consecrated French priest Fr Jean-Michel Faure in 2015 for the SSPX "Resistance," the SSPX issued a statement condemning the move, arguing that the two "no longer recognize the Roman authorities, except in a purely rhetorical manner."[41] Williamson has performed more than five similar consecrations since then, though the Society has not commented on them. Faure was one of the original priests Lefebvre asked to be consecrated in 1988 but he refused the request.[42]

One Traditional Catholic who spoke to LifeSite earlier today on condition of anonymity said if the SSPX were to consecrate one or even multiple bishops without Rome's approval, they would be acting "hypocritically" in that they would be doing precisely what they rebuked Williamson and Faure for doing.

De Jorna's letter is especially notable in that the SSPX's French district is generally considered one of its more conservative regions. In 2017, seven high-ranking priests in charge of the country's "deaneries" read a joint statement from the pulpit without permission. The letter denounced the SSPX's acceptance of the Vatican's decision to allow local ordinaries to recognize marriages of faithful who attend Society chapels. The priests argued that the measure was a deceptive act and that there is "a real danger in placing one's salvation in the hands of pastors who are imbued with this 'adulterous' spirit."[43] The priests were dismissed from their posts soon after.

Given that de Jorna's letter was published just two days after news broke

41 "Consecration of Fr Jean-Michel Faure," SSPX, Menzingen, Switzerland, March 19, 2015, https://sspx.org/en/publications/consecration-fr-jean-michel-faure-36001
42 "Interview with Fr Jean-Michel Faure," Dominicans of Avrille, https://dominican-savrille.us/interview-with-fr-jean-michel-faure/
43 Quoted in Michael Matt, "Vatican Provision for SSPX Marriages Sparks Major Controversy in French District," The Remnant Newspaper, May 11, 2017, https://remnantnews-paper.com/web/index.php/component/k2/item/3194-vatican-provision-for-sspx-marriages-sparks-major-controversy-in-french-district

that the Vatican has its sights set on canceling the Latin Mass, speculation has been rampant about the future of Tradition. It has previously been theorized that the s s p x may welcome more diocesan bishops like the late Vitus Huonder, the former ordinary of Chur, Switzerland, into their ranks. The s s p x also may simply choose to elevate priests from within to the bishopric. The number the s s p x may select and whether a tacit agreement with Rome has already been made on the matter is not readily known, though its current Superior General, Don Davide Pagliarani, has said they would ask Rome for permission and that if it was not be given they would proceed anyway.[44]

LifeSiteNews • June 20, 2024

44 Kennedy Hall, "Is the s s p x About to Consecrate New Bishops?" OnePeterFive, April 28, 2023, https://onepeterfive.com/sspx-new-bishops/

PART 2

STATE

CHAPTER VI: CATHOLIC SOCIAL TEACHING

IS THE GHETTO ALL CATHOLICS HAVE LEFT?

I'll be honest, it was difficult to watch the goings-on in the state of Arizona this past week. On second thought, "difficult" probably isn't the right word. In fact, I know it isn't. There really isn't a single term that can describe how disgusted I felt when I learned corporate interests, the mainstream media, and anti-Christian zealots successfully bullied Republican Governor Jan Brewer into vetoing a bill that would have upheld one of the most basic freedoms afforded to American citizens under the US Constitution: religious liberty.[45]

Matt Lewis, writing for the *Daily Caller*, describes the situation by noting that we have "reached a point in the gay rights debate where all the low-hanging fruit has been picked. We are now entering into the zero-sum game phase of the debate, where gay rights and religious liberty must collide."[46]

Lewis is right. I don't see things ending well for socially conservative Americans. Simply put, the country's political elite have more or less convinced the general population that religion—Christianity in particular—is the enemy of a civilized society. Toleration for it is no longer acceptable.

In an essay for *USA Today*, left-leaning columnist Kirsten Powers exhibited this dangerous worldview when she told her readers that "Christians backing this bill are essentially arguing for homosexual Jim Crow laws."[47]

Similar hyperbolic claims were regurgitated ad nauseam on networks like MSNBC. Thankfully, more than a few conservatives have responded to Powers' claims, among them Ryan T. Anderson of the Heritage Foundation. Pat Buchanan recently published a column titled "How Freedom Dies" that provides helpful insight on the situation as well.[48]

Be that as it may, I think Catholics in general have taken a rather myopic view towards the entire situation. To truly understand what happened in

---

45 Thomas Peters, "Arizona: Losing Our Religion," CatholicVote, February 28, 2014, https://www.catholicvote.org/arizona-losing-our-religion/

46 Matt Lewis, "When 'leave us alone' became 'bake us a cake!'" Daily Caller, February 25, 2014, https://dailycaller.com/2014/02/25/when-leave-us-alone-became-bake-us-a-cake/

47 Kirsten Powers, "Jim Crow laws for gays and lesbians?" USA Today, February 19, 2014, https://www.usatoday.com/story/opinion/2014/02/18/gays-lesbians-kansas-bill-religious-freedom-christians-column/5588643/

48 Pat Buchanan, "How Freedom Dies," Buchanan.org, February 25, 2014, https://buchanan.org/blog/freedom-dies-6256

NAVIGATING THE CRISIS IN THE CHURCH

Arizona we need to put it in its proper context, not only in context of the past several years but of the past several decades, even centuries. Then, and only then, will we have a better grasp as to what really happened.

Politics Will Not Save Us

It is often argued that Catholics must engage in the "battle of ideas" with those who disagree with them. Doing this is the only option we have in our pluralistic world. Anything else—calling for the restoration of the Social Kingship of Christ, for instance—is a waste of time. Catholics must seek out religious Americans, regardless of creed, and collaborate with them or none of us will survive.

As well intentioned this course of action might be, it fails to account for a few things. One, it assumes our enemies even care about having honest political discourse. Two, there are more Catholics fighting in the public square now more than any other time in history. Yet America is more anti-Catholic than ever before. Lastly, it doesn't consider the possibility that modernity and the Catholic religion are inherently at odds with one another and that efforts starting from within such a political system, no matter how noble they may be, are more or less doomed from the start.

Catholics who point these things out are sometimes referred to as inward looking and nostalgic for the Middle Ages. I have heard it said that a desire to "go back" to those "dark" times will only amplify attacks and usher in a sort of "Catholic ghetto."

This is entirely false. The ghetto has been forced upon us. And what went down in Arizona this past week is just the latest evidence in a long line of evidence of that being the case.

Our Liberal Culture Shows No Signs of Slowing Down

CatholicVote blogger Steve Skojec recently reported that federal health regulators are thinking about allowing a child to be created from the DNA of three people.[1] It hasn't been approved yet, but who can doubt that this won't be permitted, and that other countries will do the same in the near future? States like California already allow kids to have more than two legal parents.[2]

1 Steve Skojec, "Not Science Fiction: Evaluating 3-Parent Embryo Creation," CatholicVote, February 25, 2014, https://www.catholicvote.org/not-science-fiction-fda-evaluating-3-parent-embryo-creation/
2 Aaron Sankin, "California Multiple Parents Bill Passes Assembly," Huffington Post, August 28, 2012, https://www.huffpost.com/entry/california-multiple-parents-bill_n_1837806

CHAPTER VI: CATHOLIC SOCIAL TEACHING

Immoral in-vitro fertilization and surrogacy are also taking place every day. The likelihood that these will be curtailed over the long run is slim to none.

Speaking of California, have you heard about its new transgender law?[3] I don't have the time to go into it—just like I don't have the time to discuss everything included in Massachusetts' or Colorado's transgender laws[4]—but suffice it to say that no matter how many God-fearing lawmakers Catholics help get elected in those states, the chance that they will suddenly embrace the notion that "God created them male and female" is as likely as North Korea allowing its citizens the freedom of speech.

What's more, marriage laws are being knocked down across the country like dominoes. Any honest person knows there is no coming back from this. The next logical step, of course, is polygamy. Websites like *Slate* are already clamoring for that. I'd venture to say that within my lifetime such unions will be recognized as marriages.

Although I don't think I'll live to see incestuous and pedophilia marriages take place, those are undoubtedly on the radar of a number of left-wing intellectuals, who, as of late, are seemingly doing a great job of indoctrinating their students, especially the ones who attend Swarthmore College in Pennsylvania.

In a recent visit to Swarthmore, Princeton Professors Robert George and Dr Cornell West held a town hall with students. The students, however, were having none of it.

"What really bothered me is, the whole idea is that at a liberal arts college, we need to be hearing a diversity of opinion," one undergraduate complained. "I don't think we should be tolerating George's conservative views because that dominant culture embeds these deep inequalities in our society." Another student said that "when academic community observes research promoting or justifying oppression, it should ensure that this research does not continue."[5]

So, instead of academic freedom, young people are being taught that conservatives don't even deserve to be heard! That they are on their face unworthy of civil conversation. How can a Catholic hope to thrive, let alone survive, in such an inhospitable environment?

3 Perry Chiaramonte, "California's transgender law allows male high schooler to make girls' softball team," Fox News, February 14, 2014, https://web.archive.org/web/20140215020002/https://www.foxnews.com/us/2014/02/14/california-transgender-law-allows-male-high-schooler-to-make-girls-softball/

4 Stephen Kokx, "Get ready to hear the term 'transgender rights' a lot more," CatholicVote, March 25, 2013, https://www.catholicvote.org/get-ready-to-hear-the-term-transgendered-rights-a-lot-more/

5 Quoted in Jonah Goldberg, "When 'diversity' is an excuse for intolerance," The Kansas City Star, February 22, 2014, http://www.kansascity.com/2014/02/22/4840948/jonah-goldberg-when-diversity.html#storylink=cpy

Catholics Must Change Their Approach

There are dozens of other examples that indicate the modern world has rejected the Catholic faith and that Catholics have barely evangelized the culture around them. We are living in an era when the Church's teachings are viewed as anachronistic and backwards looking, to put it kindly. It's not that I don't think Catholics shouldn't be involved in politics at all. But an honest look at how things have unfolded these past several decades should force all of us to realize that fighting our enemies on *their* terms with *their* terminology isn't working.

It seems to me that we're putting too much trust in the ways of man and too little trust in the ways of God. We are in the midst of a battle that is much larger than we know and the solution isn't just going to be helping the right politician get elected to Congress—or even the White House. Catholics need to take a long, hard look at themselves and acknowledge that whether we want it or not, the "Catholic ghetto" is here and that there's very little we can do to change that without Divine Intervention. Our enemies have grown too strong and the methods we've relied upon, especially since the 1960s, aren't working. Change is desperately needed.

CatholicVote • March 1, 2014

POLITICALLY CORRECT CATHOLICISM: REFUTING THE ERRORS OF ROBERT GEORGE

Quite a few years ago, Ronald Reagan said "at the heart of conservatism is libertarianism."[6]

Having once fallen prey to libertarianism myself, I can attest to the fact that the progression out of that oversimplified (and heretical) worldview can be quite difficult. Those who do not typically end up worshipping free market economists Milton Friedman and Ayn Rand.

In a similar way, many young, impressionable "conservative" Catholics (all of whom oddly respond "John Paul II" when asked "who is your favorite pope?") are held captive to—often unbeknownst to them—Americanist-tainted political views with help from men like Professor Robert George.

Once described by the *New York Times* as "the Conservative-Christian Big Thinker," George, who teaches at Princeton—and who has garnered worldwide

---

6 Interview with Reason Magazine, July 1975, Quoted in Manuel Klausner, "Inside Ronald Reagan," Reason, https://reason.com/1975/07/01/inside-ronald-reagan/

acclaim from not only Jews and Muslims, but also from those who despise Traditional Catholics—is the poster child of "neoconservative" Catholicism.[7] When you listen to Professor George speak, you first notice his mild manner and clear communication style. In a certain way, he comes of as the secular equivalent of Bishop Robert Barron. One has to ask themselves: could this really be the man secular progressives so fear?

Indeed he is. And just like Bishop Barron, he is someone Catholics should also fear. Why? Because he presents his ideas as if they are Catholic teaching when in reality they are laced with liberal errors.

Catholicism is More Than Defending Morality

Several weeks ago Professor George, who identifies as a proud "orthodox Vatican II Catholic," spoke at the Legatus Summit in Orlando, Florida.[8] Legatus is a community of wealthy Catholic business leaders who presumably infuse their religious beliefs with their professional lives.

In his speech, George said, "it is no longer easy to be a faithful Christian, a good Catholic, an authentic witness to the truths of the Gospel."[9]

But what does George mean when he says we must be a "witness to" the "truths of the Gospel?" LifeSiteNews reported the event in the following way: "Professor George added that people can still safely identify as 'Catholic' as long as they don't believe, or will at least be completely silent about, 'what the Church teaches on issues such as marriage and sexual morality and the sanctity of human life.'"[10]

These remarks are almost word for word what George said at the 2014 National Catholic Prayer breakfast, namely, that Christian moral teaching is politically incorrect and that Catholics will be persecuted for upholding it.[11]

7 Samantha Contis, "The Conservative-Christian Big Thinker," The New York Times, December 16, 2009, https://www.nytimes.com/2009/12/20/magazine/20george-t.html
8 Ryan Shinkel, "The Catholic Church in America: An Interview with Robert P. George," Ethika Politika, November 12, 2014, https://web.archive.org/web/20160621133612/https://ethikapolitika.org/2014/11/12/catholic-church-america-interview-robert-george/
9 Patrick Novecosky, "Legates challenged to become 'Uncomfortable Catholics," Legatus, March 1, 2016, https://legatus.org/news/legates-challenged-to-become-uncomfortable-catholics
10 John-Henry Westen, "Princeton's Robert George: Are you ready to pay the price? The days of socially acceptable Christianity are over," LifeSiteNews, February 6, 2016, https://www.lifesitenews.com/news/princetons-robert-george-are-you-ready-to-pay-the-price-the-days-of-sociall/
11 Betsy Rothstein, "Catholic Leaders Sound Alarm At Prayer Breakfast: 'The Days of Acceptable Christianity Are Over," Daily Caller, May 13, 2014, https://dailycaller.com/2014/05/13/catholic-leaders-sound-alarm-at-prayer-breakfast-the-days-of-acceptable-christianity-are-

To the "conservative" Catholic mind, Professor George comes off as a sort of prophet calling out progressives for persecuting religious Americans while issuing a bold and daring call to action. In reality, things are a bit more complex.

In an interview with *Ethika Politika* following the 2014 prayer breakfast, George was asked to clarify what he meant when he said the days of "comfortable Catholicism" are over. Here is what he said:

> I mean that actively and publicly witnessing to moral truths proclaimed by, among other traditions of faith, the Catholic Church—particularly truths about the sanctity of human life in all stages and conditions and the dignity of marriage as the conjugal union of husband and wife—is no longer welcome, or in some places even tolerated, by those occupying the commanding heights of culture.[12]

It can be difficult to detect where the error is here. But Thomas Storck, a well known Catholic writer, caught wind, and in the comment section of that story, spoke up:

> Does anyone else find it odd that instead of focusing on the evangelical duty of preaching the Gospel in its fullness and converting people to the true Faith, he focuses on a subset of moral truths—even if they are important moral truths? The Apostles did not conceive of their mission as the moral reformation of pagan Greco-Roman society. They understood it to be the conversion of that society, after which the moral reform would certainly follow. Our Lord said, Go forth and preach the Gospel and baptize.[13]

Storck is absolutely right. George's intentional—and it is intentional—focus on "a subset of moral truths" instead of preaching the *theological truths* of the Gospel to convert people to the Catholic faith is a direct result of his embrace of what the Church has always condemned as "Liberal Catholicism." In other words, politically correct Catholicism.

over/
    12 Ryan Shinkel, "The Catholic Church in America: An Interview with Robert P. George," Ethika Politika, November 12, 2014, https://web.archive.org/web/20160621133612/https://ethikapolitika.org/2014/11/12/catholic-church-america-interview-robert-george/
    13 Ibid.

What is 'Orthodox Vatican II Catholicism' Anyway?

At the heart of the Catholic faith are some pretty bold, dare I say "politically incorrect" claims, claims that George himself, like Holy Mother Church, shelved at Vatican II order to improve relations with non-Catholics.

For example, instead of preaching that Christ should be recognized as King of all nations, so-called "orthodox Vatican II Catholicism" says man has a natural right to follow whatever religion they want and that "Judeo-Christian" values and a general understanding of the natural law is what can secure human flourishing and a lasting peace.

What's more, instead of proclaiming that Jesus Christ is the way, the truth, and the life, and that outside the Catholic Church there is no salvation, "orthodox Vatican II Catholicism" says non-Catholic religions possess "elements of sanctification" and have a right to spread the "special value" of their false beliefs in public.[14][15]

Lastly, instead of reminding Jews that they need to convert to be saved, and that the Old Covenant has been fulfilled, "orthodox Vatican II Catholicism" says Jews are our "elder brothers" and that we need not seek their conversion.[16]

When you right get down to it, George's "orthodox Vatican II Catholicism" is already a politically correct creation that avoids the hard sayings of the Gospel.

Tradition is the Faith

In his speech at the Legatus Summit, George asked the following question: "Will we seek to 'fit in,' to be accepted, to live comfortably in the new Babylon? If so, our silence will speak. Its words will be the words of Peter, warming himself by the fire: 'Jesus the Nazarene? I tell you, I do not know the man.'"

Odd, isn't it, to hear George speak of Peter's denial of Christ when we have a pope today who thinks proselytism is "solemn nonsense" and who just several weeks ago said followers of Judaism need not accept Christ.[17] Talk about "not knowing" Our Lord!

The sad reality is that the Church decided to "live comfortably in the new

14 *Lumen Gentium*, 8

15 *Dignitatis Humanae*, 4

16 John Paul II, Speech to Roman Synagogue, April, 14, 1986, see New York Times, https://www.nytimes.com/1986/04/14/world/text-of-pope-s-speech-at-rome-synagogue-you-are-our-elder-brothers.html

17 Rosie Scammell, "Pope Francis at Rome synagogue: God's covenant with Jews 'irrevocable," RNS News, January 17, 2016, https://religionnews.com/2016/01/17/pope-francis-rome-synagogue-gods-covenant-jews-irrevocable/

Babylon" that George speaks about when, at Vatican II, it opted to go silent on the theological truths the Church taught for centuries. Sure, she didn't go absolutely quiet on birth control, divorce, and human sexuality in the decades that followed. And it still draws down the fury of global elites for defending those doctrines. But it is precisely because Rome failed to stand by the Kingship of Christ and the prophetic papal condemnations of Liberal Catholicism in the 19th century that the culture wars have largely been won by the political left today.

What is needed now is not more vague generalities about "the Gospel" but more preaching about the Kingship of Christ. We also could use a lot less "dialogue" with false religions and more denunciations of the errors those religions promote. Catholics should also stop complaining about how hard it is to be a conservative and instead more loudly proclaim the supernatural truths of the faith they claim they adhere to. Put another way, what we need today is not more Robert George-inspired, politically correct Catholicism but more St Pope Pius X-inspired, politically incorrect Traditional Catholicism.

akaCatholic.com • February 8, 2016

ANOTHER FAILED FORTNIGHT FOR FREEDOM CAMPAIGN

From June 21st until July 4th, the United States Conference of Catholic Bishops (USCCB) will hold yet another "Fortnight for Freedom" event. 2016 marks, I believe, the fifth year the USCCB has decided to conduct this pathetic affair. The theme for this year is "Witness to Freedom."

In an effort to gin up support, American bishops have taken out ads on various Catholic media outlets. The USCCB has also published an open letter for this year's campaign. I'd like to go through that and provide commentary on each paragraph. Here is its opening statement:

> For decades, Catholics have worked to serve the common good in the United States. We have faced opposition at times, but our commitment to doing the works of mercy through our institutions, like hospitals, schools, and charities, has remained steadfast.

This sort of language is all too common in the Church today. Is the USCCB ignorant of the fact that "the common good" includes supernatural realities as well, and that doing corporal works of mercy are only half of the Church's mission? Hospitals, schools and charities are important no doubt. But what does it matter if a man is healthy, educated, and sheltered but does not have the Bread of Life in him? The one-sided focus of this first paragraph is to start out on terms acceptable to liberals. Next paragraph:

> In recent years, a new set of challenges has arisen. Laws, regulations, and executive orders have been passed that would require Catholics, as well as other people of faith both within and beyond religious institutions, to engage in activities that they believe to be immoral. In other words, ironically, we are told that we must drop our religious tenets if we want to live out our faith in service to others.

While President Obama certainly has been guilty of pushing laws that discriminate against the Church, the real blame falls on Vatican II when She decided to no longer defend the Social Kingship of Christ and instead bought into the idea that a "Free Church" in a "Free State" could actually secure the liberty necessary for Her to fulfill Her earthly mission.

In 2012, the Society of St Pius X pointed out why the Council is the real culprit in a forcefully written essay. US bishops at Vatican II "thought that cozying up to the liberal establishment would bring to the American Church peace," the SSPX rightly stated. But, "as it was not based upon Truth, it was ultimately a false peace and doomed to fail." As a result, "we are today witnessing the fulfillment of the famous quip 'the revolution eats it own.' We are now face-to-face with the outcome of the American bishops' support of religious liberty as they are being coerced to jettison the Church's moral teachings."[18]

It is also worth noting how the bishops use the phrase "other people of faith." Faith is a virtue. It allows the intellect to submit to the truths of the Catholic religion. Persons who are not Catholic, strictly speaking, do not possess faith. Thus, they cannot be considered "people of faith." Modernists, on the other hand, hold that faith is something welling up from the innermost dwellings of the human being and is a sort of sentimental belief in a higher power. This is not Catholic. The bishops are betraying their Modernist theology here.

Next, the bishops say that certain laws require Catholics to "engage in activities that *they believe to be* immoral." Why not just say, "these laws require Catholics to engage in activities that *are* immoral due to them being against the will of God and leading countless souls to hell"? Arguing that Catholics "believe these laws to be immoral" is a waste of time. It is an appeal to emotion. Instead of speaking in objective terms, the bishops are relying on subjectivism and playing into the hands of Democrats, who will simply

---

18 "Our First, Most Cherished Liberty: problematic," SSPX District of the US, April 17, 2012, sspx.org/en/news-events/news/our-first-most-cherished-liberty-problematic-706

respond: "well, *we believe* these laws *are not immoral.* Human rights demand that they be recognized!"

Next paragraph:

> The USCCB is working with Stonyhurst College in England to coordinate a US tour of relics of Saints Thomas More and John Fisher, two exemplary 16th century Catholics who bore witness to freedom in the face of a government that sought to violate the conscience rights of its citizens.

St Thomas More and St John Fisher did not die for "freedom of conscience," at least not in the sense the USCCB is using that phrase. They died as martyrs for the Catholic faith, the one true religion established by Jesus Christ. Dying for that is not the same as someone who follows a false religion and who is persecuted by their government for those erroneous beliefs. To equate the two is nothing short of blasphemy.

The bishops continue:

> St Edith Stein found freedom in the truth of the gospel. Blessed Oscar Romero found freedom in speaking out for the poor. The Martyrs of Compiègne found freedom in offering their lives as martyrs for their country, roiled by revolution.
>
> All of these Witnesses to Freedom found freedom in Jesus Christ. And that freedom was and is not a freedom of indifference, a freedom to simply do whatever we want. Rather, Christian freedom means freedom to put our faith into action by serving others, including our neighbors.
>
> One way that Catholics have served our neighbors is by building institutions, which have become vital to the fabric of American society. We seek to build up the common good through our obedience to the gospel of Jesus Christ.
>
> It is through this service that we find true freedom. We ask for the space to continue to serve the common good.

Notice how the bishops use equivocal and generic language? They are trying to appeal to as broad of an audience as possible. But employing this tactic comes at the expense of Catholic-specific language such as: "Our obedience is to the one true Church Christ established by Jesus Christ," which could have easily been used instead.

The bishops further speak about how the Church "finds true freedom" in "building institutions" that have become "vital to the fabric of American society." In truth, "obedience" to "the gospel of Jesus" requires the bishops to teach citizens the Catholic faith, and not just perform corporal works of mercy for them. The USCCB's language indicates they believe the mission of the Catholic Church is really nothing more than a non-profit concerned with the temporal well-being of men when in truth the Church "builds up the common good" of any society when it wins converts to the Catholic faith. It best "serves" nations, in other words, by giving its inhabitants the Bread of Life and forgiving them their sins. The Mass and the sacraments is what the Church truly offers the United States. It is quite telling that the USCCB did not mention this.

This year's Fortnight for Freedom campaign will be a epic failure, just as it has been the past several years. God will not allow it to succeed. Our God is a jealous God who wants society for himself. He wants bishops to "Witness to Truth" not "Witness to Freedom." The Fortnight for Freedom does not ask for this. It shamefully attempts to use the language of liberalism against itself, but in so doing turns the Church into a beggar pleading for scraps from the table of modern politics. Saints Thomas More and John Fisher are rolling over in their graves.

Magnificat Media • June 15, 2016

AMERICAN CATHOLICS OR CATHOLIC AMERICANS?

A 2015 Pew Research poll has found, among other things, that 1 in 4 Catholics living in the United States have experienced a divorce and that 4 in 10 have cohabited with a member of the opposite sex. The poll also showed that 66% of Catholics do not believe it is a sin to use contraceptives and that half of US Catholics support "gay marriage."[19]

In 2014, the Center for Applied Research in the Apostolate reported similar findings. Since the year 2000, 14 million Catholics living in the United States have left the faith. School attendance over that period dropped by 19%, infant baptisms by 28%, and marriages by 41%.[20]

With statistics like these, it's safe to say there is little to no difference in how the majority of Catholics living in the United States and their non-Catholic neighbors behave.

19 "US Catholics open to Non-Traditional Families," Pew Research Center, September 2, 2015, https://www.pewresearch.org/religion/2015/09/02/u-s-catholics-open-to-non-traditional-families/

20 "Frequently Requested Church Statistics," Center for Applied Research in the Apostolate, https://cara.georgetown.edu/faqs

Modern churchmen like to argue that this can be fixed with a more robust implementation of Vatican II. "The laity have not been properly catechized," they will often say. "More time is needed to cure what ails the People of God." St Alphonsus, on the other hand, places the blame for confused laity directly on priests: "The good morals and the salvation of the people depend on good pastors. If there is a good priest in charge of the parish, you will soon see devotion flourishing and people frequenting the Sacraments and honoring the practice of mental prayer. Hence the proverb: like pastor, like parish."[21]

Archbishop Marcel Lefebvre, the founder of the Society of St Pius X, lived by those words. He formed priests for decades according to the Church's traditional methods. But he was also keenly aware of the effects the modern world has on souls. "Our cultural and social atmosphere is so imbued with [secularism] that we are continually inhaling it and it constitutes a real danger even for souls that should be immune," he once wrote.[22]

Orestes Brownson, a 19th century Catholic intellectual who died in 1876, would have agreed with that assessment. Brownson is an oft-overlooked figure in Catholic history. Before converting to Catholicism, he subscribed to, at various points in his life, Congregationalism, Presbyterianism, Unitarianism, and Transcendentalism. In a letter written to Fr Isaac Hecker (the founder of the Paulist Order) in 1870, Brownson said the following:

> Instead of regarding the Church as having advantages here which she has nowhere else, I think she has here a more subtle and powerful enemy to combat than in any of the old monarchical nations of the world. Say what we will, we have made little impression on our old American population.
>
> Catholics as well as others imbibe the spirit of the country; imbibe from infancy the spirit of independence, freedom from all restraint, and unbounded license. So far are we from converting the country, we cannot hold our own.[23]

Three years later, Brownson offered his most mature thought on the subject in his *Brownson's Quarterly Review*:

21 Jean-Baptiste Chautard, *The Soul of the Apostolate*, TAN Books, Rockford, Illinois, 2008, p.41

22 Archbishop Marcel Lefebvre, *Pastoral Letters: 1947–1968*, Angelus Press, Kansas City, Missouri, First Printing, August 1992, p.134

23 Quoted in Russell Shaw, "The Weathercock and the Mystic: The Prophetic Friendship of Orestes Brownson and Isaac Hecker," Crisis Magazine, July 24, 2006, https://crisismagazine.com/opinion/the-weathercock-and-the-mystic-the-prophetic-friendship-of-orestes-brownson-and-isaac-hecker

Time was when I paraded my Americanism, in order to repel the charge that an American cannot become a convert to the Church without ceasing to feel and act as an American patriot. I have lived long enough to snap my fingers at all charges of that sort.

I love my country, and, in her hour of trial, I and my sons, Catholics like myself, did our best to preserve her integrity, and save her Constitution; and there is no sacrifice in my power that I would not make to bring 'my kinsmen after the flesh' to Christ; but, after all, the Church is my true country, and the faithful are my real countrymen.

Let the American people become truly Catholic and submissive children of the Holy Father, and their Republic is safe; let them refuse and seek safety for the secular order in sectarianism or secularism, and nothing can save it from destruction.[24]

Wise words from a man who more than a century and a half ago foresaw the times we live in today. I pray more Catholics will take his advice.

Magnificat Media • July 2, 2016

NATIONALISM ISN'T ENOUGH: ONLY CHRIST CAN WARD OFF LEFTIST ASSAULTS ON AMERICA

Cancel culture isn't content with getting conservatives thrown off cable television these days, though it definitely wants that. No, it has its eyes on something bigger.

What leftists are currently engaging in with their efforts to cancel Tucker Carlson is an attempt to overthrow, with help from the professional liars who run America's corporate news networks, the entirety of Western Civilization.

Their first coup attempt—to invalidate the 2016 election by removing Donald Trump from office because of "Russian interference"—failed spectacularly. Their goal now is to erase the principles that underlie the United States, as well as Christianity itself.

The Root Cause of Their Hatred

What we are seeing play out in America is not merely the product of one or two generations of failed social policies like divorce, abortion, and other

---

24 Orestes Brownson, Brownson's Quarterly Review, January, 1873, http://orestesbrownson.org/127.html

anti-family laws. What is happening is the culmination of centuries of men rejecting Jesus Christ and His Church and the placing of themselves at the center of public life over and against Almighty God.

Pope Leo XIII once taught that "[i]f the mind assents to false opinions, and the will chooses and follows after what is wrong, neither can attain its native fullness, but both must fall from their native dignity into an abyss of corruption."[25] His words directly apply to the times we are living in today. When man rebelled against the Catholic World Order (also known as "Christendom") during the 1500s, society began to decay. Slowly distancing themselves from the one true faith, men starting constructing not only their households and cities on lies, but entire nations as well. Some countries, like the United States, struck a balance between truth and error. For a long time, that seemed to work because of the goodwill of so many ordinary, God-fearing Americans. Admirably, many politicians today still push back against those who are seeking to destroy Western Civilization. President Trump's speeches in Poland and at Mount Rushmore this weekend are two such instances of someone trying to do precisely that.

But is he saying and doing enough? Said another way, is anything he or the Republican Party has done in response to the madness going on in America going to actually save the United States?

Christ or Chaos

Like Trump, many so-called "nationalists" are rising up across the US and Europe to fight the one-world globalist agenda. That's all well and good. But what is "nationalism" without God? What is populism without Christianity? Didn't Christ himself say, "without me, you can do nothing"?

The best message a politician can deliver right now is one that promotes not only Jesus Christ, but the Catholic faith specifically. In 1873, American Catholic intellectual Orestes Brownson spoke about the desperate need for the United States to convert to Catholicism. His words are prophetic.

"Let the American people become truly Catholic... and their Republic is safe," he wrote in an article written that year. "Let them refuse and seek safety for the secular order in sectarianism or secularism, and nothing can save it from destruction."[26]

Pope Pius XII made similar remarks during World War II. "Most happy

---

25 Leo XIII, *Immortale Dei*, 32, 1885, Vatican website, https://www.vatican.va/content/leo-xiii/en/encyclicals/documents/hf_l-xiii_enc_01111885_immortale-dei.html
26 Orestes Brownson, *Brownson's Quarterly Review*, January, 1873, http://orestesbrown-son.org/127.html

are those states that establish laws inspired by the doctrine of the Gospel, and do not refuse to render public homage to the majesty of Christ, the King," he declared in 1939.[27]

It is therefore inadequate to say—as many "conservative" Catholics do—that America must return to "limited government" and "faith and reason." So long as the majority of persons in the United States remain outside the Catholic Church and Her grace-giving sacraments by following false faiths, then all politics really amounts to is arranging deck chairs on a sinking ship.

Restoring All Things in Christ

Pre-Vatican II popes always taught that without the Catholic religion, man's reason will falter, his understanding of the natural law will subside, and that his will will weaken.

The intellect is a "guide" but "if it lack its companion light, the knowledge of divine things, [it] will be only an instance of the blind leading the blind so that both will fall into the pit," Pope St Pius X once wrote.[28]

Fr Francis J. Connell, one of the sharpest American minds in the 20th century, re-iterated that teaching when he published in 1951 the following remarks:

> How, then, can civil rulers know their duties of natural law unless they have recourse to revelation, as interpreted by the one authentic teacher of revealed truth, the Catholic Church?
>
> If a person tries to solve the moral problems connected with sterilization, euthanasia, contraception, etc., he will very easily go astray unless he relies on Christian revelation as proposed by the teaching authority of the Church.[29]

There is no surer foundation on which to establish a country (or to fight against those who are doing the bidding of the devil) than under the banner of the Catholic faith. If "nationalists" in the United States want to truly protect America from the revolution currently being carried out by radical leftists and Marxists, they must embrace the Catholic religion and, as St

27 Quoted in "Christ the King of Civil Rulers," SSPX District of Asia, October 26, 2021, https://web.archive.org/web/20230926131658/https://fsspx.asia/en/news-events/news/christ-king-civil-rulers-69431

28 St Pius X, *Acerbo Nimis*, 3, 1905, Vatican website, https://www.vatican.va/content/pius-x/en/encyclicals/documents/hf_p-x_enc_15041905_acerbo-nimis.html

29 Francis J. Connell, "The Theory of the 'Lay State,'" *American Ecclesiastical Review*, 125, July 1951, p.17

Pius x said, take up the "arduous task of the restoration of the human race in Christ."[30]

LifeSiteNews • July 7, 2020

WHAT FAITHFUL CATHOLICS MUST DO TO EFFECTIVELY COMBAT ABORTION, LGBT, GLOBALISM

Throughout human history, man has on many occasions scorned the sweet yoke of Christ and sought to live according to his own feeble ideas. Atheistic communism, the sexual revolution of the 1960s, and today's atomistic liberalism are just some of the most recent manifestations of depraved man's attempts to order society around his instead of his Creator's will.

Some will argue that in order to effectively combat the evils of our age, Catholics must convey their theologically-rooted arguments in a "reasonable" way so even the most hardened non-believer can entertain what they are saying. In other words, Catholics are to de-divinize the claims of the one true faith and speak only of a generalized "natural law." If they don't do this, they are told, they won't be taken seriously by non-Christians. What's worse, they will be accused of wanting to impose a theocracy.

While the natural law and the Catholic faith go hand in hand, the way in which this lowest-common-denominator approach has been implemented over the past half-century has not prevented the growth of what the late Richard John Neuhaus referred to as "the naked public square."[31]

Reading the Signs of the Times

Despite the efforts of many seemingly well-intentioned, God-fearing people, the Western world's ever-downward spiral has not slowed down. The four sins that cry to heaven for vengeance are rampant in most "first world" nations, even though more Catholics are engaged in politics today than in all Church history. Moreover, while President Trump is providing a momentary respite from leftist assaults, progressives will return to the halls of power in the not so distant future and, if past is prologue, attempt to make them

30 St Pius x, *E Supremi*, 14, 1903, Vatican website, https://www.vatican.va/content/pius-x/en/encyclicals/documents/hf_p-x_enc_04101903_e-supremi.html
31 Richard John Neuhaus, "How the Public Square Became Naked," First Things, September 2, 2008, https://www.firstthings.com/web-exclusives/2008/09/how-the-public-square-became-n

violate their consciences.

This assessment of the situation at hand, uncomfortable though it may be, is not a call for despair. It is, simply put, the reality in which we live. Indeed, the spiritual effects of original and actual sin, coupled with our hedonistic culture and the unraveling of modernity's core tenets, seem to have taken such a toll on mankind that the West has little chance of ever recovering from the dense fog it has plunged itself into. One sometimes wonders whether the effects of liberalism, as well as technology, have so disfigured man's nature that grace has anything left to build on. Those who claim we are living in a time not unlike the days of Noah are more correct than many give them credit for.

What Are Catholics To Do?

It is clear that Catholics are faced with a dilemma unlike most they have been confronted by before. One option is to continue doing what they have for decades—building ecumenical coalitions, issuing public statements, holding protests, voting for political parties that claim to stand for traditional values, and the like. No doubt there will be victories along the way if this path is chosen. But, the Culture of Death will likely remain.

Another option is to get serious about the situation at hand and, after reflecting on the real purpose of the Catholic faith, realize a different, more supernatural, course of action is needed, one that is in alignment with how the Church previously approached times of woe.

In his book *The Liberal Illusion*, 19th century French polemicist Louis Veuillot shares an insightful parable that should clarify to Catholics just what their path forward should look like. His words:

> Imagine a King deposed from his throne, the last, best hope of his conquered fatherland, who was suddenly to declare that he considered himself justly deposed and that he only aspired to enjoy his personal possessions according to the laws governing all citizens, beneath the protection of the very men who were plundering his subjects...
>
> The King, we would imagine, would disgrace himself in vain. No one would believe him. Those to whom he offered to sell his rights and his honor would tell him: "Are you mad, you are King!"

What Veuillot is saying here is that coexistence with the liberal, modern world and its anti-Christian usurpers is not what Catholics should strive for. The Social Kingship of Christ extends to all corners of the earth. All nations owe him obedience. A "free Church in a free State" is not enough. Caesar himself must give homage to his creator. A liberal, pluralistic society—even one that respects the natural law—does not, objectively speaking, fulfill its debt to God. Subsequently, it cannot be said to be pleasing to Him. If natural law truths are something Catholics want enshrined into law, such truths should be desired insofar as they are stepping stones to the eventual public recognition of the divine law, as is the case in Poland, where businesses are closed on Sundays and where Christ was recognized as "King and Lord" in 2016.[32]

No One Should be Denied the Word Of God

In the years ahead, it will become clearer that supporters of same-sex "marriage," transgenderism, abortion, and the like are, whether they themselves know it or not, engaged in a diabolical winner-take-all game.

At root of their warped ideology is an attitude that despises Christian morality and seeks to erase its influence on society as well as the next generation. The fact that such persons do not want to share power with Christ over the social sphere is plainly evident. Praying and doing penance for them, on top of seeking to convert them to the true faith, is where our efforts should primarily lie. As Pius XI wrote in his 1925 encyclical *Quas Primas*, "When once men recognize, both in private and in public life, that Christ is King, society will at last receive the great blessings of real liberty, well-ordered discipline, peace and harmony."[33]

Penn Jillette, a well-known magician and atheist, remarked in 2009 that he doesn't respect persons who don't proselytize. His comments, presented below, should motivate Catholics to once again teach their faith, and not just the natural law, to all nations.

If you believe that there's a heaven and a hell, and people could be going to hell...and you think that it's not really worth telling them this because it would make it socially awkward...how much do you have to hate somebody to not proselytize? How much do you have

---

32 Dorothy Cummings McLean, "'Time for God...and rest': Catholic Poles rejoice as Sunday shopping ban comes into effect," LifeSiteNews, March 13, 2018, https://www.lifesitenews.com/news/time-for-god...and-rest-catholic-poles-rejoice-as-sunday-shopping-ban-comes/.
Natalia Dueholm, "Polish bishops end Year of Mercy by enthroning Christ as King in presence of president," LifeSiteNews, November 23, 2016, https://www.lifesitenews.com/news/poles-end-jubilee-of-mercy-with-huge-turnout-for-mass-honoring-christ-the-k/
33 Pius XI, *Quas Primas*, 19, 1925, Vatican website, https://www.vatican.va/content/pius-xi/en/encyclicals/documents/hf_p-xi_enc_11121925_quas-primas.html

to hate somebody to believe everlasting life is possible and not tell them that?[34]

Jesus is the Prince of Peace

True peace can only be brought about by the union of hearts, wills, and minds of men united in the same doctrines in the Church Christ established. You cannot have a truly moral society without Jesus Christ at its center and you cannot truly have Jesus Christ without the Catholic faith.

The solution to the errors of our time is not convincing persons of the natural law alone. Sure, the intellect is capable of grasping the truths of the natural law, but, as taught by St Pope Pius X in *Acerbo Nimis* in 1905 and affirmed by Pope Pius XII in *Humani Generis* in 1950, without the divine law guiding man's thinking, his reason will inevitably falter and his understanding of truth will gradually subside.

The solution therefore is, as it always has been, to convert the world to Jesus Christ. As Pope Leo XIII taught in 1899, the "abundance of evils which have now for a long time settled upon the world...pressingly call upon us to seek for help from Him by whose strength alone they can be driven away."[35]

Original sin is too strong and the modern world too enticing for man to create any sort of lasting society that can survive without the grace that flows through the sacraments. The 21st century—like all centuries before it—requires a supernatural approach to the problems it faces. Novenas, First Friday and First Saturday devotions, observing Ember Days, calling for the consecration of Russia, fasting, preaching to Jews, invoking the most Holy Name of Jesus in public, and, most importantly, proclaiming the Catholic faith in its entirety in season and out will have immense salutary effects in the effort to rid the world of abortion and the rest of the rotten policies conjured up by the deceivers of our corrupt age. Let Catholics take up this crusade with great courage and conviction.

LifeSiteNews • January 4, 2019

---

34 "Atheist Penn Jillette Doesn't Respect Christians Who Don't Evangelize," Church Pop, January 16, 2016, https://www.churchpop.com/atheist-penn-jillette-christians-evangelize/

35 Leo XIII, *Annum Sacrum*, 11, 1899, Vatican website, https://www.vatican.va/content/leo-xiii/en/encyclicals/documents/hf_l-xiii_enc_25051899_annum-sacrum.html

CONSERVATIVE CIVIL WAR ERUPTS AFTER WRITER
BLASTS 'DRAG QUEEN STORY HOUR'

Sohrab Ahmari's apostasy from mainstream American conservatism (also known as "classical liberalism") and embrace of what Human Events' global editor in chief Raheem Kassam has called "a more muscular, conservative nationalism" has stirred up a hornet's nest of activity.[36]

What's got everyone so riled up? Ahmari recently suggested that the government should ban drag queen story hours at public libraries.

Ross Douthat, Rod Dreher, Matthew Schmitz, and Michael Brendan Dougherty are just some of the increasing number of right-of-center "thought leaders" commenting on Ahmari's conversion. Countless other outlets, including many liberal ones, have published essays about it as well, including *Bloomberg, Vox, The Week, The Atlantic,* the *Washington Examiner,* and *Reason,* to name a few.

Most establishment conservatives were left unpersuaded by Ahmari's argument in favor of wielding the power of the state to repress what is a clear moral evil. He's a "theocrat," whined one libertarian.[37] Believing that the government can inculcate morality is "wishful thinking at best and dangerous in the worst case," wrote a contributor to *The Federalist.*[38]

Differences aside, all interested parties should agree with Ross Douthat's assertion that Ahmari has basically lit the fuse to the debate that will decide the future of conservatism in the United States.

What Actually Happened?

On May 29, Ahmari announced his departure from "fusionist" conservatism in an essay for *First Things* magazine. What that means is that he's basically given up on the old alliance of neoconservatives, libertarians, and social conservatives and thrown his lot in with the emerging coalition of Trump-inspired economic nationalists, religious Americans, and foreign policy realists and non-interventionists.[39]

36 Raheem Kassam, "National Review is Obsessed With Itself," Human Events, June 5, 2019, https://humanevents.com/2019/06/05/national-review-is-obsessed-with-itself/

37 Stephanie Slade, "The New Theocrats Are Neither Conservative Nor Christian," Reason, June 3, 2019, https://reason.com/2019/06/03/the-new-theocrats-are-neither-conservative-nor-christian/

38 Joshua Lawson, "Conservatives Need To Stop Shooting At Each Other And Start Fighting The Left," The Federalist, June 3, 2019, https://thefederalist.com/2019/06/03/conservatives-need-stop-shooting-start-fighting-left/

39 Rod Dreher, "The Next Conservatism," The American Conservatism, May 10, 2019,

In his article, Ahmari took aim at *National Review* senior writer and Never Trumper David French for opposing a ban on drag queen story hours at public libraries. A seemingly exasperated Ahmari threw up his hands and denounced the view held by libertarians like French that says using the state as a tool for good is anathema.

"Conservative Christians can't afford" the "luxuries" of "procedural liberalism," Ahmari writes. Progressives "understand that culture war means discrediting their opponents and weakening or destroying their institutions. Conservatives should approach the culture war with similar realism."

Ahmari's main, undeniable point is that French's approach has failed to halt the advancement of the far left's agenda and the moral decay of American values. Social conservatives should fight the culture wars "with the aim of defeating the enemy and enjoying the spoils in the form of a public square re-ordered to the common good and ultimately the Highest Good," he writes.

Ahmari further admits in his nerve-striking article that "government intervention will not be the answer to every social ill," but it is not necessary to have "a great horror of the state, of traditional authority and the use of the public power to advance the common good, including in the realm of public morality."[40]

A New Conservative Movement?

Ahmari's decision to support the more populist variant of conservative thought is no small matter. For one, he's essentially creature of the establishment. An up-and-coming commentator and bestselling author with bylines at *The Wall Street Journal* and the neoconservative website *Commentary*, his rejection of the status quo likely makes him a Benedict Arnold figure to many on the right.

But Ahmari gave warning signs he was heading in this direction. In February of this year, he signed a *First Things* declaration titled "Against the Dead Consensus."[41] Other, mostly young, conservative Catholic intellectuals added their names to it as well. Some of them have "integralist" tendencies.[42]

Reading like a Viktor Orbán speech, the manifesto calls for leaving behind the "pre-Trump conservative consensus" that "failed to retard, much less

https://www.theamericanconservative.com/jd-vance-next-conservatism/

40 Sohrab Ahmari, "Against David French-ism," First Things, May 29, 2019, https://www.firstthings.com/web-exclusives/2019/05/against-david-french-ism

41 "Against the Dead Consensus," First Things, March 21, 2019, https://www.firstthings.com/web-exclusives/2019/03/against-the-dead-consensus

42 Fr Edmund Waldstein, "Integralism in Three Sentences," The Josias, October 17, 2016, https://thejosias.com/2016/10/17/integralism-in-three-sentences/

reverse, the eclipse of permanent truths, family stability, communal solidarity, and much else." The statement goes on to say the old conservatism "surrendered to the pornographization of daily life, to the culture of death, to the cult of competitiveness. It too often bowed to a poisonous and censorious multiculturalism."

First Things editor Rusty Reno wrote in a pro-Ahmari follow up essay that now is the time for religious and social conservatives to take the lead on the political right. "The libertarian and classical liberal leaders have shown that they will not confront directly multiculturalism and identity politics," he correctly argued. "Religious and social conservatives have a substantive vision of the common good, one all Americans can share. This gives us a basis on which to turn back the most destructive forces in our society."[43]

Civil War on the Right

Where does this leave things? It means there's a full-blown civil war (long overdue) between those who take an absolutist approach to free market economics, limited government, and free speech and those whose nationalistic, populist, and/or religious views make them want a more robust state that will promote virtue and more aggressively restrict vice in order to fight, among other things, secularism and globalization.

For now, social media censorship, tariffs, foreign policy, and immigration are just a few of the issues the parties involved in this battle disagree over. It's not that there hasn't been a lack of consensus on these things before. It's just that it hasn't been as stark and out in the open as it is now, thanks in large part to the election of Donald Trump.

The question now facing the emerging nationalist conservative movement—especially Ahmari, Reno, and others—is: *how* do they lead? What, specifically, are the policies they want and can they win elections, especially after Trump is out of office? Where, ultimately, are the future politicians who will represent this emerging coalition going to come from and who will be their voters?

Some of those questions have already been answered and are getting answered by various writers this very moment.[44] More will come in due time. Some were addressed in a heated hour-long discussion between Ben Shapiro and Tucker Carlson recently.[45]

43 R. R. Reno, "Time to Take the Lead," First Things, June 5, 2019, https://www.firstthings.com/web-exclusives/2019/06/time-to-take-the-lead
44 See Patrick J. Buchanan, *State of Emergency*, St Martin's Griffin, New York, 2006
45 Daily Wire+, "Tucker Carlson | The Ben Shapiro Show Sunday Special Ep. 26," YouTube,

In January, I wrote about the failure of French's strategy and its naïve faith in "proceduralism." In my article, I argued that despite the best efforts of many God-fearing people, the West is in a situation today not unlike the time before Noah. Modern man's nature has been so warped by sin that he probably can't even grasp the natural law anymore. Even if he did, he wouldn't live by it. Seeking to merely co-exist with the corrupt, modern world is not an option. Christians, I argued, must take a supernatural approach to politics. They must convert souls to Jesus Christ and advocate for policies that aid citizens on their journey to eternity.[46]

Ultimately, religious Americans must not be afraid to break ranks with mainstream Republicans and conservatives. They should promote policies that will use the authority of the state to uphold what is true and prudently restrict what is damaging to civic life. They must be pioneers in this fight and no longer be content with being what Ross Douthat has called "junior partner" status in the conservative movement.[47]

Carol Robinson, a Catholic who wrote for *Integrity* magazine in the 1940s, once said that "man thirsts for the infinite, not the wholesome. He will only be wooed away from the dynamism of the devil by Christian dynamism, and Christian dynamism comes from the supernatural." A "naturally good society is impossible to fallen man."[48]

Sound advice for today's religious conservatives if you ask me. Conservatives need to revisit voices like Robinson's if they want to properly prepare themselves for the coming tumultuous years.

LifeSiteNews • June 7, 2019

CATHOLICS FED UP WITH LIBERALISM WILL FIND INSPIRATION IN 'INTEGRITY' REPRINTS

Integrity magazine's time has finally arrived, albeit more than a half-century after ceasing publication. The only question now is whether or not religious

November 4, 2018, https://www.youtube.com/watch?v=Bh8vqof9hAk

46 Stephen Kokx, "What faithful Catholics must do in 2019 to effectively combat abortion and LGBT agenda," LifeSiteNews, January 4, 2019, https://www.lifesitenews.com/blogs/what-faithful-catholics-must-do-in-2019-to-effectively-combat-abortion-and

47 Isaac Chotiner, "Ross Douthat on the Crisis of the Conservative Coalition," The New Yorker, June 7, 2019, https://www.newyorker.com/news/q-and-a/ross-douthat-describes-the-crisis-of-the-conservative-coalition

48 Quoted in Stephen Kokx, "This prophetic 1940s Catholic magazine can help end the crisis in the Church," LifeSiteNews, March 4, 2019, https://www.lifesitenews.com/opinion/this-prophetic-1940s-catholic-magazine-can-help-end-the-crisis-in-the-church

conservatives currently getting an annulment from the "classical liberal" crowd over at *National Review* will take the time to heed its advice.

One of the positive side effects of the current civil war on the political right is that Catholics are being forced to question why they lent their support for liberal democracy in the first place and whether or not that should continue in the years ahead.

In a recent article for the *Front Porch Republic*, Darryl Hart correctly observes that before Sohrab Ahmari and David French duked it out over drag queen story hours, Brent Bozell Jr. and William F. Buckley were arguing six decades ago over the "fusion" of Catholicism with American conservatism.[49]

Unlike Buckley, Bozell—a former speechwriter for Senator Barry Goldwater,—became disillusioned with the so-called "conservative movement." In a famous 1969 letter to his former colleagues, Bozell chided them for not taking a sufficiently Christian approach to politics. "Secular liberalism...has not lost any of the battles it has had with you," he wrote. "On every front where your program has confronted secular liberalism's, you have been beaten."

The same could be said by social conservatives to the many mainstream Republicans and "conservatives" of the world today, could it not?

American Catholics Need to Look to the Past

Many young Catholics fed up with the ineffective, business as usual approach to the crisis in the West taken by outlets like *National Review* and *Public Discourse* are currently looking to Bozell for inspiration. An expat who moved to Spain and had 10 children, Bozell, a devout Catholic, launched *Triumph* magazine in 1966. *Triumph* took on not just Vatican II's reforms but many of the sacred cows held dear by the political right: "free market" capitalism, "limited" government, and the like.

As welcome as *Triumph's* newfound fame is, there exists another, even better mid-20th century publication that Catholics at *First Things* and elsewhere who are wanting to move beyond fusionism should look to: *Integrity* magazine.

Integrity was founded in New York City in 1946 by two of the most fascinating and insightful lay American Catholics of the 20th century, Ed Willock and Carol Robinson, born in 1916 and 1911, respectively. Angelus Press has already published a great deal of the pair's essays, which focus primarily on culture, family life, and St Thomas Aquinas.

Uniquely penetrating, stringently Catholic, and decidedly counter-cultural,

---

49 Darryl Hart, "Before Ahmari and French, Wills and Bozell," Front Porch Republic, June 10, 2019, https://www.frontporchrepublic.com/2019/06/before-ahmari-and-french-wills-and-bozell/

Willock and Robinson's articles on the Industrial Revolution, pop culture, suburban life, fatherhood, spirituality, and economics (to name a few of the eclectic topics they wrote about) would, if listened to, help reignite what St Pius x called the "arduous task of the restoration of the human race in Christ." Not only did this indefatigable duo expose the lie that the post-war 1940s and 50s was a sort of golden era that should be maintained, they laid out a competing, alternative political reality for Catholics in the US to go about constructing.

'The Integration of the Natural and Supernatural Orders'

Alex Barbas is a family man living in Canada doing Catholics the enormous favor of reprinting every *Integrity* that released over its 10-year lifespan. A former seminarian, Barbas has already released a book by Dr John Rao and several other rare, out of print texts. He is planning on selling a book by French Cardinal Louis Billot (1846–1931) on liberalism in the near future. Last week, his Ontario-based Arouca Press sent me a copy of *Integrity's* first three issues from October 1946 until December 1946. Each is about seventy pages in length. Barbas has compiled them into a slender 230-page paperback for sale at $18.95.

Chock full of Willock's humorous illustrations and witty poems ("Mr business went to Mass, He never missed a Sunday. Mr Business went to hell, For what he did on Monday), *Integrity's* first three editions make it clear that they, unlike many of today's leading "conservative" Catholics, had no intention of marrying their faith to the liberal principles of the American Founding, or the modern world, especially for fleeting political gain.

"We must make a new synthesis of religion and life," their flagship editorial proudly declares. "Integral Catholicism...does not mean piety so much as wholeness. It means...a consistency of theory and practice; a unity of public life and private morals; a reconciliation of commercial ethics and religious dogma." Whereas "the guiding policy of contemporary society" is to compromise, adjust, and water down, integral Catholicism "is at the opposite pole from expediency." Integral Catholicism "does not calculate its actions to please high worldly powers, or with an eye to the coming elections...we must do what is right, come what may."

Each issue of *Integrity* relies on the same straightforward format: an opening essay from the editors (usually something on how Catholics need to convert the world to Christ) followed with a half dozen or so plainly-written essays by well-qualified laymen and priests (typically on politics, spirituality, and/or economics). Willock's visually appealing cartoons and amusing quips pepper the pages throughout. "Modern economics would be shot full of holes, If personnel managers found that workers had souls," reads one poem next to a drawing of a man in a business suit.

Barbas' font choice and text size fits with the magazine's voice and tone, which is not an easy thing to accomplish. The book has no photocopied images or pages, which are all too common in re-prints these days. Willock's drawing are also formatted exceptionally well.

Dorothy Day makes an appearance in the magazine's second issue with an article on her Catholic worker project. Other essays that stand out include, "The Cross and the Dollar," "Are You Ashamed of the Gospel?", "Catholic Action in Canada," "The Worker's Apostolate," and "Apostles in Prison."

Collectively, *Integrity's* message is this: America must be viewed as a missionary country desperately in need of conversion. Modernity and its obsession with work and materialism wars against Catholic life. Followers of Christ must live out their faith by undertaking not just in politics but in their immediate and professional spheres of influence natural and supernatural efforts aimed at advancing the Kingdom of God.

'We Tend to Overly Preach the Natural Law'

The real star of *Integrity* is without a doubt Carol Robinson, who wrote under the pen name Peter Michaels. A columnist for *The Wanderer* later in life, Robinson took to task those who selectively presented or distorted the truths of the Catholic faith in order to fit in with American politics. She had no time for what she deemed the "naturalistic" proposals of parliaments, congressional committees, or the United Nations. The cure to the problems of the day was always supernatural.

"We tend to overly preach the natural law, especially in matters of social reform and economic planning," she wrote for *Integrity's* maiden issue. But "all these things the heathens do." "A man does not, by becoming more and more zealous in the practice of natural virtue, grow into supernatural life." "Are we trying to convert them to the Church via private property ... ?" she rhetorically asks. "Western society is in an unprecedented mess ... because we have been trying to run it without grace," she continues. "The salvation of America will depend not on converting Americans to the idea of goodness and unselfishness. They take to it quite readily. But they must be converted to a sense of the life of grace, a desire to do penance, a love of solitude and quiet, a respect for contemplation." Continuing on, she recalls that without grace "what is naturally good tends to become naturally bad, and what is naturally bad tends to become perverted ... only grace can restore the harmony of our natures."

Robinson's advice stands in stark contrast to that which is offered by many leading Catholic writers in America, who never tire of talking about the need to go back to the "Founding Fathers."

The Solution to the Sickness of Our Age

It is clear that *Integrity's* time has finally come. Growing numbers of Catholics are waking up to the fact that their faith and the liberal, modern world are irreconcilable. As these souls continue to break free from the Matrix-like, neoconservative Catholic narrative that blinds them from this truth, they'll need to have resources to look to in order to navigate the difficulties they'll encounter in the years ahead.

If the first three issues of *Integrity* magazine are any indication of what it produced over the ensuing decade, Catholics fed up with fusionism and liberalism will have found themselves two trusty advisers in Ed Willock and Carol Robinson.

LifeSiteNews • June 25, 2019

THIS PROPHETIC 1940S CATHOLIC MAGAZINE CAN HELP END THE CRISIS IN THE CHURCH

One of the worst lies about the Catholic Church as it existed before Vatican 11 is that it was rigid, legalistic, and imbued with clericalism.

Anyone who has read pre-conciliar papal writings on Catholic Action knows that such charges are entirely bogus. Catholics living in the late 19th and early 20th century were anything but unthinking, rosary-counting dullards who worshipped their priests. (Even if they were, at least they prayed and didn't dissent from Church doctrine, which is something that can't be said for most of today's laity).

"Catholic Action" is the name the Church previously used to describe clergy-led efforts aimed at the restoration of individuals, families, and societies to Christ. Today, the Church calls on laity to support the "New Evangelization." The two concepts are different given that the New Evangelization only asks Catholics to "witness" to their faith and not to proselytize.

One person widely known for her activism in the United States before Vatican 11 is Dorothy Day. Controversial to some, a prophet to others, Day, in her own way, sought to apply Catholic social teaching to the corrupt modern world.

Unfortunately, the amount of attention historians give to Day has resulted in Catholics in the 21st century being less familiar with other Catholic activists alive at the same time. Writers like Carol Robinson and Ed Willock, a friend of Day's about whom she wrote fondly after his premature death in 1960, are two such persons.

Born in 1911 and 1916 respectively, Robinson and Willock co-founded *Integrity* magazine in October 1946 in New York City. Their mission, according to Alex Barbas, founder of Arouca Press, was to synthesize religion and daily life.

"*Integrity* warned against complacency in the living of the faith in the modern world and often criticized American Catholics' penchant for compartmentalizing their faith," Barbas said in a phone interview with LifeSiteNews. He added: "In their first issue, Willock and Robinson said that the solution was not going to come about on the natural or ethical level. Nor would it come about through an intensification of devotions alone. The root issue, for them, was what they called 'the integration of the natural and supernatural orders.'"

Barbas, a family man who lives in Waterloo, Ontario, is re-printing every issue of *Integrity* over its 10-year existence. He has spent the better part of the last decade tracking the periodical down in libraries, on the internet, and through personal contacts. He has done the same for other rare, out-of-print Catholic books, which he sells on his website for a small profit.

Fr Kenneth Novak, the former editor of Angelus Press, released during the 1990s and early 2000s several books featuring *Integrity* essays. But Barbas believes there is untapped wisdom in the vast number of *Integrity* articles that have not yet been reprinted.

"They might not have all the answers to our problems today, but Ed Willock's and Carol Robinson's insights on family life, politics, leisure, and every other area of Catholic living are unparalleled. They are wonderful examples of how the faith can allow a soul to see through the vanity of the world and its illusory ideas," he said. "Unlike many of today's Catholics involved in political life, they didn't round off the edges of their faith or speak generally about 'the natural law.' They presented the faith integrally."

Barbas says he finds the duo fascinating because not only were their writings and speeches prophetic, they lived the faith as well. "Willock had a large family and lived on a farm as part of a Catholic community in Marycrest, New York. They practiced what they preached! There is much Catholics today can and must learn from them and their essays, which were clearly rooted in the great, anti-liberal writings of Pius IX, Leo XIII, and others."

A glance at just a few of the article headlines published in *Integrity* reveals its unique, all-encompassing perspective:

- "The Family Has Lost its Head"
- "Why Aren't Americans Contemplative?"
- "How Modern Man became Merry"
- "What is a Grown-up?"
- "Recreation and Children"
- "Accentuating the Positive"
- "Forward to the Land"
- "About Television"
- "The New Science of Society Versus the Laws of Life"

In some ways, *Integrity* is the pre-Vatican II version of Brent Bozell's *Triumph* magazine, which was founded in 1966 in response to the Second Vatican Council's liberalizing reforms. It lasted until 1976. Both called into question the sacred cows of the day (libertarianism especially) and presented the faith in a holistic, sometimes blunt manner.

A convert who obtained a master's degree in theology later in life at St John's University in New York City, Robinson was thoroughly disillusioned with Vatican II. After *Integrity* disbanded in 1955, 16 years passed until she became a columnist for *The Wanderer* newspaper in 1971 until 1987. A staunch Thomist, she gave many speeches and authored numerous books and pamphlets, often under the pseudonym Peter Michaels. She died in Connecticut in 2002. Barbas is planning on releasing Robinson's private letters, provided he gets permission to do so.

In his own essays, Willock, who was often ill, used witty illustrations to rail against everything from the vacuity of sports and the growing effeminacy of men, to the sinfulness of the stock market, the dangers of television, and the glorification of the finer things in life. The following quotes from his slender 1948 book, *Ye Gods*, which is a collection of short essays that was published by Sheed and Ward, gives ample proof of his inimitable perspective on modern life:

- "Hiroshima was the wedding feast at Cana for the omni-scientist."
- "A car or radio that is slow to warm up provides the modern speed demon with the same kind of torture formerly generated by a hair-shirt."

- "In a society that has made Economics of primary importance...having money would be considered as being in the state of grace."

- "Efficiency will be considered a virtue as long as it is profitable to reduce men to the level of automatons."

So unique were Willock's writings that a religious sister attending Marquette University in 1969 wrote her Master's thesis ("The Social Vision of Ed Willock") on him. The document is a great reminder of the penetrating insight a mind untainted by the spirit of the age can bring forth. At the risk of exaggeration, the thesis indicates that the scope, breadth, brain power, and sheer zeal for the faith behind *Integrity* was far beyond most every Catholic media outlet operating today.

It is fair to categorize Willock, as well as Robinson, as being of the same caliber and of the same anti-modernist, anti-Americanist school of thought as Fr Clifford Fenton and Fr Francis J. Connell, American priests who, during the mid-20th century, warred against Liberal Catholics like Fr John Courtney Murray (the main architect of Vatican ɪɪ's document on religious liberty).

No two clergy in the United States wrote as many essays as Fenton and Connell did for the *American Ecclesiastical Review* in the 1940s, 50s, and 60s. Their prodigious output was unequaled. Unfortunately, their wholly orthodox, Aquinas-inspired outlook was scrapped at Vatican ɪɪ and replaced by the so-called "new theology" pushed by the likes of Council *periti* Yves Congar, a progressive French Dominican who was censured in the decades prior. The Church has been suffering ever since.

One is left to wonder what would have happened if Willock lived as long as Robinson did and if the Council would never have taken place. Would *Integrity* be viewed in a higher regard than Fulton Sheen or other influential mid-20th century American Catholics? Would the United States have become a Catholic country? One can't know for sure, but in my estimation, it would have, thanks in large part to Ed Willock and Carol Robinson. Given that it's not, the work of Alex Barbas republishing their writings is all the more essential to reviving authentic Catholic Action in the 21st century and ending the worsening crisis in the Church. *Integrity's* wisdom is needed now more than ever.

LifeSiteNews • March 4, 2019

NEW CATHOLIC BOOK PUBLISHER RELEASES OUT-OF-PRINT TITLES TO RE-ESTABLISH SOCIAL KINGSHIP OF CHRIST

There are not a lot of book publishers that have a firm grip on the most pressing questions facing Catholics in the modern, post-liberal age. One that does is Arouca Press.

In my estimation, Arouca has taken the lead on a crucially important niche industry that blends political theory, Thomistic theology, and practical Catholic wisdom that can help laity save their souls from a world and Church gone mad.

One of the most unique books Arouca has released since its founding on October 13, 2018 is a reprint of an obscure, 1940s American Catholic, lay-run periodical called *Integrity* magazine.

The essays in *Integrity* are hard hitting and un-ecumenical. Any conservative or Traditional Catholic living in the US who has any interest in political affairs ought to read them.

Other titles Arouca has for sale include the memoirs of the late Antonio Cardinal Bacci, a long-time Vatican official who served under multiple popes in the 20th century, and a book critiquing liberalism written by French Cardinal Louis Billot (1846–1931). The collected works of Carol Robinson, a lay woman who wrote for *Integrity*, are also for sale. Arouca also offers many books on spirituality.

So impressive are Arouca's books that Bishop Athanasius Schneider, Fr Gerald Murray, Dr John Rao, and others have endorsed several of them.

Earlier this week, I interviewed Alex Barbas, a former seminarian turned family man who lives in Ontario, Canada, to learn about why he does what he does and what he hopes to accomplish with Arouca Press.

"My goal is quite simply to publish works which will challenge Catholics to think about the Faith so that they can make a concrete application of the Faith in their daily lives," he told me in an email (read full interview below).

Barbas, who sometimes relies on help from volunteers to transcribe manuscripts, tells me his primary aim is to re-publish out-of-print books in order to help "guide Catholics through the fog of modernity by equipping them with integrity, intelligence, true piety, and a deep love for the Faith."

As the 21st century presses on, Catholics will continue to stand at the intersection of a rapidly changing world. Globalism itself is not only increasingly being called into question but so is the Church's rapprochement with liberalism.

A growing number of articles and books on topics like religious liberty, "integralism," and Church-State relations are starting to appear. And that's a good thing. Catholics involved in these debates, and those who aren't and simply want good, quality Catholic books on spirituality, should look to Arouca Press as a guide in the years ahead.

Why did you start Arouca press and what would you like to accomplish with it?

Ever since I received the gift of Faith over 20 years ago, I've had a love for books. I think this love of books stems—partly at least—from my realization at how little I really know. I remain a student of the Faith longing for greater clarity yet delighting in the mystery of faith. It is a juxtaposition which continues to grab my attention. If I may, let me quote the theologian, Matthias Scheeben: "…the truths of Christianity would not stir us as they do, nor would they draw us or hearten us, and they would not be embraced by us with such love and joy, if they contained no mysteries….A truth that is easily discovered and quickly grasped can neither enchant nor hold" (*The Mysteries of Christianity*, B. Herder, 1946). I am continuously stirred.

It was only in 2018 that I was able to put a dream of mine into fruition. I thought that even though there were countless Catholic publishers who were doing a wonderful job of publishing contemporary works and treasures of the past, there was still room for yet another publisher.

My goal is quite simply to publish works which will challenge Catholics to think about the Faith so that they can make a concrete application of the Faith in their daily lives. I have often reflected that there can be a danger in making piety a purely abstract concept. Piety—I think—has to flow from a robust and firm knowledge of the Faith. Good books can help with this pursuit.

Now, it would be an error to view the Faith as an intellectual plaything to be used and abused through rationalistic inquiry. The Faith is rational but to *have* the Faith means to fully embrace Divine Revelation without diminution with all our *heart, mind,* and *soul* (i.e., in a holistic manner). Additionally, if we read history honestly we will realize that the Catholic Church has always been an advocate of the interplay between faith and reason (e.g., St Thomas' *Summa Theologiae*) avoiding the errors of rationalism and fideism.

Modernity, *as a set of imbibed principles orienting all of society—the "air we breathe," so to speak* – and having roots going back centuries, does present obstacles to the Catholic who wishes to take the Faith seriously. Many of our published books, in one way or another, deal with this struggle.

We hope Arouca Press can guide Catholics through the fog of modernity by equipping them with integrity, intelligence, true piety, and a deep love for the Faith. Speaking personally, founding Arouca Press has allowed me to come into contact with ideas and thinkers who have themselves challenged me with their works and discussions and whom I think will challenge others.

What sort of feedback have you received from fellow Catholics?

It has been a joy to read all the good feedback received. Many readers have expressed their appreciation for re-discovering older works or the new books we have published. It gives us encouragement that the books we are publishing are bearing some fruit and that the time invested has not been in vain! I always look forward to what the readers have to say regarding our books. I welcome all comments!

Which Arouca books are your personal favorites?

That's a difficult question to answer! Every book we published has a special place in our apostolate. The first book we published, *Meditations for Each Day* by Antonio Cardinal Bacci, takes pride of place being the book that started it all. Other than all the authors (Dr John Rao, Christian Browne, Fr Sebastian Walshe) who have decided to publish their books through Arouca Press, I am most proud of beginning two large projects: 1) republishing all of the *Integrity* periodicals (1946–1956), and 2) publishing the collected works of Carol Jackson Robinson (1911–2002). These two projects reflect ideas and considerations which I think are still relevant, and as I shall explain later, strike to the heart of the clash between Modernity and Catholicism, and how Catholics, especially in the United States, have attempted to reconcile the two. It is quite the drama

Tell me more about Carol Robinson and how her writings are relevant today...

Where do I even begin!? Due to the many gaps in my education, I cannot fully explain why I think her writings represent such an interesting and profound analysis of Modernity's grip on the Catholic mind—for that was one of the themes the *Integrity* writers and Carol Robinson tried to analyze. However awkwardly, let me at least try to say a few things. In 1941, Carol Robinson became a Catholic. There were two major influences in her life: Paul McGuire (1903–1978), an Australian diplomat, author, and Catholic Action lecturer, and the writings of St Thomas Aquinas as presented to her by the Dominican Order. Fr Francis Wendell, the head of the Third Order Dominicans in the United States, became her mentor, and was instrumental in helping her found the intrepid Catholic periodical, *Integrity*. St Thomas was always by her side, and in a personal letter from the 70s (I believe), she states that she used to wake up early in the morning to read the *Summa* rapt for hours in its brilliance.

She is relatively unknown as an American Catholic author but when I stumbled upon her writings years ago, I was enthralled by her ability to get to the root of the problems assailing a Catholic vision of life. She is one of the most quotable Catholic authors I have ever read combining wit and wisdom with a fierceness that is sorely needed today. She is not motivated by any sort of animus but out of a deep charity informed as she was by a profound faith. In her first article for *Integrity* (October 1946) she writes:

The situation is reflected in the Church by an artificial separation by the faithful of the supernatural order and the natural order; a separation of their sacramental lives from their daily lives and work. It is the true contemporary schizophrenia.

There is, I think, a tendency in the American context, to make this separation, whether consciously or not.

She was convinced that it was only through the Church's ideals and their concrete implementation in society that any sort of restoration or return to sanity was possible. She says in a 1949 *Integrity* article:

It is sad, then, to observe that so many Catholics think they defend the Church by defending liberal economics departed from fundamental Christian ideas about justice, property, usury and the common good, that it has sired such an unlovely child as Marxism. To an intolerable and unstable economic situation there are two alternative answers: either supersede the errors with worse ones which look like correctives (as Marxism does), or return to Christian principles (as is the platform of Christian "radicals").

I could quote her ad nauseam! It is all the more interesting to read these articles given the on-going debate today regarding the nature and success/failure of the liberal order in society. Carol Robinson's analysis then becomes quite prescient! We are in the process of publishing *all* of these *Integrity* articles, book reviews, and editorials in a book titled, *Thy Faith Hath Made Thee Whole.*

Her writings not only reflect social concerns but also the necessity and duty to develop the interior life as opposed to accepting worldly principles and maxims. She writes with a charm and urgency that is remarkable to read. Let me quote her again! The following passage is from a series of essays that I unearthed on the Beatitudes and the Gifts of the Holy Ghost written between 1962 and 1963 (*The Eightfold Kingdom Within*):

'Those who desire the things of this world are not made happy by possessing them; only unhappy by their absence. It is God who makes men happy, but even if God is present in our souls we cannot enjoy Him while we are attached to a thousand material and physical goods. So the process of detachment brings with it not only freedom but also joy, the true lightheartedness that made St Francis sing as he walked barefoot in the snow.'

In the mid-60s, when society was undergoing such changes and the Church was confronting the enormous pressure to adapt, Carol Robinson decided to pursue a Master's degree in theology at St John's University. Afterwards she taught for a few years at an all-girls college in upstate New York. In 1971, she became a columnist for *The Wanderer*, and it was there that she tried to make sense of all the new ideas being introduced into the Church. Her *Wanderer* articles do retain the earlier wit and vitality from her *Integrity* years. However, a stronger insistence is given on the importance of St Thomas Aquinas, whose abandonment or relegation to irrelevance, she claims, was part of the problem afflicting the clergy after the Council. Let me quote from a 1979 article:

'A paralyzed cleric is one who, while himself a believer, cannot reassure his flock that the Church has not changed her essential discipline and doctrine because he cannot meet the challenges of the progressives head on — either to point out their errors or ridicule their premises. He is not sufficiently well grounded in the philosophy of St Thomas to know why and where to go wrong. So he keeps his mouth shut. During many years we sat in the pews waiting for reassurance and it almost never came.'

Readers may disagree with her insistence on the thought of St Thomas (I know the issues are complex) but she writes as one who had studied him since the 1940s and was convinced St Thomas couldn't be abandoned without danger. This collection of articles has been tentatively titled, *An Embattled Mind: In Defense of St Thomas*. We hope to publish this book later in the year. All of her works do not suffer from a sort of "abstraction" but involve a real grounding in reality and hence relevance to the reader in 2020. We plan on publishing seven books as part of her collected works series. We are also in possession of many of her personal letters spanning nearly fifty years! That would be a project requiring years of planning and editing!

We think readers will come to appreciate the rigor and liveliness of her thinking which can contribute something of substance to the often sterile polemics of modern discourse.

What has been the most enlightening aspect of your work?

Another good question! The creative process of finding good books to publish (or receiving good manuscripts!) has given me a great source of joy. Carol Robinson often talked about having a vocation in the wider sense as opposed to merely working at a job. I think Providence has moved me towards this vocation. I also would add that the conversations I have had with all those who have helped me with publishing these books (there are so many to name!) have opened up areas of thought that I would have never encountered. I cannot fully express my gratitude and appreciation for all the things I have learned and continue to learn through these discussions.

What books are you working on now and what titles can we expect in the future?

We are currently working on publishing the memoirs of Antonio Cardinal Bacci which the translator, Dr Anthony Lo Bello, first translated privately between 1989–1990 and originally published in Italian in 1964. This book gives us a tremendous insight into the Cardinal's thoughts on the Latin language and his service under four popes (Pius XI, Pius XII, John XXIII, and Paul VI).

We are also working on publishing for the first time in English, *A Pilgrimage to Jasna Góra*, by Władysław St Reymont (1867–1925), the Nobel-Prize winning Polish author, whose works are sorely unknown in the English-speaking world. The translator, Filip Mazurczak, is also slated to translate a major work on Catholic social teaching by Stefan Cardinal Wyszyński under condition that we can raise the appropriate funds. We are waiting for a decision on our grant application.

We have so many other projects in the works such as a book on the spirituality of the Premonstratensians in the twelfth and thirteenth centuries, a book on the priesthood, a reprint of a major work on the Sacred Liturgy, and a fascinating book on one of R.A. Lafferty's works. The list is seemingly endless. May the good Lord give us enough strength to complete all these projects!

Do you have any advice for Catholics in these confusing times?

I am not comfortable in offering any advice—who am I really? I am simply a Catholic trying to publish good books. All I can say is that it seems to be of even greater importance today to really study the faith and live it integrally in these strange times which see so many rapid changes in society and the Church. We must cling to the sacraments as much as we can (it is a great tragedy that these channels of grace are withheld from the faithful); we must pray; we must develop a deep interior life with a real and infectious joy; and we must *never* get disoriented.

Liberalism, as a set of ideas born in conflict with the Church, has made tremendous inroads in how Catholics view the world. The Church offers a counter-vision (see Billot's *Liberalism*) that is as old as the moment it was founded. This vision rises above the disagreements between "conservatives" and "liberals"; it rises above party politics; it rises above certain economic theories; it rises above ideologies serving not the common good or the supernatural end of man, but offers a comprehensive view of man and society. It is the only remedy for true peace. If only more people would realize this.

May the reader forgive such verbosity!

LifeSiteNews • June 10, 2020

'CHRIST IS KING': CATHOLICS PROTEST SATANIC TEMPLE PRAYER AT COUNTY BOARD MEETING

More than 100 Catholics and Protestants prayed and sang songs to express opposition to and make reparation for an invocation delivered by a "minister" of The Satanic Temple in West Michigan this past week.

Faithful from across the area filled the boardroom at the Ottawa County Commissioners' meeting on Tuesday. Many more stood and kneeled outside in the jam-packed entryway where they held Christian-themed flags and posters that read, "My Jesus Mercy" and "Satan has no rights." Their prayers could be heard inside as the individual gave his remarks.

Grassroots conservatives first started planning for the evening when news broke on March 21 that county chairman Joe Moss would not prevent a representative of the Temple from delivering his "prayer." Moss told LifeSite that his hands were tied due to the new invocation policy he and his fellow board members revised last year. He also said the county would likely face a lawsuit if he acted otherwise.

Medical freedom activist Teresa Cichewicz, a local Traditional Catholic, coordinated with America Needs Fatima to hold a Rosary Rally at the meeting. "We thank the Mother of God for allowing us to pray uniformly with more than 60 Catholics the 15-decade Rosary outside the boardroom," she told LifeSite.

Cichewicz and her also group sang Latin hymns, invoked the help of the Blessed Virgin Mary, and held a large banner that read, "Satanism is part of the problem not part of the solution." Several members addressed the commissioners later in the evening about the need to scrap the revised policy.

The four-and-a-half hour meeting began with Luis Cypher stepping up to the podium. Commissioner Jason Bonnema, who voted against the invocation guidelines last year, immediately asked Moss to have Cypher provide his real name, as Satanic Temple members use pseudonyms. To which Moss threatened to bring the meeting into recess. A frustrated Bonnema eventually left two hours later during the public comment session, during which more than 45 people spoke.

With dozens of concerned citizens looking on and cameras from several media outlets pointed towards him, Cypher began his remarks by asking everyone to reject "arcane doctrines" and to "embrace the Luciferian impulse to eat of the tree of knowledge and dissipate our blissful and comforting delusions of old." While wearing a Satanic Temple pin as well as what appeared to be mock Rosary beads around his neck, Cypher closed his brief 2 1/2-minute remarks by calling on commissioners to "stand firm against any and all arbitrary authority that threatens the personal sovereignty of one or of all. That which will not bend must break, and that which can be destroyed by truth should never be spared its demise. It is done. Hail Satan! Thank you very much." Scant applause from what appeared to be less than 10 individuals could be heard in the room.

According to the *Holland Sentinel*, Commissioners Gretchen Cosby and Kendra Wenzel prayed silently during Cypher's remarks.[50] Commissioner

---

50 Mitchell Boatman, "Satanic Temple invocation forces Ottawa County to reckon with the meaning of religious freedom," Holland Sentinel, April 24, 2024, https://www.holland-

Rebekah Curran handed out cookies with "John 3:16" stickers on their packaging to protesters before the meeting. Curran was also the first to speak during public comment, during which she said a prayer.

Later in the evening, commissioners approved a pro-life measure that appeared to be designed to temper blowback by showing that they still support traditional values. Ottawa County is one of the state's most religious and conservative areas. The global headquarters of the Reformed Church in America and the Christian Reformed Church in North America are located 30 miles east in the city of Grand Rapids. The two denominations also maintain colleges in the region. Moss' political action group, OttawaImpact, won a super majority of seats on the 11-person commission in 2022 by courting those communities by running on an anti-woke, pro-constitutional platform.

While some attendees and commissioners defend the County's policy on libertarian grounds by arguing that the First Amendment requires speech that may sometimes "be offensive," the majority of public comments condemned the invocation as a sorry excuse for legalized blasphemy.

"All power on earth, civil and religious, is given to men by God himself. And those men are expected, nay required, to use that power according to the will of the one who gave it to them," Catholic graduate student Joseph Amoros said while holding a crucifix. "The foremost duty of political leaders is to orient the social life of man to assist him in the salvation of his soul … you have all failed miserably in your primary responsibility," he exclaimed.

Amoros further called on the commissioners to "make reparation" for the "unspeakable violation of justice" that they committed against the Kingship of Christ. He recommended they seek out the local Catholic bishop to perform a consecration of Ottawa County to the Sacred Heart of Jesus.

The evening was a pivotal moment in West Michigan politics as numerous prominent local leaders and media were in attendance, making it something of a turning point after years of infighting among activists. Brian Burch, a former Holland city councilman, posted on X last month that Moss' Ottawa Impact commissioners "enable, defend, and protect the rights of Satan over the protection of our souls. Stop this, you cowards. Satan has no place in Ottawa County or anywhere on Earth."[51]

LifeSiteNews • April 24, 2024

sentinel.com/story/news/politics/county/2024/04/24/satanic-temple-invocation-forces-ottawa-county-to-reckon-with-the-meaning-of-religious-freedom/73432933007/
51 Stephen Kokx, "Christians to hold Rosary rally against Satanic Temple member's invocation at Michigan county meeting," LifeSiteNews, April 4, 2024, https://www.lifesitenews.com/news/christians-to-hold-rosary-rally-against-satanic-temple-members-invocation-at-michigan-county-meeting/

CHAPTER VII: US POLITICS

REPUBLICAN PARTY MUST EMBRACE NATIONALIST, SOCIALLY CONSERVATIVE AGENDA

A 2017 report by an organization called The Democracy Voter Study Group found that in the last presidential race Donald Trump won socially conservative, economically liberal voters who previously supported Democrats.[1]

The upcoming 2020 elections present the Republican Party with an historic opportunity to build on this newly forged coalition of blue-collar moderates and religious Americans. If the GOP chooses to ignore their concerns about the effects of globalization and growing economic inequality and instead treats Trump's presidency—and the populist re-alignment he's ushered in—as a mere blip on the screen, the party will fade into obscurity. Demographic changes alone will ensure that that occurs. However, if Republicans embrace the president's nationalist agenda and fix unfair trade deals, stop endless wars, prevent abortions, block social media censorship, improve infrastructure, and halt unchecked immigration, the party of Lincoln has the potential to dominate American politics for decades to come.

National Review editor Rich Lowry spoke about the future of conservatism at the Aspen Ideas Festival several weeks ago. "The Republican Party is never going to be the same," he said. "And I don't think it's going back to what it was. I don't think there will ever be a figure like Trump again...but I do think the party will have to be more populist, will have to be more nationalist, socially conservative, not quite as libertarian."[2]

Lowry is right. Republicans have to run candidates in the 2020 elections who can solidify for the party the working class voters Trump convinced to support him in 2016. Tucker Carlson, the Buckley-esque de facto leader of this populist brand of conservatism, implicitly endorsed that strategy last month on his Fox News show.

"There isn't a caucus that represents where most Americans actually are: nationalist on economics, fairly traditional on the social issues," he lamented. "Imagine a politician who wanted to make your healthcare cheaper, but wasn't

1 Lee Drutman, "Political Divisions in 2016 and Beyond," Voter Study Group, June 2017, https://www.voterstudygroup.org/publication/political-divisions-in-2016-and-beyond

2 Rick Carroll, "GOP does soul searching at Aspen Ideas Festival," The Aspen Times, July 1, 2019, https://www.aspentimes.com/news/gop-does-soul-searching-at-aspen-ideas-festivalri/

ghoulishly excited about partial birth abortion. Imagine someone who genuinely respected the nuclear family, and sympathized with the culture of rural America, but at the same time was willing to take your side against rapacious credit card companies bleeding you dry at 35 percent interest."
"Would you vote for someone like that?" he asked. "My gosh. Of course. Who wouldn't? That candidate would be elected in a landslide. Every single time. Yet that candidate is the opposite of pretty much everyone currently serving in congress."[3]

Carlson made similar comments at the recently concluded National Conservatism conference in Washington DC in his talk, "Big Business Hates Your Family," which excoriated libertarian economic principles.[4]

Promoting the True Common Good

Perhaps it's my Catholic faith that attracts me to Bobby Kennedy (by far the most devout of all the Kennedy brothers), but I can't help but think he can act as a sort of inspiration for nationalist conservatives in the years ahead.

I could be wrong about that[5], but consider that in 1968, Kennedy, who by then was the father of 10 children, gave a speech at the University of Kansas about his opposition to the Vietnam War. The most frequently cited part of his now famous remarks is when he shared his thoughts on economics.

While praising America's schools, families, and civic patriotism, Kennedy observed that for "too much and for too long America seems to have surrendered personal excellence and community values in the mere accumulation of material things." Our gross national product, he added, "if we judge the United States of America by that" does not consider "the health of our children, the quality of their education or the joy of their play … it measures everything in short, except that which makes life worthwhile. And it can tell us everything about America except why we are proud that we are Americans."[6]

3 Ian Schwartz, "Tucker Carlson: Elizabeth Warren's 'Economic Patriotism' Plan 'Sounds Like Donald Trump At His Best," Real Clear Politics, June 6, 2019, https://www.realclearpolitics.com/video/2019/06/06/tucker_carlson_elizabeth_warrens_economic_patriotism_plan_sounds_like_donald_trump_at_his_best.html

4 Jonathon van Maren, "Tucker Carlson: big business is now at war against your family," LifeSiteNews, July 15, 2019, https://www.lifesitenews.com/blogs/tucker-carlson-big-business-is-now-at-war-against-your-family/

5 See Ann Coulter, "Ann Coulter Column: Bill O'Reilly Is Killing History with Factually Challenged Praise of RFK," News Busters, July 31, 2013, https://www.newsbusters.org/blogs/nb/ann-coulter/2013/07/31/ann-coulter-column-bill-oreilly-killing-history-factually

6 Robert F. Kennedy, Remarks at the University of Kansas, Mach 18, 1968, Quoted in JFK Library, https://www.jfklibrary.org/learn/about-jfk/the-kennedy-family/robert-f-kennedy/robert-f-kennedy-speeches/remarks-at-the-university-of-kansas-march-18-1968

Kennedy was a man of vast wealth from Massachusetts yet he appealed to working class folks and non-whites because his populist message spoke to their hearts and made them feel part of something bigger, something that had purpose and scope. He was also loved by the African-American community and spent time with Cesar Chavez (a vehement opponent of illegal immigration). Kennedy also stood up for workers abused by corporations.

Why, then, are Republican lawmakers, many of whom claim to be Christians, not borrowing from his speeches? Why do conservatives who identify as "pro-family" and "pro-Trump" accept campaign contributions from groups like the US Chamber of Commerce, one of the loudest voices in Washington for open borders and cheap, illegal immigrant labor?[7]

Simply put, Republican elites seem to prefer talking only about market share, stock swaps and the consumer price index rather than address the harmful effects of, say, internet porn consumption, our nation-wide addiction to Facebook, the impact absent dads have on young boys, how universal daycare is bad for families, and how drag queen story hours warp the minds of children.

Conservatives should be as concerned with big business as they are with big government. A truly free market respects the human person as a creature of God instead of viewing him or her as a piece of machinery in service of maximizing capital gains for shareholders. The Republican Party must elect nationalist politicians with a more tradition-minded, solidarity-focused outlook. They should run candidates passionate about protecting middle-class American workers and their communities. Not only is a victory in 2020 likely assured if it does that, blue-collar voters who are squeemish about the extreme pro-infanticide, pro-LGBT policies pushed by the Democratic Party would become its new base, probably for good.

LifeSiteNews • July 22, 2019

CHRISTIANS SHOULD SUPPORT TUCKER CARLSON'S PRO-FAMILY ECONOMICS

The Inquisition has begun. Tucker Carlson is guilty of heresy. His crime? Arguing free markets tend to erode, instead of promote, the overall well being of a country, especially its families.

7 Nick Manes, "The campaign for Rep. Jim Lower says it raised $200,000," Twitter, July 9, 2019, https://x.com/nickrmanes/status/1148664573282660355. Sean Higgins, "Chamber president warns US is 'out of people,' needs more immigration," Washington Examiner, October 30, 2018, https://www.washingtonexaminer.com/news/2280387/chamber-president-warns-us-is-out-of-people-needs-more-immigration/

"Anyone who thinks the health of a nation can be summed up in GDP is an idiot," the preppy intellectual asserted last week on his television show. "Culture and economics are inseparably intertwined."[8] The Pat Buchanan-esque Fox News host has drawn the ire of pretty much every conservative thinker over the past several days. And for good reason. Carlson has violated the cardinal sin of the modern day Republican Party: questioning the infallibility of the market.

During his impassioned 15-minute monologue, Carlson convincingly argued that middle America has been hollowed out by globalist policies and that the real goal of right-wing economics has been to "make the world safe for banking."

Taking aim at Senator Mitt Romney specifically, Carlson pointed out that he spent "the bulk" of his career taking over companies, firing their employees, and extracting their wealth. "Romney became fantastically rich doing this."

The Establishment Goes Berserk

Predictably, Carlson's apostasy stirred up a hornets nest of activity among the cult-like conservative commentariat, which, unsurprisingly, accused him of Bernie Sanders-type thinking.[9]

National Review, a magazine that previous ran columns equating the taxation of soda to socialism,[10] leapt into action as if the republic itself were on the verge of collapse, publishing multiple articles that amounted to telling Carlson to shut up and stop acting like a victim.[11] "The market cures all!" the outlet seems to think.

The fresh perspective Carlson brings to policy discussions in the age of globalization should be most welcomed by pro-family Christians, who should long for an economy built not on rugged self-interest but what *Triumph*

8 Fox News, "Tucker: Leaders show no obligation to American voters," YouTube, January 2, 2019, https://www.youtube.com/watch?v=mSuQ-AyiicA

9 Ben Shapiro, "America Needs Virtue before Prosperity," National Review, January 8, 2019, https://www.nationalreview.com/2019/01/tucker-carlson-populism-america-needs-vir-tue-before-prosperity/

10 Tyler Arnold, "The Troubling Soda-Tax Trend," National Review, June 12, 2017, https://www.nationalreview.com/2017/06/soda-tax-trend-seattle-joins-berkeley-boulder-levies-sin-tax-kills-jobs/

11 David French, "The Right Should Reject Tucker Carlson's Victimhood Populism," National Review, January 4, 2019, https://www.nationalreview.com/2019/01/the-right-should-re-ject-tucker-carlsons-victimhood-populism/. Kevin Williamson, "The Non-Debate," National Review, January 8, 2019, https://www.nationalreview.com/2019/01/tucker-carlson-popu-lism-status-games/

magazine founder L. Brent Bozell Jr. once called radical "self-denial."[12]

Carlson pricks the conscience of those who generally only think in terms of dollars and cents. He shines a light on the very real, often intentionally overlooked communal damage done by slavish devotion to profit. He seems to understand that markets affect persons, their families, and towns in totalizing ways, and that economics is not just about individuals pursuing mammon in a cordoned-off sphere of life.

"One of the biggest lies our leaders tell us that you can separate economics from everything else that matters," Carlson said in his monologue. We are told "economics is a topic for public debate" while "family and faith and culture" are only "personal matters."

But "we are not servants of our economic system. We are not here to serve as shareholders. We're human beings and our concerns are real," he told an annoyed Ben Shapiro during an interview in November.[13]

A More Authentic, Christian Conservatism

The rise of Carlson's star at Fox is reflective of the larger political emergence of what is often incorrectly labeled "the populist movement." In reality, what Carlson is arguing for is a more traditional variant of conservative thinking that regrettably lost out to William F. Buckley's big business, pro-war, (and possibly CIA-backed) neoconservative coalition in the 1960s.

Sometimes referred to as "paleoconservatism," Carlson's outlook generally sees international finance, multinational corporations, and deregulated markets not as benevolent forces showering upon mankind a cornucopia of unreserved benefits, but as intentional tools of the rich and powerful that over the long haul have probably done more harm to Americans and their communities than good.

"There are a lot of ingredients to being happy," Carlson has said, reflecting his multilayered outlook. "Dignity, purpose, self-control, independence—above all, deep relationships with other people. Those are the things that you want for your children," not cheap plastic possessions and soul-crushing jobs where "mercenaries who feel no long-term obligation" to the American people rule over them.

Ultimately, Carlson seems to be siding with the Catholic Church's social teachings, which essentially hold that taking away as many restrictions on

12 L. Brent Bozell, *Mustard Seeds: A Conservative Becomes a Catholic,* Trinity Publications, Manassas, Virginia, 1986, p.316

13 DailyWire+, "Tucker Carlson | The Ben Shapiro Show Sunday Special Ep. 26," YouTube, November 4, 2018, https://www.youtube.com/watch?v=Bh8vqof9hAk&t=1s

man's economic behavior as possible creates a space where the worse effects of original sin are given the most room to run rampant. As Pope Leo XIII taught in *Rerum Novarum*, the state must prudentially intervene in the economy, especially when the family—the basic building block of society—is threatened.

America Needs Laws That Promote Virtue

While some conservatives have made the argument that a sound economy simply needs a "moral and virtuous citizenry," it seems nonsensical to say that being privately virtuous is the sole solution to the mess we've gotten ourselves into. After all, America's current economic system a) strongly entices all of us to behave un-virtuously and b) not only doesn't take into account family life (and the importance of local communities) but actively wars against them.

How can persons who live in an economic system that undermines the very things that help make men moral in the first place remain moral? Isn't the whole point of "being virtuous" to eventually change public policy so authentic human flourishing can spread and so others can more easily attain virtue as well?

Pro-family Europeans seem to understand this. In Italy, the nationalist party there is giving land to large families.[14] In Poland, parents who have multiple children are awarded with tax credits while stores are required to shut down on Sundays.[15] Advocate for such things in the United States and you'll be accused of fascism. Recall that when Republican Senators Marco Rubio and Mike Lee fought to expand the child tax credit in 2017, not a few conservatives threw a temper tantrum.[16]

Carlson is Not the First to Identify the Problem

The tidal wave of attacks launched by market fundamentalists against Carlson is a sure sign as any that he and his pro-family economic outlook is a threat to Wall Street's grip on the GOP.

14 Tim Wyatt, "Italy's far-right government offers free land to parents who have third child in 'neo-medieval' policy," Independent, November 4, 2018, https://www.independent. co.uk/news/world/europe/italy-far-right-free-land-third-child-family-government-matteo-salvini-birth-rate-children-a8616781.html

15 Dorothy Cummings McLean, "'Time for God...and rest': Catholic Poles rejoice as Sunday shopping ban comes into effect," LifeSiteNews, March 13, 2018, https://www.lifesitenews. com/news/time-for-god...and-rest-catholic-poles-rejoice-as-sunday-shopping-ban-comes/

16 Doug Mainwaring, "As tax reform vote looms, Senators Rubio, Lee fight for improved child tax credit," LifeSiteNews, November 30, 2017, https://www.lifesitenews.com/news/as-tax-reform-vote-looms-senators-rubio-lee-fight-for-improved-child-tax-cr/

As it currently stands, the old guard is on the ropes and struggling to stay in the fight. Their imperialist foreign policies were put on the endangered species list the day Donald Trump won the presidency.[17] Now, they're worried their economic ideas may become extinct so they want to make an example out of Carlson.

In many ways, Carlson is making arguments similar to those marshaled by Robert F. Kennedy, another original thinker who viewed economics holistically and from a Christian point of view. In 1968 at the University of Kansas, Kennedy delivered a famous speech anathematizing the idolatrous worship of America's gross domestic product.

"Too much and for too long, we seemed to have surrendered personal excellence and community values in the mere accumulation of material things," Kennedy said. "Our Gross National Product...if we judge the United States of America by that...counts air pollution and cigarette advertising, and ambulances to clear our highways of carnage."

"It does not include the beauty of our poetry or the strength of our marriages, the intelligence of our public debate or the integrity of our public officials. It measures neither our wit nor our courage, neither our wisdom nor our learning, neither our compassion nor our devotion to our country." The GDP, Kennedy concluded, measures everything "except that which makes life worthwhile. And it can tell us everything about America except why we are proud that we are Americans."[18]

Amen to that. More conservative Christians need to line up behind this sort of thinking. Carlson would be wise to continue promoting the message that economic life is a means to an end, not an end itself. The more converts he wins, the better.

LifeSiteNews • January 10, 2019

17 Julian Hattem, "Trump warns against 'false song of globalism'," The Hill, April 27, 2016, https://thehill.com/policy/national-security/277879-trump-warns-against-false-song-of-globalism/
18 Robert F. Kennedy, "Remarks at the University of Kansas," Quoted in John F. Kennedy Presidential Library and Museum, March 18, 1968, https://www.jfklibrary.org/learn/about-jfk/the-kennedy-family/robert-f-kennedy/robert-f-kennedy-speeches/remarks-at-the-university-of-kansas-march-18-1968

US BISHOPS SIDE WITH GLOBALISTS IN CONDEMNING TRUMP'S BORDER WALL

Last Friday, the president of the US bishops' conference, Cardinal Daniel Di-Nardo, and the chairman of the committee on migration, Bishop Joe Vásquez, unsurprisingly rebuked President Donald Trump for declaring a national emergency in order to build a wall on America's southern border. "'The wall first and foremost is a symbol of division and animosity between two friendly countries," their joint statement reads. "We remain steadfast and resolute in the vision articulated by Pope Francis that at this time we need to be building bridges and not walls."[19]

While one is certainly free to disagree with the way in which Trump went around Congress to get what he wanted, I'm not exactly sure what the rest of this document means. Are they proposing the United States shouldn't have a border wall at all? Are the bishops calling for the feds to construct actual concrete bridges between the United States and Mexico?

Borders are a Good Thing

The problem with this sort of sentimental, ambiguous, and ultimately doctrinally-unfounded statement is that it fails to defend in a rational way what it puts forth. Sadly, sloppy remarks like this are all too common among bishops these days. But such is Catholicism in the age of Pope Francis, the most confusing, imprecise, and modernist pontiff in Church history.

How, after all, is a wall a "symbol of division?" Why are symbols of division bad anyway? Christ himself announced he came "not to bring peace" but a sword. He caused a lot of "division" during his earthly life. Many of his disciples left him after he told them they needed to eat his flesh. He also said a Catholic's enemies will be members of their own family.

Far from being evil, walls are a good thing if they provide security, protect life, and ensure a country's common good is upheld in the face of those who would seek to destroy it. Trump's wall accomplishes this.

The bishops' statement reminds me of how progressive Democrats claim that Jesus was an "undocumented immigrant" and that Christians who want a border wall probably would have thrown Jesus, Mary, and Joseph into a detention center if given the opportunity.

---

19 "President of US Bishops' and Chairman of Bishop's Committee on Migration Respond to President's Order to Fund Construction of Border Wall," United States Conference of Catholic Bishops," February 15, 2019, https://www.usccb.org/news/2019/president-us-bishops-and-chairman-bishops-committee-migration-respond-presidents-order

Aside from the fact that it was an angel that told Joseph (the bread-winning head of the household) to escort his stay-at-home wife Mary into Egypt (which was under Roman rule and therefore not a separate country at the time), the Holy Family didn't receive public housing and free daycare upon arrival. They went back to Joseph's place of origin where he made a living as a carpenter after their brief journey.

Are US Bishops Complicit in the Destruction of the West?

The political left and, apparently, the US bishops' conference, does not want immigrants to return to their native lands. Ever. One possible reason is because they need them to fill their empty churches, as Steve Bannon, former adviser to President Trump, has recently argued.[20]

Another is because a flood of low-skilled laborers from Latin America into the United States will secure government grant money for Catholic Charities.

Ultimately, these migrants will have the long-term effect of providing the Democrat Party with a reliable voting bloc for decades. Texas is already on its way to being a toss-up state for the Electoral College. Give it another 15 years and a Republican might not be able to win the presidency ever again. Do American bishops really want to have blood on their hands for having played a key role in ensuring pro-abortion liberals run the executive branch until the second coming of Christ? Part of me thinks some of them would be fine with that.

Democrats hate the idea of a border wall because it would hamper their efforts to "diversify" and "multiculturalize" America, a plan rooted in anti-Christian and anti-Western Civilization attitudes. Again, can the bishops really not see what's going on here? I think Bannon was right to accuse them of being "one of the worst instigators of this open borders policy."[21]

Regardless if they can or can't realize that they're doing the bidding of the godless New World Order, they seem to think that whatever happens, things will turn out just fine because, at the end of the day, we're all brothers sailing in the same ark of human fraternity, as Pope Francis recently stated.[22]

20 Alana Abramson, "Steve Bannon: Bishops Support the Undocumented So They Can Fill Pews," TIME Magazine, September 7, 2017, https://time.com/4931496/steve-bannon-daca-catholic-church-60-minutes/

21 Quinn Scanlan, "Not necessary to justify separating kids, parents at border, 'it's zero tolerance': Bannon," ABC News, June 17, 2018, https://abcnews.go.com/Politics/justify-separating-kids-parents-border-tolerance-bannon/story?id=55946718

22 Stephen Kokx, "Pope's Abu Dhabi Speech More Freemasonic Than Catholic," Catholic Family News, February 15, 2019, https://www.catholicfamilynews.org/blog/2019/2/15/popes-abu-dhabi-speech-more-freemasonic-than-catholic

Welcoming the stranger is what the Gospel demands. It'll all work out. Or something.

Countries Also Have a 'Right to Life'

Good intentions aside, Catholic teaching on international law and the rights of nations cannot be reduced to a few fuzzy Bible verses. Providing temporary refuge for persons fleeing war zones is indeed part of the Catholic faith, but in no way does it teach that everyone has a universal right to migrate anywhere at anytime; charity must first be extended to those nearest to us and in most need.

Nor does Catholicism hold that borders are immoral or that laws that maintain a country's integrity deserve contempt. Chief among a country's rights is the right to life and preservation, and to be free from outside, international aggressors. A nation's borders, language, and culture can and should be defended, most especially if the country has a Christian orientation.

Given that the millions of persons currently invading America at its Mexican border are being used as pawns by international elites to destroy the last vestiges of Christianity in the United States, politicians who are resisting open borders initiatives should generally be praised, not vilified, by clergy for their efforts.

If bishops today were aware of the intricacies of Catholic teaching on international relations and the ins and outs of contemporary geopolitics, laity might have read a statement from the USCCB expressing appreciation for President Trump for fighting the enemies of Almighty God who are trying to impose a one-world, pro-abortion, anti-Christ government. Instead, what they got was a bland, 89-word press release that sounded more like a Tweet from socialist Congresswoman Alexandria Ocasio Cortez. As the Psalmist so often cried out in lamentation, "How long must we wait, O Lord, how long?"

LifeSiteNews • February 21, 2019

SOCIAL CONSERVATIVES CAN'T LET GOP BECOME THE PARTY OF 'GAY FAMILY VALUES'

In case you missed it, Ric Grenell, the former Acting Director of National Intelligence, gave an outstanding speech at the Republican National Convention last month. It was a historic broadside against the Deep State and neoliberal internationalists who have been in power for pretty much the last 40 years. I'm sure their blood was boiling as they watched it.

Just days before Grenell, a homosexual, delivered his remarks, he made a video declaring Donald Trump the "most pro-gay president in American history." Trump, in turn, retweeted the video, stating that it was his "great honor" to receive the title.

The Trump administration has walked a fine line the past several years with its social conservative base and the LGBT community. No one can deny that Trump is quite possibly the most pro-life president we ever had. He's also admirably defended the religious liberty of the Little Sisters of the Poor and others. He's to be praised for those efforts. But, and this is a big but, he has said nothing against the abomination that is same-sex "marriage." In fact, he supports it.

In 2016, just before assuming office, Trump told *60 Minutes* that he's "fine" with legalized sodomy. "It's irrelevant because it was already settled. It's law. It was settled in the Supreme Court. I mean, it's done," he told Leslie Stahl.

It's hard to say that if any other Republican had been elected in 2016, they would express opposition to gay "marriage" either. The party simply gave up on it after *Obergefell v. Hodges* was handed down by the Supreme Court in 2015. I can see a President Ben Carson calling out homosexual relations, but a President Jeb Bush? Or even a President Cruz? I doubt it.

Sadly, it seems that the country—and even religious conservatives—have moved on from the issue, even though God surely hasn't and will no doubt exert His vengeance on America at some point for allowing this scourge to continue.

Politically speaking, President Trump and his advisers have made the calculation that courting moderate, pro-LGBT voters won't hurt them in the slightest with his Evangelical and pro-life base. They're right to think that. He has delivered all and then some for those voting blocs. There's no way they won't support him even if he continues to move to the left on homosexuality.

In my own Congressional district here in Michigan, moderate Republican Peter Meijer has received Grenell's endorsement. Grenell went to high school in the area several decades ago. Meijer sent out a Tweet recently claiming that the GOP "has become a party that celebrates diversity and inclusion."

It seems to me that a Trump-led GOP will continue to reward social conservatives with laws that restrict abortion and uphold their religious liberty. Meanwhile, for the LGBT crowd, he will ensure that homosexuality is not viewed or treated as anything out of the ordinary. Whether this arranged marriage can be sustained over the long run remains to be seen.

Charlie Kirk, the Evangelical founder of Turning Point USA, has taken a leading role in encouraging young people to have a more laissez-faire attitude toward homosexuality, despite often saying that he, as a Christian, believes there are "only two genders." He's frequently tweeted and often "liked" other tweets that normalize the gay agenda.

Other influencers, like pro-abortion Fox News commentator Tomi Lahren, have also expressed support for "LGBT rights" on libertarian grounds. Donald Trump Jr. has previously said he's also "totally for" gay "marriage."[23]

But some Christians aren't having it.

Dave Reilly, a devout Traditional Catholic who lives and works in Indiana, confronted Kirk at one of his rallies in 2019.

"How does anal sex help us win the culture war? ... Why are you promoting it?" he bravely asked in front of hundreds of attendees while carrying a rosary in his hand.

Kirk was caught flat-footed. "Like, I don't care what two consenting adults do ... and your hyper-focus on it is kinda ... weird," he replied.

Apparently, Kirk has never read the part of the Bible that says men lying with other men is an abomination and that sin makes nations miserable.

Rob Smith, the homosexual black man who was co-hosting the event with Kirk, was on stage with him. He didn't have a good answer to Reilly's question either, opting instead to hurl empty LGBT talking points at him.

The altercation didn't end there. Popular "conservative" influencer Benny Johnson, who works for Kirk, slammed Reilly for his remarks online, absurdly claiming that his question was "homophobic."[24]

Social conservatives are going to see more of these sorts of baseless attacks if they let moderates like Meijer and Kirk (and gay men like Grenell) run the show. It's up to grassroots Christians to ensure Republicans will reverse homosexual "marriage" the same way they've successfully forced them to take up the cause of overturning abortion.

If religious Americans are content with getting pro-life laws, so be it. In truth, they need to strive for much more than that. If they don't, the realignment currency underway on the political right will continue to push for the

23 "Short Episode: Donald Trump, Jr. Opens Up About Gay Marriage, Women's Rights, and His Love of Hunting," The Huffington Post, March 15, 2012, https://www.huffpost.com/entry/the-six-pack-donald-trump-jr_b_1348643

24 Benny Johnson, "There's a difference between asking genuine questions & trolling," Twitter, October 30, 2019, https://twitter.com/bennyjohnson/status/1189573349254598656?lang=en

acceptance and normalization of homosexual behavior in the United States and across the world.[25] And that is not a good thing.

LifeSiteNews • October 21, 2020

WASHINGTON ELITES (NOT ORDINARY CITIZENS) ARE UNDERMINING AMERICAN 'DEMOCRACY'

There's one thing our corrupt leaders in Washington are right about these days: America *is* under attack. But not from the people they claim it is.

Hours after the January 6 "insurrection" in 2021, Democrat lawmakers Chuck Schumer and Nancy Pelosi decried what they called an assault on our "sacred" democracy.[26]

"These hallowed halls," crowed Schumer (as if Capitol Hill is some bastion of morality and righteousness), were trampled on by "rioters." This "temple to democracy was desecrated."[27]

Give me a break. Anyone who falls for this nonsense is either purposefully ignorant of what really goes on in Washington or is brainwashed.

First off, Congress gets steamrolled by an army of corporate, foreign, and social justice lobbyists all the time. Most everything these oily characters want, they get. If Schumer was being honest, he'd admit there is an insurrection waged against ordinary Americans in our nation's capital every day of the year.

Second, the US is not a democracy. It's a constitutional republic with three separate branches of government. Additionally, "the people" rarely decide public policy. Woke multinationals, tech oligarchs, Big Pharma executives, the media, and a cabal of lawyers and judges largely determine what our laws are.

Furthermore, if Black Lives Matter has taught us anything, it's that burning down small businesses and holding entire cities hostage is the surest way to get what you want.

The so-called "hallowed halls" Schumer speaks about are anything but that.

25 Josh Lederman, "Trump administration launches global effort to end criminalization of homosexuality," NBC News, February 19, 2019, https://www.nbcnews.com/politics/national-security/trump-administration-launches-global-effort-end-criminalization-homosexuality-n973081

26 Nancy Pelosi Press Release, "Pelosi Remarks Upon Reconvening of the House of Representatives," January 6, 2021, https://pelosi.house.gov/news/press-releases/pelosi-remarks-upon-reconvening-of-the-house-of-representatives

27 "READ: Chuck Schumer's Statement to the Senate on the Storming of the Capitol," US News, January 6, 2021, https://www.usnews.com/news/elections/articles/2021-01-06/read-chuck-schumers-statement-to-the-senate-on-the-storming-of-the-capitol

Backroom deals, corrupt bargains, billion-dollar tax breaks, and corporate carveouts have caused the stench of iniquity to seep deeply into the walls of the buildings these ethically-challenged quislings work in. Trump was right to call DC a "swamp" in need of draining.

Democrats will predictably recycle talking points about the need to protect our "sacred democracy" every January 6 from here on out. Really what they're doing is ensuring the on-going persecution of patriots who only wanted to reclaim America from the traitors who are selling it out.

LifeSiteNews • January 7, 2022

BIG TECH, DEEP STATE TEAM UP TO USHER IN COMMUNISM IN THE US

Corporate authoritarianism has come to the United States. Liberal businesses, backed by the uni-party Deep State, now get to decide what is and isn't acceptable political speech. This is an all-out assault not only on our constitutional freedoms, but on conservative Christians specifically.

The collective purging of Donald Trump (and others) from social media last week was a concerted effort meant to destroy him and the populist, nationalist movement he led. It was intended as a warning shot to any future political candidate who wants to run on the America First agenda.

It's patently ridiculous to claim, as many have, that Trump was inciting an actual "insurrection" on January 6. Not only did he call for a "peaceful" protest, Antifa and Black Lives Matter activists (some of whom seem to have been involved in the breaking into the Capitol building) have inflicted far greater damage on our country these past few years than the protesters in Washington ever did.

Nancy Pelosi's ridiculous impeachment vote was held for one reason and one reason alone: to act as the final nail in the coffin of President Trump's political coalition. Shame on the 10 Republicans that went along with it.

Other cultural institutions are jumping on board the de-personing of President Trump as well. The Professional Golf Association of America (PGA) just announced that one of its biggest tournaments will no longer be held at Trump's New Jersey golf course. Already there are reports of airlines and banks denying services to Trump-supporting Americans. Some are allegedly getting fired from their jobs simply for having been in DC on the 6th. This ruthless purge is likely not going to stop anytime soon.

Corporate America's real goal in the months and years ahead is to introduce a sort of social credit system not unlike the one used by the Chinese Communist Party. They want to ban anyone who supports America First policies from using their services under the totally bogus claim that they're basically domestic terrorists who may end up "storming our nation's Capitol again" if they're not punished.

America is sliding into dangerous territory right now. Liberal fascism shows no sign of stopping. A country where unaccountable, trillion-dollar tech companies are allowed to manipulate, suppress, and censor the people—and even the president himself—is not a free country. It's a dictatorship. Big Tech is waging a merciless war on our bedrock principles and no one, not even Republicans, are seemingly willing to take a stand against them.

President Trump said many times that the real reason the establishment hated him is because they hate you and me. That's still true today. And no matter how hard the likes of warmonger Liz Cheney and RINO's in Congress will try to extricate the GOP of America First patriots, nothing can disprove the fact that 75 million Americans voted for Donald J. Trump in 2020. Those voices must band together and do everything they can to ensure the gains made by him are sustained in the future. Patriots must put on the armor of Jesus Christ and His Blessed Mother as they go forward into this battle. God's truth is the only weapon that's guaranteed to simultaneously bring down those who plot evil while bringing peace to the world. May His wisdom guide the hearts of all of us in the years ahead.

LifeSiteNews • January 14, 2021

BISHOPS CAVE UNDER PRESSURE, WON'T DENY PRO-ABORTION BIDEN HOLY COMMUNION

How much do Catholic bishops in the United States really care about unborn babies? Or infallible church teaching on the Eucharist for that matter? By the looks of it, not that much.

The Spring General Assembly of the US Conference of Catholic Bishops came to a close a week ago. Unsurprisingly, they failed to issue a statement on the need for pro-abortion politicians to be denied Communion. Although such a denunciation was always a long shot, it would have been entirely in keeping with Canon Law (and a clear sign as any that they take seriously 1 Corinthians 11:29, which states that those who unworthily receive Communion "drink judgment on themselves").

Bishop Kevin Rhoades of Fort Wayne, Indiana has said that the document the bishops plan to release later this year will "present a clear understanding of why the Church has these laws."[28] Ho-hum! This is nothing more than kicking the can down the road. Even if they do issue something stronger than the typically mealy-mouthed statements bishops are known for these days, it won't be anything more than a paper tiger. Biden's bishop, Washington DC's Wilton Gregory, has already said he won't refuse him Communion. Others have hinted they won't either.[29]

The entire situation should infuriate faithful Catholics, and not necessarily because of the politics involved, but rather because the bishops don't seem to understand, or care about, the theological implications of their actions.

In his book *The Blessed Eucharist*, 19th century German priest Fr Michael Müller explains that when a soul in a state of sin receives Holy Communion, it is comparable to dragging Christ "as a prisoner" into a "horrid and filthy dungeon."

"Would it not be far better that the Sacred Host should be thrown upon a dunghill ... [than] be received into a heart defiled with mortal sin?" he asks.[30] If Joe Biden, who has presided over multiple "gay marriage" ceremonies and has fought to expand abortion for decades, doesn't fit this category then no one does.[31]

At the same time, one could potentially argue that Biden doesn't know any better, and that he's been more or less incentivized to support these soul-killing policies. After all, US bishops have never held liberal Catholic politicians who brazenly flout Church teaching accountable. Just look at Rep. Ted Lieu (D-CA). He went on Twitter recently to "dare" the bishops to deny him Communion after expressing his support for a laundry list of pro-abortion and pro-LGBT policies.[32]

28 Gretchen Crowe, "Rhoades: 'There's a great need to better understand Eucharist's centrality," Catholic News Service, June 21, 2021, https://web.archive.org/web/20210621205730/ https://www.catholicnews.com/rhoades-theres-a-great-need-to-better-understand-eucharists-centrality/

29 Cindy Wooden, "Washington's soon-to-be cardinal says he won't deny Joe Biden Communion," Catholic News Service, November 24, 2020, https://web.archive.org/web/20230131035511/https://www.americamagazine.org/politics-society/2020/11/24/cardinal-wilton-gregory-joe-biden-communion-dialogue. Dorothy Cummings McLean, "These bishops stand in the way of prohibiting Communion for Biden, pro-abortion politicians," LifeSiteNews, June 8, 2021, https://web.archive.org/web/20230205164645/https://www.lifesitenews.com/news/these-68-us-bishops-reject-discussion-on-communion-for-pro-abortion-politicians-like-biden/

30 Fr Michael Müller, CSSR., *The Blessed Sacrament*, TAN Books and Publishers, Rockford, Illinois, 1994, pp. 162–163

31 Curtis M. Wong, "Joe Biden Officiated A Gay Wedding Over Memorial Day Weekend," Huffington Post, May 30, 2017, https://web.archive.org/web/20221209023831/https://www.huffpost.com/entry/joe-biden-memorial-day-gay-wedding_n_592dc142e4b0c0608e8bed5c

32 Thomas Williams, Ph.D., "Pro-Abortion Congressman Ted Lieu 'Dares' Bish-

It would have been a glorious moment in Church history—perhaps something akin to when St Ambrose rebuked Emperor Theodosius in the 4th century—had the bishops taken a stand and defended Catholic doctrine at their June meeting. Instead, they caved to media and Vatican pressure and are now complicit in the continued profanation of the Body of Jesus Christ.[3334] May God have mercy on their souls.

CNSNews.com • July 8, 2021

CATHOLICS PROTEST MICHIGAN ABORTION LAWS WITH EUCHARISTIC PROCESSION AT STATE CAPITOL

Jesus Christ and his mother, the Blessed Virgin Mary, toured the Michigan state capitol this week.

On Wednesday, a Eucharistic procession organized by GOP state Rep. Jim DeSana took place on capitol grounds. A statue of a crucifix and another of Our Lady of Fatima were carried by attendees and placed on the steps of the capitol building at the conclusion of the hour-long event.

Nearly 200 Catholics primarily from the east side of the state attended the ceremony, which was led in the rosary by Fr John Hedges of St Stephen's parish in New Boston, located just south of Detroit.

DeSana is serving his first term in elected office. He currently represents the 29th District in the Statehouse, where Republicans are in the minority. They are also the minority in the Michigan Senate. A devout pro-life Catholic who supports homeschooling, DeSana told LifeSite it was a great experience.

"I hope to be a prayerful witness out here at the capitol for everybody to see that we as Catholics care about the unborn child," he said. "If people in Michigan would continue to be faithful, we would have a pro-life state."

Michigan voters overwhelmingly passed a ballot proposal that overturned the state's constitutional ban on abortion last month. The new measure

ops to Deny Him Holy Communion," Breitbart, June 20, 2021, https://web.archive.org/web/20230319200031/https://www.breitbart.com/politics/2021/06/20/pro-abortion-congressman-ted-lieu-dares-bishops-to-deny-him-holy-communion/

33 "Abortion Giant NARAL Pressures Bishops to Give Communion to Biden," CatholicVote, June 16, 2021, https://web.archive.org/web/20230321212220/https://catholicvote.org/abortion-giant-naral-pressures-bishops-to-give-communion-to-biden/

34 Jason Horowitz, "Vatican Warns US Bishops: Don't Deny Biden Communion Over Abortion," The New York Times, June 14, 2021, Updated October 29, 2021, https://web.archive.org/web/20230104195433/https://www.nytimes.com/2021/06/14/world/europe/biden-vatican-communion-abortion.html

likely means abortion will be legal up until birth, depending on how future lawsuits shake out.

According to the *Washington Post*, women who live in neighboring pro-life states are coming to Michigan for abortions.[35] Michigan's current governor, Democrat Gretchen Whitmer, runs an unapologetically pro-abortion administration.

DeSana's father James served as an elected official in the 1960s and 70s. A dad to eight children and a grandfather to many more, DeSana was sworn into office on the day of the procession. He told LifeSite that the Catholics he talked to on Wednesday were overjoyed to be there.

"People were saying that they were happy to be here ... and to have [it] be a penitential act on behalf of the unborn."

The procession began around 10:30 a.m. on a street just north of the capitol near the headquarters of the Diocese of Lansing. Despite the chilly 40-degree temperature, Catholics young and old, including parents with young children and several high school students, took part in the march. Several local media outlets covered the event as well.

A group of men led the march while carrying a statue of a crucified Christ on their shoulders. Four teenage girls followed behind them with a statue of Our Lady of Fatima. Loudspeakers played chants and prayers in Latin throughout the procession, which was approved by capitol police beforehand. At the event's culmination, the two statues were placed on the steps of the capitol building and a brief Benediction service took place.

One young man from Grand Rapids was thrilled with the day's events. "To see Jesus here, at the capitol, enshrined—at least temporarily—at the seat of our government was beautiful. I hope our lawmakers will recognize and accept what we are standing up for. Christ is King!" he exuberantly told LifeSite.

LifeSiteNews • December 8, 2022

REFLECTIONS ON CPAC: CONSERVATIVES MUST EMBRACE CHRIST, NOT LGBT IDEOLOGY

I attended my first Conservative Political Action Conference (CPAC) this year. I'm grateful to have gone and to have met the people I did. But what struck

---

35 Rachel Roubein with McKenzie Beard, "Fresh off abortion rights victory, Michigan providers embrace out-of-state patients," Washington Post, November 10, 2022, https://www. washingtonpost.com/politics/2022/11/10/fresh-off-abortion-rights-victory-michigan-providers-embrace-out-of-state-patients/

me the most after seeing up close and personal the so-called leaders of the "conservative" movement is just how much coalition politics is a dirty, sad state of affairs, and that Jesus Christ is sorely missing from most of it.

Earlier this week I spoke with Brian McCall from *Catholic Family News* about my time in Orlando. That interview is set to be released in the coming days on their YouTube channel. I told him that CPAC made me long for Christendom. I told him that it made me yearn to live during a time in human history when elected officials and others in public life wanted to actually help those who were under their protection get to heaven. Nowadays, politics is little more than power-hungry individuals employing whatever schemes they can cook up to take each-other out. Sure, human beings have always done this to varying degrees, even in Catholic nations prior to Martin Luther's revolt in the 1500s. But everything is far, far worse today now that the world has rejected the true faith.

The way I see it, politics in recent centuries is God telling us, "Okay you stiff necked rabble, you want to reject my teachings? Let's see you manage things better without the sacraments at the center of public life. Good luck!"

If nothing else, CPAC 2021 confirmed to me that democracy, pluralism, and modernity easily brings out the worst in people and that we're all on a sinking ship until God decides to intervene. Until then, Christians can have minor political victories here and there, but if Jesus Christ is not recognized as the ruler of nations, we're just re-arranging deck chairs on the Titanic.

The 'Conservative Movement' is not Pro-Christ

The political right has been trending in favor of the LGBT agenda for a while now, and under President Trump its relationship with the gay lobby has only grown closer. Anti-LGBT groups like Mass Resistance and Americans for Truth about Homosexuality aren't allowed at CPAC anymore. Fortunately, Abby Johnson called out CPAC organizers for going soft on family issues during a panel discussion this year. I was in the front row when she did that and was glad to have witnessed it.

To be fair, there *was* a session held on the main stage about the importance of fatherhood. Terry Schilling from the American Principles Project also moderated a talk about keeping boys out of girls' sports. But that was all low hanging fruit. Everyone knows the GOP wants to move on from *Obergefell v. Hodges* and that it is seeking to appease the LGBT faction, whose influence is only going to grow over the long term. The camel's nose is already under the tent, in other words, and Schilling and others like him, though clearly well-intentioned, are between a rock and a hard place. I don't envy them.

The conservative movement will always talk about the importance of being pro-life. And they did at this year's CPAC with a panel discussion that featured Alison Centofante of Live Action. They also premiered Nick Loeb's new *Roe v. Wade* movie. CPAC organizers clearly understand that abortion motivates millions of people to donate their money to politicians and to go to the polls every election cycle.

Perhaps the most shocking thing I saw at CPAC—really, couldn't help but notice—was the way the women were dressed. You think Fox News has a problem with modesty? Come to CPAC. And it's not just the twenty-something talking heads on "conservative" media who are problematic. Even the teenagers are bad.

Overall, attendees at CPAC are an interesting lot. The older folks tend to be die hard activists who border on making an idol out of politics. They willingly fork over hundreds, if not thousands of dollars for the chance to see corrupt lawmakers up close and personal. The younger high school and college students all seemingly want to be the next Tomi Lahren or Ben Shapiro.

A drag queen named "Lady Maga" was at CPAC this year. I asked him if he thinks the Republican Party is moving in his direction. He immediately said that conservatives across America "love freedom" and that they love him too. How wonderful.

The Kingship of Christ is the Only Way Forward

What should Christians be doing amid this chaos? Should they simply demand that they be left alone in the name of religious liberty? Should they file lawsuits that will allow them to teach what the Bible says in their own communities?

While it's true that we need to be able to do those things—and that politics can help achieve those ends—our real goal should be the total reclaiming of the public sphere for Jesus Christ, who has dominion over all creation.

I told Brian McCall on his show that what I truly miss is good old fashion Catholic Action, where bishops lead the laity in public life. I said that we should "care little for what the left or the right thinks of us. Let's be considered fools for Christ!"

I'm sick of the rat race of modern politics where ordinary lay people too often twist and contort the Christian faith to fit in with this or that political movement. Usually what happens is the truth gets watered down somewhere along the way. I don't pretend to have all the answers, but a good start in the years ahead would be for Catholics to boldly proclaim the truth of the Gospel and to be a thorn in the side not only of all politicians but most especially the "conservative" ones. Conservatism won't make America great again. Only Christ can. Let's never tire of reminding our fellow citizens of that.

LifeSiteNews • March 5, 2021

CHRISTIAN NATIONALISM AND THE NATURAL LAW: EXPOSING LEFTIST FEAR-MONGERING

Heidi Przybyla is not a household name in the United States. But she said something recently that earned her nationwide attention.

Przybyla is a left-wing journalist who joined *Politico* in 2022. Raised Catholic and highly educated, she previously worked for *USA Today*, *Bloomberg*, and *NBC News*. She ignited a firestorm during an appearance on *MSNBC*'s "All In With Chris Hayes" last month."[36] She was on the program to promote her purportedly groundbreaking 1,700-word essay, "Trump allies prepare to infuse 'Christian nationalism' in second administration."[37]

While seated next to former GOP Chairman Michael Steele, Przybyla argued that "Christian nationalists" are an existential threat to the United States. "The thing that unites them as Christian nationalists...is that they believe that our rights as Americans, as all human beings, don't come from any earthly authority. They don't come from Congress, they don't come from the Supreme Court. They come from God."

Convinced that she had made an effective point, Przybyla continued. "The problem with that is that they are determining—man, men, it is men—are determining what God is telling them."

Undeterred, she added that "so-called natural law" is "a pillar of Catholicism." It "has been used for good in social justice campaigns, Martin Luther King evoked it in talking about civil rights, but now you have an extremist element of conservative Christians who say that this applies specifically to issues including abortion, gay marriage, and it's going much further than that."

36 Tim Hains, "Heidi Przybyla: Extremist Conservative Christian Nationalists Believe Your Rights Come From God, Not Government," Real Clear Politics, February 23, 2024, https://www.realclearpolitics.com/video/2024/02/23/heidi_przybyla_extremist_conservative_christian_nationalists_believe_your_rights_come_from_god_not_government.html
37 Alexander Ward and Heidi Przybyla, "Trump allies prepare to infuse 'Christian nationalism' in second administration," *Politico*, February 20, 2024, https://www.politico.com/news/2024/02/20/donald-trump-allies-christian-nationalism-00142086

Religious Voices Push Back

Among those who criticized Przybyla were Evangelical Tony Perkins of the Family Research Council and CatholicVote president Brian Burch. Both added their names to a joint letter addressed to *Politico*'s upper management that decried her comments as a "smearing of the Christian faith." The letter also said her words indicated she has a "disqualifying lack of knowledge" with the fact that "our own Republic was founded on the belief that our rights come from God, not earthly kings or government."[38]

One of the more surprising voices that pushed back against Przybyla was Bishop Robert Barron.[39]

Barron had uncharacteristically injected himself into the political world in 2020 when socialist Congresswoman Alexandria Ocasio-Cortez slandered St Damien of Molokai for preaching the Gospel to natives in Hawaii. She had indirectly accused the saint, whose statue resides in Statuary Hall of the US Capitol building, of upholding "white supremacist culture." At the time, Barron called A O C's remarks "outrageous" and "insulting."[40]

Barron spoke with the *Washington Examiner* about Przybyla's remarks. He delivered what has become the most common way conservatives tend to refute liberal assertions of this kind. "To say that our rights come not from God but from the government opens the door to totalitarianism, for the very government that gave them can take them away. To hold that our rights come from God is to affirm that there is a power greater than the state, and such a conviction is essential to the preservation of our freedom," he said.[41]

Zionists Condemn 'White Christian Conservatives'

Przybyla's remarks cannot be viewed in a vacuum. They are part of an

38 Joseph Wulfsohn, "Christian groups send letter to *Politico* demanding apology over reporter's viral comments: 'Deeply disturbing,'" Fox News, February 28, 2024, https://www.foxnews.com/media/christian-groups-send-letter-politico-demanding-apology-reporters-comments

39 Bishop Robert Barron, "Friends, I wanted to share some reflections with you concerning a recent clip I saw," X, February 23, 2024, https://twitter.com/BishopBarron/status/1761125620388356603

40 Doug Mainwaring, "US bishop: A O C calling St Damien white supremacist 'crazy, outrageous, insulting,'" LifeSiteNews, August 3, 2020, https://www.lifesitenews.com/news/us-bishop-aoc-calling-st-damien-white-supremacist-crazy-outrageous-insulting

41 Peter Laffin, "Bishop Robert Barron on the growing leftist secular threat," Washington Examiner, March 3, 2024, https://www.washingtonexaminer.com/restoring-america/faith-freedom-self-reliance/2898047/exclusive-bishop-robert-barron-on-the-growing-leftist-secular-threat

emerging trend in the mainstream media that is meant to intensify the delegitimization of otherwise normal Americans who want nothing more than common-sense, pro-family, and pro-life policies.

Movie producer Rob Reiner has been one of the most dutiful foot soldiers in this battle as of late. A longtime sufferer of Trump Derangement Syndrome, Reiner recently decided to make a documentary entitled *God and Country*. Its purpose was to expose what he sees as the "troubling rise of Christian nationalism."

In its review of the film, which unsurprisingly flopped at the box office,[42] *The Times of Israel* quotes Reiner as saying that Christian nationalists "believe that America … is ordained by God to be a white Christian nation." He then added, without proof, that they are "willing to go to the lengths of violence to get their way."[43]

I'm not sure I know of any mainstream "white Christians" who are engaging in or promoting violence to realize their political goals. I do know, however, many liberals and non-Christians—the Anti-Defamation League being one—who inflict spiritual harm on souls by indoctrinating children with LGBT ideology, by pushing artificial intelligence, by encouraging open borders, and by weaponizing the FBI to investigate Traditional Catholics.

Reiner is not alone in his efforts to vilify those who just 15 years ago would have passed for middle-of-the-road Democrats opposed to multiculturalism. Tom Schaller and Paul Waldman have focused their attention on them as well.

In March, Schaller and Waldman, both of whom, like Reiner, are Jewish, released a new book entitled *White Rural Rage: The Threat to American Democracy*.

Schaller has argued that "white people" in the United States are "the most racist, xenophobic, anti-immigrant, anti-gay, geo-demographic group in the country." They're also "the most strongly White nationalist and White Christian nationalist … [and] they're most likely to excuse or justify violence as an acceptable alternative to peaceful public discourse."[44]

The collective message being sent by Przybyla, Reiner, Schaller, and Waldman is not difficult to discern: white conservative Christians will destroy America if Donald Trump is elected in 2024.

42 John Nolte, "Nolte: Like All Rob Reiner Movies, 'God and Country' Flops with $38K Opening," Breitbart, February 20, 2024, https://www.breitbart.com/entertainment/2024/02/20/nolte-like-all-rob-reiner-movies-god-and-country-flops-38k-opening

43 Stephen Silver, "In documentary 'God and Country,' Rob Reiner shines a light on Christian nationalism," The Times of Israel, February 17, 2024, https://www.timesofisrael.com/in-documentary-god-and-country-rob-reiner-shines-a-light-on-christian-nationalism

44 Nathan J. Robinson, "Are Rural White People The Problem?" Current Affairs, March 4, 2024, https://www.currentaffairs.org/2024/03/are-rural-white-people-the-problem

The Natural Law, Properly Understood

By and large, Catholics have not been lumped into the category of "Christian nationalists." Przybyla, Reiner, and others are generally referring to Evangelical Protestants with their remarks.

That being said, there are many policies Catholics can support that "Christian nationalists" currently back. A safe and secure border, for instance, is one such law. As is keeping America's religious and cultural makeup fairly homogeneous.

It is important to push back on Przybyla's claim that "so-called natural law" is "a pillar of Catholicism," as she has said it has been "used for good in social justice campaigns" in the past but "now you have an extremist element of conservative Christians who say that this applies specifically to issues including abortion, gay marriage, and it's going much further than that."

St Thomas Aquinas teaches that there are four types of law: eternal law, divine law, natural law, and human law. Eternal law pertains to God and His plan for all things. Divine law is that which God has revealed "by the prophets" and especially "by His Son" (Heb. 1:1) in order to direct man to his supernatural end (eternal beatitude in Heaven). Natural law is that which is inscribed on the "hearts of men" (Romans 2:15) and leads them to participate in the eternal law. Human or civil laws are those which man derives from the natural law to govern society and nations in a just manner in accordance with the common good.

Przybyla attempts to belittle natural law by arguing that it is not clear what it demands. "The problem with that is that ... man, men, it is men—are determining what God is telling them."

In saying this, Przybyla betrays a fundamental misunderstanding of natural law, which is based not on men's opinions about divine revelation ("what God is telling them") but on human nature itself. "Man's nature is a rational nature," explains Fr Austin Fagothey, SJ, in his classic work *Right and Reason*, "and he finds the natural law by the use of his reason in drawing conclusions about his own nature." And further, "The natural law is manifested to reason not by any external sign [i.e., decree], but simply by a rationally conducted examination of human nature with all its parts and relations, and particularly in its relation to God, the Supreme Lawgiver."[45]

Now, it is true that man can darken his conscience and dull his sensitivity to precepts of the natural law. He does this by sinning but also by rejecting the Catholic Faith. "How, then, can civil rulers know their duties of natural

45 Fr Austin Fagothey, SJ, *Right and Reason: Ethics in Theory and Practice*, TAN Books and Publishers, Inc., Rockford, 2000, p. 174

law unless they have recourse to revelation, as interpreted by the one au-thentic teacher of revealed truth, the Catholic Church?" American priest Fr Francis Connell wrote in 1951. "If a person tries to solve the moral problems connected with sterilization, euthanasia, contraception, etc., he will very easily go astray unless he relies on Christian revelation as proposed by the teaching authority of the Church."[46]

This doesn't change what the natural law entails, however. That abortion and gay "marriage"—two policies singled out by Przybyla—are violations of the natural law is knowable by basic reason: abortion is willful murder of another human being while homosexual activity is contrary to biology in that it leads to disease and ultimately death.

One need not be, as Przybyla argues, an "extremist element of conservative Christians" to come to these conclusions. Hillary Clinton herself said in the year 2000 that "marriage has got historic, religious, and moral content that goes back to the beginning of time, and I think a marriage is as a marriage has always been, between a man and a woman."[47]

Anti-Christian Globalists are the Real Threat

There was a time in the not too distant past when the United States was led by political leaders who better understood the natural law and what it entails. Civil laws by and large reflected that reality. But since the 1960s, the sexual liberation movement, the infiltration of college campuses by woke professors, and scores of other political victories by anti-Christian forces have led to the passage of bills that are contrary to not only the natural law but to the divine and eternal law as well.

These laws are, as St Augustine famously said, unjust and no laws at all. The real threat to America is not "Christian nationalists" but rather anti-Christian globalists who want to maintain these unjust laws. Przybyla, Reiner, and others like them are woefully misguided in fighting on behalf of those forces.

Catholic Family News • April 2024

---

46 Fr Francis J. Connell, "Theory of the Lay State," *American Ecclesiastical Review*, 125, July 1951, p. 17

47 Amy Sherman, "Hillary Clinton's changing position on same-sex marriage," PolitiFact, June 17, 2015, https://www.politifact.com/factchecks/2015/jun/17/hillary-clinton/hillary-clin-ton-change-position-same-sex-marriage

'CHRIST IS KING' GOES VIRAL FOLLOWING CANDACE OWENS' DEPARTURE FROM THE DAILY WIRE

The phrase "Christ is King" was trending on X this past weekend, as well as on Monday, the start of Holy Week, following news that Candace Owens was no longer working for the *Daily Wire*, a website co-founded by Ben Shapiro, who is Jewish.

Traditional Catholics, Evangelicals, Zionist Jews, and others have been responding to one another, sometimes aggressively, on X over the past 72 hours about whether or not the phrase "Christ is King" is itself or is being used for "anti-Semitic" purposes.

The kerfuffle has drawn the attention of many prominent conservatives who otherwise broadly agree on culture war issues but are theologically divided on the topic. "Watching certain people OBJECT to Christians saying 'Christ is King' is VERY revealing. Taking notes," Catholic author Taylor Marshall posted.[48]

The situation appears to have stemmed from interactions that Owens, whose husband is Catholic, had with two Jewish Rabbis last week. One of them, Shmuley Boteach, attempted to cancel her with help from the Anti-Defamation League after a contentious back and forth he had with her online that ultimately lead to her calling the perverse sex store he and his daughter operate "filth."[49]

Schmuley later mocked Owens in a video he released on the Jewish holiday of Purim while acting like he was drunk on "Gentile blood." The move was criticized as being below the belt by influencers on the platform, including *InfoWars*' Alex Jones.

Another incident was when Owens interviewed a Rabbi on her podcast about the conflict in Gaza. His position was that Jewish suffering is a particularly unique evil. Owens responded by telling him Christianity is "actually the most persecuted religion in the world."[50]

Shapiro and His Allies Unite Against Owens

In November 2023, a leaked video of *Daily Wire* co-founder and arch-Zionist Ben Shapiro showed him telling a crowd of people at a private event that

---

48 Dr Taylor Marshall, "Watching certain people OBJECT to Christians," X, March 25, 2024, https://x.com/TaylorRMarshall/status/1772286037374517496

49 Candace Owens, "As I said... everyone can see what is happening.," X, March 21, 2024, https://x.com/RealCandaceO/status/1770936309949100393

50 Classic Groyper, "Uniquely evil? That's very hard for me to say," X, March 24, 2024, https://x.com/classicsgroyp/status/1771892963406213492

Owens' commentary on the war had been "disgraceful."[51] He later publicly urged her to quit. To date, more than 30,000 Gaza civilians have been killed by Israeli forces.

One of the first individuals to comment on Owens' departure was *Daily Wire* contributor Andrew Klavan. Catholic *Daily Wire* employees Matt Walsh and Michael Knowles, Knowles being godfather to one of Owens' children, have thus far offered little opinion on the matter, with Knowles simply sharing that he is close friends with all involved.

Klavan is ethnically Jewish but was baptized an Anglican twenty years ago. Among other things, he supports homosexual relationships.[52] In a recent podcast, he argued that there are some people who use the term "Christ the King" to offend Jewish people.

"I'm a Jew, I'm proud of my race... Christians have welcomed me with open arms, except this 'Christ the King anti-Semitic' crowd," he said, without specifying who he was referring to. "When you use that phrase to mean that God has abandoned His chosen people the Jews... and that He's broken his promise, His covenant with the Jews, you are quoting Scripture like Satan does in the Bible," he added. "You are quoting Scripture to your purposes."[53]

Klavan further chastised Christians who "spit that phrase at Ben Shapiro" because "if Ben were to embrace Jesus Christ it would cause devastation to his family, to the people who love him, to the people who listen to him, to his position in the world."

The Old Covenant is No Longer Valid

Reaction to Klavan's video has fallen along denominational lines. Former Trump legal adviser Jenna Ellis came to his support by issuing multiple posts on X.

"Some prominent voices who use the term 'Christ is King'... do so as an antisemitic dog whistle against Jews, indicating that God has abandoned them

51 Stephen Kokx, "Candace Owens gives epic response to Ben Shapiro, charges of 'anti-Semitism' during Tucker Carlson interview," LifeSiteNews, November 16, 2023, https://www.lifesitenews.com/news/candace-owens-rejects-charge-of-anti-semitism-during-viral-interview-with-tucker-carlson/

52 Heather Clark, "Evangelical College's Invite to Pro-Life Screenwriter Who Believes Homosexuality Doesn't 'Offend God' Questioned," Christian News Network, July 13, 2019, https://christiannews.net/2019/07/13/evangelical-colleges-invite-to-pro-life-screenwriter-who-believes-homosexuality-doesnt-offend-god-questioned/

53 AF Post, "Jewish Daily Wire host Andrew Klavan says 'Christ is King' is an anti-Semitic dogwhistle," X, March 23, 2024, https://x.com/AFpost/status/1771614691925598599

for Christians," she argued.[54] Calvinist Allie Beth Stuckey sympathetically remarked that "using 'Jesus is King' for any other reason than to share the gospel is evil. It's not a catchy saying or motivational mantra."[55] *Daily Wire* co-founder Jeremy Boreing shared a lengthy X post claiming that the phrase is "not innately antisemitic" but "may be antisemitic" in certain contexts. He warned others to not "use His Name as a cudgel to bash those in whom the Light of God yet flickers. If you do, you are a blasphemer and an antisemite and a piece of crap generally, and the fear of the Lord is clearly not in you."[56]

Conservative Catholics have responded almost universally with support for "Christ the King" messaging. They also maintain that the Bible actually does support the theology Klavan and others condemn.

"Jenna, the New Testament clearly teaches that the Old (Mosaic) Covenant was made 'obsolete' by the New Covenant (Hebrews 8:13) and that the Church is the true 'Israel of God' (Galatians 6:16)," *Catholic Family News* managing editor Matt Gaspers said in an X post responding to Ellis.[57]

"All Catholics should obviously hold that Christ is King" and believe the "New Covenant in Christ fulfills the Old," *Crisis Magazine* editor in chief Eric Sammons likewise said. "Opposing the modern government of Israel is not antisemitic," he added.[58]

Owens herself has issued several follow up messages on X reiterating her support for the phrase. "The reason why some people believe that with enough insistence they can convince American Christians that the basic truth, 'Christ is King' is actually antisemitic, is because they have been successfully spiking the ball on Christianity for the past 60 years," she said.[59] Amen to that!

LifeSiteNews • March 26, 2024

54 Jenna Ellis, "For those confused, the debate over the term 'Christ is King' IS NOT over the question of whether Christians believe Jesus is Lord," X, March 24, 2024, https://x.com/JennaEllisEsq/status/1771905695073382602

55 Allie Beth Stuckey, "Just to make sure this is perfectly clear," X, March 24, 2024, https://x.com/conservmillen/status/1771997639355048211

56 Jeremy Boreing, "How is saying 'Christ is King' antisemitic?," X, March 25, 2024, https://x.com/JeremyDBoreing/status/1772253907319669011

57 Matt Gaspers, "Jenna, the New Testament clearly teaches that the Old (Mosaic) Covenant was made 'obsolete'," X, March 25, 2024, https://x.com/MattGaspers/status/1772308859647885375

58 Eric Sammons, "A few beliefs that all Catholics should *obviously* hold," X, March 25, 2024, https://x.com/EricRSammons/status/1772231967872020956

59 Candace Owens, "The reason why some people believe," X, March 25, 2024, https://x.com/RealCandaceO/status/1772273631818612756/history

WILL THE DEEP STATE ACTUALLY ASSASSINATE
DONALD TRUMP?

The inevitability of another Trump nomination—and possible electoral victory next November—is something Beltway elites are coming to grips with. Robert Kagan, the neocon husband of liberal Zionist Victoria Nuland, said as much in a recent column for CIA mouthpiece *The Washington Post*.[60]

Nuland is a bureaucratic parasite (what the media calls a "diplomat") who currently serves in the Biden regime. Her primary job right now is to ensure yours and my tax dollars are funneled to Volodymyr Zelensky's ever-widening pockets.

Kagan's article is several thousand words long. It is Exhibit A of why he belongs in an insane asylum. It is an unhinged rant about how Trump will usher in a "dictatorship" if he ever gets re-elected, which, Kagan admits, is looking very possible. Kagan theorizes that if Trump wins the presidency he will "immediately become the most powerful person ever to hold that office" given the obstacles he has overcome.

Kagan ominously asks his audience—most of whom are probably intelligence agents—what they are going to do to prevent this from happening. "If we thought there was a 50 percent chance of an asteroid crashing into North America a year from now, would we be content to hope that it wouldn't?" he wonders. "Or would we be taking every conceivable measure to try to stop it, including many things that might not work but that, given the magnitude of the crisis, must be tried anyway?"

A Trump election might result in "the loss of property and possibly the loss of freedom," Kagan added, apparently aloof to the fact that numerous Traditional Catholics, conservatives, and pro-lifers have been sentenced to jail time or had their homes violated during Joe Biden's time in office. America is "closer to that point today than we have ever been, yet we continue to drift toward dictatorship, still hoping for some intervention that will allow us to escape the consequences of our collective cowardice."

Kagan is skilled in the art of deception. What he calls "dictatorship" is actually, as liberals themselves so often say, "what democracy looks like." A Trump re-election would not be "tyranny" but a reflection of what the popular sentiment of the people currently is. Simply put, if voters are fed up with Biden's open borders policies, his support for Ukraine, and awful record on domestic issues then they have the right to oust him. To describe that as

---

60 Robert Kagan, "A Trump dictatorship is increasingly inevitable. We should stop pretending," The Washington Post, November 30, 2023, https://www.washingtonpost.com/opinions/2023/11/30/trump-dictator-2024-election-robert-kagan/

an embrace of communism-light is to merely deflect from the kleptocracy Americans live under and have lived under for decades.

The most disturbing aspect of Kagan's remarks is not so much his misleading characterization of what a Trump victory in 2024 would mean. It is his own response to the question, "are we going to do anything about it?" Again, Kagan argues that the court system, conservative media, and political leaders like Mitch McConnell have thus far prevented Trump from rising to the top of the GOP field. Only after pointing this out does he say: "We continue to drift toward dictatorship, still hoping for some intervention that will allow us to escape the consequences of our collective cowardice."

It seems to me that what he is trying to say with the words "still hoping for some intervention" is to urge the Deep State to assassinate Trump.

That Kagan would make such brazen remarks in one of the most powerful newspapers in the country speaks volumes about where the US is at the moment.

Are We Being Programmed to Accept a Trump Assassination?

A possible Trump assassination has been raised by other political observers as well. Tucker Carlson told comedian Adam Carolla in August he thinks it is a real possibility. "If you begin with criticism, then you go to protest, then you go to impeachment, now you go to indictment and none of them work. What's next? Graph it out, man," he said. "We're speeding towards assassination, obviously… They have decided—permanent Washington, both parties have decided—that there's something about Trump that's so threatening to them, they just can't have him."[61]

Carlson himself asked Trump about this possibility before. Trump simply responded by saying "they're savage animals. They are people that are sick."[62]

Alex Jones, the founder of *InfoWars*, likewise told Carlson that assassination is the next logical step because Trump cannot be stopped. "The Deep State does kill people. And that's their only next move," he predicted earlier this month.[63]

---

61 Daniel Arkin, "Tucker Carlson stokes conspiracies, claims US is 'speeding towards' assassination of Trump," NBC News, September 1, 2023, https://www.nbcnews.com/news/tucker-carlson-says-us-speeding-assassination-trump-stoking-conspiraci-rcna102976

62 LifeSiteNews Staff, "Donald Trump talks assassination, Epstein and indictments in interview with Tucker Carlson," LifeSiteNews, August 23, 2023, https://www.lifesitenews.com/news/donald-trump-talks-assassination-epstein-and-indictments-in-interview-with-tucker-carlson/

63 Stephen Kokx, "Alex Jones rips mask off New World Order's 'designed global collapse' on Tucker Carlson's show," LifeSiteNews, December 8, 2023, https://www.lifesitenews.com/

There are two ways to think about these prognostications. One way is to view them as nothing more than the informed opinions of pundits who are familiar with the way politics and the Deep State operate. Another way is to understand them as a sort of programming tool meant to telegraph what is to come.

If Trump were to be assassinated, the America First movement would be without its leader. Having been decapitated, it would likely flail about until breaking into various factions. Who would benefit from that? Quite obviously the establishment wing of the Republican Party, especially the military industrial complex, which has been rallying behind Nikki Haley in her presidential race.

If Trump somehow does make it to election day alive—and ends up winning—my guess is the Deep State will never forgive him or the American people for putting him back in the Oval Office. At that point they would be emboldened to take revenge by collapsing the entire country with false flags, energy grid attacks, and sowing domestic chaos that ultimately leads to civil war. I hope I am wrong about that and that our prayers will prevent such wicked plans from being realized. But perhaps that is what we deserve for mocking God with all the sins we allow to take place in our country. If ever there was a time to put our trust in God and not in men, now is that time.

LifeSiteNews • December 18, 2023

THE TRUMP ASSASSINATION ATTEMPT: A FAILED COUP ON THE UNITED STATES

The assassination attempt on Donald Trump's life—as well as his recent debate with Joe Biden—reminded me of a scene from *The Godfather: Part II*.

Michael Corleone (played by Al Pacino) was in Cuba visiting Jewish gangster Hyman Roth (played by Lee Strasburg). Roth had become a sort of mentor to him after his father's passing. But Michael, who was upset over the attempted murder of Corleone family capo Frank Pantangelli, confronted him.

"Who gave the go ahead? I know I didn't," he emphatically asked.

Roth, immediately aware that Michael probably knew he was the one who approved it, denounced the daring question with a monologue about his former friend Moe Greene, who Michael assassinated for standing in the way of his business dealings in Las Vegas.

news/alex-jones-rips-mask-off-new-world-orders-designed-global-collapse-on-tucker-carl-sons-show/

"No one knows who gave the order. When I heard it, I wasn't angry. I knew Moe, I knew he was head-strong, talking loud, saying stupid things. So when he turned up dead, I let it go," Roth sternly replied. "And I said to myself, this is the business we've chosen! I didn't ask who gave the order, because it had nothing to do with business!"

After watching what unfolded this past month, I was left wondering: "Who gave the order for the media to turn on Joe Biden, the man they have been covering up for since 2016? Who gave the go-ahead to assassinate President Trump? Who, in other words, directed them to implode the Democratic Party and then follow it up with an attempt on the life of the man most likely to be the next president? More importantly, *why* did they do this?"

Foreign Policy and Israel

Despite the fact the liberal American and global media empire hates Trump for many of his domestic policies, what is most alarming for them this time around—and is what likely motivated the assassination attempt—is his pro-peace stance on the wars in Israel and Ukraine.

It goes without saying that Joe Biden has had a frosty relationship with Israeli Prime Minister Benjamin Netanyahu. Not only has Biden publicly speculated that Netanyahu is prolonging the war in Gaza to stay in power (which he is), he dragged his feet on giving Israel weapons out of fear they would end up being used on civilians.[6465]

Furious over the decision, Netanyahu recorded a video complaining about how "it's inconceivable that in the past few months, the [Biden] administration has been withholding weapons." He then remarked that "during World War II, Churchill told the United States, 'Give us the tools, we'll do the job.' And I say, give us the tools and we'll finish the job a lot faster."

During his debate with Biden, Trump echoed Netanyahu's talking points by saying Israel needs to "finish the job." He also disgustingly said Biden has "become like a Palestinian" by not being more supportive of Israel's demands. Current estimates place the Gaza death toll just north of 35,000, with most of the casualties being women and children. Some reports claim it is closer to 186,000.[66] Latin Patriarchate Cardinal Pierbattista Pizzaballa has repeatedly

64 Rebecca Shabad, "Biden says 'every reason' to believe Netanyahu is prolonging war for political gain," NBC News, June 4, 2024, https://www.nbcnews.com/politics/white-house/biden-netanyahu-israel-hamas-war-rcna155386

65 Jacob Magid, "Biden: I won't give Israel offensive weapons to attack in populated parts of Rafah," Times of Israel, May 9, 2024, https://www.timesofisrael.com/in-bluntest-threat-yet-biden-says-israel-will-have-to-choose-between-rafah-op-us-arms/

66 Frank Wright, "Christian persecution continues in Gaza as death toll climbs," LifeSite-

exposed the war crimes carried out by the Israeli Defense Force.[67]

At first glance, it appears Trump has adopted the Nikki Haley approach, and that he has given his carte blanche support for Israel and Netanyahu. "Support Israel whatever they need whenever they need it, no questions asked," Haley has previously said.[68] At the same time, Trump's own relationship with Netanyahu, as well as his official position on the conflict, is not so simple.

Just two months into his presidency in 2017, Trump urged Netanyahu at a press conference to stop erecting settlements. "I'd like you to hold back ... a little bit," he said.[69] In a 2021 interview, Trump accused Netanyahu of betraying him after the 2020 election. "There was no one who did more for Netanyahu than me. There was no one who did for Israel more than I did. And the first person to run to greet Joe Biden was Netanyahu," Trump exclaimed. "I've not spoken to [Netanyahu] since. F**k him."[70] What's more, after the October 7 attack in Israel (which Netanyahu reportedly knew about beforehand), Trump criticized him for not being better prepared.[71] Ron DeSantis and Nikki Haley, Trump's main opponents during the primary, rebuked him for saying that, as clear a sign as any of their fealty to the Zionist lobby. During an interview with Jewish journalist Barak Ravid in 2021, Trump also said he felt Netanyahu was leading him along in peace negotiations. He praised Palestinian Authority

News, July 10, 2024, https://www.lifesitenews.com/analysis/christian-persecution-continues-in-gaza-as-death-toll-climbs/

67 Stephen Kokx, "Israeli forces kill two Christian women in Gaza parish, destroy convent: Jerusalem Patriarchate," LifeSiteNews, December 16, 2024, https://www.lifesitenews.com/news/israeli-forces-kill-two-women-in-gaza-parish-destroy-convent-jerusalem-patriarchate/. Frank Wright, "EXCLUSIVE: Catholic bishop in the Holy Land reveals the war's devastating impact on Christians," LifeSiteNews, February 7, 2024, https://www.lifesitenews.com/opinion/exclusive-catholic-bishop-in-the-holy-land-reveals-the-devastating-impact-on-christians-of-the-war/. Andreas Walzer, "Latin Patriarchate of Jerusalem condemns Israeli raid on Catholic school complex in Gaza," LifeSiteNews, July 8, 2024, https://www.lifesitenews.com/news/latin-patriarchate-of-jerusalem-condemns-israeli-raid-on-catholic-school-complex-in-gaza/

68 Vincent James, "Nikki Haley: 'Give Israel whatever they need whenever they need it, no questions asked'," X, October 26, 2023, https://x.com/davincentjames/status/1717615446894211367

69 Andrew Rafferty, "Trump to Netanyahu 'I'd Like to See You Hold Back on Settlements a Little Bit'," NBC News, February 15, 2017, https://www.nbcnews.com/news/us-news/trump-netanyahu-i-d-see-you-hold-back-settlements-little-n721351

70 Andrew Carey and Amir Tal, "Trump accuses Netanyahu of disloyalty for congratulating Biden after 2020 win: 'F**k him'," CNN, December 11, 2021, https://www.cnn.com/2021/12/10/politics/donald-trump-benjamin-netanyahu/index.html

71 Adriana Gomez Licon and Jill Colvin, "Trump's criticism of Israel's Netanyahu draws strong condemnation from GOP rivals," AP News, October 12, 2023, https://apnews.com/article/donald-trump-benjamin-netanyahu-israel-hamas-republicans-63295565c0abe5b-30da5898a6b8eb01a

President Mahmoud Abbas as being "almost like a father" figure with whom he "had a great" meeting. "I thought the Palestinians were impossible, and the Israelis would do anything to make peace and a deal," Trump said, frustrating Zionists. "I found that not to be true."[72]

So why does any of this matter? After all, Trump and his son-in-law Jared Kushner put into place many policies that benefitted Israel when he was president, including the United States' recognition of the Golan Heights and Jerusalem as its capitol. Well, big-time Jewish donors were not supporting Trump in the G O P primary in 2024. An article published by the *Times of Israel* earlier this year reported that "the [Jewish Republican] establishment" was "pulling their checkbooks out" for Nikki Haley. "They don't want Trump as the nominee," the *Times* said.[73] *Politico* likewise found that Haley's political advocacy group, Stand For America, Inc., received $250,000 donations in 2019 from former Trump mega-donor Sheldon Adelson (who died in 2021) and his wife Miriam Adelson, both of whom are staunch Zionists.[74] Haley, who met with Miriam while attending a Republican Jewish Coalition event in 2021, told radio show host Hugh Hewitt last October that she would "give Israel whatever they need" in its war in Gaza.[75] Axios reported that Mike Pence flew to Israel in 2023 on Adelson's private jet.[76]

This is all crucial to note as it shines light on the dynamics at play with Trump's stance on Israel, which is more transactional than anything. Indeed, Adelson herself has allegedly pledged to spend more than $100 million to ensure Trump gets back in the White House. But according to Jewish website *Haaretz*, she "wants Israeli sovereignty over the West Bank" in return.[77] In

72 "Trump: I thought Israelis would do anything for peace, but found that not to be true," Times of Israel, December 11, 2021, https://www.timesofisrael.com/trump-i-thought-israelis-would-do-anything-for-peace-but-found-that-not-to-be-true/

73 Ron Kampeas, "Nikki Haley a favorite for Jewish Republican donors seeking credible Trump alternative," Times of Israel, January 13, 2024, https://www.timesofisrael.com/nikki-haley-a-favorite-for-jewish-republican-donors-seeking-credible-trump-alternative/

74 Alex Isenstadt, "Document reveals identity of donors who secretly funded Nikki Haley's political nonprofit," Politico, August 26, 2022, https://www.politico.com/news/2022/08/26/donors-secretly-funded-nikki-haleys-nonprofit-00053963

75 Zachary Leeman, "Nikki Haley Declares She'd Give Israel 'Whatever They Need', But Says They're 'Too Prideful' To Ask For Ground Troops," M SN, October 18, 2023, https://www.msn.com/en-us/news/world/nikki-haley-declares-she-d-give-israel-whatever-they-need-but-says-they-re-too-prideful-to-ask-for-ground-troops/ar-AA1iruKS

76 Jonathan Swan and Lachlan Markay, "Scoop: Pence took Adelson private jet to Israel," Axios, March 9, 2022, https://www.axios.com/2022/03/10/pence-adelson-private-jet-israel

77 Nettanel Slyomovics, "Trump Is Desperate for Miriam Adelson's Cash. What Will She Expect in Return?" Haaretz, June 3, 2024, https://www.haaretz.com/us-news/2024-06-03/ty-article/.premium/trump-is-desperate-for-cash-but-donors-have-conditions/0000018f-df3a-db29-a3ef-ff3a27530000

other words, she wants complete Israeli hegemony in the region. Netanyahu wants the same, and is seeking to expand his conflict to Lebanon and Iran to create a Greater Israel in order to build the third temple. But Trump already prevented him from annexing the West Bank during his first term. "I got angry and I stopped it, because that was really going too far. That was going way too far," he said in his interview with Ravid.[78]

Importantly, Trump also informed *Time Magazine* in April he would not rule out withholding aid to ensure the war in Gaza comes to an end.[79] Cell phone footage at an Ultimate Fighting Championship also showed Trump telling one of the competitors that he will "stop the war" in Palestine.[80] In March, he told *Israel Hayom*, an Israeli daily newspaper founded by Adelson, that, "Israel has to be very careful, because you're losing a lot of the world, you're losing a lot of support, you have to finish up, you have to get the job done. And you have to get on to peace, to get on to a normal life for Israel, and for everybody else."[81] These are all clear signs that Trump, unlike Haley, is not willing to go along with whatever Netanyahu wants in an expanded campaign. Netanyahu is obviously aware of this, and knows the clock is running out for him if Trump is re-elected, and that Trump's victory likely means the breakup of his coalition government and a possible guilty verdict in his corruption trial, which could land him in jail.[82][83][84]

78 "Trump: I thought Israelis would do anything for peace, but found that not to be true," Times of Israel, December 11, 2021, https://www.timesofisrael.com/trump-i-thought-israelis-would-do-anything-for-peace-but-found-that-not-to-be-true/

79 "Read the Full Transcripts of Donald Trump's Interviews With TIME," Time Magazine, April 30, 2024, https://time.com/6972022/donald-trump-transcript-2024-election/

80 Frank Wright, "Trump says Israel must 'finish the job' in Gaza, makes false charge regarding October 7 'deniers'," LifeSiteNews, June 18, 2024, https://www.lifesitenews.com/analysis/trump-says-israel-must-finish-the-job-in-gaza-makes-false-charge-regarding-october-7-deniers/

81 Timothy H.J. Nerozzi, "Trump tells Israel to 'finish up' Gaza offensive because nation is 'losing a lot of support'," Fox News, March 26, 2024, https://www.foxnews.com/politics/trump-tells-israel-finish-gaza-offensive-nation-losing-lot-support

82 "Netanyahu's corruption trial resumes amid Israeli war on Gaza. What to know," Al-Jazeera, December 5, 2023, https://www.aljazeera.com/news/2023/12/5/netanyahus-corruption-trial-resumes-amid-israeli-war-on-gaza-what-to-know

83 Bruno Nota, Jordana Miller, and Ella Torres, "Israeli Prime Minister Benjamin Netanyahu indicted for bribery, fraud, breach of trust," ABC News, November 21, 2019, https://abcnews.go.com/International/israels-prime-minister-benjamin-netanyahu-indicted-bribery-fraud/story?id=67199981

84 Farnoush Amiri, "House passes proposal sanctioning top war-crimes court after it sought Netanyahu arrest warrant," Associated Press, June 4, 2024, https://www.pbs.org/newshour/politics/house-passes-proposal-sanctioning-top-war-crimes-court-after-it-sought-netanyahu-arrest-warrant

Ukraine and Israel are Connected

It is not unreasonable to think that the attack on Trump's life on July 13, the date of Our Lady of Fatima's third appearance in Portugal in 1917, is tied to his resistance to Israel's desire for a wider conflict. Think back to the JFK assassination. The same people who gave the order for his death seem to be the same ones who tried to take out Trump. They wanted to send the same message they did with President Kennedy by using the same method of execution—blowing the president's head off on live television. And who was it that Kennedy was standing up to? Well, the CIA wanted him to invade Cuba, and he wouldn't. But he and his brother, then-Attorney General Robert Kennedy, had also taken steps to have the American Zionist Council register as a foreign entity. Doing so would have limited its influence on political affairs.[85] Their failure to do so has resulted in the Council's successor, the American-Israel Public Affairs Committee, sending "babysitters" to monitor lawmakers to ensure they vote the way they want them to, or so Kentucky GOP Congressman Thomas Massie told Tucker Carlson recently.[86]

Additionally, Kennedy opposed Israel's efforts to build a nuclear weapons program, infuriating then-Prime Minister David Ben-Gurion.[87] He insisted that the US conduct regular inspections of their Dimona facility. It doesn't take a rocket scientist to conclude that Israel had the most to gain from Kennedy no longer being president.

It doesn't seem unreasonable, therefore, to believe that the Zionist-controlled Western media apparatus threw Joe Biden overboard after the debate in order to bolster Trump's candidacy. Then, with Trump being the frontrunner, he would be taken out and replaced by the unapologetically pro-Israel Nikki Haley, who would be named the GOP's nominee by the party's wealthiest donors—folks like Miriam Adelson—at its convention in Milwaukee, thereby handing Netanyahu a controllable asset in his desire for a world war.

The reason why that possibility seems even more probable to me is the fact that Haley herself is 100% supportive of more bombs being dropped in the Middle East—and in Ukraine. But Trump has been opposed to war in Ukraine

85 "DOJ orders the AZC to Register as a Foreign Agent," Israel Lobby, https://www.israel-lobby.org/azcdoj/

86 Stephen Kokx, "GOP Congressman Thomas Massie exposes Zionist lobby's power over Congress," LifeSiteNews, June 10, 2024, https://www.lifesitenews.com/news/gop-congress-man-thomas-massie-exposes-zionist-lobbys-power-over-congress/

87 "The Battle of the Letters, 1963: John F. Kennedy, David Ben-Gurion, Levi Eshkol, and the US Inspections of Dimona," National Security Archive, May 2, 2019, https://nsarchive.gwu.edu/briefing-book/nuclear-vault/2019-05-02/battle-letters-1963-john-f-kennedy-david-ben-gurion-levi-eshkol-us-inspections-dimona

for years. Recall that during a CNN town hall in May 2023, Trump called for peace in the country so that people will "stop dying." After rejecting the moderator's repeated attempts for him to call Putin a "war criminal," Trump replied by noting, "Russians and Ukrainians, I want them to stop dying. And I'll have that done in 24 hours. You need the power of the presidency to do it."[88]

Trump's desire for peace in Ukraine—which is really just a money laundering scheme for Satan-worshipping, corrupt politicians in the West at this point—has drawn the ire of pro-Israeli commentators as well. "Ukraine and Israel are the military frontlines of this struggle—autocracies versus democracies," Andrew Fox has said on X. "The Iranian regime is … providing Russia with artillery shells and drones to fight in Ukraine."[89] Fox further remarked that Iran "will have more rockets to fire at you when they no longer need to provide them to Russia for the war in Ukraine."[90] Shaiel Ben-Ephraim has also explained that "the only way Israel wins is if Ukraine wins and vice versa. We have to stop this multi-headed hydra at the source: the Kremlin."[91]

One curious development that makes one pause and think about who may have given the order is that US intelligence communities are now claiming that Iran has been caught working on a plan to kill Trump. In my eyes, this is an obvious attempt to deflect any and all attention from Israel. It also lays the groundwork for the media to blame any future assassination carried out on Trump (which is very likely) on Iran. Doing that would make it easy to shift public opinion of patriotic Americans away from Trump's pro-peace policy to a 9/11 level of support for the US to get more heavily involved in the region, which is exactly what Netanyahu wants. As influencer Michael Cernovich said in an X post, "The Deep State wants war with Iran. What better way than for them to 'kill two birds with one stone' by removing Trump and leaving the body on Iran? That's what they want. Beware!"[92]

88 Stephen Kokx, "Media melts down after Trump tells CNN town hall that the 'killing' in Ukraine must end," LifeSiteNews, May 11, 2023, https://www.lifesitenews.com/news/media-melts-down-after-trump-tells-cnn-town-hall-that-the-killing-in-ukraine-must-end/

89 Andrew Fox, "You think the war in Gaza is just about 'Free Palestine'?" X, June 28, 2024, https://x.com/Mr_Andrew_Fox/status/1806877786574848179

90 Andrew Fox, "Israeli friends, I'd be very wary about celebrating the Vance VP pick," X, July 15, 2024, https://x.com/Mr_Andrew_Fox/status/1812941617516483046

91 Shaiel Ben-Ephraim, "There is no way to be an anti-Ukraine isolationist and be pro-Israel," X, July 15, 2024, https://x.com/academic_la/status/1812972637586661839

92 Michael Cernovich, "The deep state wants war with Iran," X, July 16, 2024, https://x.com/Cernovich/status/1813278807840989376

A Pro-Peace Alternative to the NWO

If Donald Trump had been killed on July 13, what would have happened? One possibility is that CIA-backed "patriot" groups would have started a pseudo "insurrection" and burned the country down Black Lives Matter style. In response, Joe Biden would have activated the National Guard, invoked Martial Law, and perhaps cancelled the election altogether.

Whatever might have taken place, God spared us from it by protecting Trump on that stage. Only He knows where things go from here. The media—and those who gave the order to take Trump out—did not have a Plan B. They are in uncharted territory.

The questions now being asked are whether a real or false flag attempt will be made on Joe Biden if he doesn't step aside. Many are also wondering if there will be another effort made on Trump's life. Some are speculating that cyber attacks and energy grid outages might occur on the American homeland.

While we don't know if any of that will happen, what is for certain is that the liberal world order, what my LifeSite colleague Frank Wright calls the "long 20th century," is coming to an end.[93] It is not a question of when, but how. Trump was merely the latest target in its last desperate attempt to cling to power. Recall that in recent months, Slovakia's Robert Fico and Hungary's Viktor Orbán, both of whom have been calling for peace in Ukraine, were victims of assassination plots as well. Hopefully, Trump, who welcomed Orbán to Mar-a-Lago to discuss a peaceful solution in Ukraine, will not be put under the bullseye again.

Unsurprisingly, Ukraine's President Volodymyr Zelensky said just two days after the Trump assassination attempt that he hopes a representative from Russia will attend his planned November peace summit. This is the first time he has said something to that effect. Is he seeing the writing on the wall and looking for an off-ramp to save his own life?

Archbishop Viganò has recognized the connection between Fico, Orbán, and Trump. In an X post, he called for prayers while noting the sinister attacks made on each of them. "Their staunch opposition to the New World Order and their defense of national sovereignty unite them with President Trump," His Excellency said. "Adding to the previous criminal attacks against avowedly anti-globalist political leaders, is now this terrible attempt to eliminate President Donald J. Trump, the leading opponent of the radical globalist Left."[94]

93 Frank Wright, "TICK TOCK - IT'S WAR O'CLOCK," Substack, June 21, 2024, https://frankwright.substack.com/p/tick-tock-its-war-oclock

94 Archbishop Carlo Maria Viganò, "Adding to the previous criminal attacks against avowedly anti-globalist political leaders," X, July 14, 2024, https://x.com/CarloMVigano/sta-

Leading America Back to God?

It is no small thing what happened to Donald Trump on July 13. He should not be alive. Despite his personal flaws and his policy failures on social issues, he is a historic figure who has escaped death by a miracle. That alone seems to make him a vessel chosen by Our Lord for this moment in history. As atheist Jewish author Yuval Harari said earlier this year, "If [Donald Trump is elected again], it is likely to be…the death blow to what remains of the global order."[95] We should pray he accomplishes that.

While it is right to be critical of Trump, it cannot be forgotten that Catholic layman Tom Zimmer, the famous "hermit of Loreto," prophesied in the 1980s that Trump would "lead America back to God."[96] Private revelation is not binding on Catholics, but it is certainly interesting to ponder if that is what he will end up doing.

Most Catholics would probably agree with Archbishop Viganò's assessment of Trump over the past several years. In October 2020, just one month before the presidential election against Joe Biden, Viganò described Trump as a "*kathèkon*" who was standing in the way of the "mystery of iniquity." In December 2022, His Excellency rebuked him for hosting the Log Cabin Republicans at Mar-a-Lago, calling the event a sign that "the deep state has contaminated the entire political elite without distinction, even involving Donald Trump, who up until now seemed to be a source of hope for the future of the United States." Then, Viganò clarified to *Catholic Family News'* Matt Gaspers in August 2023 that Trump "can be a sort of *katechon* if he is clear about the global *coup d'état* perpetrated by the deep state." Finally, after Trump's assassination attempt last weekend, Viganò heralded him as "the leading opponent of the radical globalist Left" and one of the few remaining "avowedly anti-globalist political leaders" in the West.

At the end of the day, Trump is a representation of the contradiction of the modern age. He is a non-Catholic, seemingly on a righteous crusade, but without being particularly close to Christ. Yet he also appears to have a justified anger towards the global ruling class, a class he was part of for decades. He now wants to fight against them by undoing their unjust policies and bringing peace to war-torn nations, all while simultaneously looking

tus/1812386354392617079

95 Ben Bartee, "World Economic Forum Capo: Trump Will Be 'Death Blow' to 'Global Order," PJ Media, February 6, 2024, https://pjmedia.com/benbartee/2024/02/06/world-economic-forum-capo-trump-will-be-death-blow-to-global-order-n4926200

96 John-Henry Westen, "President Trump will 'lead America back to God,' according to 1983 prophecy," LifeSiteNews, June 30, 2020, https://www.lifesitenews.com/blogs/president-trump-will-lead-america-back-to-god-according-to-prediction-from-1980/

the other way on abortion and homosexuality but also pledging to defend the rights of Christians to live without being harassed by their government. In some ways, this mimics all of us in our spiritual lives, does it not? Some days, we are saints. Others, sinners. When we fall, we go to Confession and promise to do better the next time. Hopefully, Mr Trump, having been given a second chance at life, will do that in the years he has left on this earth. Our prayers can certainly help him in that regard.

Catholic Family News • July 18, 2024

SHOULD CATHOLICS CELEBRATE PRESIDENTS' DAY?

Presidents' Day, which was observed on Monday, is an odd thing for a Catholic to celebrate. America, after all, is essentially a Freemasonic experiment. It was constructed by individuals who not only despised the Catholic faith but who sought to erect a nation where fallen man and his corrupted reason—and not Christ and supernatural truth—would be the basis for political life. Too few Catholics living in the United States realize this.

In an effort to get them up to speed with how the Founding Fathers really viewed the one true religion, it would be worthwhile to compile some of their quotes and provide some feedback. But before I do that, I want to draw your attention to this tweet by EWTN anchor Raymond Arroyo:

"The advancement and diffusion of knowledge is the only guardian of true liberty."—James Madison #PresidentsDay.

Arroyo is a full-blooded Americanist. He is how Catholics in America should not celebrate Presidents' Day. I'll go more in depth with what "Americanism" is in another essay, but for now realize it is an error common among Catholics living in the West that drives them to think "the diffusion of knowledge" is the only guardian of "true liberty" instead of recognizing that *the diffusion of sanctifying grace* is the only guardian of true liberty. In any case, on to the presidents. First up, Thomas Jefferson:

• "Almighty God hath created the mind free, and manifested his supreme will that free it shall remain by making it altogether insusceptible of restraint."[97]

97 Quoted in Thomas Jefferson, "A Bill for Establishing Religious Freedom," 1779, https://www.monticello.org/research-education/thomas-jefferson-encyclopedia/virginia-statute-re-

- "Truth is great and will prevail if left to herself. She is the proper and sufficient antagonist to error, and has nothing to fear from the conflict."[98]

Jefferson's first error lies in the claim that because "the mind" is created "free" it must be left "free" from all restraint.

While it it true that man possess free will, as Frank Sheed has written in *A Map of Life*, man's freedom has a purpose. It is not to be used in any manner whatsoever that the individual sees fit. Sheed comments thus:

Now every faculty of man has first its own proper action; and second its own proper object. Thus the eye has its action—namely, to see—and its object—namely, colored surface. So the intellect has its action, which is to know or be aware of, and its object, which is truth. Likewise, the will has its action, which is to love, and its object, which is goodness. In other words, the intellect knows things insofar as they appear to the soul true, and the will loves things insofar as they appear to the soul good. Now the supreme truth is God, so the intellect's highest task is to know God. And the supreme goodness is God, so the will's highest task is to love God.[99]

In other words, our intellect is not "free" to reject truth, which is Jesus Christ, as He himself said, "I am the Way, the Truth and the Life."[100] By its nature, the intellect must adhere to truth.

Furthermore, the will is only "free" insofar as it chooses that which is good. As Pope Leo XIII wrote in his 1888 encyclical *Libertas*, "Nothing more foolish can be uttered or conceived than the notion that, because man is free by nature, he is therefore exempt from law." Yet Jefferson constructs his entire political philosophy on the rejection of the intellect and will to the revealed truths of God, as interpreted by the Catholic Church.

While Jefferson is correct to observe that "truth is great," he is mistaken to believe that it will prevail if left to itself while competing with falsehood in a marketplace of ideas. History attests to the fact that human nature has been too weakened by Original Sin and that the lure of the world, the flesh, and the devil is too strong for men to live virtuously without the law encouraging them to do so. Put another way, "neutral" laws that allow man a wide latitude

ligious-freedom/
98 Ibid.
99 Frank Sheed, *A Map of Life*, Ignatius Press, San Francisco, 1994, p.126
100 John 14:6

to choose between truth and error usually end in a nation where men choose that which is objectively wrong. Leo XIII wrote about this when he said truth will be "gradually obscured" from society when unbridled liberty is granted to all forms of speech. "Nothing will remain sacred and inviolate," he also recalled.[101] Who can deny that this is exactly what has happened in America? Next up, Jefferson's right hand man, James Madison in his *Memorial and Remonstrance Against Religious Assessments.*

The religion of every man must be left to the conviction and conscience of every man; and it is the right of every man to exercise it as these may dictate. This right is in its nature an unalienable right.

In matters of Religion, no man's right is abridged by the institution of Civil Society...Religion is wholly exempt from its cognizance.

The Bill implies that the Civil Magistrate is a competent Judge of Religious Truth...[this] is an arrogant pretension.[102]

It must be stressed that man does not possess a "right" to *not submit to the teachings* of Holy Mother Church. He is certainly *free* to do so, and may at times possess a civil right to propagate the beliefs of a false religion. But if he possessed an "unalienable right" to reject the Catholic faith, the First Commandment would be a lie and God would have given equal rights to truth and error.

Pope Gregory XVI of happy memory, in his encyclical *Mirari Vos*, had the following to say about "liberty of conscience":

Now we examine another prolific cause of evils by which, we lament, the Church is at present afflicted, namely indifferentism, or that base opinion which has become prevalent everywhere through the deceit of wicked men, that eternal salvation of the soul can be acquired by any profession of faith whatsoever, if morals are conformed to the standard of the just and the honest.

This shameful font of indifferentism gives rise to that absurd and erroneous proposition which claims that liberty of conscience must be maintained for everyone. It spreads ruin in sacred and civil affairs, though some repeat over and over again with the greatest impudence that some advantage accrues to religion from it. 'But the death of the soul is worse than freedom of error,' as Augustine was wont to say.

---

101 Leo XIII, *Libertas*, 23, 1888, Vatican website, https://www.vatican.va/content/leo-xiii/en/encyclicals/documents/hf_l-xiii_enc_20061888_libertas.html
102 James Madison, "Memorial and Remonstrance Against Religious Assessments," 1785

Experience shows, even from earliest times, that cities renowned for wealth, dominion, and glory perished as a result of this single evil, namely immoderate freedom of opinion, license of free speech, and desire for novelty.

As far as Madison's claim that no one may "abridge" another man's religious beliefs goes, let it be said that the Church has always maintained that a Catholic State may disallow the public dissemination of heresy. Moreover, coercion itself is not sinful. Fr François Laisney is a priest of the Society of St Pius x. In an essay for *The Angelus* magazine, he explains why:

...the underlying error here is that any coercion is always against the dignity of man. If man were supreme, thus his own ruler, then any coercion would indeed be opposed to his dignity. [But] God is Supreme [and] man received his being from God...

As intended by God, authority is a help to do good. The authority of parents over children is a good example ... Where the authority is good, it helps many to be good.

Thus there can be good coercion (reasonable and moderate) that, far from opposed to human dignity, protects it from falling into error and sin...

Thus the refusal of coercion under the guise of human dignity is in fact a refusal of divinely instituted authority...[103]

Fr Laisney is merely echoing the words of St Alphonsus, who once wrote: "Fools regard as prosperity to be free from correction, or to despise the admonitions which they receive; but such prosperity is the cause of their ruin."

Madison's claim that the state is not a competent judge when it comes to recognizing religious truth is also at odds with Catholic teaching. Yet again, Leo xiii tells us why:

God has made man for society, and has placed him in the company of others like himself, so that what was wanting to his nature, and beyond his attainment if left to his own resources, he might obtain by association with others.

Wherefore, civil society must acknowledge God as its Founder and Parent, and must obey and reverence His power and authority. Justice therefore forbids, and reason itself forbids, the State to be godless; or

103 Fr Francois Laisney, "Toleration or Religious Liberty," sspx, https://web.archive.org/web/20160914065112/http://sspx.org/en/node/1490

to adopt a line of action which would end in godlessness-namely, to treat the various religions (as they call them) alike, and to bestow upon them promiscuously equal rights and privileges.

Since, then, the profession of one religion is necessary in the State, that religion must be professed which alone is true, and which can be recognized without difficulty, especially in Catholic States, because the marks of truth are, as it were, engravers upon it.

This religion, therefore, the rulers of the State must preserve and protect, if they would provide—as they should do—with prudence and usefulness for the good of the community.[104]

Next on our list is second President John Adams, one of the most anti-Catholic men to ever hold the office. His words:

- "Since the promulgation of Christianity, the two greatest systems of tyranny that have sprung from this original, are the canon and the feudal law. By the former of these, the most refined, sublime, extensive, and astonishing constitution of policy that ever was conceived by the mind of man was framed by the Romish clergy for the aggrandizement of their own order. All the epithets I have here given to the Romish policy are just, and will be allowed to be so when it is considered, that they even persuaded mankind to believe, faithfully and undoubtingly, that God Almighty had entrusted them with the keys of heaven, whose gates they might open and close at pleasure."[105]

- "This afternoon's entertainment was to me most awful and affecting; the poor wretches fingering their beads, chanting Latin, not a word of which they understood; their *Pater Nosters* and *Ave Marias;* their holy water; their crossing themselves perpetually; their bowing to the name of Jesus, whenever they hear it."[106]

- "[These United States were] founded on the natural authority of the people alone, without pretense of miracle or mystery."[107]

104 Leo XIII, *Libertas*, 1888, Vatican website, https://www.vatican.va/content/leo-xiii/en/encyclicals/documents/hf_l-xiii_enc_20061888_libertas.html
105 John Adams, "Draft of 'A Dissertation on the Canon and the Feudal Law," Papers of John Adams, Volume I, 1765, https://www.masshist.org/publications/adams-papers/index.php/view/ADMS-06-01-02-0052-0003
106 Letter from John Adams to Abigail Adams, Massachusetts Historical Society, October 9, 1774, https://www.masshist.org/digitaladams/archive/doc?id=L17741009ja
107 John Adams, A Defense of the Constitutions of Government of the United States of America, 1787

Finally, here are some remarks from George Washington:

- "All possess alike liberty of conscience and immunities of citizenship. It is now no more that toleration is spoken of, as if it was by the indulgence of one class of people, that another enjoyed the exercise of their inherent natural rights. For happily the Government of the United States, which gives to bigotry no sanction, to persecution no assistance requires only that they who live under its protection should demean themselves as good citizens, in giving it on all occasions their effectual support."[108]

- "We have abundant reason to rejoice that in this land the light of truth and reason has triumphed over the power of bigotry and superstition... in this enlightened age and in this land of equal liberty, it is our boast, that a man's religious tenets will not forfeit the protection of the laws, nor deprive him of the right of attaining and holding the highest offices that are known in the United States."[109]

When Washington says "in this enlightened age" where "truth and reason has triumphed over the power of bigotry and superstition," what he means to say is that "America has proudly rejected the Catholic World Order of centuries gone by and founded a glorious Masonic Order based on man's reason against it."

Ultimately, it would be better for Catholics to approach Presidents' Day more as a day of prayer and fasting and less of a day of celebration. No doubt they can look with esteem at these men's natural virtues and leadership abilities. Indeed, on a certain level, they are to be admired. Loving one's country, after all, is a virtue.

At the same time, Catholics should consider spending the day not fawning over men who espoused ideas completely at odds with the Catholic faith (and who saw themselves as the sworn enemies of Christendom) but rather, they should pray that the men who will wield the enormous amount of earthly power that comes with the American presidency in the future may use it to advance the truths of the Catholic religion. Lord knows too many of them haven't in the past.

akaCatholic.com • February 16, 2016

108 George Washington, Letter to the Hebrew Congregation in Newport, Rhode Island, August 18, 1790
109 George Washington, Letter to the Members of the New Jerusalem Church of Baltimore, January 1793

TRUMP VS THE NEW WORLD ORDER

Super Tuesday and Super Saturday came and went. As expected, Donald Trump dominated the competition.

Sort of.

While Trump did exceptionally well in states like New Hampshire, South Carolina, and elsewhere in the South, The Donald has stumbled as of late, coming in second to Texas Senator Ted Cruz in a number of contests.

Trump will likely expand his delegate lead in the coming weeks, though he probably won't arrive at the Republican convention with enough of them to secure the nomination. If that happens, the oligarchs in the Republican Party will do everything they can to deny him that which is rightfully his.

It has been rumored that the establishment may call upon Mitt Romney to save the GOP from a Trump nomination. Some Republicans say they won't vote for Trump even if he is their candidate. Others suggest running a third party "conservative" as the best option.

Before discussing what a Trump victory would mean for the Republican Party, I'd like to put his candidacy into context. If possible, into a Catholic context.

American 'Leadership' is an Orchestrated Deception

Since the end of the Second World War, a small but influential group of intellectuals have convinced many in the West that it is America's duty to advance "freedom" and "democracy" across the world in order to bring about a "lasting peace."

While that might sound good on paper, these words are actually smoke-screens that conceal more sinister ends. What "freedom" actually means in practice is upending traditional values and opening up markets so multinational corporations can reap massive profits off cheap labor. "Democracy" is nothing more than rigged elections between controlled candidates handpicked by globalist puppeteers who work in tandem with establishment media to push a one-world agenda. Advancing the cause of "peace" is likewise a fraudulent business. Below are just a few of the ways the West has promoted this over the past seventy years:

- Bribed countries to join the North Atlantic Treaty Organization (NATO) in order to encircle Russia.

- Assassinated the political enemies of foreign leaders who are hostile to the West's goals and blamed the murder on said leader in order to tarnish their image and paint them as a "thug" who is a "threat" to "democracy."

- Provoked revolutions by funding non-governmental organizations that seek to oust leaders in the Middle East and elsewhere who are not compliant with American demands.

- Funneled billions of taxpayer dollars to "moderate rebels" to stoke regional conflicts and overthrow heads of state while simultaneously boosting revenues for the military industrial complex in Washington.

Using the GOP to Promote Neocon Policies

Those who espouse this warped ideology are usually called "neoconservatives." To put it in Catholic terms, neoconservatives seek to obliterate the Social Kingship of Christ and replace it with a world run on the Freemasonic Kingship of Man.

For decades, neocons have preyed on the patriotism of ordinary Americans to lure young men and women to fight unjust wars on behalf of the Zionist lobby, the real behind-the-scenes power broker in the United States.

While paying lip service to social conservatism, limited government, and constitutionalism, neoconservatives hijacked the Republican Party and transformed it into an open borders, bloodthirsty Frankenstein in the service of international elites.

Despite insurgent presidential candidates like Pat Buchanan warning voters about the direction this clandestine group of war criminals has been taking not only the GOP but the Democratic Party as well, Buchanan's message that globalization, open borders, and endless wars are bad for America was diminished thanks to a corporate media and two-party system that was able to sideline him on the national stage.

Trump Against the Neocons

Donald Trump has the temperament of an eight-year-old child. He mocks. He condescends. He can't give specifics for half the things he talks about. And I don't trust him on social issues. For good reason, these facts—and many others—have a large number of voters, including Catholics, deeply disturbed about his candidacy.

At the same time, much of his public image is an act, and he has turned out be a far shrewder political operator than I expected. Few predicted he would have this much success. At least I didn't.

Americans support Donald Trump because he represents the frustration ordinary, mostly white, voters have towards politics in general but also the feckless politicians the Republican Party has nominated over the past thirty years, all of whom have failed to halt the social and economic decay of the United States.

Despite his inconsistency and immaturity, Trump has been strong on several important policies that should be appreciated by Catholics.

In an article for the Ron Paul Institute for Peace and Prosperity, Daniel McAdams outlines five areas where Trump differentiates himself from the neocons.

McAdams first notes that Trump helped expose just how "disastrous" the Iraq war was. This was long overdue and helped debunk the lie of "nation building" oversees instead of here at home.

Second, Trump wants to "actually speak with Russian President Vladimir Putin to see if US/Russia differences can be worked out without a potentially world-ending nuclear war."

Third, although Trump says "he is hugely pro-Israel" he has also said "the US side should...take a neutral role in the [peace] process."

Fourth, Trump has been calling out the "idiotic neocon advice" that resulted in the overthrowing of Muammar Gaddafi in Libya and resulted in "the red carpet" being "laid down for ISIS" in that country.

And lastly, McAdams notes that Trump is "suggesting that it may be a good thing that Russia be bombing ISIS into oblivion and that we might want to just sit back and let that happen for once."[110]

Globalists Will Resist Trump Every Step of the Way

Neoconservatives are apoplectic over a possible Trump presidency. His success could mean their demise, if only for a short while.

To be sure, it is difficult to know who Trump would surround himself with if he won the presidency. Would he call up warmonger Henry Kissinger? Would he seek the advice of the Council on Foreign Relations? I don't know.

110 Daniel McAdams, "Neocon Armchair Warhawks Panic Over Trump Foreign Policy," AntiWar.com, March 3, 2016 https://original.antiwar.com/daniel-mcadams/2016/03/02/pan-icked-neocon-armchair-warhawks-penning-harshly-worded-letter-on-trump-foreign-policy/

NAVIGATING THE CRISIS IN THE CHURCH

But what I do know is that as of right now Trump appears to have all the right enemies, including the neocons, as McAdams points out.

Republican elites will not go silently into the night. The attacks on Trump in the coming days and weeks will only get more vicious. We've already seen how quickly some of them compare him to Hitler. 50 self-identified members of "the Republican national security community" have also signed an open letter excoriating him for his foreign policy views.[111] Unsurprisingly, not a few of them have said they are supporting Hillary Clinton in the general election. So much for party loyalty.

In brief, a Trump nomination would mean that globalist Republicans would no longer dictate the terms of America's economic and foreign policy. Far from breaking the GOP in two, his victory would return the party to serving the will of the American people instead of international elites.

akaCatholic.com • March 7, 2016

ARE 'AMERICA FIRST' CONSERVATIVES BECOMING HEART AND SOUL OF THE GOP?

Bobby Jindal, where have you been these past eleven years?

For those who have forgotten who Bobby Jindal is—and I don't blame you—may I remind you that he was the Governor of Louisiana from 2008 until 2016. During that time he was touted as a possible top-tier contender for president.

But Jindal, an Indian-American who converted to Catholicism in college, saw his star crash and burn literally overnight after delivering an abysmal response to President Obama's State of the Union address in 2009. He tried to run for president in 2016 but gained next to no traction. Eventually, he endorsed Marco Rubio.

Jindal has remained largely quiet during the Trump presidency. He wrote an article in December of 2019 about "populist patriots" rejecting the establishment.[112] But other than that, he's been rather muted. Until this past weekend.

In an essay published in the *Wall Street Journal* Sunday, Jindal argued that the "new world order" touted by George H. W. Bush in the 1990s is "no

---

111 Pamela Engel, "50 top GOP national security officials sign letter warning Trump would be 'the most reckless president in American history," Business Insider, August 8, 2016, https://www.businessinsider.com/gop-national-open-letter-donald-trump-2016-8?op=1

112 Bobby Jindal, "Trump Wins the Populist Patriots," The Wall Street Journal, December 2, 2019, https://www.wsj.com/articles/trump-wins-the-populist-patriots-11575330486

longer relevant." He urged Republicans to reject the party's antiquated talking points about trade, immigration, and foreign policy. Voters are looking to "back candidates that pledge to continue [Trump's] fight against elites in both parties," he declared.[1]

Although Jindal has been relegated to political obscurity, he's clearly betting on the growth of the America First movement within the GOP. If he becomes more boisterous in his support for Trump's brand of populism in the coming years, he might just add an element of intrigue to what's shaping up to be a titanic battle for the heart and soul of the Republican Party.

The Evolving GOP

I've written before about why the Republican Party needs to maintain the new coalition of socially conservative, blue-collar voters President Trump has forged together.[2] Whereas the GOP can and should move to the center on economics—while also maintaining their law and order, pro-life message—Democrats can't moderate on any social issues without infuriating their base. They're beholden to the radical left. It would be a monumental blunder for Republicans to not solidify this once-in-a-generation realignment.

Donald Trump Jr. seemed to understand that when he told *The Hill* newspaper recently that, "we're still the party of endless wars and there are still some neocons who are really into that and we are not ... I just think that mentality is really out of place in the Republican Party right now but there are going to be those dinosaurs who do not evolve."[3]

Trump's absolutely correct. It's high-time America First, religious conservatives kicked to the curb once and for all establishment, country-club RINOs who treat the US like a multinational corporation and who only care about the size of the Gross Domestic Product. The future of the party, and arguably the country, depends on it.

LifeSiteNews • August 28, 2020

1 Bobby Jindal, "After Trump, a Different GOP," The Wall Street Journal, August 23, 2020, https://www.wsj.com/articles/after-trump-a-different-gop-11598197856

2 Catherine Lucey, "Donald Trump Presides Over GOP Remade in His Image," The Wall Street Journal, August 26, 2020, https://www.wsj.com/articles/donald-trump-presides-over-gop-remade-in-his-image-11598473437

3 Jonathan Easley, "Trump Jr. seeks to elect 'new blood' to Republican Party," The Hill, August 25, 2020, https://thehill.com/homenews/campaign/513599-trump-jr-seeks-to-elect-new-blood-to-republican-party/

EUROPE'S EMBRACE OF MULTICULTURALISM
WILL BE ITS DOWNFALL

The city of Brussels was just hit with a terrorist attack. Pray for those who died, as well as for their loved ones. In the coming days we will be told by Western media outlets that this murderous act is in no way a reflection of the religion of Islam. "Our strength comes from our diversity. We must remain welcoming and tolerant of those who differ from us," or so we are told.

Meanwhile, back on planet earth, Viktor Orbán, the Prime Minister of Hungary, delivered a powerful speech last week shining a light on the threat migrants pose to the safety of Europeans.[4] Orbán speaks the truth about the crisis going on there. One wishes the princes of the Catholic Church had as much courage as he does. Alas, Pope Francis spent Palm Sunday chastising Catholics for being "indifferent" towards "refugees."[5] How naive those words are now.

The situation unfolding across the Atlantic requires some deep reflection, as it isn't as simple as Francis suggests. Europe decided long ago to cut itself loose from its Christian roots. Secularism and liberalism thoroughly permeate the hearts and minds of most of her people. One example of just how bad it is over there is the recent decision of François Hollande of France to rename his country's "Ministry for the Family" to the more inclusive, pro-LGBT sounding "Ministry for Families." Hollande explained that he changed the name because "it would be reactionary to believe that there is only one model of the family."[6]

Perhaps in His infinite wisdom, God is using these terrorist attacks as punishment for Europeans who are rejecting His laws. Maybe this is His way of telling them that they, like the prodigal son, must fall on their knees, return to the true faith, and beg for forgiveness if they want to be saved from the scourge of Islamic violence.

Of course, that really can't happen unless the Catholic Church takes the lead. And at the moment the Church doesn't want to take the lead. Although men like Orbán and others are resisting globalist efforts to make Europe a

4 Viktor Orbán, "Speech by Prime Minister Viktor Orb6n on 15 March," Budapest, https://2015-2022.miniszterelnok.hu/speech-by-prime-minister-viktor-orban-on-15-march/

5 Diane Montagna, "Pope Francis Decries Indifference to Refugees in Palm Sunday Homily," Aleteia, March 21, 2016, https://aleteia.org/2016/03/21/pope-francis-decries-indifference-to-refugees-in-palm-sunday-homily

6 Quoted in Fr Alain Lorans, "A most singular use of the plural," DICI, March 11, 2016, https://web.archive.org/web/20160510175719/http://www.dici.org/en/news/a-most-singular-use-of-the-plural/

more "open society," the Vatican has been more than content to help that process along.

Angela Merkel of Germany has also been a key player in turning Europe into a road apple ripe for the taking. During New Year's celebrations in Cologne this year, thousands of third-world "refugees" sexually assaulted German women.[7] Similar attacks took place in Sweden.[8] Both were covered up by Western media.[9] In Amsterdam, a severed head was recently found lying in the street following an altercation between warring migrant gangs from North Africa.[10] Earlier this month, the film crew for *60 Minutes Australia* was attacked in Stockholm.[11] Such is life in post-Christian Europe! As the late French Archbishop Marcel Lefebvre would often say, "where Christ does not reign, the devil will." Truer words have never been spoken.

Several months ago I saw an insightful post on Facebook about immigration. I forget exactly which page it was posted on but it was attributed to Fr Mauro Tranquillo, an Italian priest of the Society of St Pius x. I do not know for certain if he himself shared the comment or if the translation from Italian to English is even accurate. Either way, it aptly summarizes the situation at hand:

Invoking the Gospel to support indiscriminate hospitality is a fallacious sophism for several reasons. First, it is true that there is an order in charity: to help someone by damaging someone else is complete nonsense. Those who rule a society cannot ignore the common good. It is therefore not necessary to welcome masses of people into a society already in crisis. Also, true charity cannot lose sight of the eternal salvation of souls, which you can get only through the Roman Church. The entry of people of other faiths in large numbers does not facilitate their conversion but feeds into an indifference, even if they do not take

7 "Germany shocked by Cologne New Year gang assaults on women," BBC, January 5, 2016, https://www.bbc.com/news/world-europe-35231046

8 "Youth gangs assaulted women in several Swedish cities on NYE—local media," RT News, January 12, 2016, https://www.rt.com/news/328674-sweden-migrant-assault-women/

9 Ivar Arpi, "It's not only Germany that covers up mass sex attacks by migrant men ... Sweden's record is shameful," Spectator, January 16, 2016, https://web.archive.org/web/20170218194707/http://www.spectator.co.uk/2016/01/its-not-only-germany-that-covers-up-mass-sex-attacks-by-migrant-men-swedens-record-is-shameful/

10 Chris Tomlinson, "Migrant Gangs Leave Severed Head On Amsterdam Street," Breitbart, March 20, 2016, https://www.breitbart.com/europe/2016/03/20/migrant-gangs-leave-severed-head-on-amsterdam-street/

11 Alex Griswold, "Video Released of 60 Minutes Film Crew Being Attacked in Sweden by Migrants," Mediaite, March 21, 2016, https://web.archive.org/web/20170312033549/http://www.mediaite.com/tv/video-released-of-60-minutes-film-crew-being-attacked-in-sweden-by-migrants/

control of the society and do not impress it with their faith. There is a clear plan behind the entry of Muslims in Europe, which is to give the final blow to what little remains of Christian identity. I do not think that those who govern the Church can ignore a matter so obvious. I can only conclude that they are accomplices.

akaCatholic.com • March 22, 2016

PRAY THAT EUROPE FOLLOWS THE LEAD
OF HUNGARY, NOT THE VATICAN

In a recent interview with journalist Edward Pentin, Hungarian Foreign Minister Péter Szijjártó said his country wants to remain a "Christian nation" and to preserve Europe "as a Christian Europe" in the face of a "migratory crisis" that is endangering the continent's Christian heritage.[12] Such remarks stand in stark contrast to comments made by Pope Francis these last few years.

During his 2016 acceptance speech for the Charlemagne Prize, an award that is given to those who help bring about European "unification," Pope Francis said, "I dream of a new European humanism" where "being a migrant is not a crime."[13]

Francis repeated his "dream" a year later while addressing 27 European heads of state at the Vatican. "As leaders, you are called to blaze the path of a new European humanism made up of ideals and concrete actions," he said.[14]

In 2014, he called on the European Parliament to rediscover its memory, its courage, and "a sound and humane utopian vision."[15]

The future Pope Francis wants for Europe and the future Mr Szijjártó's country wants for Europe couldn't be more different. The continent now faces, as Ronald Reagan once said in 1964, a "time for choosing."

12 Edward Pentin, "Hungarian Foreign Minister: We Want a Christian Hungary, a Christian Europe," National Catholic Register, September 14, 2018, https://www.ncregister.com/blog/hungarian-foreign-minister-we-want-a-christian-hungary-a-christian-europe
13 Francis, Papal Address, Vatican website, May 6, 2016, https://www.vatican.va/content/francesco/en/speeches/2016/may/documents/papa-francesco_20160506_premio-carlo-magno.html#_ftn10
14 Francis, Papal Address, Vatican website, March 24, 2017, https://www.vatican.va/content/francesco/en/speeches/2017/march/documents/papa-francesco_20170324_capi-unione-europea.html
15 Francis, Address to the Council of Europe, Vatican website, November 25, 2014, https://www.vatican.va/content/francesco/en/speeches/2014/november/documents/papa-francesco_20141125_strasburgo-consiglio-europa.html

Europe at a Crossroads

As it stands currently, Hungary, Poland, and a few other courageous nations are resisting the global left's efforts to tear asunder their Christian identity by opening their borders, flooding them with immigrants, and imposing on them homosexuality, secularism, and feminism.

Fortunately, some Catholic clergy are aware of what these orchestrated attacks really are. In July, Bishop Athanasius Schneider told an Italian newspaper that there is a "long-prepared plan by international powers to radically change the Christian and national identities of the European peoples."[16]

Some of the people responsible for this plan include Germany's Angela Merkel, France's Emmanuel Macron, and their pal George Soros. All of them are openly pushing the gay agenda, abortion on demand, radical environmentalism, and an array of other policies under the umbrella of "diversity."

But even the Dalai Lama, who himself supports same-sex "marriage," believes those who are concerned with immigration aren't acting unreasonably. At a conference in Sweden two weeks ago, he told his audience that "Europe belongs to the Europeans." He also said refugees should return to their native lands to begin the rebuilding process. Germany "cannot become an Arab country," he correctly observed. "Germany is Germany."[17]

Two Paths Forward

The battle between secular EU technocrats and Christian nationalists has reached a boiling point. Right now, Hungary is being threatened with sanctions by the European Union that may force it to recognize homosexual "marriage" and accept Muslims from the third-world. Likewise, Poland has faced strong opposition from the EU for trying to ensure their country upholds traditional values. Its parliament is currently in the beginning stages of instituting a new holiday commemorating the Christianization of their country in the 10th century.

In the midst of this titanic battle for the heart and soul of Europe lies Rome. Historically, popes have defended the rights of sovereign nations and have encouraged, as Pope Benedict did, the continent to recognize the

16 Dorothy Cummings McLean, "Bishop: Mass migration part of plan to water down Europe's Christian identity," LifeSiteNews, July 2, 2018, https://www.lifesitenews.com/news/bishop-mass-migration-part-of-plan-to-water-down-europes-christian-identity/

17 Lukas Mikelionis, "Dalai Lama says 'Europe belongs to Europeans' and refugees should ultimately go back home," Fox News, September 15, 2018, https://www.foxnews.com/world/dalai-lama-says-europe-belongs-to-europeans-and-refugees-should-ultimately-go-back-home

threat of Islam and come back to Christ.[18] But not Francis. His embrace of population control activists and support for radical environmentalism and open borders have aligned him more closely with the international left than with the God-fearing leaders of Hungary and Poland.[19][20]

Multiculturalism Undermines Christianity

A motivating factor for Pope Francis appears to be the slogan "unity in diversity," which he often invokes. It just so happens that "unity in diversity" is the official motto of the European Union.

Former British Prime Minister David Cameron appeared to grasp the dangers of having too much "diversity" when, in 2011, he admitted that "state multiculturalism [has] failed."[21] Former French President Nicolas Sarkozy echoed the same sentiments less than a month later.[22]

Catholic author Dr Peter Kwasniewski has argued in an essay for Life-SiteNews recently that a religiously "neutral" public square inevitably turns into an anti-Christian one. Why? Because Christ himself said without Him we can do nothing. No nation, in other words, can stand on its own two feet for long if it publicly refuses to recognize Christ as its King.[23] Viktor Orbán seems to know this. Pope Francis, not so much.

The Vatican Promotes Globalist Policies

In 1917, Our Lady of Fatima spoke about the "annihilation of nations." Many believed this to be a reference to Communism and atomic warfare. Could it also be a reference to the "annihilation" of the Christian identity of European

18 Phillip Pullalla, "Pope criticizes EU for excluding God," Reuters, August 9, 2007, https://www.reuters.com/article/us-eu-anniversary-pope-iduSL2421365520070324/
19 Lisa Bourne, "Globalists want Church to serve 'New World Order': Italian journalist," LifeSiteNews, October 20, 2017, https://www.lifesitenews.com/news/population-control-promoters-infiltrate-vatican-italian-journalist/
20 Pete Baklinski, "Photo directory of population controllers influencing the Vatican," LifeSiteNews, November 22, 2017, https://www.lifesitenews.com/news/photo-directory-of-population-controllers-influencing-the-vatican/
21 "State multiculturalism has failed, says David Cameron," BBC News, February 5, 2011, https://www.bbc.com/news/uk-politics-12371994
22 "Nicolas Sarkozy declares multiculturalism had failed," The Telegraph, February 11, 2011, https://www.telegraph.co.uk/news/worldnews/europe/france/8317497/Nicolas-Sarkozy-declares-multiculturalism-had-failed.html
23 Peter Kwasniewski, "Why a 'religiously-neutral' public square always turns out to be anti-Christian," LifeSiteNews, September 12, 2018, https://www.lifesitenews.com/blogs/why-a-religiously-neutral-public-square-always-turns-out-to-be-anti-christi/

nations in the 21st century? Could it likewise have been a warning about multiculturalism and "unity in diversity" emerging in historically Christian lands? I'm fairly certain that Francis isn't interested in calling on Europe to return to the Catholic faith. What he will likely do in the years ahead is continue to promote "integral humanism" and build relationships with social justice, population control, and open borders advocates. The Vatican's current Secretary of State, Cardinal Pietro Parolin, a rumored front-runner to succeed Francis, has given us an indication that this is what will happen.

Just this year, Parolin visited the shadowy Bilderberg gathering.[24] In 2017, he spoke at the World Economic Forum in Davos, Switzerland.[25] In 2016, during an address at the United Nations, he expressed frustration with European countries that aren't doing more to welcome immigrants.[26] If he is ever elected pope, Parolin would undoubtedly continue to position the Church as a cog in the globalist's machine.

Hungary and Poland have laid out their vision for the future of Europe. Pope Francis has laid out his. Let's pray he joins those countries, and, like his predecessors, takes up the cause of defending Christianity in Europe against Islamic invaders and international forces once again. As unlikely as that sounds, miracles do happen.

LifeSiteNews • September 26, 2018

NBC SMEARS 'ULTRA CONSERVATIVE,' ANTI-GLOBALIST CATHOLICS

NBC chief foreign correspondent Richard Engel has launched a new "On Assignment" series where, purportedly, he "doesn't just get the story, he goes to the center of it."

Engel kicked off his show on April 14 with a report on how "ultra conservative" Catholics are "taking aim" at Pope Francis, a "humble" leader who "reaches out" to the marginalized.[27]

24 Dorothy Cummings McLean, "Top Vatican Cardinal to join elite globalists in secretive 'Bilderberg' meeting," LifeSiteNews, June 6, 2018, https://www.lifesitenews.com/news/top-vatican-cardinal-to-join-elite-globalists-in-secretive-bilderberg-meeti/
25 World Economic Forum, "Davos 2017—An Insight, an Idea with Cardinal Pietro Parolin," YouTube, https://www.youtube.com/watch?v=iF1rWoSglEM
26 Cardinal Parolin, Address at the United Nations Summit for Refugees and Migrants, Vatican website, September 20, 2016, https://press.vatican.va/content/salastampa/en/bollettino/pubblico/2016/09/20/160920b.html
27 Richard Engel and Kennett Werner, "Steve Bannon and US ultra-conservatives take

The episode is pretty much what you'd expect from someone who spends most of his time on television talking with liberal feminists Rachel Maddow and Andrea Mitchell, the wife of former Federal Reserve Chairman Alan Greenspan.

Without getting into all the details, Engel's "investigation" is nothing more than an attempt to thwart the rising tide of criticism inside and outside the Catholic Church of Pope Francis.[28]

But why, one has to wonder, would a left-wing MSNBC correspondent (and member of the Council on Foreign Relations) come to the aid of the Church? After all, Catholicism is opposed to gay "marriage," abortion, transgenderism, and every other position the political left holds dear.

As a card-carrying member of the international elite, Engel likely senses that an increasing number of Catholics—as well as nationalist politicians—are fed up with this heterodox, open-borders Pontiff, and that if their anti-globalist message spreads, the anti-Christian world order Engel's buddies want to usher in could be in jeopardy.

Engel therefore recognizes that Francis is essentially the face of the global left and that he is among the last, best hope that cosmopolitan elites have to stop the growth of populism across the West.

To his credit, Engel grants a good chunk of airtime to Church Militant's Michael Voris and the Acton Institute's Fr Robert Sirico. Respectively, they expose liberal clergy in Rome and argue that Francis' economic views are erroneous. The viewer easily understands the two are from the "conservative" wing of the Church.

Engel also profiles former Trump adviser Steve Bannon, though he is a bit tougher on him than he was on Voris and Sirico. The two talk mostly about immigration while strolling through Vatican Square.

Engel's ultimate goal is to portray the former presidential adviser as a mean-spirited manipulator who is trying to, as he says, "Bannonize" the Church.

Meanwhile, he depicts Francis as an open-minded, welcoming, and loving pastor who is on the receiving end of unjustified "attacks" from malicious-minded Catholics.

To accomplish this, Engel enlists the help of dissident pro-LGBT priest James Martin. At one point, Martin tells Engel that Catholics who criticize

aim at Pope Francis," NBC News, April 12, 2019, https://www.nbcnews.com/news/world/steve-bannon-u-s-ultra-conservatives-take-aim-pope-francis-n991411

28 On Assignment, "The ultra-conservative crusade against Pope Francis," MSNBC, April 14, 2019, https://www.msnbc.com/on-assignment/watch/the-ultra-conservative-crusade-against-pope-francis-1493172291746

Francis are, at root, just racist toward migrants and that Bannon is basically a bigot.

I laughed out loud when I heard Martin say that, primarily because he himself has declared his support for homosexual couples kissing during the exchange of peace at Mass. What could be more hateful than leading souls into sin?

The Vatican is Partnering with the Global Left

Engel's report is instructive in that it helps clarify (as if it were not obvious already) whose side the media are on in all this. Recall that pedophile priests and Vatican corruption was the stuff of blockbuster movies and front-page stories in the early 2000s. But now that the pope is pushing many of the same policies the political left is, the media have said nary a word about the abuse crisis that has been exposed by Italian Archbishop Carlo Maria Viganò.

Not only does the corporate press recognize the danger anti-globalist attitudes pose to the pope's agenda, so too does the Vatican.

Starting today and lasting until May 3, the Pontifical Academy of Social Sciences will host a conference on nationalism and the "nation-state." Honduran Cardinal Walter Kasper, among others, will deliver remarks at the gathering.[2930]

Given Francis's recent comments expressing his opposition to border walls, it's not hard to imagine that this three-day gathering will use a lot of flowery language about "welcoming migrants" while condemning "xenophobia" and the "fear of the other."

In previous years, the Pontifical Academy of Social Sciences welcomed Bernie Sanders, former California Democrat Governor Jerry Brown, and population control activist Jeffrey Sachs to speak at its events. Its current head, Bishop Marcelo Sánchez Sorondo, believes communist China is the "best" at "implementing the social doctrine of the Church."[31]

Italian journalist Riccardo Cascioli has argued that the Vatican's collaboration with such individuals is part of an infiltration effort aimed at placing "the great moral force that the Catholic Church undoubtedly exercises...at

29 "Vatican conference warns of dangers of resurgent nationalism," Associated Press, May 1, 2019, https://www.yahoo.com/news/vatican-conference-warns-dangers-resurgent-nationalism-112732379.html

30 The Pontifical Academy of Social Sciences, "Nation, State, Nation-State," https://web.archive.org/web/20191118112211/https://www.pass.va/content/dam/scienzesociali/booklet/booklet_2019plenarysessionpass.pdf

31 Claire Chretien, "Vatican bishop praises Communist China as 'best' at implementing Church's social doctrine," LifeSiteNews, February 6, 2018, https://www.lifesitenews.com/news/vatican-bishop-communist-china-is-the-best-at-implementing-the-social-doctr/

the service of the New World Order." The Church "was—and it is—the only point of resistance to … the idea of a world-led government guided by technocratic elites," he has said. "For this reason, the Catholic Church was a target."[32] Cascioli is correct. So long as Francis remains in the Vatican, international elites will have an ally sitting on the Throne of St Peter and they'll do everything in their power to keep it that way. The only question now is whether more Catholics will stand up and, as Steve Bannon is doing, defend the Church from their sinister schemes.

LifeSiteNews • May 1, 2019

HAVE US BISHOPS SOLD OUT TO THE DEEP STATE'S OPEN BORDERS AGENDA?

A group of 14 Catholic bishops who live on both sides of the Texas-Mexico border have signed a statement rebuking President Trump's immigration policies. It's a mixed bag of some good but mostly bad arguments.

I've previously written about how the bishops rely on proof-texting Bible verses to support their open borders stance. Unsurprisingly, their latest statement begins by quoting Matthew 25:35 (one of their favorites): "I was a stranger and you welcomed me."

Quite obviously, Catholics must do this. But always with prudence. There is an order to charity that, at least when it comes to matters of national policy, must be extended to fellow Americans first.

To my knowledge, US bishops have never called for a limit on the number of years refugees should stay in the United States. Nor have they endorsed a cap on how many of them should be admitted in the first place. On this, they're in lockstep with the Democratic Party, which wants a steady flow of persons coming over the southern border to ensure future electoral victories. I'd be shocked to learn if any of the bishops were in favor of putting ceilings on either figure, despite unlimited flooding of strangers into a country being a violation of Catholic principles on the rights and duties of nations to protect their common good.[3334]

32 Quoted in Lisa Bourne, "Globalists want Church to serve 'New World Order': Italian journalist," LifeSiteNews, October 20, 2017, https://www.lifesitenews.com/news/population-control-promoters-infiltrate-vatican-italian-journalist/
33 Thomas Williams, Ph.D., "Why Saint Thomas Aquinas Opposed Open Borders," Breitbart, January 31, 2017, https://www.breitbart.com/politics/2017/01/31/saint-thomas-aquinas-opposed-open-borders/
34 Fr Gregoire Celier, SSPX, "Immigration: Principles, Rights, and Practices," Fideliter,

In their letter, the bishops argue that violence and poverty is what drives many immigrants to the border. They also say Americans shouldn't "assume they are criminals, as they are sometimes perceived." Many of them are "victims of criminal elements in their own countries."

True. But why don't the bishops call for improvements to the Mexican economy or for the police forces in their native countries to be more effective? Isn't that the root of the problem?

Gangs and the multinational corporations in the US that lure workers to cross the border illegally are also at fault here. Yet Trump has been the toughest president ever on Mexican drug cartels and on opioid addiction in the United States. Very few, if any, American bishops praise him for those efforts. Catholic author and activist Deal Hudson is right to wonder if the bishops are plotting to make sure Trump doesn't get re-elected in 2020.[35]

Mexico is in Need of Conversion

What the bishop's statement also embarrassingly implies is that Mexican clergy have done such a poor job at preaching the Gospel that their country has become a barren wasteland of corruption, so much so that every single person should be allowed to claim refugee status in the United States.

If the bishops were serious about solving the border crisis they would issue a statement imploring the Mexican people and their leaders to live out their Catholic faith so true peace and harmony will flourish, thus eliminating the need for persons to flee in the first place. Human beings have a duty to better their home country first before giving up on it and jetting off to another.

Rather than act as if Mexico is a failed state like Libya—which it obviously is not—the bishops should throw their support behind policies that streamline the legal immigration process in the United States instead of turn a blind eye to those crossing illegally. They should also be more vocal in calling for economic assistance for Mexico's poorest citizens, which is precisely what the Trump administration has been doing. Last year, Trump announced $5.8 billion in aid and investment for government and economic development in Central America.[36] He awarded $4.8 billion for southern Mexico alone. Why

January-February, 2007, Reprinted for Angelus Press' August 2007 edition, Featured on SSPX. com, https://sspx.org/en/immigration-principles-rights-and-practices

35 Deal Hudson, "Are US bishops plotting to take down Trump in 2020?," LifeSiteNews, June 25, 2018, https://www.lifesitenews.com/opinion/will-the-2020-election-be-the-catholic-bishops-versus-donald-trump/

36 José Cárdenas, "Stop the Central American migration wave at its source," New York Post, March 10, 2019, https://nypost.com/2019/03/10/stop-the-central-american-migration-wave-at-its-source/

didn't the bishops praise him for that?

The remainder of the bishops' statement calls for changes in the way the US handles court cases with asylum seekers. It also asks for God's help to "welcome, protect, promote, and integrate immigrants, as requested by Pope Francis." Fine. But I can't remember the last time the bishops (or Pope Francis) actually called for immigrants to be truly integrated into the country they arrive in. Isn't this the man who believes in "unity in diversity" and apologizes to aboriginal peoples?[37]

What is Catholic Teaching on Immigration?

When it comes to immigration, US bishops never tire of using language that guilts Americans into thinking they are committing a sin by supporting a border wall. This is entirely un-Catholic. As St Thomas Aquinas taught, the number of persons let in to a country must be balanced with the common good of the country receiving them.[38] In other words, economics, costs to the taxpayer, the education system, social harmony, religious cooperation, and the entire gamut of other cultural issues related to a nation's overall spiritual and temporal health must be part of the equation. A country has the right to preservation and to be free from groups of persons that would radically disrupt its equilibrium. Immigrants also have the duty to integrate themselves into the welcoming land.

Germany is a prime example of how not to do immigration. Right now, Germany is learning its lesson the hard way after letting in millions of Muslims from the Middle East, the vast majority of whom are young men. Not only is day to day life there witnessing civil unrest and rampant sex crimes, it may not even be German in thirty years if its low birth rate doesn't pick up. The entire country is being over-run by Islam.

Some say that the United States is better off with more foreigners. "Diversity is our strength! We are a nation of immigrants," it is often remarked. But is it really? How is social cohesion enhanced when more and more Americans have fewer and fewer things in common with their neighbors?

At the end of the day, immigration is being used by the Democrat Party to grow their base. It's also being pushed by international elites who want every

37 ICT Staff, "Pope Francis Apologizes to Indigenous Peoples for 'Grave Sins' of Colonialism," ICT News, September 12, 2018, https://ictnews.org/archive/pope-francis-apologizes-to-indigenous-peoples-for-grave-sins-of-colonialism?redir=1

38 Thomas Williams, Ph.D., "Why Saint Thomas Aquinas Opposed Open Borders," Breitbart, January 31, 2017, https://www.breitbart.com/politics/2017/01/31/saint-thomas-aquinas-opposed-open-borders/

country to be demographically the same. Recall that former Secretary of State John Kerry admitted in 2016 to graduates of Northeastern University that they need to prepare themselves to enter "a complex and borderless world."[39] Count me among those who see this issue the same way Bishop Athanasius Schneider and Cardinal Robert Sarah do. Both men have on multiple occasions said there is an orchestrated, globalist plot utilizing mass migration to de-Christianize the West and to create a blended, post-national, one-dimensional world.[40][41] Shame on US Bishops for not echoing their remarks.

LifeSiteNews • March 13, 2019

2020 ELECTION IS TRUMP/VIGANÒ VS BIDEN/FRANCIS FOR FUTURE OF GLOBAL ORDER

A decade ago, journalists could barely contain themselves when news of misbehaving clergy came across their desk. Almost every time Pope Benedict said something about homosexuality or abortion, the media instantly reminded their audiences that the Catholic Church is a hypocritical organization filled with predatory pedophiles.

Fast forward to today. Despite the fact that Archbishop Carlo Maria Viganò has blown the lid off rampant abuse in the Church, news networks the world over have largely remained silent on his claims.

NBC's chief foreign affairs correspondent Richard Engel drew some attention to Viganò a year ago. But Engel's reporting was merely an attempt to link His Excellency to what Engel called the "far right" in the Church.[42] In other words, it wasn't a serious investigation. It was a hit piece meant to delegitimize him.

The reason why the West's Marxist media has zipped its lips on Viganò's statement is because it sees in Pope Francis a willing partner for its globalist,

39 Victor Davis Hanson, "Imagine There's No Border," City Journal, Summer 2016, https://www.city-journal.org/article/imagine-theres-no-border

40 Dorothy Cummings McLean, 'Bishop: Mass migration part of plan to water down Europe's Christian identity," LifeSiteNews, July 2, 2018, https://www.lifesitenews.com/news/bishop-mass-migration-part-of-plan-to-water-down-europes-christian-identity/

41 Dorothy Cummings McLean, "Cdl. Sarah: Some people 'exploit the Word of God' to promote multiculturalism, immigration," LifeSiteNews, October 27, 2017, https://www.lifesitenews.com/news/cardinal-sarah-some-people-exploit-the-word-of-god-to-promote-multicultural/

42 Stephen Kokx, "NBC report on 'ultra-conservative' Catholics smears Steve Bannon, anti-globalists," LifeSiteNews, May 1, 2019, https://www.lifesitenews.com/blogs/nbc-report-on-ultra-conservative-catholics-smears-steve-bannon-anti-globalists/

liberal agenda. As such, they've been running interference for him. They know that if they were talking about the corruption going on during his reign, they would be undermining his open borders and pro-environmentalist message.

Fortunately, Donald Trump is president of the United States. And thanks to his Catholic wife Melania, he seems to be clued up on the crisis in the Church, as well as on its partnership with the New World Order. He has already expressed thanks to Archbishop Viganò for warning him about the "Deep Church" in a public letter. He's also mentioned author Taylor Marshall on Twitter. And he's directed his state department to take a hard stance on communist China—something the Vatican wholly disagrees with.[43]

Which brings me to the latest twist: Pope Francis's new encyclical *Fratelli Tutti*.

Plain and simple, *Fratelli Tutti* is the planting of the Church's flag firmly in the Joe Biden camp over and against President Trump, whom Francis previously scolded for "building walls and not bridges."[44]

In this rambling document, Francis waxes like an elderly John Lennon about a utopian brotherhood of man while portraying Our Lord and Savior as nothing more than a good-hearted humanitarian. While Francis often invokes the name of "Jesus" in his letter, he never uses Our Lord's divine titles (Son of God, Christ the King, etc). Mary is also denied the honor of being called "the Blessed Virgin." Instead, she's simply called "the Mother of Jesus." No doubt this was done to not offend Protestants.

Sounding more like leftover lecture notes from a social justice course at UC-Berkeley, *Fratelli Tutti* is not merely a list of Democratic talking points about diversity and immigration (although it is that). It is a blueprint for the socialist world order that Francis and his allies want to help usher in should Joe Biden become president. Without a doubt, it was deliberately released to coincide with the US election. The Vatican desperately wants "Sleepy Joe" to win. He would help fulfill many of Francis' goals on sustainability, immigration, China, and more.

LifeSiteNews • October 12, 2020

43 Calvin Freiburger, "Pope Francis snubs Pompeo visit over criticism of Vatican-China deal," LifeSiteNews, September 29, 2020, https://www.lifesitenews.com/news/pope-francis-snubs-pompeo-visit-over-criticism-of-vatican-china-deal/

44 Gerard O'Connell, "Pope responding to questions on Trump: 'A person who only thinks of building walls, and not building bridges, is not Christian,'" America Magazine, February 18, 2016, https://www.americamagazine.org/content/dispatches/aboard-plane-home-mexico-pope-francis-responds-questions-donald-trump

IS JOE BIDEN TRYING TO DISTRACT VOTERS FROM HIS FAILED COVID POLICIES BY PROVOKING WAR WITH RUSSIA?

Despite the best efforts of our so-called military and political "experts," fewer than 1 in 6 Americans favor sending US troops into Ukraine should armed conflict break out with Russia.[45] Polling from the Charles Koch Institute shows 73% of Americans prefer their elected officials focus on domestic issues right now instead of on foreign affairs.[46]

This is good news. It indicates Deep State actors posing as intelligence officials on Western media networks are failing to convince people that the US should involve itself in yet another overseas quagmire.

Most of the people I talk to suspect Ukraine is being used to distract voters from Biden's failures at home. I think they're onto something. Massive supply chain shortages, runaway inflation, and a relentless push for vaccines are rightly causing the president's poll numbers to crater. All indications point to disastrous midterm elections for the Democrats. Beating the drum of war, while making Putin (instead of Joe Biden) the most hated man in America, could trick some voters into forgetting about the freedom-robbing policies the White House and Congress have been pushing for the last year-and-a-half.

One of the strangest arguments I've heard in defense of US entanglement in Ukraine was given by Biden's Deputy National Security Adviser Jonathan Finer on CNN last month. When asked why the American people should care about what's going on over there, the poor sap said because "borders should be inviolate" and "sovereignty should be respected."[47] Who knew the Biden administration was filled with America First patriots?!

Finer's reasoning might sound nice on paper, but it's not why the US is concerned with Ukraine. For decades, the West has been obsessed with unnecessarily encircling—and provoking—Russia with NATO expansion. While defending "human rights" and "protecting democracy" is what Beltway elites might say they're doing in Ukraine (and elsewhere), those with eyes to see and ears to hear—which seems to be most of the voting electorate these days—are aware there's a much larger, and more sinister game being played that isn't worth the lives of American boys and girls.

45 Darragh Roche, "Fewer Than 1 in 6 Americans Want US Soldiers in Any Ukraine-Russia War: Poll," Newsweek, January 21, 2022, https://www.newsweek.com/few-americans-want-soldiers-deployed-ukraine-russia-war-invasion-poll-1671546

46 "NEW POLL: Americans still want focus on domestic issues, weary of war over Ukraine," Stand Together Trust, December 17, 2021, https://standtogethertrust.org/news/poll-americans-wary-of-war-over-ukraine/

47 RNC Research, "Biden's Deputy National Security Adviser says Americans should care about Ukraine," X, January 25, 2022, https://x.com/RNCResearch/status/1485996227875463173

Whatever course of action Joe Biden decides to take in the future, it's pretty rich to hear his deputy national security adviser talk about national autonomy, let alone cite it as a reason to go to war. After all, isn't this the administration that's letting thousands of foreigners walk across America's southern border with impunity every day? Yes it is. The irony of that was not lost on Donald Trump.

At a rally in Conroe, Texas on January 29, the former president blasted Biden's glaring hypocrisy. "Everyone in Washington is obsessing over how to protect Ukraine's border. But the most important border in the world is not Ukraine's border, it's America's border," Trump thundered. "Before Joe Biden sends any troops to defend a border in Eastern Europe, he should be sending troops to defend our border right here in Texas."[48]

As Trump continues his journey back into the public eye with what appears to be the embryonic stages of his 2024 presidential bid, he'd be smart to make immigration, border security, and anti-globalist policies top-tier campaign themes. He won the Oval Office by running on those the first time around in 2016 and, as recent polling data suggests, the American people would support him on those issues again.

LifeSiteNews • February 18, 2022

WHY I STAND WITH ARCHBISHOP VIGANÒ AND HIS ANALYSIS OF THE RUSSIA-UKRAINE CONFLICT

An increasing number of Catholics are attacking Archbishop Carlo Mario Viganò for his insightful analysis of the situation in Ukraine. Catholics I respect, and know, have accused His Excellency of being a "conspiracy theorist" pushing "Kremlin propaganda" and "carrying water for the KGB."[49]

The blowback Viganò is receiving deserves our attention, as does the way establishment traditionalists are talking about the Ukrainian conflict itself. We live in a significant moment in Church history. It would be a mistake almost beyond compare to cancel the archbishop at the exact time we need him most.

48 Abigail Adcox, "Trump touts borders at home and abroad during Texas rally," Washington Examiner, January 30, 2022, https://www.washingtonexaminer.com/news/877158/trump-touts-borders-at-home-and-abroad-during-texas-rally/
49 Claire Giangravé, "Archbishop Viganò pushes conspiracy theories about Ukraine and Russia in 10,000-word letter," Religious News Service, March 7, 2022, https://www.americamagazine.org/faith/2022/03/07/vigano-ukraine-242526. Peter Kwasniewski, Facebook, March 12, 2022, https://www.facebook.com/photo?fbid=4809045955816879&set=p-cb.4809046022483539

First, let me say I believe Archbishop Viganò is the answer to decades of prayers and penance by Catholics who have begged God to send them a prelate who can see through the lies of the world and guide them through the fog that has enveloped the Church. In this regard, I view him as a sort of Old Testament prophet.

This isn't to say he's impeccable, for no human being is, but I can't recall a single public statement His Excellency has made that doesn't read like one of the great social encyclicals of the 19th century. Even his critics would be hard pressed to deny the gifts of the Holy Spirit are plainly visible in his writings. It seems to me God is giving him graces otherwise reserved for a pope.

What Did Viganò Actually Say?

Far from being Russian "propaganda," Viganò's well researched summary of the Ukraine-Russia conflict is a balanced explanation of what's going on in the region—and why it's taking place. It's less of an op-ed arguing for one side over the other and more of a 10,000-foot view of current geo-political realities. Few, if any, bishop statements I've read so far possess half the understanding of the situation as Viganò's does.

It takes a decent amount of time to wade through His Excellency's analysis given its breadth and scope. I've done so twice now. Here, in perhaps a grossly oversimplified manner, is what he said:

- The entire conflict is a trap designed by the global Deep State to purposefully provoke a war.

- The West knows expanding NATO upsets Russia but is doing it anyway despite previously saying it wouldn't.

- NATO and various other countries are illegally pouring ammunitions into Ukraine, thereby violating international law. This is making Ukraine a tinderbox ready to explode.

- There are many economic factors at play in Ukraine—gas pipelines, bio-labs, other technologies—that make it attractive to outside parties.

- President Zelensky is a corrupt individual acting as a puppet of Klaus Schwab and the Great Reset. He is selling out Ukraine to the West and not preventing neo-Nazi forces trained by the US from wreaking havoc on Russian-speaking Ukrainians.

- Joe Biden has been tied to Ukraine since his time as Barack Obama's

Vice President. His son Hunter is connected to the Ukrainian energy company Burisma.

* There was a Color Revolution in Ukraine backed by George Soros and other Western groups. This has caused great social unrest since taking place in 2013/2014.

* Rhetoric has been ratcheted up in the last several months by Zelensky (and the West) about nuclear and atomic weapons, thereby heightening Putin's mistrust and prompting him to dissolve the Minsk agreement.

* The media cannot be relied on to report fairly what is going on in Ukraine. Their COVID track record is proof they can't do anything but lie. They are purposefully trying to entice Westerners to support an escalation.

* The US, EU, and NATO promise the Ukrainian people prosperity if they side with them but in reality, they seek to enslave Ukrainian citizens to the same freedom-robbing and culturally depressing policies that have destroyed the now godless West.

* The West needs to return to Christ and seek peaceful relations with Russia so all people can live in harmony. Rome has fallen silent about the true crimes being committed across the world. Perhaps God is going to use Russia as His bulwark against the secular West.

I do not see anything His Excellency has written that can be characterized as pro-Russian talking points or Kremlin "propaganda." He's charted a decidedly non-ideological course by taking into consideration a variety of factors.

In my estimation, Viganò's essay betrays a solid understanding not only of the behaviors (and corruption) of Ukrainian leaders—past and present—but also of the foreign and domestic policies pursued by Ukrainian lawmakers in recent years. He also displays a sober grasp of the history and relationship between Europe, Ukraine, and Russia and how the current conflict fits into the larger goals of the Great Reset and the future plans of international elites.

If I had been consulted by His Excellency on what to include before his statement went to print, I would have asked him to include some additional citations for a few of his claims. Saying something pastoral about Ukrainian Catholics and how he sympathizes with them and other innocent victims in this conflict would have gone a long way as well. I would have also asked him to share more thoughts on the actions taken by Vladimir Putin. Perhaps he will do this in the future.

Pushback from Traditional Catholics

His Excellency's statement has not been well-received by establishment traditional Catholic media outlets and public figures. I needn't repeat what they've said in this space. Most of their comments can be found online. Broadly speaking, they amount to nothing more than vague accusations and uncharitable remarks that fail to put forth a cogent counterargument.[50]

The only substantive response I've seen so far is an interview with Fr Jason Charron on Matt Fradd's *Pints with Aquinas* podcast, and even he gets a few of the archbishop's remarks wrong.[51] Ultimately, the personal attacks and snide comments made about Archbishop Viganò reflect more poorly on those who made them than on the archbishop himself, whatever his personal failings.

One possible reason Catholics aren't seeing this conflict for what it is is because they are looking at it through an Americanist or "conservative" political lens. The influence of Deep State-owned corporate news networks is likely to blame for this. For decades, Western outlets have been repeating Cold War-era talking points and using terms like "oligarchs" and "propaganda" only when speaking about Russia. This has had the lamentable effect of blinding many Americans to the reality that the same terms can be used for powerful individuals like Bill Gates and outlets like CNN, the BBC, and many others. Americans are also, by and large, unaware of just how many revolutions, how much social discord, and numerous unjust wars the US has had its hand in over the last several decades under the guise of spreading "freedom" and "democracy." Too many Catholics think that only Russia is evil and the US is good, when in reality things are far more complicated than that.

President Trump, for his part, was able to cut through the media's spin on all this. In a 2017 interview with Bill O'Reilly, Trump was asked how he could work with Putin, a man O'Reilly called "a killer." Trump promptly responded, "There's a lot of killers. What, you think our country's so innocent? ... take a look at what we've done ...[there's] a lot of killers around, believe me."[52]

50 New Catholic, "Carlo Maria Viganò is Not a Traditionalist," Rorate Caeli, March 8, 2022, https://rorate-caeli.blogspot.com/2022/03/carlo-maria-vigano-is-not-traditionalist.html

51 Pints with Aquinas, "Responding to Archbishop Viganò & What's Going on in Ukraine w/ Fr Jason Charron," YouTube, March 14, 2022, https://www.youtube.com/watch?v=EVGm-J7nhnY8

52 Abby Phillip, "O'Reilly told Trump that Putin is a killer. Trump's reply: 'You think our country is so innocent?'" The Washington Post, February 4, 2017, https://www.washingtonpost.com/news/post-politics/wp/2017/02/04/oreilly-told-trump-that-putin-is-a-killer-

Is it not the case that Archbishop Viganò is in a certain sense saying the same thing but in regards to the Ukraine-Russia conflict? And, like President Trump, is he also not being vilified by his critics as a Putin "supporter" for doing so?

Seeing Through the Lies of the World is a Gift From the Holy Spirit

Another point worth mentioning is that Viganò's analysis tracks closely with the views taken by more than a few conservative reporters. *The Columbia Bugle*, Pedro Gonzalez of *Chronicles*,[53] Raheem Kassam of *The National Pulse*, and Jack Posobiec from *Human Events* have been providing invaluable coverage of the Ukraine-Russia conflict. They all deserve an award for revealing Western media corruption.[54] They've also been instrumental in explaining how neoconservatives, Deep State actors, and leaders of the Great Reset are pushing for war in Ukraine.

And yet, when Archbishop Viganò puts forth statements similar to theirs, Catholics call him a "conspiracy theorist." I do wonder how some so-called Traditionalists reconcile their low appraisal of Archbishop Viganò with their adulation for, say, Leo XIII, a pope who wrote an entire encyclical in 1884 on how global Freemasonry is trying to ensnare the world to its diabolical ways. Would they have laughed him off and called him a "conspiracy theorist" if they were alive back then? If not, what makes them say such things about Archbishop Viganò today?

The Holy Spirit gives us the graces needed to see through the empire of lies built by the devil. If COVID-19 has taught us anything, it's that evil men are plotting the destruction of not only the Church but the world as a whole and that the term "conspiracy theory" really isn't an effective smear anymore. Most of the time, it's a conspiracy *fact*.

Catholics may disagree with Archbishop Viganò's analysis, but if they do decide he's wrong and then go public with their views they should at least provide a substantive critique of his statement, and not be so quick to casually throw him under the bus. They should also humbly pray to God about whether His Excellency has been sent specifically for this moment

trumps-reply-you-think-our-countrys-so-innocent/

53 Pedro Gonzalez, "The Fog of Information War in Ukraine," Human Events, March 15, 2022, https://humanevents.com/2022/03/15/the-fog-of-information-war-in-ukraine/#google_vignette

54 Natalie Winters, "US Funds Ukrainian Former Bioweapons Facility Handling 'Dangerous Materials... With Windows Wide Open," The National Pulse, March 10, 2022, https://thenationalpulse.com/archive-post/u-s-funds-former-ukraine-based-soviet-bioweapons-facility/

in order to get us to see through the many falsehoods around the world. I for one support Archbishop Viganò's statement and await the day the worldwide Church does as well.

LifeSiteNews • March 17, 2022

MEDIA MELTS DOWN AFTER TRUMP TELLS CNN THE 'KILLING' IN UKRAINE MUST STOP

During a combative CNN town hall that felt more like a debate with liberal moderator Kaitlan Collins Wednesday night, former US President Donald Trump caused the media flip out after calling for peace in Ukraine.

After an agenda-driven Collins pressed Trump repeatedly about which side he wants to see victorious, he simply replied, "I don't think in terms of winning and losing. I think in terms of getting it settled so we stop killing all these people."

"They're dying," he further exclaimed. "Russians and Ukrainians. I want them to stop dying. And I'll have that done in 24 hours."

Trump's diplomatic tone stands in stark contrast to the decidedly pro-Ukrainian, neoconservative platitudes that have dominated corporate media and Capitol Hill, where Democrats and Republicans have continually voted to send billions of dollars in so-called "aid packages" to the corrupt Ukrainian President Volodymyr Zelensky.

Reaction to Trump's remarks has predictably fallen along ideological lines. Republican Senator J.D. Vance of Ohio praised him by tweeting, "This is real statesmanship."[55] Vance represents an emerging strain of populist conservatism that breaks with the GOP establishment's commitment to interventionism overseas.

Former GOP New Jersey Governor Chris Christie, on the other hand, echoed what many liberal outlets have made their key takeaway. "Donald Trump refused to say tonight that he wanted Ukraine to win the war with Russia. More proof that he continues to be Putin's puppet," he ridiculously tweeted.[56]

A number of media personalities were on the verge of tears following the

55 Senator J.D. Vance, "This is real statesmanship," X, May 10, 2023, https://x.com/JD-vance1/status/1656481403842822144

56 Chris Christie, "Donald Trump refused to say tonight that he wanted Ukraine to win the war with Russia," X, May 10, 2023, https://x.com/GovChristie/status/1656466180624744449

town hall, which was allegedly cut short due to Trump's effectiveness at swatting away Collin's biased questions. Former MSNBC anchor Keith Olbermann described the broadcast as the "Hindenburg disaster of TV news." He called for CNN's CEO Chris Licht to be fired and declared Collins' career "over."[57] MSNBC host Joe Scarborough and CNN reporter Jake Tapper were also emotionally shaken. Both suggested the event was "dangerous" for democracy.[58]

Seeking Peace With Russia

Collins, 31, relentlessly interrupted Trump throughout the telecast, which took place at St Anselm College in New Hampshire, a key state in the upcoming 2024 Republican presidential primary race. At one point Trump called Collins a "nasty person," to which the audience broke out in applause.

Ukraine was first mentioned when a student asked Trump if he would continue Joe Biden's policy of sending weapons to the war-torn country. Trump explained that he would sit down with leaders from both nations to seek consensus so the fighting would come to an end.

Putin's a "smart guy" but "he would have never gone in [to Ukraine] if I was president," Trump asserted. "And his pipeline would have never [blown up]," a reference to the still unsolved explosion of the Nord Stream gas pipeline in the Baltic Sea, which some have speculated was a false flag carried out by the United States to frame Russia.[59]

Trump also refused to go along with Collins' characterization of Putin as a war criminal. "If you say he's a war criminal, it's going to be a lot tougher to make a deal," he said. Trump additionally voiced frustration with the growing disparity between the amount of money the US is sending Ukraine.

Never Trump Republican strategist Rick Wilson unleashed a profanity-laced tirade on Twitter that seemed to sum up the views of many on the left. CNN has "set a match to democracy," he complained. This is "bad for every other Republican candidate in the primaries" because "you can't beat

57 Keith Olbermann, "THE HINDENBURG OF TV NEWS," X, May 11, 2023, https://x.com/KeithOlbermann/status/1656511378939674624

58 "Trump crushes town hall... video roundup... Jake Tapper on the verge of tears," Revolver, May 12, 2023, https://revolver.news/2023/05/trump-crushes-town-hall-video-round-up-jake-tapper-on-the-verge-of-tears/. The Columbia Bugle, "Joe Scarborough sounds like he's going to cry," X, May 11, 2023, https://x.com/ColumbiaBugle/status/1656641520525619207

59 WND Staff, "Pulitzer-winning journalist suggests US retrieved an unexploded bomb from the Nord Stream pipeline," LifeSiteNews, April 6, 2023, https://www.lifesitenews.com/opinion/pulitzer-winning-journalist-suggests-us-retrieved-an-unexploded-bomb-from-the-nord-stream-pipeline/. Frank Wright, "Nord Stream pipeline sabotage dealt a blow to Europe and Russia but not the US," LifeSiteNews, October 28, 2022, https://www.lifesitenews.com/opinion/nord-stream-pipeline-sabotage-dealt-a-blow-to-europe-and-russia-but-not-the-us/

[Trump] on the stage ... it's time to go to work. He's going to be the nominee."[60] Former Trump adviser Steve Bannon expressed great satisfaction with Trump's performance, as well as with the media meltdown it caused. "What has freaked the media out is that MAGA is ascendent," he said. "And they understand we're going to win the primary, we're going to win the general, and Donald John Trump is going to be the 47th President of the United States."[61]

LifeSiteNews • May 11, 2023

CHRISTIANS SHOULD GIVE PUTIN CREDIT FOR WAGING WAR ON LGBT PROPAGANDA

Russian President Vladimir Putin continued his war on woke ideology Sunday by signing into law a bill that strengthens his country's opposition to "LGBT propaganda."

Western media predictably lashed out at the Orthodox Christian president, who, unlike European and North American politicians, has rejected international pressure to embrace transgenderism and state-sanctioned sodomy.

Putin has been routinely been vilified by the press for decades as being one of the most evil men to have ever lived. The reason is because he stands in the way of the US military industrial complex's plans for global hegemony.

To be sure, Putin, who is divorced, is no saint. But I have friends who would rather have him as their president than Joe Biden. I don't blame them. After all, earlier this year he said that "the overthrow of faith and traditional values ... has taken on the features of ... outright Satanism."[62] Name one Western head of state who speaks like this.

The bill Putin signed into law broadens the scope of a 2013 measure in order to prohibit LGBT content not only for children but for Russians of all ages. It also bans pedophilia and gender "reassignment" in films, books, media, and advertising.

According to Russian outlet *RT News*, the bill passed with unanimous support in both the upper and lower houses of Russia's Federal Assembly.

---

60 Rick Wilson, "I have words," X, May 10, 2023, https://x.com/TheRickWilson/status/1656460186184298496

61 The Columbia Bugle, "Steve Bannon Reacts To President Trump's Dominant CNN Town Hall Performance," X, May 11, 2023, https://x.com/ColumbiaBugle/status/1656685683312869376

62 Aila Slisco, "Putin's 'Satanism' Speech Compared to Rhetoric From MAGA Republicans," Newsweek, September 30, 2022, https://www.newsweek.com/putins-satanism-speech-compared-rhetoric-maga-republicans-1748094

To that I say: Bravo! American lawmakers should follow suit.

This isn't the first time Putin has the social justice left up in arms. At the Valdai International Discussion Club in Sochi last year, he denounced those who promote "cancel culture," equating them to the Bolsheviks who instigated the 1917 communist revolution in Russia. It is "monstrous" that "children are taught from an early age that a boy can easily become a girl and vice versa," he rightly noted at the time.[63]

Putin's Sochi speech was so on target that he earned the praise of *The American Conservative's* Rod Dreher. "Putin, Orbán, and all the illiberal leaders … are all completely clear and completely correct on the society-destroying nature of wokeness and post-liberal leftism," he wrote.

Under the new law, individuals reportedly risk incurring a penalty of up to 400,000 rubles ($6,600). Corporate entities could be fined up to five million rubles (around $83,000).

It is also worth recalling that in the summer of 2020, Russian voters outlawed homosexual "marriage."[64] European Union authorities have frequently condemned Russia for such "anti-LGBT" laws. Although abortion is currently legal until the 12th week of pregnancy, when compared to the rest of the developed world, Russia is arguably more Christian than most Western nations.

It has been said that even a broken clock is right twice a day. I hope Christians who consider Putin an irredeemable villain will recognize the good he has done with this and other laws that defend Biblical morality against the diabolical forces of wokeism. Leaders who support such bills are hard to come by in our post-Christian world. Let's give credit where credit is due.

LifeSiteNews • December 5, 2022

TUCKER CARLSON TORCHES WOKE AUSTRALIAN JOURNALISTS OVER JULIAN ASSANGE, PUTIN, COVID

Remarks made by Tucker Carlson in response to biased questions posed to him by liberal journalists while on tour in Australia this week are going viral.

Earlier today, Carlson posted clips to his X account from his appearance at

---

63 "Putin Rails Against 'Monstrous' West in Valdai Speech," The Moscow Times, October 22, 2021, https://www.themoscowtimes.com/2021/10/22/putin-rails-against-monstrous-west-in-valdai-speech-a75373

64 "Russian Parliament Begins Legalizing Ban on Same-Sex 'Marriage,'" Reuters, July 15, 2020, https://www.reuters.com/article/us-russia-politics-gaymarriage/russian-parliament-begins-legalising-ban-on-same-sex-marriage-idUSKCN24G1CJ/

an exclusive lunch event at the Hyatt Hotel in Canberra. Carlson is nearing the end of a five-city tour with billionaire businessman Clive Palmer for his "Australian Freedom Conference." According to Newsweek, ahead of Carlson's visit the Australian Institute of International Affairs "warned that his presence would mean more mimicking of Kremlin propaganda."[65]

Carlson took a flamethrower to the flimsy attempts made by several reporters to depict him as a pro-Putin, xenophobic stooge who opposes science and free speech.

"A lot of (reporters) are insecure and weak and suck up to power," he said at one point. "This alignment between media organizations and the government, I find disgusting."

Before fielding their questions, Carlson gave preliminary remarks about the recently freed Julian Assange, which he called "wonderful news."

"Typically, the way it works... [is] the guy who discovers the crime doesn't go to jail. It's the guy who commits the crime that goes to jail. And that's been inverted in his case," he said.

Carlson made special mention of former Trump CIA Director Mike Pompeo and Trump Vice President Mike Pence. He called Pence, who posted on X that he disagreed with Assange being freed, a "sad, weak man," while noting that his remarks were "incredibly shameful." Carlson also described Pompeo as a "criminal" who "tried to murder" Assange while he was detained in the United Kingdom.

The Sydney Morning Herald's political correspondent Paul Sakka was one of several journalists who asked Carlson a question. Carlson laughed off Sakka's agenda-driven inquiries.

"Did [Vladimir Putin] make you take the COVID shot?" Carlson shot back at him.

"The COVID shot saved probably tens of millions of dollars," Sakka started to respond.

"Oh yeah, definitely," Carlson mockingly retorted.

Carlson also took umbrage with Sakka's comment that former British Prime Minister Boris Johnson and other "right wingers" consider Putin an enemy of "democracy" and of the "rule of law."

"Boris Johnson is a criminal buffoon who, like so many who claim to love Ukraine, is single-handedly responsible for the deaths of hundreds of thousands of Ukrainian men in this war," he replied. "Boris Johnson, on orders from the Biden administration, shut down... the peace negotiations almost two years ago."

65 Nick Mordowanec, "Tucker Carlson's Viral Confrontation With Reporter Cheered by Conservatives," Newsweek, June 27, 2024, https://www.newsweek.com/tucker-carlson-me-dia-conservatives-viral-1918159

Carlson then shamed Sakka and Australian journalists generally for allowing "the Biden administration to push us into nuclear war" in Ukraine while they dare talk about how Putin "doesn't respect human rights or the rule of law." To further emphasize his point, Carlson noted that the Australian government "did nothing" while Assange was in custody for 12 years. "In the free world, we don't hold people who haven't been charged with a crime," he said. "You tell me how that's consistent with the rule of law or democracy. It's not. It's rule by the intel agencies. It's lawlessness."

Carlson also clarified to Sakka the numerous harmful effects of the COVID shot, which he said, "are everywhere."

"There's a database publicly available in the United States that shows you… [the] Pfizer [shot] has caused more injuries than all self-reported injuries than all the previous vaccination campaigns for the last 50 years combined. And no one in the media has written a story about it," he noted.

Carlson was referring to the Vaccine Adverse Event Reporting System database, which includes hundreds of thousands of adverse reactions to the COVID jab. The latest conservative estimate is that over 17 million worldwide died from receiving the injections, making it the worst man-caused medical catastrophe in history.[66]

Carlson argued that the reason the media has been silent about the shot's harmful side effects is because Pfizer is "one of the largest advertisers on television in the United States."

The "media should be like holding these people to the fire on that," but they're not, he exclaimed. "If you're a journalist, your job is to challenge power on behalf of the powerless. It's not to align with the powerful against the powerless. And that is precisely what you have done."

Carlson also swatted off a question from *Associated Press* reporter Kat Wong, who tried to paint him as a racist and insensitive to gun violence by asking about demographic changes in the United States that are making whites a minority.

"Native-born Americans are being replaced, including blacks, native-born Americans," he replied. When "leaders shift their concern from the people whose responsibility it is to take care of to people around the world, to put their priorities above those of their own citizens, that's immoral."

"The movement of millions of people, mostly with low skills, and no native command of the language, and no shared culture of people who already live there… [is] the most destructive thing you can do to a country."

---

66 Doug Mainwaring, "Study: approx. 17 million COVID-19 vaccine deaths have occurred globally up to September 2, 2023," LifeSiteNews, October 6, 2023, https://www.lifesitenews.com/news/study-shows-COVID-19-vaccines-more-likely-to-cause-deaths-than-to-save-lives/

Carlson was also asked by an audience member for his take on the 2020 election and the security of elections going forward in the US. He replied by noting the phrase "conspiracy theory" was invented by American intelligence agencies in 1964 to use as a "control tool" to shut down persons who were noticing anomalies with the government's investigation into the assassination of President John F. Kennedy. He said those who invoke the term today are "discredited" and that concerns over future elections are reasonable given that even Republicans have not attempted to make them more secure.

Carlson concluded by warning his audience that Australia is a place with "almost no problems" and that it can be a global leader but only "if you don't screw this country up on purpose through mass immigration," which is what Britain, Canada, and the United States have done. "One of the great lies that we in the modern world have been told is that prosperity is generated by banks and real estate. And that money lending is the engine of prosperity," he said. "That's a lie. What creates wealth is productivity, and what's required for productivity are resources, and you have more resources than virtually anybody."

Carlson urged Australians to not be "taking orders" from the U.K. and to not think the US will save them in the long run because "in the end, countries act in their own interests."

LifeSiteNews • June 27, 2024

GOP CONGRESSMAN EXPOSES ZIONIST LOBBY'S POWER OVER CONGRESS

Representative Thomas Massie informed Tucker Carlson that the influential American-Israel Public Affairs Committee (AIPAC) has "babysitters" who monitor US politicians to keep them in line.

AIPAC is one of the most powerful lobbying groups in Washington, DC. With roots dating to the 1950s, the group spends millions of dollars every year to pressure elected officials from both parties to promote Zionist interests.

"Last month, we voted like 15 or 16 times on issues related to Israel," Massie explained. "We haven't had 16 votes in April on [issues related to] the United States!"

Less than two dozen lawmakers, mostly Democrats, routinely oppose AIPAC's goals. US Senator Bernie Sanders and pro-abortion members of "the Squad," including Rashida Tlaib and Alexandria Ocasio-Cortez, are among them.

A website called Track AIPAC keeps tabs on GOP and Democrat lawmakers who take the group's money. A *Politico* op-ed published this past weekend described it as a "fundraising juggernaut," noting that in recent years it has raised "more money for candidates than any similar organization this [election] cycle."[67]

What are Massie's Main Complaints?

A self-described "libertarian Republican," Massie has consistently supported America First policies since winning Kentucky's 4th Congressional District in 2012. His efforts have put him in hot water with AIPAC in recent years, especially his "no" vote on the recently passed "Anti-Semitism Awareness Act," a bill that the even the left-leaning *Washington Post* said was meant to "silence criticism of Israel."[68]

"I vote my conscience, which [AIPAC] won't tolerate," Massie proudly explained to Carlson. "I'm against sending our money overseas. I'm against starting another proxy war. I'm against sanctions because it's going to weaken the dollar. I'm for free speech."

Massie won his primary this year with over 70% of the vote. He told Carlson he was initially "neutral" toward AIPAC and that he would even meet with them to discuss foreign affairs, but now he does "not like" them due their spending $400,000 to oppose him in his last campaign.

"They're worried that I'll run for (Mitch) McConnell's (Senate) seat. And so they're trying to send me a message."

Massie further maintained that the group, which claims it is nothing more than American citizens lobbying for their particular interests, should register as a foreign entity with the US government. Doing so would force them to reveal details about how they operate, he said. "Let's look and see if you're getting any money from that foreign country. Are you a dual citizen with that foreign country? ... Is Netanyahu speaking to your group, advising you on your next move? Are you getting money from the military industrial complex?"

Massie also explained that AIPAC pays for lawmakers to take vacations to Israel and that it has "co-opted Evangelicals" by funding a grassroots organization called Christians United for Israel that encourages them to oppose lawmakers who don't comply with their demands. "It's actually a top-down

67 Jessica Piper and Haley Fuchs, "Bipartisanship or Republican meddling? AIPAC is biggest source of GOP donations in Dem primaries," *Politico*, June 9, 2024, https://www.politico.com/news/2024/06/09/aipac-republican-donors-democratic-primaries-00162404
68 Abigail Hauslohner, "House passes antisemitism bill over complaints from First Amendment advocates," The Washington Post, May 1, 2024, https://www.washingtonpost.com/national-security/2024/05/01/antisemitism-awareness-act-campus-protests/

movement from AIPAC so that people who aren't even Jewish will feel like they've got to support Israel ... even if it's a secular state that funds abortions."

A 'Babysitter' Representing a Foreign Country

Massie also told Carlson that the group sends lawmakers an "AIPAC person" who basically tells them what to do. "It's like your babysitter. Your AIPAC babysitter who is always talking to you for AIPAC. They're probably a constituent in your district, but they are, you know, firmly embedded in AIPAC," he said.

He added that when the person visits Washington, they have lunch with Congressmen and often do political favors for them.

"Why would they want to tell their constituents that they've basically got a buddy system with somebody who's representing a foreign country?" Massie asked Carlson. "It doesn't benefit the congressman for people to know that. So they're not going to tell you that."

"Nobody" on Capitol Hill has a "Britain guy ... an Australian guy ... a Germany dude," he exclaimed.

Massie concluded that despite the group's influence, AIPAC is "exposing their weakness" because a growing number of GOP lawmakers are telling him they agree with his opposition even if they can't stand with him publicly yet. "If one person starts speaking the truth, [AIPAC is] afraid it could be contagious," he said.

LifeSiteNews • June 10, 2024

WHY THE US DEEP STATE HATES EL SALVADOR'S NATIONALIST PRESIDENT NAYIB BUKELE

Corrupt Western media outlets are following a well-known playbook amid the rise in popularity of El Salvador's 41-year-old pro-life, nationalist president, Nayib Bukele, who has a 90 percent approval rating.[69]

Like Donald Trump before him, Bukele rose to power on a wave of populist support. He is perhaps most loved by his people (and equally hated by the Deep State) for jailing over 60,000 gang members that were threatening the stability of his 6.6 million-person country. As a result of his law-and-order

---

69 Kennedy Hall, "Bitcoin-supporting, pro-life president of El Salvador rips Biden for meddling in country's affairs," LifeSiteNews, December 10, 2021, https://www.lifesitenews.com/news/pro-bitcoin-pro-life-el-salvador-president-rips-biden-over-foreign-meddling/

policies, crime in El Salvador has reached historic lows. For putting the safety of his people first, Bukele has been given the honor of being smeared by a growing number of left-wing news organizations in the US. Bukele is "[taking] steps that eat away at the country's democracy," the *Associated Press* groaned recently.[70] "El Salvador's authoritarian president is becoming a regional role model," an article from *The Economist* lamented. "That is dangerous for democracy and human rights."[71]

While no politician is perfect in today's godless world, Bukele (who is not particularly religious, though does have Palestinian Christian roots[72]) has admirably pushed back against the globalist agenda after he won 53 percent of the vote in 2019. He has been a thorn in the side of neo-liberal imperialists ever since. Below are a few of the many reasons why he is disliked by the West's cosmopolitan elite.

Despite backing a 30-day lockdown and the experimental COVID shot during the plandemic, Bukele encouraged citizens to exercise, take vitamins, and eat healthy to prevent the virus' worst side effects.[73] He also distributed government-backed medical packages that included ivermectin.[74]

When Canada's Justin Trudeau forcibly removed the peaceful Freedom Convoy truckers from Parliament Hill in Ottawa in February 2022, Bukele took to Twitter to call out his hypocrisy. "Are these the people who give lessons to other countries about democracy and freedom?" he asked. "[Trudeau's] credibility on these topics is now worth 0."[75]

70 Megan Janetsky, "Amid criticism over his war on gangs, El Salvador's President Bukele turns to sports," Associated Press, July 7, 2023, https://apnews.com/article/nay-ib-bukele-sportswashing-el-salvador-17b7a710d63f0c0a1c4b2d397a74155d

71 "El Salvador's authoritarian president is becoming a regional role model," The Economist, March 16, 2023, https://www.economist.com/the-americas/2023/03/16/el-salvadors-authoritarian-president-is-becoming-a-regional-role-model

72 Raphael Ahren, "His dad was an imam, his wife has Jewish roots: Meet El Salvador's new leader," The Times of Israel, February 7, 2019, https://www.timesofisrael.com/his-dad-was-an-imam-his-wife-has-jewish-roots-meet-el-salvadors-new-leader/

73 "El Salvador: Police Abuses in COVID-19 Response," Human Rights Watch, April 15, 2020, https://www.hrw.org/news/2020/04/15/el-salvador-police-abuses-COVID-19-response. Gerardo Arbaiza, "El Salvador to Begin Giving Third Dose of COVID-19 Vaccine," Reuters, September 25, 2021, https://www.usnews.com/news/world/articles/2021-09-25/el-salvador-to-begin-giving-third-dose-of-COVID-19-vaccine. Kennedy Hall, "Pro-life president of El Salvador encourages healthy living, vitamins to fight COVID-19," LifeSiteNews, January 5, 2022, https://www.lifesitenews.com/news/pro-life-president-of-el-salvador-encourages-citizens-to-fight-COVID-the-natural-way/

74 Kennedy Hall, "El Salvador distributes medical packages that include ivermectim to COVID patients and their families," LifeSiteNews, January 14, 2022, https://www.lifesitenews.com/news/el-salvador-distributes-medical-packages-that-include-ivermectim-to-COVID-patients-and-their-families/

75 LifeSiteNews Europe Staff, "Trudeau has 'zero credibility' on 'democracy' following

Bukele has also been outspoken against the murder of unborn children. For decades, El Salvador has upheld the right to life for the preborn without exceptions. In 2021, Bukele affirmed his support for that position while also refusing to legalize euthanasia and "same-sex marriage."[76] The bloodthirsty, pro-LGBT US State Department despises him for that alone.

Joe Biden has been a target of Bukele as well. A proponent of unifying Central America into a European Union-styled confederation, Bukele pushed back against Biden for meddling in El Salvador's affairs in December of 2021.[77] "It is clear that the interests of the United States Government have NOTHING TO DO with democracy, in ANY COUNTRY," he tweeted.[78]

It's not difficult to understand why the military-industrial complex dislikes Bukele and is labeling him a "threat to democracy." Whatever his flaws, he's refusing to promote their woke, globalist ideology. And for that, he's been targeted for cancelation. The CIA simply does not want a long-serving vassal state to go rogue.

Running Interference for Corrupt Politicians

The blowback Bukele has been receiving in the press is the classic Deep State strategy of accusing your enemy of what you yourself are guilty of. Hillary Clinton did this in her debates with Donald Trump. Joe Biden and Volodymyr Zelensky are doing the same.

Just this year, Zelensky suspended all upcoming elections, citing the easily avoidable conflict with Russia as the reason why. He's also nationalized the news and banned 11 opposing political parties.[79] Yet how did the

Emergencies Act: President of El Salvador," LifeSiteNews, February 15, 2022, https://www.lifesitenews.com/news/trudeau-has-zero-credibility-on-democracy-following-emergencies-act-president-of-el-salvador/

76 Nelson Renteria, "Salvadoran president rules out allowing abortion, same-sex marriage," Reuters, September 17, 2021, https://www.reuters.com/world/americas/salvadoran-president-rules-out-allowing-abortion-same-sex-marriage-2021-09-17/

77 Oscar Cruz, "Nayib Bukele proposes a Central American union that would make the region one of the world economic powers," El Salvador Times, September 27, 2018, https://www.elsalvadortimes.com/articulo/politicos/nayib-bukele-propone-union-centroamericana-convertiria-region-potencias-economicas-mundiales/20180925050649049018.html

78 Kennedy Hall, "Bitcoin-supporting, pro-life president of El Salvador rips Biden for meddling in country's affairs," LifeSiteNews, December 10, 2021, https://www.lifesitenews.com/news/pro-bitcoin-pro-life-el-salvador-president-rips-biden-over-foreign-meddling/

79 Grayson Quay, "Zelensky nationalizes TV news and restricts opposition parties," The Week, March 20, 2022, https://theweek.com/russo-ukrainian-war/1011528/zelensky-nationalizes-tv-news-and-restricts-opposition-parties. Julia Shapero, "Zelensky announces ban on 11 Ukrainian political parties with ties to Russia," Axios, March 20, 2022, https://www.axios.com/2022/03/20/ukraine-ban-political-parties-russian-ties

"pro-democracy" press respond to these dictatorial decrees? By defending it! "Voting in the middle of the Russian invasion is legally and practically unworkable," read a supportive article in *Foreign Policy*.[80] Not only that, Zelensky was given the rare honor of speaking to a joint session of Congress in December 2022. That tells you everything you need to know about how bad the rot in Washington is these days.

And what about Joe Biden? After weaponizing the FBI against pro-lifers, demonizing American patriots as domestic terrorists, and sicking the Department of Justice on Donald Trump and his supporters, Biden has been hailed as a hero who is fighting extremism and hate instead of being decried as the tyrant he is. The lengths Western "news" outlets will go to gaslight the American public is truly astonishing.

At the end of the day, "defending democracy" simply means defending dictatorship by the media. So, whenever you hear that someone is a "threat to democracy," what they really are is someone who is engaging in an un-authorized battled against the Deep State and its fascist agents who push left-wing propaganda on media outlets all day. Whatever his faults, Bukele should be applauded for his efforts to improve the lives of his people.

LifeSiteNews • July 28, 2023

BRAZILIAN LAWMAKER DEMOLISHES LEFTISTS IN UN SPEECH, WINS PRAISE FROM ELON MUSK

A rising star in Brazilian conservative politics has earned praise from Elon Musk and other anti-woke social media users for a riveting speech he delivered at the United Nations.

Twenty-seven-year-old Chamber of Deputies member Nikolas Ferreira excoriated his country's socialist president Lula da Silva, who he said "should be in jail," while also launching a blistering attack on LGBT ideology.

"The left replaces Jesus … [and] the cross, which represents injustice against an innocent person, with symbols that represent nothing other than selfishness," Ferreira explained. "The rainbow is not yours, but ours. Read the Bible. You'll find out."[81]

80 Lea Reaney and Joel Wasserman, "Wartime Elections in Ukraine Are Impossible," Foreign Policy, July 11, 2023, https://foreignpolicy.com/2023/07/11/ukraine-democracy-wartime-elections-russia-zelensky/

81 Nikolas Ferreira, "This was my speech at United Nations Headquarters," X, April 9, 2024, https://x.com/nikolas_dm/status/1777667806097543634

Ferreira, who Musk described as a "brave man" in an X post linking to his speech, has achieved global name recognition in recent years thanks to his popularity on social media. He currently has 3.3 million followers on X (formerly Twitter), 10.6 million followers on Instagram, and 1.82 million subscribers on YouTube. Born in 1996, he was elected to the Chamber of Deputies in 2022 with a historic 1.4 million votes, the most ever received by a candidate.

Ferreira stated on X that his remarks (which were made in 2023) resulted in autocratic Supreme Court justice Alexandre de Moraes investigating him. In that same year, de Moraes fined messaging app Telegram for not suspending Ferreira's account, which he alleged was spreading "criminal manifestations."[82]

As previously reported by LifeSite, X owner Elon Musk is engaged in a legal battle over free speech in Brazil against de Moraes, who has been running the country as if it were his own fiefdom in recent years. Since the 2022 presidential election between Lula and incumbent Jair Bolsonaro, de Moraes has personally suspended bank accounts and banned reporters, elected officials, and citizens from social media all in the name of "defending democracy."

Musk announced on X that de Moraes ordered certain X accounts suspended, and that the details of his order be kept private. Musk refused, even in the face of heavy fines. He also called on de Moraes, who he said has "brazenly and repeatedly betrayed the constitution and people of Brazil," to resign.

Last week, journalist Michael Shellenberger released the "Twitter Files Brazil." The files reveal that the FBI, George Soros, and the Supreme Court of Brazil are engaged in an assault on both the Brazilian and US Constitutions.[83]

Many ordinary citizens in Brazil believe the 2022 presidential race was fraudulent. Hundreds of thousands of citizens protested in the streets afterwards. Former president Jair Bolsonaro returned to Brazil in March 2023 after temporarily fleeing to Florida only to have his home raided by federal authorities two months later. He is currently prohibited from running for office until 2030 for allegedly provoking a riot that occurred at the Brazilian Capitol on January 8, 2023, even though he condemned the event and was not in Brazil at the time. Bolsonaro's son Eduardo, who visited former US

82 Sahar Akbarzai and Julia Jones, "Brazil fines Telegram for not suspending far-right congressman's account," CNN, January 25, 2023, https://www.cnn.com/2023/01/25/americas/brazil-telegram-intl-latam/index.html

83 Michael Shellenberger, "The FBI, George Soros, and Brazil's government say they defend free speech and democracy," X, January 30, 2024, https://x.com/shellenberger/status/1752433572496232874

President Donald Trump at his Mar-a-Lago estate in March this year, has said lawyers are attempting to overturn that ruling. Tucker Carlson recently interviewed Eduardo, telling him he believes it is "pretty clear" the election was "stolen" and that it was "rigged with help from the CIA."[84]

LifeSiteNews • April 10, 2024

GEORGE SOROS PANICS, BEGS EUROPEANS TO PREVENT EU FROM DISSOLVING LIKE SOVIET RUSSIA

Notorious liberal financier George Soros is calling on Europeans to "mobilize" in order to prevent the European Union from dissolving in the same way the USSR did in 1991.

In a hyperbolic opinion piece published Tuesday, Soros claimed Europe is facing a "revolutionary moment." Among other concerns, he warned that if nationalist politicians are victorious in the upcoming European Parliament elections, "the dream of a united Europe could become a 21st-century nightmare."[85]

Soros has long been the subject of criticism from conservatives and pro-lifers due to his immense influence on world affairs. In recent years, he has funded radical organizations like Occupy Wall Street, Black Lives Matter, and Antifa. During the 2016 presidential election, he was one of Hillary Clinton's largest donors.[86] Hungarian Prime Minister Viktor Orbán has accused him of being *the* driving force behind Muslim migration into Europe.

Soros has directly and indirectly interfered in the domestic affairs of a number of countries, including Ukraine, Poland, Colombia, Hungary, the United States, and many others, including Ireland, where he funded the campaign that led to the legalization of abortion there. His activism so infuriated conservative actor James Woods last October that he called him "satanic" for

---

84 Stephen Kokx, "Eduardo Bolsonaro, canceled journalist expose human rights abuses by Brazil's socialist president," LifeSiteNews, March 14, 2024, https://www.lifesitenews.com/news/eduardo-bolsonaro-canceled-journalists-expose-human-rights-abuses-by-brazils-socialist-president-lula/

85 George Soros, "Europe, Please Wake Up," Project Syndicate, February 11, 2019, https://www.project-syndicate.org/commentary/political-party-systems-undermining-european-union-by-george-soros-2019-02

86 Mark Hodges, "Clinton donors could fund Planned Parenthood for 120 years: report," LifeSiteNews, August 4, 2016, https://www.lifesitenews.com/news/clinton-donors-could-fund-planned-parenthood-for-120-years-report/

having "undermined the stability of Western democracies."[87]

In his article this week, Soros blamed everything from populist movements in Germany, the United Kingdom, Italy, and elsewhere to Brexit and "an outdated party system in most European countries" for creating what he calls a period of "radical disequilibrium."

"It is difficult to see how the pro-European parties can emerge victorious from the election in May unless they put Europe's interests ahead of their own," the billionaire opined. "The first step to defending Europe from its enemies, both internal and external, is to recognize the magnitude of the threat they present," he continued. "The second is to awaken the sleeping pro-European majority and mobilize it to defend the values on which the EU was founded."

Sowing Discord in the Church

The Catholic Church has not been immune to Soros' machinations either. WikiLeaks revealed that he spent $650,000 to influence Pope Francis' September 2015 visit to the United States with the goal of having more American bishops "publicly voice support of economic and racial justice."[88]

Soros has also financed dissident groups like Catholics for Choice, Catholics in Alliance for the Common Good, and Catholics United, all of which support left-wing and Democratic policy goals.[89]

Daniel McAdams is the executive director of the Ron Paul Institute for Peace and Prosperity. He told me Soros is worried because he's spent billions of dollars to create a Europe that is free from national identity and religious values but that he is seeing his investment fall flat.

"Meddling in internal affairs and undermining national sovereignty have been two pillars of the worldwide Soros movement, including in the United States," he said. The possibility of the EU being dismantled has left Soros "depressed and desperate."

"The lesson is that even billions of dollars cannot change human nature," McAdams continued. "History can be temporarily shaped by such figures as Soros and indeed the post-communist era particularly for Europe could

87 James Ridson, "Hollywood actor blasts billionaire George Soros as 'satanic,'" LifeSite-News, October 18, 2018, https://www.lifesitenews.com/news/hollywood-actor-blasts-billion-aire-george-soros-as-satanic/

88 John-Henry Westen, "Leaked e-mails show George Soros paid $650K to influence bishops during Pope's US visit," LifeSiteNews, August 23, 2016, https://www.lifesitenews.com/news/breaking-leaked-e-mails-show-george-soros-paid-to-influence-bishops-during/

89 Lisa Bourne, "How billionaire George Soros is trying to hijack the Catholic Church for his progressive agenda," LifeSiteNews, September 1, 2016, https://www.lifesitenews.com/opinion/soros-lurks-in-the-shadows-trying-to-bring-down-catholic-church/

definitely be considered the Soros era. But all of that is coming apart."

During an interview with *The Washington Post* in June 2018, Soros said that when Donald Trump was elected president, "everything that could go wrong has gone wrong."[90] He had donated more than $25 million dollars to Democrat politicians during the 2016 election cycle.

Soros is the founder of the nefarious grant-giving Open Society Foundations, which claims to support humanitarian and democratic initiatives but in reality foments social discord by installing globalist politicians, provoking riots, spreading propaganda, and pouring money into pro-abortion groups across the world.[91]

LifeSiteNews • February 15, 2019

90 Michael Kranish, "'I must be doing something right': Billion George Soros faces renewed attacks with defiance," Washington Post, June 10, 2018, https://www.washingtonpost.com/politics/i-must-be-doing-something-right-billionaire-george-soros-faces-renewed-attacks-with-defiance/2018/06/09/3ba0e2b0-6825-11e8-9e38-24e693b38637_story.html?noredirect=on
91 Natalie Dueholm, "George Soros may be part of biggest 'international political collusion in history': UK politician," LifeSiteNews, November 21, 2017, https://www.lifesitenews.com/news/soros-may-be-part-of-biggest-level-of-international-political-collusion-in/. Sonia Mota, "George Soros admits playing an integral part in the Ukraine crisis - CNN interview May 27, 2014," YouTube, https://www.youtube.com/watch?v=0sAArjOBf_c

CHAPTER IX: CULTURE

COVID PASSPORTS AND SECRET CONSECRATIONS

International travel regulations are heading in a direction that could mean individuals won't be able to enter (or leave) a given country without proof of having received the COVID shot. If that comes to fruition, it could imperil the future of the Catholic faith.

Dr Peter Kwasniewski recently penned an article for *OnePeterFive* arguing that papally-unapproved ordinations may need to take place in the years ahead given the proliferation of Liberalism and Modernism in the church.[92]

His essay makes a comparison between the actions of French Archbishop Marcel Lefebvre in 1988—who consecrated four bishops against the wishes of John Paul II—and other instances of clergy acting without the pope's support.

Kwasniewski points to the examples of Ukrainian Cardinal Josyf Slipyj and Polish Cardinal Karol Wojtyła, both of whom clandestinely passed on holy orders behind the Iron Curtain without Paul VI's explicit knowledge during the middle part of the 20th century.

What's interesting about Kwasniewski's article is that when read in light of vaccine passports and COVID lockdowns, it should remind Catholics that we're on the precipice of not just another "Iron Curtain" situation where a handful of countries in one section of the world are shrouded in spiritual darkness but rather a planetary blackout that could leave entire continents without the true faith.

Take Germany, for instance. Home to arguably the most dissident group of bishops in the West, Germany is seeing its clerics sow so much discord that the faith is practically disappearing in their land. Who will ordain the next generation of orthodox priests? Pro-LGBT Cardinal Reinhard Marx?

One could also look at the sad state of Catholicism in Ireland. As Life-SiteNews has previously reported, St Patrick's Seminary in Maynooth has announced that a measly four men have entered to study for the priesthood for 2021. That's believed to be the lowest number since the seminary's founding

---

92 Peter Kwasniewski, "Clandestine Ordinations Against Church Law: Lessons from Cardinal Wojtyła and Cardinal Slupyj," One Peter Five, October 13, 2021, https://onepeterfive. com/clandestine-ordinations-against-church-law-lessons-from-cardinal-Wojtyła-and-cardinal-slipyj/

in 1795.[93] The light of Christ has all but gone out on the Emerald Isle. It is not difficult to foresee a situation in the near future where countries ban un-vaccinated bishops from entering to perform ordinations. If that happens, entire states will become spiritual concentration camps with only the modernist priests and bishops inside its borders to rely on. If those nations don't have Traditional clergy willing to ordain solidly formed seminarians, then the faith may be in great danger there. It goes without saying that the gates of hell will not prevail against the Church. But that doesn't mean international Freemasonry can't successfully stamp out the Church's presence from entire continents for a duration of time.

To Whom Shall Catholics Go?

Catholics need to ask themselves the following question: how many orthodox cardinals and bishops are left in the Church? I myself think the number is extremely low. I agree with Archbishop Viganò that the true Church is being eclipsed by a "conciliar" imposter that is acting as a New World Order vassal institution working to bring about the Great Reset and lay the foundations for the coming of the anti-Christ.

No doubt there are bishops across the world who are "friendly" toward groups like the Fraternal Society of St Peter, the Institute of Christ the King, and others who want to celebrate the traditional liturgy. But if the Modernist usurpers in Rome are going to use *Traditionis Custodes* to stifle those communities—as it appears they will—the faith could get pretty bleak for Catholics in countries where leftist bishops occupy positions of power. They'll simply refuse to ordain (and consecrate) traditional candidates.

Some Trads might think that the Society of St Pius x (sspx) will always be there for them to fall back on, and that if things get bad enough, diocesan priests and laity will just join up with them. Well, at the moment the sspx has just three bishops and more than 700 priests in the entire world. Three bishops, the youngest of whom is 63, is simply not enough to service the worldwide traditional community, which has grown exponentially since Archbishop Lefebvre's consecrations in 1988. Moreover, what if one of them succumbs to old age or sickness, or is prevented from leaving Europe because they don't have a Green Pass? What will happen to the traditional communities across the world then?

93 Tim Jackson, "Ireland's last diocesan seminary hits new low, admits just 4 new men to study for priesthood," LifeSiteNews, October 7, 2021, https://www.lifesitenews.com/news/irelands-last-diocesan-seminary-hits-new-low-admits-just-4-new-men-to-study-for-priesthood/

I think it's safe to say that history will have a high regard for Catholic bishops who are and have been taking actions to ensure the survival of the faith in as many places of the world as possible. The enemies of Christ who run this planet are undoubtedly scheming to put an end to the Catholic faith. COVID passports are a strong weapon in that fight right now, and perhaps will be again in the future.

Catholics need to take precautions immediately and make sure they are living in a country and/or state that is not far from bishops who are willing to ordain seminarians and consecrate clergy without Vatican approval. It may be the only way they will have access to the sacraments in the years ahead.

OnePeterFive • October 28, 2021

WHY CATHOLICS SHOULD AVOID 'FAST FOOD'

God could have chosen to not create food. He could have made man in a way such that he did not need to eat in order to survive. But, in His infinite wisdom, God did.

Because God's splendor is best shown forth in variety, there exists thousands of differently textured, colored, and tasting foods containing various nutrients and vitamins for man to enjoy.

Children (and perhaps not a few adults) may be shocked to learn that food doesn't come from the grocery store. It comes from the earth. As punishment for Original Sin, man must work the earth by the sweat of his brow, sometimes for many months, in order to bring forth that which sustains him during this brief life.

God's Plan for Food

Food is mentioned numerous times in the Old Testament as well as during the life of Christ, Who is frequently recorded as teaching and reclining at table. Preparing meals, as St Martha did in John 12:2, and eating in common, is also something God reminds us is a good and holy thing.

God has elevated certain foods above others—fish, bread, and the drink of wine being the most obvious. Wholesome and containing much of what is needed to keep man's body functioning properly, those serve as a reminder to abstain from what is unhealthy and to eat what is good.

God made man's relationship with food in a way that is similar to his spiritual life. Take broccoli, asparagus, and all the other "green foods" that men tend to shy away from because they aren't the most delectable. Do they not require a bit of sacrifice to eat? Are they not perhaps a form of light penance imposed on us by God in exchange for a healthy and long life? Food is also intended to sustain us and should not be eaten for the pure enjoyment of it, which easily leads to gluttony and idolatry. Taken collectively, it seems God's plan for food is that all men must eat, that food comes from the earth and requires work to cultivate and prepare it. Certain foods are favored by God and nourish the body while others harm it. Food is a means to an end and should be eaten with others.

The Harm of 'Fast Food'

The "fast food" industry attacks each and every aspect of God's plan for food. For starters, fast food is not real food. It contains inordinate levels of sugar, salt, preservatives, calories, and fats. Fast food is shipped thousands of miles from its point of origin to its destination where it is microwaved, deep fried, and prepared in seconds. High blood pressure, clogged arteries, obesity, heart problems, and intestinal damage are just a few of its worst side effects.

Prepared by workers who often earn unjust wages, fast food "meals" are accompanied by a 32-ounce jug of flavored high fructose corn syrup, which some studies show can lead to cancer.[94] Low-grade poison seems to be an apt description for what passes as fast food these days.

In addition to its lack of nutrition, fast food is generally meant to be consumed not with others but on your own. It is intended for the "man on the go" and to be eaten within seconds. Far from replenishing bodily needs, fast food disrupts our digestive process in a matter of seconds.

An Unnatural Order

The animals that sustain the fast food industry are in no way raised according to God's plan. Pumped full of hormones so they can increase in size unnaturally fast, these genetically modified animals are more man-made mutants than creatures of God.[95]

To make even more profits, arrogant corporations who think God's timeline for the growth of plants and animals isn't fast enough apply harmful

94 Dr Josh Axe, "High Fructose Corn Syrup Dangers and Healthy Alternatives," DrAxe.com, September 29, 2016, https://draxe.com/nutrition/high-fructose-corn-syrup-dangers/
95 Julia Calderone, "The way some meat producers fatten up cattle is more bizarre than you might think," Business Insider, April 6, 2016, https://www.businessinsider.com/farmers-fatten-cattle-hormone-implants-2016-4

herbicides and pesticides to the earth, leaving the land unable to reproduce, like a husband that just underwent a vasectomy.

In every way, fast food represents a parallel, prideful food pyramid that spits in the face of God's plan for food. It is liberalism applied to nutrition. Many fast food "restaurants" are open 24 hours a day nearly 365 days a year, requiring workers to slave away on Sundays, Easter, and other Holy Days of Obligation.

Prime, Sext, and Compline are replaced with the liturgical calendar of "the morning rush," "the office lunch crowd," and "fourth meal." Catholics seriously need to ask themselves: "If Christ walked among us today, would He eat at McDonald's or Burger King?"

Fast food is akin to unlimited cell phone data but for calories. It requires no sacrifice, no inconvenience, and no suffering. Anything our taste buds want our taste buds get within minutes. Whereas God separated the night from the day, fast food unites them under the dollar menu at places that are "open late" until 4am, when we should be sleeping.

Purposefully added salts, oils, and un-pronounce-able ingredients also give fast food the needed flavor required to lure man back for more, making him a slave to his belly until he is unrecognizable from his previous healthy self.

Damage to Family Life

Fast food relies on the motor car for its sales. It tears asunder family life by providing a cushion to the petroleum-dependent, suburban lifestyle, which insulates persons from inconvenience and encourages them to enjoy the luxuries of life—air conditioning, cable TV, hot tubs, etc. A forgetfulness of the virtues of patience and long-suffering are the hallmarks of suburban living.

Rather than enjoying a dinner cooked by a loving and dutiful wife, fast food hands you a meal not on a plate but in a brown paper bag prepared not with love but with that most capitalistic of terms: "efficiency."

Instead of discussing the day's activities with those entrusted to his care, fast food encourages a husband to eat in the solitude of his SUV, scorning the tradition of preparing, sometimes for hours, "grandma's recipe" together as a family with his children.

To Eat or Not to Eat?

God's plan for food involves patiently working the soil and relying on nature to bring forth crops from the earth. Fast food is created in laboratories with artificial ingredients from chemically-treated land and animals.

Whereas Christ reclined at table with others and used meals as an opportunity to teach the faith, fast food encourages the consumption of deep-fried burgers and chicken nuggets on your own as quickly as possible.

Whereas preparing meals has historically been done by loving spouses, fast food relies on strangers to microwave obesity-inducing ingredients for unjust wages every day of the week, 24 hours a day.

Whereas Catholicism calls on man to fast and abstain from certain foods, fast food tells you to satisfy your cravings, whatever they may be, whenever they occur.

Catholics must resist the fast food system created by modern man. They should avoid it altogether and amend their eating habits accordingly. They should strive to have a garden of their own and prepare meals at home with their families, knowing that the fast food industry wars against God's plan for food in every way.

Catholic Family News • June 20, 2018

BIG PHARMA DOESN'T WANT HEALTHY PEOPLE, IT WANTS CUSTOMERS

If there's one thing that's obvious in this coronavirus-insane world, it's that the global medical establishment not only rejects but detests the idea that the human body is a temple of the Holy Spirit.

The pressure being put on every man, woman, and child to get the COVID shot is an all-out assault on the human person as a creature made in the image and likeness of God. Not only are the ingredients in this jab from hell having terrible side effects on those who get it, it doesn't even protect them from contracting the virus in the first place. We're basically living through a world-wide experiment that's genetically altering the human race.

True as that is, the misleadingly-labeled "vaccine" isn't the root of the problem. The real threat is the international "healthcare" industry run by Big Pharma that's promoting it.

Several years ago, I was severely overweight despite living by the food pyramid's guidelines. I ate low-fat foods, got my fair share of breads and pastas, and drank milk every day. I also ran on the treadmill for 30 minutes three times a week. It wasn't until I confronted my primary care doctor about some heart palpitations and muscle fasciculations I was experiencing in 2018 that I decided to pay more attention to what I was putting into my body. I quickly signed up with a personal trainer. He told me everything I

CHAPTER IX: CULTURE

had been doing was completely backwards.

"Fats are not bad. We need them," he said. "Buy some olive oil. Also, cut out carbs, eat more protein, lift weights, and restrict alcohol. It's processed by the body as sugar."

It took me a couple months to get on board with what he wanted but it started to make sense when I began looking more closely at the labels on my favorite foods. Sucrose, corn syrup, and maltodextrin were in everything.

"Why is there 35g of sugar in SlimFast?" I asked a friend of mine. "What is canola oil doing in tortilla chips? There's 800mg of sodium in chicken broth? Cough medicine has the same ingredients as a can of cola!?"

I soon realized the entire food system is stacked against us. Everywhere I went I noticed some terrible substance that ruined the nutritional value of what I wanted to eat. Even "organic" protein powders had artificial junk pumped into them.

Simply put, human beings aren't designed by God to process the food, or drugs, they are being forced to consume today. Sure, MRI's, surgeries, and other advances in modern medicine should be praised for their benefits. But if you look at the big picture, the "healthcare" industry isn't real medicine. Real medicine heals the body. It relies on what God made it to run on (vitamins, minerals, macro-nutrients) in order to rid it of toxins and ward off disease. Yet doctors who prescribe supplements and who recommend natural remedies to their patients are forced to open independent practices that aren't covered by insurance. All the big "research" money goes to hospitals backed by the pharmaceutical companies.

Big Pharma likes to say that human being live longer now (and with less pain) than ever before. To that I say: To what end? Who cares if we're alive until we're 85 and choking down 10 pills every 24 hours to numb ourselves while paying thousands of dollars a month for prescription drugs? What sort of quality of life is that? This world is a valley of tears. No one can escape suffering.

People should do their best to remain in good physical shape for as long as they can, and not throw away the health God gave them on poor dietary choices or alcohol abuse. If they get sick, they should seek out doctors who will treat them not as a guinea pig in a lab but as a member of the Mystical Body of Christ. They should reject becoming part of Big Pharma's system of fake medicine.

The "holy trinity" of health is pretty simple: eat right, lift weights, and get sleep. More people should do those three things and keep their focus on eternity. Let God worry about how long they'll live.

LifeSiteNews • May 6, 2021

CHRISTIANS MUST RESIST PRESSURE TO GET THE COVID SHOT

It's generally a truism that things speed up near the end. Whether we are getting closer to the reign of the anti-Christ only God knows. What *is* undeniable is that the "Great Reset" is being implemented at breakneck speed by sinister men like Klaus Schwab, who is seemingly trying to re-create mankind from the bottom up in a diabolical mimicking of the one and only Great Reset—the death of Christ on the cross that freed us from the chains of original sin.

It seems to me that the COVID jab represents a baptism into the New World Order, a sort of satanic cleansing ritual whereby one is granted basic human rights. Those who reject it are judged as heathens deserving to be excommunicated from public life.

I predict that until everyone submits to it, new variants will continue to be "discovered" and hyped by the media. Eventually, booster shots will be released every few months so that it will be impossible for ordinary people to resist getting at least one shot.

Where Do Things Go From Here?

Everywhere you look, more and more countries and businesses are requiring proof that you've been injected with this de-population cocktail. International travel will likely require it in the not-so-distant future as well. Already at the Vatican, visitors need to show a Green Pass before visiting its museums.[1] Pope Francis himself, who once called getting the shot "an act of love," shamefully joined in with the media's mocking of Cardinal Burke, who ended up in the hospital after contracting the virus.[2]

Another reason the COVID injection is concerning is that it has a transhumanist element to it. Just like the artificial food we eat and the bogus pharmaceutical drugs we take, it is geared toward subtly changing what we are as human beings. What's more, many pregnant women have reported miscarriages after receiving the shot.[3] Young people are having major heart

---

1 David McLoone, "Vatican demands COVID-19 'Green Pass' for entry to historic museums," LifeSiteNews, August 9, 2021, https://www.lifesitenews.com/news/vatican-to-demand-COVID-19-green-pass-for-entry-to-historic-museums/

2 CNA Staff, "Pope Francis on COVID-19 Vaccines: 'Even in the College of Cardinals There Are Some Deniers," National Catholic Register, September 15, 2021, https://www.ncregister.com/cna/pope-francis-on-COVID-19-vaccines-even-in-the-college-of-cardinals-there-are-some-deniers

3 Celeste McGovern, "Former Pfizer VP: COVID vaccines pose 'severe risk' of infertility for women," LifeSiteNews, August 19, 2021, https://www.lifesitenews.com/news/pfizer-vp-vaccination-women-is-stupid-infertility/

problems in response to it, too. The human body is simply not designed by God to safely process its ingredients.

Millions of people may die this coming fall and winter thanks to having compromised immune systems, which may not be able to fight off a common cold. The "unvaccinated" will likely be blamed if and when that happens. This has all been predicted in dystopian Hollywood movies for decades.

Ultimately, what we're witnessing is a complete re-vamping of mankind in the image and likeness of the prince of this world. Many will seek religious exemptions to not receive it. Some may get them while others will just retire early. But evil knows no limits. Satan does not tolerate dissent. He's a jealous demon and wants everything for himself. Pray that you, me, and our fellow Christians will withstand whatever the next stage he and his servants are planning in the coming months and years. It's likely only going to get worse before it gets better.

LifeSiteNews • September 20, 2021

BACK TO THE LAND: UNPLUGGING FROM THE ENERGY GRID

MSNBC host Rachel Maddow has been criticized by not a few conservatives for asking her audience to imagine what would happen if Russia "killed the power" to the electrical grid in the upper Midwest during the polar vortex last month, when wind chill temperatures reached 40 below.

"What would you do if you lost heat indefinitely as the act of a foreign power on the same day the temperature in your front yard matched the temperature in Antarctica?" she wondered.[4]

While many of the views espoused by Maddow, a former Catholic who is "married" to a woman, deserve contempt, this particular hypothetical shouldn't be met with derision.

City vs Country Living

At their core, Maddow's remarks touch on a pressing matter that all Catholics should be concerned with, namely, how utterly dependent upon others, especially faceless energy corporations, modern man is.

---

4 Julio Rosas, "Rachel Maddow Theorizes Russian Attack on Power Grid During Polar Vortex: 'What Would You and Your Family Do," Mediate, January 31, 2019, https://www.mediaite.com/tv/rachel-maddow-theorizes-russian-attack-on-power-grid-during-polar-vortex-what-would-you-and-your-family-do/

They also should remind us about how much of a precarious situation we are in vis-a-vis those who control our resources.

Astute observers of today's cultural, political, and economic patterns will notice that there is a deliberate attempt to not only gin up disgust for those who live in small towns but to actively destroy, sometimes indirectly, but often times directly, the Christian way of life that goes along with it.

Consider the disturbing phenomenon of suburban sprawl. It is increasingly difficult today to take a leisurely Sunday drive into the country and find quiet space where birds and not Buicks make the most noise. This is due, at least in part, to a growing number of farmers selling off hundreds of acres of God's green earth and in its place erecting soul-less subdivisions with $450,000, hot tub-equipped homes occupied by two-income, two-child families.

The net result of these pseudo-communities is an immense amount of pressure on Christian parents who want to raise their children away from the corrupting world and on healthy soil so they have can an appreciation for the majesty of creation. It is, simply put, more difficult to "get away" now.

Consider also the migration of young people away from small towns and their deep-rooted traditions to large metropolitan areas. Perhaps this has been the case for quite some time, but it seems to me to have sped up in recent decades thanks to television and movies promoting the idea that rural areas are where, as Barack Obama once famously said, "bitter" Americans who "cling to guns or religion" live.

The effect of all this is two-fold. One, it creates a sort of class conflict between those in the cities and those who live in the country. Two, it's aim is to deplete the number of independent, self-sufficient citizens living off the land and to increase the number of dependent, controllable persons living in condensed cities.

Consider a family man who owns land, raises animals, grows his own food, burns wood for heat, and uses solar panels for energy. He is far more independent, and thus more of a threat to the goals of global Freemasonry, than the subway-riding, childless 30-something who rents a room on the 18th story of a gas-heated apartment building and whose cooking skills amount to pressing the microwave's "on" button.

Ultimately, what Maddow should have asked her viewers was not to imagine Russia hacking their power supply, but rather to imagine the CIA doing it. Better yet, she should have asked them to imagine not being on the grid at all!

The Land Helps Man Grow Closer to God

In his book *De Regno*, St Thomas Aquinas says the more self-sufficient a thing is, the more dignified it is. As such, the more dependent a man is on others the less dignified he is. Yet this is precisely the situation the modern world has created. Today, entire continents are reliant on a handful of powerful CEOs. It is thus for good reason that French Archbishop Marcel Lefebvre, during remarks made on his Jubilee Anniversary in 1979, said:

I wish that, in these troubled times, in this degenerate urban atmosphere in which we are living, that you return to the land whenever possible. The land is healthy; the land teaches one to know God; the land draws one to God; it calms temperaments, characters, and encourages the children to work.[5]

Solange Hertz, a long-time columnist for *The Remnant*, and author of many insightful essays on modern life, commented on this subject many times. In her provocative book *Beyond Politics* she describes electricity as "Lucifer's anti-grace."

"Pervading the universe before the sun was created on the fourth day, electromagnetism cannot be evil in itself … but as Prince of this world, Lucifer was apparently at liberty to appropriate it to his own purposes," she writes. She continues:

Many an aged citizen today can look back on a youth spent without electricity. For thousands of years generations have lived happily without it, relying on simple mechanics and water power to provide their creature comforts, when suddenly, with the onslaught of the Enlightenment of the eighteenth century, it became a necessity.

"Without electricity," Hertz further adds, "civilized existence was deemed no longer possible. To civilize meant to electrify."

"Usurping the role of the Holy Ghost as Paraclete and Consoler, electricity is the very soul of the city of man, indispensable elixir of progress."[6]

5 Archbishop Marcel Lefebvre, Jubilee Sermon, September 23, 1979, SSPX Asia, https://www.sspxasia.com/Documents/Archbishop-Lefebvre/Jubilee-Sermon-of-Archbishop-Lefebvre.htm

6 Quoted in Stephen Hand, "Hell's Amazing Grace by Solange Hertz," In the Alternative, July 20, 2017, https://stephenhand2012.wordpress.com/2017/07/20/hells-amazing-grace-by-solange-hertz/

Modern Man Needs to Fast From Electricity

Hertz's point is well taken. It makes me wonder just how long can modern man live without technology and electricity. My guess is about as long as it takes for a priest to say Mass.

Imagine, for instance, the chaos that would ensue if New York or Los Angeles lost power and day traders on the stock exchange couldn't practice the sin of avarice, or if the diabolical producers of the filth that passes for "entertainment" these days weren't able to spread promiscuity on the silver screen. Satan would be disabled momentarily but his servants would do everything in their power to get those impious currents of sin up and running again as soon as possible.

At the same time, how long do people today go without confessing their sins or receiving Holy Communion? Weeks, months, years, and sometimes decades. But if the power went out the day of the Super Bowl, a revolution might break out by night's end if it isn't restored before kickoff.

If there ever was a time when the rulers of this world wanted to carry out their maniacal plans against billions of God's children, now is as good as ever. At present, more persons are totally dependent on them and the energy they control—and less dependent on God and His never-ending flow of supernatural charity—than ever before.

Catholic Family News • March 5, 2019

WHAT WOULD THE MARTYRS THINK ABOUT BELGIUM'S EUTHANASIA LAW?

Late last week the country of Belgium became the first nation in the world to allow terminally ill persons *of any age* to be euthanized. The controversial bill was passed by Belgium's Parliament 86–44 and is expected to be signed by Catholic King Philippe in the coming days.[7]

Despite 60% of the Belgium population identifying as members of the Catholic Church, their country now has the dubious distinction of being home to the most progressive assisted suicide laws on the planet.

There's little need to discuss how barbaric this policy really is. Hiding behind the mask of empathy, fanatical worshippers of the idol of choice will now be able to entice society's most vulnerable members into making

---

7 "Belgium's parliament votes through child euthanasia," BBC News, February 13, 2014, https://www.bbc.com/news/world-europe-26181615

the gravely sinful act of meeting our Lord—the Author of Life—not on His terms but on theirs.

Proponents of the measure claim that euthanasia of minors will only occur in specific circumstances and that it will be carefully regulated. In other words, only during "safe, legal, and rare" occasions will the procedure be carried out on children.

Sounds familiar, doesn't it?

The truth is that like abortion, this law will be abused and will also lead to other countries adopting similar reckless end-of-life policies.

Dying as Christ Died

However noble supporters of euthanasia think their intentions are, they are blinded by the fact that suffering is something we all must go through, and that it is part of God's divine plan that we do so. For some, poor health is the heavy cross they will be asked to bear for the duration of their lives. For others, it will be something different. Either way, we should remind ourselves that no servant is greater than their master. And Jesus Christ underwent a most barbaric death. Not only was He nailed to a piece of wood, He was scourged at a pillar, adorned with a crown of thorns, and rejected by mobs of Jews who just days earlier claimed him as their king. What makes us think that we have a right to a pain-free passing to the next world?

The last moments of our lives are a special time that God has prepared for us from all eternity. If we trust in Him like the martyrs did, we will endure the suffering He sends us with great joy. St Lawrence, for example, accepted his fate when he was burned alive on a gridiron. His resignation to God's will won special graces that have helped sustain the Church for two thousand years. Imagine if he had listened to the Belgium Parliament. What graces would have been lost had he ran away and killed himself with a mega-dose of morphine!

The suffering Our Lord has planned for us in our final days serves a greater purpose than we know. Those moments are not only designed to lessen the time we will have in purgatory, they will help procure the salvation of those we are closest to on earth. Assisted suicide, by virtue of the fact that it cuts that suffering short, denies those opportunities. By partaking in it, we reject God's will.

Just like how you and I didn't get to decide when our life began, we don't get to decide when our life ends. Pray for those lawmakers in Belgium—as well as those persons across the world—who wrongly think that we do.

CatholicVote • February 17, 2014

THE MORTARA AFFAIR: *FIRST THINGS* REIGNITES JEWISH-CATHOLIC DEBATE

In 1858, a six-year-old Jewish boy named Edgardo Mortara was escorted by Vatican officials away from his family's home in Bologna. His crime? As an infant, he was on death's door after falling ill and his Catholic housekeeper, Anna Morisi, baptized him without his parents' knowledge. Young Edgardo eventually survived and was taken to Rome as a ward of the Papal States, where Blessed Pope Pius IX oversaw his upbringing. Years later, he became a priest and, in his memoirs, defended the pope against international criticism.

The so-called "Mortara Affair" captured the attention of the neoconservative commentariat last month when *First Things* published an article defending Pius's decision. The author, Fr Romanus Cessario, OP, a professor of theology at St John's Seminary in Boston, laid out an airtight case in favor of the decision.

In his article, Cessario provided a detailed account of the effects that baptism has on the soul. He then explained how Morisi took the correct course of action in baptizing the ailing child. Cessario cited St Thomas Aquinas to show that Mortara's removal from his parent's home at the hands of the state was justified given their refusal to grant him the Catholic upbringing he had a right to receive.[8]

Neoconservatives were predictably apoplectic, especially because the essay was published in their flagship magazine (interestingly enough, Richard John Neuhaus, *First Things'* founder, did not think it was a "kidnapping," as some of his acolytes have argued it was).

First Things' readers immediately demanded that the magazine "disavow" the article and "reaffirm the journal's historical commitment to the freedom of religion as understood in liberal states."[9] A well-choreographed, multi-front attack involving Catholic as well as non-Catholic writers was launched in the weeks that followed.[10] The reason why is obvious. Defending the "Mortara Affair" runs the risk of calling into question Vatican II's teachings on religious liberty and Catholic relations with non-Catholics, especially the Church's position towards the Jews.

8 Fr Romanus Cessario, O.P, "Non Possumus," First Things, February 2018, https://www.firstthings.com/article/2018/02/non-possumus
9 Robert T. Miller, "The Mortara Case and the Limits of State Power: *First Things* Should Disavow Fr Cessario's Defense of Pius IX in the Mortara Case," Public Discourse, January 11, 2018, https://www.thepublicdiscourse.com/2018/01/20868/
10 Rod Dreher, "The Edgardo Mortara Case," The American Conservative, January 9, 2018, https://www.theamericanconservative.com/the-edgardo-mortara-case/

Putting Human Respect Ahead of God

One of the first arguments marshaled against Fr Cessario was that Pius IX failed to respect the natural rights of Edgardo's parents over their son. Charges of "anti-Semitism" were also leveled against Cessario. Everyone from the left-wing *Commonweal* magazine to Zionist Princeton Professor Robert George weighed in on the matter.[11] Their collective message was thus: the Mortara Affair was an embarrassment for the Church and a toxic stain on Jewish-Catholic relations. Those who defend it are probably bigoted towards Jews and are helping lay the groundwork for the rise of fascism in the West.

The sad, sorry, and incoherent responses Fr Cessario's review elicited can be chalked up to the corrosive, paranoid-inducing effects that liberalism (and being concerned with human respect) have on the Catholic mind. If Catholics were truly convinced they had a divine duty to preach the truth in season and out of season—and that they are obligated to please God rather than man, knowing full well they'd be persecuted like Christ was for doing so—the Mortara Affair would be something priests and laity would defend instead of decry as a "monstrous" embarrassment.

Despite *First Things'* capitulation, we should be thankful that editor Rusty Reno allowed it to go to print in the first place. For one, it has shown ordinary Catholics who among them means what they say when it comes to putting God first and ridding the Church, and world, of liberalism and human respect. It has also allowed the faithful to witness firsthand the utter lack of fortitude many so-called Catholic thought leaders possess when it comes to defending the faith when it upsets Jews.

At the end of the day, Fr Cessario and those who bravely defended him on social media and elsewhere provided bullet proof Catholic teachings on baptism, state power, and family rights to prove he was right. His critics shamefully spit in the face of Our Lord by putting fleeting political alliances before the truth. If anything, their actions prove what *Catholic Family News'* long-time editor John Vennari knew long ago, namely, that Liberal Catholicism is driven by a desire to tone down Church teaching because of what non-Catholics think so as to maintain inter-religious collaboration, which ultimately leads to indifferentism.

---

11 Tara Isabella Burton, "Why a 150-year-old kidnapping case has Catholics arguing today," Vox, January 26, 2018, https://www.vox.com/identities/2018/1/26/16933192/edgardo-mortara-kidnapping-case-catholics

Neoconservatives are a Disgrace to Catholicism

The implication made by neoconservatives over the last few weeks that Pius IX was some sort of tyrant is beyond shameful. Orestes Brownson, an eminent 19th century American Catholic thinker, defended his decision at the time. "We cannot excuse their attempt to magnify and misrepresent it as an act of kidnapping," he wrote.[12]

What's more, Edgardo himself sided with the pope as well. Shouldn't that be enough to end the discussion? Yet for neo-Catholics like Professor Robert George and others, the fact that he became a priest is of no importance. Pius IX violated the cardinal sin of "limited government" and did something that damaged Jewish-Catholic relations. Whatever positive effect his decision had later on doesn't matter.

Pray, dear reader, that you and I will never succumb to such diabolical disorientation. Who could imagine there would come a day when Catholics would be so horrified by the idea of a licitly baptized child being raised according to the one true faith that they would deny essential Church doctrines so not to offend non-Catholics? Surely, "an enemy hath done this" (Matthew 13:28).

Catholic Family News • February 24, 2018

CATHOLIC RACE THEORY, PART I:
BROTHERHOOD AMONG GOD'S CHILDREN

From school boards to Capitol Hill, Critical Race Theory is being jammed down the throats of ordinary Americans. What is desperately needed in order to combat this diabolical ideology is *Catholic Race Theory.*

What is Catholic Race Theory? In brief, its is an understanding of the origins of the peoples of the wold rooted in the divinely revealed truth that all mankind descend from one of the three sons of Noah—Shem, Ham, and Japheth—and that they are designed by God to complement each other in supernatural fraternity in both civil and ecclesial society.

Modern Churchmen are Not Helping

Fewer things have been more politicized and exacerbated in recent decades than the issue of race. Groups like Black Lives Matter (BLM) have stated

12 Orestes Brownson, Bronson's Quarterly Review, April, 1859, http://orestesbrownson. org/178.html

that one of their primary aims is the eradication of the family unit, which is understood by Christians to be the "domestic church."[13] Critical Race Theory's loudest proponents, of which BLM is, also oppose fundamental tenants of English common law and other basic principles that underlie Western Civilization.

For the most part, mainstream churchmen have taken their cues from liberals on the subject. "Systemic racism," "racial equity," and "social justice" are just a few of the many buzzwords left-leaning laity and clergy have used while talking about the topic in the last several months. On August 7, for instance, John Stowe, the current Bishop of Lexington, Kentucky delivered a talk entitled "Why Black Lives Matter: A Catholic Perspective on Racism" to his diocese. The lecture sounded as if it was written by an anti-white, social justice warrior who lives in San Francisco.

So-called "conservative Catholics" have not provided a robust theory on race either. Organizations like the Cardinal Newman Society have done little more than make general arguments about how "the dignity of the human person" requires Christians to respect of all God's children.[14]

In totality, it seems as if Catholics have been caught flatfooted on the issue and are not equipped to think about race from a truly Biblical perspective.

Problems with Contemporary Race 'Theories'

What is an authentically Catholic view of race and race relations? What should the Church be saying in response to the growing cancer of Critical Race Theory? We seek to provide such a response in this article and in future ones.

First, it must be noted that contemporary "race theories" are rooted in ideas first presented by anti-Christian, evolutionist thinkers. Charles Darwin taught in his 1871 work *The Descent of Man* that "negroid" peoples were less evolved than "caucasoids," and that the extermination of the "savage races" would be for the betterment of the human species.[15] Contemporaries of Darwin such

13 Martin Bürger, "Black Lives Matter quietly scrubs website of goal to 'disrupt' the 'nuclear family'," LifeSiteNews, September 22, 2020 https://www.lifesitenews.com/news/black-lives-matter-quietly-scrubs-website-of-goal-to-disrupt-the-nuclear-family/

14 Cardinal Newman Society Staff, "10 Ways Catholic Education and Critical Race Theory Are Incompatible," Cardinal Newman Society, July 15, 2021, https://cardinalnewmansociety.org/10-ways-catholic-education-and-critical-race-theory-are-incompatible/

15 "The western nations of Europe, who now so immeasurably surpass their former savage progenitors, and stand at the summit of civilization, owe little or none of their superiority to direct inheritance from the old Greeks, though they owe much to the written works of that wonderful people. ... At some future period, not very distant as measured by centuries, the civilized races of man will almost certainly exterminate, and replace, the savage races throughout the world," Charles Darwin, *The Descent of Man and Selection in Relation to Sex*,

as Thomas Huxley and Charles Kingsley also argued that "negroid peoples" are genetically inferior to whites. Darwin's own cousin, Sir Francis Galton, was so obsessed with creating the perfect race that he is known as the "father of eugenics." He even wrote a lewd novel in which he introduces his readers to this genetic utopia.[16]

Catholic Race Theory, on the other hand, is rooted in Divine Revelation, which teaches that man is designed to live in harmony with his brethren. This is evident in the Book of Genesis. Most of what is known about the earliest peoples and their dissemination after the Flood is found in Genesis Chapter 10, also known as the "Table of Nations." These verses discuss the descendants of Noah, starting with his three sons Shem, Ham, and Japheth. Each is recorded as founding a familial bloodline called a "generation of Noah."

All people today descent from one of these three tribes. Over the centuries, these bloodlines have largely blended together due to migration and inter-marriage. Genesis also describes where some of Noah's sons and their families first settled. Historians have commented on the genealogies of Noah, including Josephus in his *Antiquities of the Jews* and Church Doctors such as St Isidore of Seville in his *Etymologies*. The subject has been touched on very little by Catholics, however. Most of what we know about the Table of Nations or the Generations of Noah we derive directly from Scripture.

Characteristics of Noah's Sons and Their Descendants

According to Judeo-Christian tradition, Japheth was the father of Europeans whose descendants settled modern-day Turkey and Greece. Jesuit priest Fr James Meagher in his book *How Christ Said the First Mass* argues that Japheth's household is characterized by a propensity for order and industriousness. This is easily seen in the entrepreneurialism as well as in the legal and constitutional structures found among European peoples and their diaspora in the United States. Ancient Rome, with its emphasis on order, law, and hierarchy, was, in many ways, the apex of Japhethite culture. That culture—which is synonymous with Western Civilization—is what Critical Race Theory seeks to destroy.

Shem was the grandfather of Heber, from whom the term Hebrew is derived. Shem is the father of many Middle Eastern peoples, including the Jews, as well as Arabs, Asians, and Native Americans who crossed into the Western Hemisphere by way of the Bearing Straight. His offspring are characterized by deep spirituality and a high intellect. When God sent His only-begotten

Second Edition, D. Appleton and Company, New York, 1896, pp. 141, 156.

16 See *Kantsaywhere*

Son into the world, He decreed that He descend from the line of Shem. Modern-day Jews are most associated with the "Semitic" tribe but this is not wholly accurate, as non-Jews are Semites as well.

Ham is the father of the Mesopotamian and African peoples. Ham's son, Mizraim, settled Egypt. The line of his first son, Cush, settled Mesopotamia and Ethiopia. The house of Ham founded the most ancient and longest-lasting civilizations in history. Their propensities tend toward community and artistry, as seen in the grandeur of ancient Egypt. Dark-skinned Africans are often associated with the Hamitic tribe, but most Hamites would have been light-skinned. The "white" indigenous North-African Berbers are one example of this, as is, quite possibly, the Guanches People of the Canary Islands, who may be related to the white inhabitants of Northern Britain and Ireland, whose ancestors likely migrated up the Iberian coast after crossing North Africa to the west out of Egypt.[17] St Augustine of Hippo was a light-skinned Hamite.

Grace and Interdependence in God's Plan

Each "generation" appears to possess their own talents as well as dominant faults. No generation can be said, in the eyes of God, to play a lesser role in the safeguarding and development of His religion. Consider that Japethites (whom Genesis 10:5 refers to as "Gentiles") were chosen to spread the Gospel after the Crucifixion and Resurrection of Christ. It could be argued that their innate desire to build, to go forth, and expand is why God selected them as the heirs to the Old Covenant. "May God enlarge Japheth," Genesis 9:27 states.

At the same time, God deigned that the Semitic Jewish people, because of their innate zeal and spirituality, were to steadfastly preserve the faith of Abraham and keep the Commandments as given by God to Moses until the coming of Christ.

Hamites also contributed to the development of the Catholic religion primarily by their musical and architectural talents. It is not difficult to see how Hamitic culture could have influenced the colors and patterns of the chasuble and dalmatic used in the Mass. That same attention to detail can be seen in the utensils, statues, and altars in churches. This may also explain the beauty that's obvious in the structures built in the kingdoms of Egypt and Mesopotamia.

While God undoubtedly bestowed blessings and gifts on each tribe, each has dominant faults. In other words, Japethites, Semites, and Hamites possess

17 Alice Baghdjian, "Half of European men share King Tut's DNA," Reuters, August 1, 2011, https://www.reuters.com/article/oukoe-uk-britain-tutankhamun-dna-iduKTRE-7704OR20110801/

innate tendencies that, unless aided by the grace of the sacraments—as well it might be argued by the assistance of the other tribes—might lead to destructive excesses.

The Japhethite inclination to work and order, for example, can easily devolve into an obsession with material goods and earthly wealth. The so-called Protestant work ethic comes to mind. A certain moral rigidity or austerity can also become ingrained in a purely non-Catholic, Japhethite culture that lacks true spirituality and the conviviality and expressiveness found among Hamitic peoples. Early American Puritanism is an example of this.

A Semitic nation, meanwhile, may slide into superstition without the true faith. Myths, combined with intellectual pride, can also give way to blind loyalty to earthly deities. Here, one is reminded of the communist dictatorships of China and North Korea in the 20th and 21st centuries as well as the Japanese emperors of the past.

A Hamitic culture that lacks the rigor of Semitic discipline and the ambition of the Japhethite peoples may easily fall into a state of social atrophy or anger, vengeance, and lack of respect for communal and family structure. Present-day South Africa, where looting and violence are rampant, as well as inner-city America, seem to be an example of this.

All men today descend from a common bloodline (cf. Acts 17:26) and are designed by God to complement one another's talents and gifts on their journey to heaven in society and in the Church. Catholic Race Theory maintains that we are made in the supernatural image of God with particular gifts as well as weaknesses that can only be "healed" with sanctifying grace.

The Correct View of the Curse of Ham

Why, it may be asked, has the Bible been used to justify the taking of African slaves and the belief that the "curse" of Ham makes Africans and other dark-skinned Hamites inferior to the peoples of Europe and North America? The answer is that for many years certain Protestant denominations promoted the idea that the descendants of Ham, some of whom settled Africa, were cursed because he mocked Noah's drunkenness in Genesis Chapter 9. This opinion states that African (Hamitic) peoples are inferior to others and are destined for slavery.

This claim falls flat on its face for a number of reasons. First, the curse of indefinite servitude was placed on Canaan, Ham's son, not Ham himself (Genesis 9:20–27). Canaan's brother, Cush, is believed to be the father of the Sub-Saharan African peoples, and he is never cursed by his father. In fact, Scripture goes out of its way to say that not all of Ham's sons would be cursed. These verses make clear reference not to Ham, but only to Canaan, who would eventually settle ancient Palestine and not Africa. This is affirmed by Jewish historian Josephus:

> And when Noah was made sensible of what had been done, he prayed for prosperity to his other sons; but for Ham, he did not curse him, by reason of his nearness in blood, but cursed his prosperity: and when the rest of them escaped that curse, God inflicted it on the children of Canaan. [18]

Additionally, many descendants of Ham listed in Scripture settled outside of Africa, and were not dark-skinned. Some of Ham's descendants were "white."

The example of Ismael, the son of Abraham and the brother of Isaac, is helpful in debunking this theory. According to the Book of Genesis, Abraham, a descendant of Shem, took Agar, the handmaid of his wife Sara, as a concubine. She was likely an Egyptian Hamite. From their union, Ismael was born. Since Abraham's wife Sara was barren, it was presumed that Ismael would be the heir of Abraham until God finally blessed Sara with a son of her own, Isaac. Instead of despising the "cursed" son of the Hamite bondwoman, Ismael, God blesses Agar and Ismael (cf. Gen. 17:20). It is also recorded in Genesis Chapter 21 that Ismael eventually took an Egyptian wife, which suggests that the Hamite peoples were forever linked with the blessing of Ismael.

The Curse of Cain

Another erroneous opinion promoted by certain Protestants and non-Christians has been the a misinterpretation of the curse of Cain, the son of Adam and Eve. Many Protestants, wishing to justify the African slave trade, once claimed that all African peoples inherited the curse of Cain. But as is clear from the Biblical text in Genesis Chapter 4, Cain himself was cursed to poverty and wandering, not his progeny. Cain even asked God to protect him from his brothers, whom he believed would hunt him down for murdering Abel. God obliged and placed a mark on him to distinguish him from the others, not as punishment but to assure him of His protection.

There is much speculation as to what constitutes the "mark of Cain." Some have speculated that it could have been black skin. Even if true, Scripture notes that the mark was meant for Cain alone, and, being a symbol of protection, is, in a sense, a favor from God.

18 Josephus, *Antiquities of the Jews*, Book I, Chapter 6

What's more, St Augustine of Hippo refers to the curse as the wickedness of Cain's line in a spiritual sense, using the sin of Cain as an allegory for those who choose evil over goodness.[19] St Augustine further notes that all people living on the earth except Noah and his family were annihilated by the Flood, not just Cain's offspring. Alcuin of York, in his Questions on Genesis, Chapter 4, Question 89, likewise says that the mark of Cain is the "trembling and moaning" of a fugitive.

As of the publication of this essay, we are yet to discover a prominent Catholic commentator who has stated that the mark of Cain is black skin.

From a merely secular perspective, Cain's household also cannot not be necessarily considered cursed since it later produced important innovations in human history. For example, Jabel was Cain's great-great-great-great grandson. According to Scripture, he was the first to dwell in tents and pasture animals. Jabel's brother, Jubal, invented stringed instruments and organs. Their other brother, Tubalcain, invented metallurgy and was a "hammerer and artificer in every work of brass and iron" (Genesis 4:22). Cain's line also built the first cities in the world.

The Three Kings: An Example of Racial Harmony

The harmony of the races as equal and complimentary in the eyes of God is represented in the persons of the Three Kings.

Little is known about the "Magi"—Caspar, Balthazar, and Melchior—except that they were from "the east" (Matthew 2:1) and that they were probably converts from the Zoroastrian religion. Based on ancient tradition, and maybe even the etymology of their names, we can speculate on their origins.

Casper, who is sometimes referred to as "Jasper," likely came from a Japhethite nation like Syria or Armenia. Balthazar was probably a Babylonian Hamite, which seems to be affirmed with the closeness in pronunciation of his name to Belshazzar, Nebuchadnezzar, or Beltshazzar, the Babylonian name given to the prophet Daniel. According to Medieval tradition, Melchior came from Persia, which was originally settled by Elam, a son of Shem. Melchior therefore was a representative of the Semite tribe, to which Christ Himself belonged. Melchior also has the same suffix as Chedorlaomor, who was an Elamite king that made war on Sodom and Gomorrah.

Whatever else can be said about the Three Magi, it seems that they represented the three different tribes of Noah's sons and that not one of them was so "accursed" as to not be invited to Christ's presence at his birth. All were

19 St Augustine, *City of God*, Book XV, Chapter 8

equal in dignity before the cradle of Our Savior.

We hope this can serve as a starting point for any future discussion on race relations from a Catholic perspective.

Catholic Family News (Co-authored with Daniel Vasko) • September 2021

CATHOLIC RACE THEORY, PART II:
THE TRIBE OF JAPHETH

There is no better villain than "white" European Christians these days. According to the media's version of history, white Christians have been responsible for the oppression and subjugation of African, Native American, Indian, Middle Eastern, Asian, and every other group of people on the planet.

The media likes to attack Christian Japhethites and their history because they want to link them to violence and hatred. This is most evident in the way Christopher Columbus has been vilified in recent decades.

Another reason Japhethites are besmirched is because Semites who control most cultural institutions in the West seem to have a deep-seated, historical resentment over God's decision to favor them. "May God enlarge Japheth," Genesis 9:27 states. As such, tearing down Western Civilization is for them a sort of act of revenge.

The State of Japhethites Today

Some criticisms of contemporary Japhethites do possess a grain of truth in them. After the Protestant Revolt, when Japhethites in Europe and America lost the true faith, they essentially became what the media today says they are: a materialistic colonizer that has little respect for non-Japhethite peoples and cultures.

This seems to be confirmed by the fact that Europe is largely a barren wasteland when it comes to religion and spirituality. The same can be said for the United States, where divorce is rampant, church attendance has dropped to historic lows, and the average family has shrunk to less than two children.[20] In Latin America, the Middle East, and other nations where Semites and Hamites live, religious observance and family size is not as diminished.

American and European Japhethites are a shadow of what they used to

---

20 "Average number of people per family in the United States from 1960 to 2022," Statista Research Department, June 2, 2023, https://www.statista.com/statistics/183657/average-size-of-a-family-in-the-us/

be when they possessed the Catholic faith and when they understood that their God-given mission was to go forth and preach the Gospel. The result of this has been the adoption of a neo-Protestant, materialistic mentality that has resulted in them fighting misguided crusades for "liberal democracy" across the world. Although Western Japhethites believe they are defending "freedom" overseas, history shows that most of the conflicts they instigate are waged for profit, natural resources, or on behalf of corporations so they can open up overseas markets. It's also important to recall that non-Japhethite countries—especially those in the Middle East—tend to resist Japhethite social, political, and religious norms.

A Brief History of the Tribe of Japheth

According to Genesis Chapter 10, Japheth is the patriarch of European peoples. He is recorded as having seven sons. Among the most notable are Gomer, who settled central and modern-day Turkey, and Javan, who settled the Greek isles. Japheth's offspring also settled the mountainous regions around Mount Ararat where Noah's Ark came to rest. They lived in those lands that, although fertile, were not as lush as the Nile Delta or the Tigris and Euphrates River valleys, where the sons of Ham settled. They likely established a hunter-gather or even trading society there, as opposed to the farming communities of Hamites and Semites.

From Gomer came Ashkenaz, whose progeny settled the Caucus Mountains in present-day Armenia. Japtheth's son Magog settled the Russian steppes. According to archaeological and genealogical evidence, his offspring migrated into Eastern and Northern Europe. They are widely recognized as the progenitors of the Vikings and the Celts, who shaped Europe for the next several centuries until they were more or less domesticated by Christianity with the conversion of pagan warlords like St Vladimir, Clovis, and others. The sons of Magog tamed horses and produced the chariot, which was later adopted by nations that they raided, including Mesopotamia, Egypt, and India.[21] They also invented trousers in order to ride horses more effectively.

Historical Traits of Japhethites

As was discussed in Part I of this study, Japheth's line is characterized by order and industriousness, as well as expansion. This can be seen in their history,

21 Rodrigo Quijada Plubins, "Chariot," World History Encyclopedia, March 6, 2013, https://www.worldhistory.org/chariot

both for good and evil. In fact, this is one of the most consistent traits of the Japhethite line.

Like the Magogites, the Japethite Mitanni and Medians periodically raided the Hamitic lands of Mesopotamia. Around 1,200 BC, "sea peoples" from the Aegean Sea invaded and settled the Egyptian delta. Historians believe that these are the ancestors of the Philistines who later colonized the land of Canaan.[22] The Philistine giant Goliath would have been the archetypical Japhethite colonizer—tall and warlike, common features for those who were from the north of the Caucasus Mountains.

The prophet Ezekiel (Ezekiel 38) called Gog of Magog a scourge of God from the north, writing that they would punish Israel for their sin with their horses, horsemen, and spears. In the Book of the Apocalypse (20:7), they are portrayed as an warring horde.

The Generations Grow Closer

The Persian Empire is an instance of cultural mixing between the Japhethite sons of Madai in the mountainous north of the country and the Semitic Elamites in the lower regions on the coast of the Persian Gulf. In fact, its history is a ping-ponging back and forth between the influence of the Medians and the Elamites. It even had multiple capitals in several areas belonging respectively to the two separate tribes, from Ecbatana in the north to Susa and Persepolis in the south.

According to the extra-canonical Book of Jubilees, Chapter 10:35–36, Madai, a son of Japheth, did not like the portion of land that his brothers took, so he admonished his Semitic wife's brother, Arphaxad, and settled north of Elam, afterwards called Media in his honor.

This heterogeneous amalgam of tribes that made up the Persian Empire would eventually conquer Babylon in the sixth century BC, as recorded in Scripture. But they, in turn, were overrun by the small Japhethite army of Alexander the Great, which was legendary for its rapid conquests.

Complementarity Among the Generations

Despite the fact that Japhethites enjoyed a near-continual expansion of their territory since the days of Magog, they arguably lacked civilizational maturity. For example, the sons of Shem and Ham in Mesopotamia and Egypt were leaps and bounds ahead of them until around the sixth century BC "The

22 Fred C. Woudhuizen, Ph.D., "The Ethnicity of the Sea Peoples," Academia.edu, https://www.academia.edu/7287651/The_Ethnicity_of_the_Sea_Peoples_dissertation

descendants of Ham built the first civilizations," the late Fr Victor Warkulwicz has noted. "The advanced civilizations of Sumer and Egypt were the products of the Hamitic genius for organizing, building, and inventing."[23]

The sons of Javan who settled Greece eventually did adopt and then elaborated on and popularized the insights of the early Hamites. "The Hamitic people developed arithmetic, geometry and astronomy to solve practical problems in commerce, surveying and navigation," Fr Warkulwicz has also said. "They were the original explorers and settled in all parts of the world following the dispersion at Babel."[24]

Some of the greatest Greek philosophers credit the Hamitic Egyptians for the origins of philosophy. Plato, for instance, states that it was the Egyptian Theuth who invented numbers, arithmetic, geometry, astronomy, and, "most important of all, letters." (Phaedrus, 274d).

The earliest recorded work of Egyptian philosophy, *The Maxims of Ptahhotep*, was written as wise advice from fathers to their sons. That subject matter seems to fall in line with the familial and communal predilections of Hamites. The Bible's Book of Proverbs is written in a similar style.

Northern European Japhethites like the Goths, Visigoths, Vandals, and Celts eventually conquered Rome, their close Japhethite cousins. In the modern era, Spain and Portugal expanded into the New World. Great Britain and the United States, which possess more of an untamed and irreligious commercialism, have taken on a leading influence in global affairs in more recent centuries. It is simply in the Japhethite D N A to exert themselves on others.

The True Faith and the Tribe of Japheth

The expansionist and brutal excesses of Japhethites were tempered by the Catholic faith, particularly when the barbarian Gauls and Vikings were made protectors of the Church. The Crusades could not have had better proponents than Christianized Japhethites.

But without Catholicism, Japhethites embrace their dominant faults. Today, they have given way to blind expansionism in the name of commodities and material gain—even resorting to barbarism and war crimes. In other words, when unmoored from the Gospel, Japhethites tend to view their success as being measured on the ability to procure wealth and conquer new territory.

As has been previously mentioned, spirituality can be particularly difficult for Japhethites. It is "the line of Shem" according to Fr Warkulwicz, that is

---

23 Fr Victor P. Warkulwicz, M.S.S., *The Doctrines of Genesis 1–11: A Compendium and Defense of Traditional Catholic Theology on Origins*, iUniverse, Lincoln, 2007
24 Ibid.

"characterized by a strong spiritual and religious sense."²⁵ This weakness can be noticed at Western Japhethite get-togethers today. Japhethite gatherings tend to be overly conversational, focusing on sports and work-related pursuits. This stands in contrast to the more festive and rhythmic aspects of gatherings of Latin American peoples, who enjoy dancing and music. Moreover, Protestant sects that originally sprang up out of Northern Europe have become extremely businesslike in the current age. A brief reading from the Bible and a long sermon are almost universally the norm in Evangelical and other communities today. Mormonism is also an example of this. Mormons have a "president" similar to the US Constitution. The Church of Scientology is likewise organized like a corporation, complete with members, by-laws, and a board of directors. This is the natural way a Japhethite understands religion without the real faith.

The Mission for Japhethites Today

Japhethites are the number one enemy of proponents of Critical Race Theory. Their culture and way of life has been targeted for extinction by global elites. Their Semitic brothers in Noah are primarily to blame of the undermining of Japhethite nations. Japhethites today must recognize this and defend themselves against such efforts. What that looks like will be touched on in a future article. The short answer is that Japhethites must re-embrace the Catholic faith so they can be properly equipped to once again lead their brothers to temporal and eternal flourishing as they did for centuries before.

Catholic Family News (Co-authored with Daniel Vasko) • November 2021

CATHOLIC RACE THEORY, PART III:
THE TRIBE OF SHEM

The term "Semitic" means one who descends from the line of Shem. Today, Jews are most commonly associated with the term Semite. Indeed, of the three sons of Noah—Japheth, Shem, and Ham—only "Semites" are consistently mentioned by name in the media. Usually this is done in reference to "anti-Semitism." Socialist congresswoman Ilhan Omar (D-MN), as well as Rashida Tlaib (D-MI), are often given this label by Western media outlets.

What is ironic about that is that both Omar and Tlaib are Muslim, which

25 Ibid.

is a Semitic religion conceived and spread by Arabs, who are also Semites. Omar, who hails from Ethiopia, is a Hamite. Tlaib's parents were born in the Holy Land, making her a Semitic Arab. It is not logical to suggest either of them are "anti-Semitic."

According to Fr James Meagher's book *How Christ Said the First Mass*, people from the Far East and South and Central America are also Semites. He maintains that they migrated east after the Great Flood.[26] The Semitic line is therefore the most numerous tribe of Noah's sons in the world. It is a complete misnomer to equate "anti-Semitism" with being "anti-Jewish" on this basis alone.

Catholicsm is Not an 'Anti-Semitic' Religion

Modern churchmen who follow the Second Vatican Council's teachings in *Nostra Aetate* constantly seek to denounce so-called "anti-Semitism." This is primarily done to suppress missionary efforts towards Jews and to hide the fact that Catholic doctrine teaches that the Old (Jewish) covenant is no longer valid (see Hebrews 8:6–13 and the Council of Florence (1431–1445) for more on this subject).[27]

It is undeniable that the line of Shem, Abraham specifically, was blessed by God, for they are the House which brought God's only Son into the world. But to say, as the modern Church does in the name of combatting "anti-Semitism," that Jews don't need to accept Christ as the Messiah is heresy, not to mention downright hateful toward their soul.

The Apostles were themselves Jewish Semites who came to recognize Christ, also a Semite, as the fulfillment of the Old Law. Their example serves as a reminder that Christ came for all people, and that in Him "there is neither Gentile nor Jew" (Colossians 3:11). Rather, all are one in His Mystical Body,

26 Fr James Meagher, *How Christ Said the First Mass*, TAN Books and Publishers, 1985, p. 220

27 "[The Holy Roman Church] firmly believes, professes, and teaches that the legal prescriptions of the Old Testament or the Mosaic law, which are divided into ceremonies, holy sacrifices, and sacraments, because they were instituted to signify something in the future, although they were adequate for the divine cult of that age, once our Lord Jesus Christ Who was signified by them had come, came to an end and the sacraments of the New Testament had their beginning. Whoever, even after the Passion, places his hope in the legal prescriptions and submits himself to them as necessary for salvation, as if faith in Christ without them could not save, sins mortally. She does not deny that from Christ's Passion until the promulgation of the Gospel they could have been retained, provided they were in no way believed to be necessary for salvation. But she asserts that after the promulgation of the Gospel they cannot be observed without the loss of eternal salvation."—Council of Florence, Bull Cantate Domino (Decree for the Jacobites), Denzinger 712; D.S. 1348

the Holy Catholic Church. The Catholic faith cannot be "anti-Semitic." It is itself a Semitic religion.

A Brief History of Ancient Semites

According to Genesis Chapter 9, Noah planted a vineyard after the Flood. Likely not knowing the potency of the post-diluvian wine due to the change in atmospheric pressure and oxygenation, he became inebriated after drinking it. While his youngest son Ham mocked him, his other sons, Japheth and Shem, covered him with a cloak. Noah awakened from his slumber and, as Scripture says, "blessed the Lord God of Shem." He also prophesied that God would "enlarge Japheth" while making Canaan, the son of Ham, Shem's servant.

Shem's line was indeed blessed, as hundreds of years later God made a covenant with Shem's progeny Abraham and his descendants. Before Abraham, however, the Semitic tribe was just another tribe in the Noahide tree.

According to Genesis Chapter 10, Shem had five sons—Elam, Lud, Arphaxad, Aram, and Ashur. It seems that each son along with his particular clan migrated from the original location of the Ark in Turkey down the Euphrates River into the plain of Shinar, otherwise known as Mesopotamia. Elam ventured through Syria to the coast of the Persian Gulf in modern day Iran. Lud and his tribe stopped in Northern Syria and Southern Anatolia, present day Turkey. Aram likewise settled in Syria. Arphaxad, according to Josephus in his *Antiquities of the Jews*, settled the land of Chaldea, which was on the coast of the Persian Gulf in modern day Iraq at the mouth of the Tigris and Euphrates Rivers on the other side of the Persian Gulf from his brother Elam. Ashur settled the land by the same name, which would later be conquered and subdued by the Hamitic Assyrians, eventually becoming their capital, Nineveh. Arphaxad is the great-grandfather seven times over to Abraham, who was born at Ur of Chaldea around 1950 BC Chaldea is where historians generally believe that the first civilization of Sumer began.

Sumer is credited with many intellectual discoveries such as the earliest writing system, cuneiform. Sumerian Semites produced the first law codes as well, those of Urukagina and Ur-Nammu, which predated the Hamite Babylonian code of Hammurabi by 300 years. This seems to lend credence to the idea that Shem and his descendants had high levels of intelligence. The Jewish Encyclopedia affirms this by stating that the Chaldean people were Semites of a "very pure blood" who were not only experts in reading and writing but also incantation, sorcery, and astrology.[28]

Semitic Developments and Tribal Interactions

Despite the advancements of Semites in this period, there was steady conflict between them and their Hamitic brothers who settled north of Sumer/Chaldea. Those middle-Mesopotamian Hamites later became known as the Akkadians. Starting around 2300 BC, the Akkadians began to dominate the Semites in the region, and eventually conquered their cities.[29]

Akkadian histories will be touched on in a future article on the Hamitic tribe. For now, it suffices to say that they borrowed from the intellectual discoveries of their Semitic counterparts, including their cuneiform script as a result of their conquests. The Greek Japhethites would one day, in turn, borrow those discoveries from the Egyptian Hamites and build on them.

Josephus states that it was the progeny of Joktan, great-grandson of Shem, who inhabited the Cophen, now known as the Hindus River Valley in modern India. Therefore, the Hindus Valley civilizations emerged from Joktan. As will be shown in Part IV of these essays, there was a large amount of Hamitic influence in this region as well.

From southeast and northeast Asia, Semites migrated to the New World. North and South Americans are well known for their spiritual tendencies, which they inherited from their Semitic ancestors. One here is reminded of the practices of American Indians, the Aztecs, and other aboriginal peoples.

Semitic Advances and the Blessing of Abraham

Scholars agree that the language of Sumer was within the same family as Abraham's Hebrew dialect. It is reasonable to believe that Hebrew was spoken in the city of Ur. According to Fr Victor Warkulwicz, Hebrew could have been the original pre-diluvian (i.e., pre-Flood) language preserved from the division of languages at the Tower of Babel.[30] This is not a far-fetched theory given that Shem, according to Biblical genealogy, was still alive for most of Abraham's life. Therefore, Abraham could have spoken with him directly.

What's also fascinating is that Fr Meagher says that the Talmud as well as

---

28 Emil Hirsch, J. Frederic McCurdy, et al., "Chaldea," Jewish Encyclopedia, https://www.jewishencyclopedia.com/articles/4213-chaldea

29 Ibid.

30 Fr Victor P. Warkulwicz, M.S.S., *The Doctrines of Genesis 1–11: A Compendium and Defense of Traditional Catholic Theology on Origins*, iUniverse, Lincoln, 2007

other rabbinic and Christian sources claim that Melchizedek, the priest-king of Salem and founder of Jerusalem, was none other than Shem himself and that it was he who personally blessed Abraham.[31] St Paul seems to validate this theory when he says that Melchizedek was "without genealogy" which, again, according to Fr Warkulwicz, is indicated by the fact that after Noah's death Shem would be considered at the top of his family tree. Fr Warkulwicz also believes that the purported blessing of Abraham by Shem/Melchizedek would have been an act typical of a father towards his son or blood descendant. This makes sense since Shem was the heir to Noah, who died just two years before the blessing of Abraham took place. Shem/Melchizedek, therefore, would have been within his legitimate right to bless on behalf of the family given that Noah was deceased.

The Gifts and Traits of Semitic Peoples

As already mentioned, Semites are not only Jews but also peoples from Asia. The primary gifts of Asian peoples is spirituality and intelligence. In a 1982 study that appeared in the periodical *Nature*, British psychologist Richard Lynn found that the average IQ for Japan's younger generation was about 111, the highest in the world at the time.[32] In 2019, *Forbes* published an article on a study ranking the top 25 most intelligent countries in the world. Unsurprisingly, Semitic nations were featured prominently.

"Asia and Europe dominate the list, with Japan taking the top spot," it read. China, South Korea, Hong King, Taiwan, and Singapore were all ranked within the top six.[33] Canadian psychologist Jordan Peterson, citing many studies, has often argued in support of the claim that Jewish people possess some of the highest IQ in the world.[34]

As far as Semitic spirituality goes, Arabs, Hindus, and South Americans seem to be the only cultures in the world that still take religion seriously. Semites are also well learned in the areas of alternative and holistic medicines. In some countries in Latin America, it is common to go to a "plant store" for remedies with approval from the state. In more legalistic minded Japhethite

31 Fr James Meagher, *How Christ Said the First Mass,* TAN Books and Publishers, 1985, p. 220

32 Robert Cowen, "Are People Smarter in Japan?" The Christian Science Monitor, June 16, 1982, https://www.csmonitor.com/1982/0616/061626.html

33 Duncan Madden, "Ranked: The 25 Smartest Countries in the World," Forbes, January 11, 2019, https://www.forbes.com/sites/duncanmadden/2019/01/11/ranked-the-25-smartest-countries-in-the-world/?sh=1f49ab35163f

34 Jordan Peterson, "On the so-called 'Jewish Question,'" JordanPeterson.com, March 23, 2018, https://www.jordanbpeterson.com/psychology/on-the-so-called-jewish-question/

nations, there is a tendency to regulate everything pertaining to medical care through insurance, waivers, and other documents. Semitic peoples are also naturally patriarchal. They emphasize the role of the male head of the family and society. Their women are often required to be modestly dressed, though sometimes this is taken to an extreme with head-to-toe as well as facial coverings in Muslim cultures. Semites are famous for upholding their patriarchal traditions whereas Japhethites and Hamites often succumb to matriarchy as a result of weak men.

Semitic Spirituality

Today, Catholicism is all but forgotten by the sons of Noah. Modern-day Semites that lack the Catholic religion all too easily fall into mythologies and superstitions. They also embrace false religions like Islam, Hinduism, and Buddhism. Most Semitic peoples prefer a hierarchical and religiously pervasive political system, which is the case in Muslim countries like Saudi Arabia, Iran, and Thailand. In the past, Japan considered their emperors divine beings.

The predominantly Semitic people in India, while having converted in great numbers to Catholicism thanks to Jesuit missionaries centuries ago, are a perfect example of how a lack of Japhetic order and true spirituality can lead to superstitions. Strange gods like the elephant headed Ganesa are present everywhere in India and featured in extravagant religious festivals such as Durga Puja. Many of the same bizarre gods have been worshiped in India for centuries. In Hinduism, the excesses of the spiritual tendency of the Semite to cling to tradition is on full display.

Semitic spirituality is famous for having influenced many European and American Japhethites fed up with the dryness of Western culture and religion. Celebrities like John Lennon and others have long looked toward Hinduism, Buddhism, and other eastern sects. Whatever their faults, these persons are able to see through the aridity of an overly Japhethite spirituality.

Russia is an interesting case as it is a combination of very strong Japhethitic and Semitic influences. Culturally, Russians seem to possess a propensity for European order and industriousness but they also have an attraction toward Eastern spirituality. The Churches of the East are a perfect example of this as they have for centuries safeguarded ancient liturgies and traditions that have otherwise been updated in the West in recent centuries. Regrettably, many Orthodox communities seem to have adopted an excessive ethnocentrism and affinity for particular national cultures and religious traditions.

Catholicism Benefits All Peoples

Rome sits neatly between the Japhethite nations of Europe, the Hamitic countries of Africa, and the Semitic lands of the Middle East. This is an apt location for the Catholic faith to call home.

The Traditional Latin Mass itself could be said to perfectly synthesize the unique gifts and talents of the Japhethites, Semites, and Hamites. As such, it has the ability to round off the excessive tendencies of those who live in a place where the majority of the population is almost exclusively one of the tribes of Noah. Consider that persons living in the Japhethitic country of 13th-century Norway would have benefitted greatly from the Latin Mass with its hymns and devotions. This would have had the effect of educating them on that part of spirituality that is natural to the sons of Shem but perhaps foreign to Japhethites.

Sadly, this entire dynamic is thrown out the window with the *Novus Ordo Missae*, which too often incorporates many of the norms and general ethos of whatever country it is celebrated in. In other words, the *Novus Ordo* cuts off the influences that the other sons of Noah contributed to the Latin Mass as it developed over time. As a result, modern Catholics in the West are left spiritually stunted in some ways.

The Eastern "Orthodox" communities can often be charged with this same fault. Although quite appealing to spiritually-starved Westerners, Orthodoxy seems to be gaining a large number of former Catholics who attended *Novus Ordo* liturgies. These persons look to the admittedly richer liturgical practices of the Orthodox communities for a more stable spiritual life. More will be said on this in a future article.

The Path to Harmony

Our Lady at Fatima asked for Russia to be consecrated to her Immaculate Heart. Why didn't she ask for a Japhethite county like the United States or Canada to be consecrated? What is so particular about Russia?

One reason could be that Russia is a type of cultural bridge between Japhethite Western nations and Semitic peoples of the Middle and Far East. Once converted to Catholicism, Russia could theoretically serve as a sort of spiritual superhighway that influences both the neighboring European, Arab, and Asiatic countries with a newly acquired Catholic faith.

Whether Russia will be consecrated to the Immaculate Heart of Mary in our lifetimes only God knows. What is important to understand about Semitic spirituality is that the peoples of the Middle and Far East are, by virtue of their Noahide ancestry, in possessions of different characteristics than their Hamitic and Japhethitic brethren. Any evangelizing endeavors towards them will certainly need to take this into account. We pray that God will soften their the hearts of Semites around the world so they will embrace the true Messiah, who was of their own household and who preached to before the Gentiles. When they do this, they will no longer possess the disdain they seem to have for their Japhethite and Hamite brothers.

Catholic Family News (Co-authored with Daniel Vasko) • December 2021

CATHOLIC RACE THEORY, PART IV: THE TRIBE OF HAM

Of all the tribes of Noah, the offspring of Ham are the most oppressed and manipulated, particularly those who descend from his son Cush, who settled sub-Saharan Africa.

As has been noted in previous articles, the sons of Ham built some of the longest-lasting civilizations in history, including Egypt and Ethiopia. Today, however, Ham's household is often the target of oppression by Japhethites and Semites. Among other things, Hamites have been taught to embrace many erroneous ideologies and to indulge in their excessive tendencies. This has had the lamentable effect of preventing Hamitic peoples, especially Cushites (descendants of sub-Saharan African peoples), from fully realizing their God-given potential.

A Genealogical History of the Tribe of Ham

Genesis Chapter 10 records Ham as having four sons: Mesraim, Phut, Canaan, and Cush. Mesraim settled the Nile Delta in Egypt while Phut lived in Libya in North Africa. Canaan settled modern-day Israel whereas Cush is considered the father of the Ethiopian and sub-Saharan African peoples.

Each son and his tribe migrated southward along the Euphrates River from the Ark in modern-day Turkey, along with the sons of Shem, into Mesopotamia. The Mesopotamian plain, or the "plain of Shinar" or "Senaar" was, at the time, an extremely fertile land, even more fertile than today. It was a hotbed of activity for the first century after the Flood.

It was in middle Mesopotamia where a son of Cush named Nimrod emerged. Nimrod, according to Genesis, was the first great king on the earth, one who was a "great hunter before the Lord" (Gen. 10:9) and who united the entire region. He is believed to have ordered the construction of the Tower of Babel. St Augustine accuses Nimrod of being a "deceiver" and an "oppressor."[35]

At the time, everyone in the world spoke the same language, the language that had been spoken on the Ark and in the pre-Flood world in the Garden of Eden (though some variations were likely present, as is the case in the United States where regional accents are easily discernible).

Nimrod purportedly first popularized the worship of false gods, whereas before mankind recognized the one true God, Who resembled more or less the God of Noah and his sons—all of whom were all still alive at the time.

According to Fr James Meagher, the Tower of Babel could have been conceived as a means to survive another flood. God, however, was offended by these efforts and confounded man's speech as a result, thereby diversifying languages and scattering the people.

Fr Victor Warkulwicz says that the Tower may have been built around the time of Pheleg's birth. Pheleg was the son of Heber in the line of Arphaxad, a son of Shem. Fr Warkulwicz notes that Scripture says it was during the time of Pheleg that "the earth was divided" (Gen. 10:25). This indicates a period of time relatively soon after the Flood around 3,000 BC.

Further Expansion After the Flood

Hamites not only settled in the Plain of Shinar but also migrated westward across North Africa, reaching the Atlantic coast. Genealogical and archaeological evidence suggests Hamites then turned northward and migrated through Spain and France, and as far north as England and Ireland.

In 2011, news agency Reuters reported on a study that found "up to 70 percent of British men and half of all Western European men are related to the Egyptian Pharaoh Tutankhamun."[36] If true, this suggests that modern-day Irish people have DNA genetically more similar to Hamitic pharaohs then even the pharaohs had with their Semitic neighbors the Arabs.

This finding also appears to be confirmed by discoveries of Egyptian mummies, many of which were found to have red hair not unlike North African and Berber tribes of today. Forensic experts have shown that some of the most famous pharaohs in history, such as Rameses II, were "redheads." It is therefore entirely possible that the gene for red hair was born and carried by

35 Fr Victor P. Warkulwicz, M.S.S., *The Doctrines of Genesis 1–11: A Compendium and Defense of Traditional Catholic Theology on Origins*, iUniverse, Lincoln, 2007, p.395

36 Alice Baghdjian, "Half of European Men Share King Tut's DNA," Reuters, Aug. 1, 2011, https:// www.reuters.com/article/oukoe-uk-britain-tutankhamun-dna/half-ofeuropean-men-shareking-tuts-dna-idUKTRE-7704OR20110801

North African Hamites into modern day England and Ireland. According to Josephus in his *Antiquities of the Jews*, the sons of Cush migrated southward into Ethiopia and sub-Saharan Africa. Josephus believes that "all men of Asia" were Cushites. If true, this means that Cushites blended with the ancestors of Joktan, a son of Arphaxad the Semite, who lived in what is now modern-day India. This suggests that the Indian people are a mix of Cushites and Semitic Joktanites. This Cushite-Joktanite mix would have later migrated through Asia to the east, eventually ending up in Northern and Southern America. These tribes eventually became the Olmec, Aztec, Mayan, and Inca cultures. Migration could have even driven these peoples from the islands of Polynesia into South America directly.

Civilizational Growth, Tribal Conflicts, Cultural Development

As has been stated in a previous article, the Semitic people of ancient Sumer introduced writing and law codes. This indicates a high level of intelligence. However, the world immediately after the Flood was dominated by Hamites, who were known as great architects. "The advanced civilizations of Sumer and Egypt were the products of the Hamitic genius for organizing, building, and inventing," Fr Warkulwicz has said. "The Hamitic people developed arithmetic, geometry and astronomy to solve practical problems in commerce, surveying, and navigation. They were the original explorers and settled in all parts of the world following the dispersion at Babel."[37]

Most of the earliest monuments built across the world before the six century BC were erected by dark and light-skinned Hamites, including the Hagar Qim and Mnajdra temples on Malta, as well as the Great Pyramids of Giza. It may have been the Hamitic propensity for building that inspired the early Semitic Chaldean ziggurat builders. The Aztec temples that were discovered by Europeans who came to the new world were also the result of Hamitic knowledge.

As stated above, Hamite and Semite cities existed in Mesopotamia alongside each other for centuries until the Hamitic people from the city of Achad (known as the "Akkadians") conquered Mesopotamia. From there, the region traded hands between Hamites and Semites. Centuries later, as the Mesopotamian civilizations crumbled, both the Akkadians and Sumerians were raided by Japhethites who hailed from the Zargos Mountains in northern Iran. These were the Gutian people.

37 Warkulwicz, op. cit., p.390

According to several renowned archaeologists, the Gutians had blonde, long hair and were fair-skinned Indo-Europeans from the lands of Madai or Media. They were known for raiding cities—almost like Vikings—and securing tributes, then retreating back to the north.[38]

At the time of Abraham's birth around 1950 BC, the empires of Sumer and Akkad were in ruins. This is generally considered an "intermediate period" in Mesopotamian history. In fact, from that time on, the region was changed forever due to the influx of nomadic Amorites, who were descendants of the Canaanites, the progeny of Ham's son Canaan. Abraham would have been quite familiar with the Amorites and Canaanites from his youth, as they would have seemed almost omnipresent given that they were thoroughly dispersed throughout all of Mesopotamia as a type of barbarian ruling class.

Amorites merged with middle-Mesopotamian people to form the Babylonians. Future Babylonian kings such as the famous Hammurabi were descendants of the Amorites. Abraham would have also encountered the Amorites specifically throughout his extensive travels as the son of Terah, who was a merchant. After taking over his father's caravan following his death, Abraham was inspired by God to settle in a land that was dominated by both Egyptian and Canaanite Hamites—the land of Canaan.

Gifts and Tendencies of Hamitic Peoples

Hamites have a propensity for community and artistry. This seems to be supported by the fact that they were the first great builders, since to erect great structures implies a coordinated, communal effort.

Apart from their building talents, Hamites produced some of the most magnificent pieces of art in history at a time when Japhethites were still living as hunter-gatherer nomads in the north. Indeed, the Hamitic genius for creativity can still be seen today in places like India, where the Cushite-Joktanite people hold some of the most awe-inspiring and ornate religious festivals in the world.

This tendency is also present in South America, where over-the-top displays of religion, music, and dancing is a staple of many countries. It might even be argued that Japhethite buildings and art in ancient cities like Rome were inspired by the previous accomplishments of the Hamites.

It is also worth noting that descendants of sub-Saharan African Cushites dominate the sports, music, and "entertainment" industries in the West, indicating physical as well as creative talents.

38 Kerry Barger, *The True Story of Noah: Discovering Where the Ark Came to Rest*, 2014, p.43

Hamites approach business and relationships quite differently than their brothers in Noah. Japhethites often pursue economic success to a point where personal and familial relationships are ignored in favor of material gain. They are also a more reserved, even stoic people. The Hamitic tendency toward community and relationships often betrays a lighter, more convivial perspective. A Saturday evening basketball tournament in Brooklyn, New York, for instance, are where Hamitic peoples are easily seen living out their innate desire for community.

The Hamitic contribution to the Mass and the Church is predominantly seen in its aesthetic aspects. Whereas Semites contributed the actual Messiah, Our Lord and Savior Jesus Christ, Hamitic Egyptians and Babylonians spurred the use of mosaics, gold, and priestly vestments that later Jews and Christians adopted. Fr Meagher himself gives credit to the Egyptians and Babylonians for inspiring Moses and Abraham. He states that "during the Babylonian captivity the Hebrews saw kings and nobles clothed in silk which the Israelites brought back with them to Palestine."[39] Fr Meagher also says that Israelites brought the royal sandal (which is frequently seen on Egyptian monuments) from Egypt. The cope or chasuble worn by priests and described in the Bible were also depicted in Babylonian sculptures, he has written.[40]

Hamitic influence is evident in the symbolism and fashion of the ancient Israelites and the Catholic faith today. This fact alone may account for why African Catholics seem to take their faith more seriously than European and American Catholics. For all its faults, the *Novus Ordo* liturgy could be a factor in higher Mass attendance rates in Africa than in the West, as it places a particular emphasis on "active"participation and the integration of cultural practices, all of which are natural to Hamites. Whereas Japhethites and Semites seem to have a sort of repulsion to expressive liturgy, Hamites enjoy clapping hands and having a more charismatic Mass service.

This should not, however, discount the undeniable fact that pre-Vatican II missionary efforts in Africa were effective at converting Hamitic peoples with the Latin Mass. If the Latin Mass was restored to its rightful place, and the *Novus Ordo Missae* was done away with completely, there would be even more salutary effects on African peoples, who would likely convert in droves.

---

39 Fr James Meagher, *How Christ Said the First Mass*, TAN Books and Publishers, 1985, p. 293–294
    40 Ibid.

Hamites Today

Like modern-day Japhethites and Semites, Hamites in the 21st century are given over to their dominant faults and excesses, particularly apathy, matriarchy, sensuality, and familial and cultural breakdown, often at the pressure and under the direction of their godless brothers in Noah.

In previous centuries, Japhethites and Semites oppressed Hamites, especially Cushites, by reducing them to mere merchandise in the slave trade. Today in the United States, Cushites are treated with disdain if they don't vote for the Democratic Party. It is also a particularly sad fact that a 2016 study found that while black women only comprise 6% of the American population, they account for 35% of all abortions.[41] Planned Parenthood itself was started by the white eugenicist Margaret Sanger, who infamously wrote in 1939, "we don't want the word to go out that we want to exterminate the Negro population."[42]

As was discussed in Part I of this series, evolution has been used to claim that dark skinned Hamites are less evolved then Japhethites and Semites. Charles Darwin's book *The Descent of Man* (1871) is filled with comparisons of the "evolved white European" to the "savage" Cushite peoples.

North African light skinned Berbers have been treated in a similar way by their Muslim Semitic Arab rulers. For centuries, Berbers were a proud and independent Christian people composed of many tribes throughout North Africa. Islam emerged in the seventh century A.D. and its followers quickly enslaved the native Christian population.

Hamitic peoples have contributed greatly to civilizational advancement since the Flood. Like their brothers in Noah, they must rediscover their Catholic roots in order to rise above the suppression of an atheistic and materialistic world that seeks to oppress them. This will begin when Hamites reject the propaganda taught to them by their brothers in Noah and embrace the Catholic faith so they can once again have strong families and communities.

Catholic Family News (Co-authored with Daniel Vasko) • January 2022

---

41 Mark Hodges, "CDC: 35% of aborted babies are black," LifeSiteNews, Dec. 5, 2016, https://www.lifesitenews.com/news/cdc-statistics-indicate-abortion-rate-continues-to-be-higher-among-minoriti/

42 Becky Yeh, "7 shocking quotes by Planned Parenthood founder Margaret Sanger," LifeSiteNews, February 23, 2015, https://www.lifesitenews.com/opinion/7-shocking-quotes-by-planned-parenthood-founder-margaret-sanger/

CATHOLIC RACE THEORY, PART V:
HARMONY BETWEEN THE SONS OF NOAH

Now that we have established the histories of the sons of Noah (and discussed in detail their respective tendencies and talents), it is necessary to explain how and why Catholic Race Theory can and should be adopted in the 21st century. Doing this will enable men of the world to enter into more harmonious relationships with one another and to live as God intended.

Implementing Catholic Race Theory

The first and most important step is to re-assert the validity of Genesis as a true account of historical events. Part of modern man's rebellion against God stems from his viewing Scripture as a "figurative" retelling of the past. While parts of the Bible are indeed symbolic, Scripture is not Greek mythology. Sadly, many who call themselves Catholic view it in this manner. What's more, many non-Catholics believe the Bible is simply a contradictory collection of words written by hypocritical men who didn't practice what they preached. Efforts must immediately be undertaken to affirm that the Bible's teachings on the origins of man and creation are literal and true.

Second, evolution (i.e. the idea that mankind came from apes and/or other lower creatures) needs to be attacked head-on. This noxious theory undermines basic truths of Catholicism and assaults the divine worth of each human person. It also perpetuates (as Darwin intended) the falsehood that some human beings are innately inferior in their human dignity to light-skinned people. In contrast, Catholic Race Theory holds that the peoples of the earth are brothers who share a common father, Noah, and that they are designed by God to complement each other. This is a far richer, more supernatural view of human beings than the vengeful-driven ideology put forth by proponents of Critical Race Theory.

Third, all the tribes of Noah are currently in a state of excess. In other words, they have spurned the Catholic faith and are now given over to their dominant faults. As such, countries across the world are in a fragile, even dangerous situation where basic knowledge of even the natural law is waning. Until Catholicism is recognized by the nations of the world as the one true religion, countries should put a moratorium on immigration policies so the social conflicts that are too often brought on by religious, cultural, and ethnic differences between clashing Hamites, Semites, and Japhethites can be minimized.

Fourth, the Catholic Church must reacquire the wisdom that priests, historians, theologians, and scholars have written about the tribes of Noah.

Although there appears to be very few figures in Church history that have commented on this subject, Fr James Meagher, St Isidore of Seville, Fr Victor Warkulwicz, and groups like the Ohio-based Kolbe Center for the Study of Creation are some of the best resources Catholics today can draw from for insights on the origins of peoples and the sons of Noah.

Ultimately, the enemies of Christ are seeking to inflame racial tension, erase borders, create a one world government, and, under the guise of "multiculturalism," do away with the Social Kingship of Christ. The Catholic Church has the obligation to oppose these initiatives in the years and decades ahead. Simply put, the Church must present Catholic Race Theory as the solution to these problems instead of issuing boilerplate statements about the importance of "human dignity" and the need to "treat all people with respect."

Practical Approaches and Steps Toward Harmony

Critical Race Theory as well as evolution must be taken out of school systems. Prayer, the teaching of religion, morality, creationism, and teaching about the sons of Noah should replace them. Homeschooling, Catholic co-ops, and more traditional forms of learning must also be encouraged.

Groups like Black Lives Matter spread pernicious ideas. Racial harmony will not be obtained if society adopts their agenda. Nor will policies like affirmative action and reparations help ease racial tensions. Harmony among the sons of Noah will occur when each tribe recognizes that they have something to learn from their brothers.

Although priests and bishops must ultimately be the ones who introduce Catholic Race Theory into their parishes and dioceses, for now it appears that lay Catholics must take up the arduous task of promoting it at the grassroots level. This can be done on social media, blogs, websites, journals, books, and elsewhere. Highlighting different saints from each of the Semitic, Japhethitic, and Hamitic tribes, as well as delving deeper into their respective histories, talents, and gifts, would be beneficial topics for laity to research as well.

Banning the *Novus Ordo Missae* and re-establishing the Latin Mass as the Roman Church's "ordinary form" (while also allowing other ancient and venerable Eastern and Western Rites) would be of great benefit to racial harmony, as the *usus antiquior* perfectly blends the different gifts of each tribe.

The Benefits of Catholic Race Theory

Catholic Race Theory first and foremost removes classifications of people based on degrees of evolutionary superiority. It teaches that the races of the world are equal in dignity and that people should appreciate different cultures, though they should neither be ashamed of their own. Pope Pius XI's 1937 encyclical *Mit Brennender Sorge* is a helpful resource on this subject. Catholic Race Theory rejects racism in its true form. While it is true that God "enlarged" Japheth and sent His only Son into the world as a Semite, all three tribes were represented at the birth of Christ (as symbolized by the Three Kings). Each is loved by God and *can* and *should* learn from one another.

Catholic Race Theory helps Catholics understand how the peoples of the world interact and how God designed mankind to reflect His beauty. It allows Catholics to appreciate the talents and traits of each tribe and how each fits into God's plan. Catholic Race Theory also aids Catholics in knowing how to understand the different non-Catholic peoples of the world when attempting to evangelize them or work with them on social and political affairs.

It is our hope that a greater conversation can now be had regarding Catholic Race Theory. The Church has a duty to help mankind overcome racial and ethnic strife and to ensure harmony among the peoples of the world. We pray that our efforts here have and will contribute to this in some way.

Catholic Family News (Co-authored with Daniel Vasko) • February 2022

CHAPTER X: FAMILY LIFE

JUSTICE KENNEDY TURNED HIS BACK ON CHILDREN

When oral arguments for the Defense of Marriage Act (DOMA) and Proposition 8 took place in March, Supreme Court Justice Anthony Kennedy acknowledged that if the Court allowed homosexual couples to participate in the institution of marriage, society would head into "uncharted waters" because we "have five years of information to weigh against 2,000 years of history or more."

"On the other hand," he remarked, "there is an immediate legal injury ... and that's the voice of ... 40,000 children in California that live with same-sex parents."

Rather presumptuously, Kennedy argued that these children "want their parents to have full recognition and full status. The voice of those children is important in this case, don't you think?"

We now know which way Justice Kennedy went. He ruled against 2,000 years of history and sided with five years of social experimentation.

Though not mentioned until page thirteen of his opinion, the needs of children seem to be what convinced Kennedy to strike down DOMA, which he claimed "humiliates tens of thousands of children now being raised by same-sex couples."

While never explicitly defining what he means when he uses the term "marriage," Justice Kennedy concludes that the Defense of Marriage Act "makes it even more difficult for children [of same-sex couples] to understand the integrity and closeness of their own family and its concord with other families in their community and in their daily lives."

DOMA "writes inequality into" law, he proceeded to conclude. It ignores the "dignity" that is conferred upon same-sex "marriages" via state ordinances.[43]

That an allegedly Catholic jurist wrote this opinion is deeply disturbing. By haphazardly invoking terms such as "dignity," "integrity," and "equality" and applying them to legalized sodomy, Justice Kennedy willfully ignores not only human nature but natural law itself. Simply put, there is no "dignity" in a disordered "union" that flies in the face of God's commandments.

43 "Full text of Supreme Court ruling on DOMA," Chicago Tribune, June 26, 2013, http://www.chicagotribune.com/news/chi-full-text-supreme-court-doma-ruling-20130626,0,4403697.htmlpage

Instead of relying on reason and specifics in formulating his opinion, Kennedy employs sentimentality and emotional appeals to rationalize his radically un-Catholic perspective. Such a malnourished understanding of sin shouldn't be surprising. After all, it was he who ridiculously declared in an opinion for the 1992 case *Planned Parenthood v. Casey* that "at the heart of liberty is the right to define one's own concept of existence, of meaning, of the universe, and of the mystery of human life."

Kennedy compounds his egregious ruling on DOMA by glossing over the purported "closeness" of families headed by homosexual couples. He apparently believes that there is no meaningful difference between the way "married" homosexual couples start a family (often by renting a womb of a woman through paid surrogacy) and how married heterosexual couples begin a family (through a total self-giving, one-flesh uniting, procreative act).

While it is noble Justice Kennedy wants to look out for the well being of children, it is most unfortunate that he has chosen to ignore basic truths about the human person in order to do so. His upside down opinion cites no scientific evidence for his position and wholly disregards what basic reason tells us about family life and human dignity. He self-righteously throws out more than 2,000 years of history and arrogantly pushes the United States into what he himself called "uncharted waters." This is judicial usurpation at its worst and children, as they have in the past when marriage laws were changed, will get hurt as a result.

CatholicVote • June 30, 2013

WHY DO A MAJORITY OF CATHOLICS DISAGREE WITH CHURCH TEACHING ON MARRIAGE?

Here's a fun fact for the start of your week: 53% of Americans support redefining marriage to include same-sex couples. While that might not be a "fun" statistic, you might be surprised to learn that only ten short years ago only 30% of Americans supported homosexual "marriage."

According to a recent poll conducted by the Public Religion Research Institute (PRRI), increasing numbers of Catholics are joining in on the trend to turn their backs on God's teachings for the family.[44] According to the PRRI,

44 Daniel Cox, Juhem Navarro-Rivera, Robert P. Jones, Ph.D., "A Shifting Landscape: A Decade of Change in American Attitudes about Same-Sex Marriage and LGBT Issues," Public Religion Research Institute, February 26, 2014, https://www.prri.org/research/2014-lgbt-survey/

roughly 60% of white Catholics and 56% of Latino Catholics now favor recognizing homosexual unions as a form of marriage.

The institute also found that 72% of white Catholics and 66% of Latino Catholics think homosexual couples can be "as good as parents as heterosexual couples."

What's more, they found that 63% of white Catholics and two-thirds of Latino Catholics think it's acceptable for same-sex couples to adopt children.

These sad statistics will surely be used to pressure the Catholic Church to change its teachings and further argue that those who favor redefining marriage are on the right side of history—as if "history," and not God, is the side we need to worry about being on.

No matter how malnourished and poorly formed the consciences of Catholic laity are today, God's laws pertaining to marriage, children, and the family are as unchangeable as the sun rising in the east. No human authority can alter them. Full stop.

What, then, should Catholics make of this apostasy? What's driving and who is to blame for this confusion? Well, schools for one.

In December of 2013, Mark Zmuda, the vice principal of Eastside Catholic High School in Seattle, was asked to resign after the diocese learned he exchanged wedding vows with his "partner" earlier in the year. He complied but Eastside students immediately conducted sit-ins and protests with signs that had glitter and pink writing on them that read "Love is Love" and "Who am I to judge?" They even wrote a petition for Change.org that gained over 15,000 signatures. Here's a snippet of what it says: "We are uniting in order to change the Catholic Church's opposition of gay marriage. It is time to revisit the policy and act as Jesus would have, loving and supporting every person regardless of their marital status."[45]

The question I have is: Who is educating these children about the faith because they sure as heck aren't teaching them what the Church maintains.

Another reason a growing number of Catholics are in favor of homosexual unions is the lukewarm leadership Churchmen have had on the issue.

In recent decades, there's been very little, if any, reprimanding taking place for Catholic politicians who speak out against the Church's moral teachings on abortion, marriage, and similar topics. When the laity see this, they become emboldened. Eventually, they convince themselves that no one, not even the clergy, has the right to tell them they are wrong.

Pop culture, mass media, and television also bear a large burden for the

---

45 Sabrina Elfara, "Protests Follow Resignation of Gay Vice Principal Who Married Partner," ABC News, December 20, 2013, https://abcnews.go.com/blogs/headlines/2013/12/protests-follow-dismissal-of-gay-vice-principal-who-married-partner/

general apostasy in the Church. When laity consume thousands of hours of what passes for comedy, music, and entertainment, they're slowly infected with the pro-homosexual agenda that is presented to them. Given that the culture we live in is vehemently anti-Catholic, Catholics are breathing in air that is polluted with error.

Bishops, priests, principals, and educators need to get a grip on their curriculum, and if they aren't already, more forcefully teach what the Catechism says about marriage to young Catholics. If they don't, the Church will continue to see its members fall away from her teachings at an even more alarming rate.

CatholicVote • March 3, 2014

'FEMINISM IS A LIE': YOUNG CATHOLIC WOMEN
DEFEND TRADITIONAL FAMILY VALUES

Being a young woman isn't easy these days. Planned Parenthood, liberal politicians, and pop culture all tell them that they need a career and the right to kill their unborn child in order to be a strong and successful woman.

But the young women that attended this year's Bringing America Back to Life convention in Cleveland, Ohio, told me that they reject those ideas.

"Feminism in today's society is not something that is really supporting women at all. In fact, it's hurting women more than anything," one young Catholic woman told me.

"God created woman to do everything a man cannot do: carry children, nurture them, and raise them. God made us to be the heart of the home rather than the head… being too much like a man, you lose what it means to be a woman," remarked another.

Claire Dyson of the Ohio-based Center for Christian Virtue also rejected the idea that abortion is a form of empowerment.

"It is a lie to tell young women that they can't be authentically feminine, that we can't live out our call to life, to nurture. It is a lie that we can't do that and have full lives because it is built into our very DNA that women in general are nurturers."

Dyson added that, "the great tragedy of the day is that men and women don't understand what it is to be men and women. We have been fed a lie for decades that each must be the same. We equate equality with sameness when really our true strength lies in our differences."

It wasn't just young women like Dyson who believe feminism is wrong. College student Kaitlyn Hogg from Franciscan University does as well.

"I think where some feminists get it wrong is that women were created to be nurturing and to be caregivers," she said. "That does not mean women are weak in any sense. It means that they are strong. Where early feminists got it wrong is they took the family out of womanhood. And womanhood begins in family; it begins in being a mother, in being a daughter, in being a sister."

Of all the women that spoke to me at this year's Bringing America Back to Life convention, one 9-year-old girl gives me reason to hope that the pro-family and pro-life movement is in good hands.

"Being pro-life is the saving of people from getting murdered. And I believe that it matters to save people because it's horrible to kill them. It's sad that people don't understand that even though they're in the womb. They're people. They have their own body. They have their own mind. And it's just terrible how people don't believe that."

LifeSiteNews • May 21, 2021

FAR-LEFT DEMAND FOR UNIVERSAL DAYCARE IS REALLY ABOUT INDOCTRINATING CHILDREN

One issue Democrat candidates for president are sure to discuss this election season is universal daycare, a policy socialist Senator Bernie Sanders tweeted support for on Sunday.

"While psychologists tell us that ages 0–4 are the most important years of human development, we have a dysfunctional childcare system which underpays staff and is too costly for working families. We need universal, publicly funded childcare," Sanders said.[1]

Aside from the fact that the first nine months a baby spends in the womb (you know, before "age 0") are also vital to their development, it's a bit odd to hear the pro-abortion Sanders call for having strangers (as opposed to a newborn's own mother) raise a child during their "most important years."

Then again, maybe it's not that strange. After all, the left hates that parents are allowed to raise their children with Christian values. Recall that in 2013, MSNBC host Melissa Harris-Perry declared that "we have to break through our kind of private idea that kids belong to their parents, or kids belong to their families, and recognize that kids belong to whole communities."[2]

1 Bernie Sandes, "While psychologists tell us that ages 0–4 are the most important years of human development," Twitter, Febuasry 10, 2019, https://x.com/SenSanders/status/1094644973591584768
2 LifeSite Staff, "MSNBC Host: Children belong to 'whole communities,' not their parents,"

Just one year earlier at the 2012 Democratic National Convention, a bizarre video was played that said, "government is the only thing we all belong to."[3] Delegates at that convention also booed when references to God were voted into the party's platform.[4]

Consider also that in recent years progressive lawmakers have been extremely effective at pushing propaganda in school districts across the country. From drag queen story hours to mandatory transgender history lessons, Democrats have been relentless in forcing their extremist ideology onto other people's children.[5]

A Deceptive Proposal

In his tweet, Sanders linked to an op-ed that appeared in the *New York Times*. It was written by Katha Pollitt.

While it is no doubt true that, as Pollitt explains, child care is "one of the biggest costs a family faces," the reason she wants it paid for by taxpayers is anything but altruistic.

"The child care crisis has a huge effect on women's employment. It keeps women at home who need and want to work," she claimed without proof. Universal daycare "would help more people and do more to change society for the better." It would "allow lots of people to go to work."[6]

But here's my question: why is that such a good thing? Thousands of years of evidence suggests most women actually don't want to work. They prefer strong husbands who provide for them while they raise children at home. Not until the past 50 or so years in all of human history have women been working full-time. Many of them are now speaking out about how it actually makes them miserable.[7]

LifeSiteNews, April 9, 2013, https://www.lifesitenews.com/news/msnbc-host-children-be-long-to-whole-communities-not-their-parents/

3 Freedom Works Staff, "We All Belong to the Government," Freedom Works, September 5, 2012, https://www.freedomworks.org/we-all-belong-to-the-government/

4 Fox News Staff, "Convention floor erupts as Dems restore references to God, Jerusalem in platform," Fox News, November 5, 2012, https://www.foxnews.com/politics/convention-floor-erupts-as-dems-restore-references-to-god-jerusalem-in-platform

5 Calvin Freiburger, "California school district says parents can't pull kids from new LGBT sex ed," LifeSiteNews, April 19, 2018, https://www.lifesitenews.com/news/california-school-district-says-parents-cant-pull-kids-from-new-lgbt-sex-ed/

6 Katha Pollitt, "Day Care for All," The New York Times, May 17, 2019, https://www.ny-times.com/2019/02/09/opinion/sunday/child-care-daycare-democrats-progressive.html

7 Joy Pullman, "The Feminist Life Script Has Made Many Women Miserable. Don't Let It Sucker You," The Federalist, December 11, 2018, https://thefederalist.com/2018/12/11/the-fem-inist-life-script-has-made-many-women-miserable-dont-let-it-sucker-you/

What's more, the number of sexual abuse cases at the work place is anecdotal proof that men and women have a difficult time being together and not acting inappropriately. Isn't there more to womanhood than being a wage slave for some profit-driven corporation anyway? Apparently not for liberals.

I remember back to August 2018 when Chelsea Clinton boasted how *Roe v. Wade* was a boon to our nation's economy. "The net, new entrance of women [into] the labor force from 1973 to 2009 added three and a half trillion dollars to our economy," she proudly stated, seemingly forgetting that money is the root of all evil.[8]

Ivanka Trump is also pushing women into the workforce as an unqualified good with her "Women's Global Development and Prosperity Initiative." This is not something pro-family activists should be enthusiastic about.

One solution to the cost of childcare could be to use the tax code to reward and/or incentivize married, stable families with children. In Hungary, anti-globalist Prime Minister Viktor Orbán wants to allow families that have four or more children to never pay income taxes again. Similar schemes in the US could easily solve the concerns raised in Politt's article.

But feminists like her scoff at such proposals because they only reinforce the traditional, male-headed household family unit, the strongest bulwark against their Marxist ideology. Predictably, this is what Pollitt complained about in her essay.

"Lack of child care also promotes the less quantifiable but real tendency of parenthood to turn previously egalitarian couples into gender stereotypes. He becomes the chief breadwinner, she's responsible for children and home, and it stays that way even if she goes back to work," she writes.

Has this woman ever met a stay-at-home mom? They are some of the most loving, humble, joy-filled people around—not to mention many of them will tell you they love being able to raise their kids while using their professional "skills" in unique ways.

Feminists like Pollitt seem to believe it's a form of liberation when a woman does what her overbearing boss demands of her in exchange for money but that it's a form of indentured servitude when asked by her caring husband to do something for him out of love.

At the end of the day, universal daycare is a woefully inadequate and wrongheaded proposal with a malicious intent. Only when the lie of feminism is repudiated by young women—and when men take up their duty of provide

8 Calvin Freiburger, "Chelsea Clinton: Roe v. Wade freed women to add $3.5 trillion to US economy," LifeSiteNews, August 15, 2018, https://www.lifesitenews.com/news/chelsea-clinton-roe-v.-wade-freed-women-to-add-3.5-trillion-to-u.s.-economy/

for their spouses, just as Christ did for His bride the Church—will the issues related to raising American children be properly addressed.

LifeSiteNews • February 12, 2019

THE BATTLE OVER THE FAMILY: HARRISON BUTKER'S COMMENCEMENT SPEECH

By now, Harrison Butker's commencement address at Benedictine College in May feels like ancient history. Since then, "Pride Month" came and went, Joe Biden made a fool of himself at a D-Day event in France,[9] and Pope Francis greeted a group of homosexuals and "transgender" men at one of his general audiences at the Vatican.[10]

All par for the course in this upside down world of ours.

The media frenzy that resulted from Butker's speech was primarily due to his not so subtle, but cleverly phrased suggestion that women should put aside their professional goals and focus on their family instead.

"For the ladies present today...some of you may go on to lead successful careers in the world, but I would venture to guess that the majority of you are most excited about your marriage and the children you will bring into this world," he said. "I can tell you that my beautiful wife, Isabelle, would be the first to say that her life truly started when she began living her vocation as a wife and as a mother." He also argued that "one of the most important titles of all" is "homemaker."

Feminists Find Butker's Defiance Intolerable

The attacks launched by America's most well known, Deep State-allied individuals and press outlets the week after Butker delivered his courageous speech predictably smeared him as misogynistic, sexist, anti-woman, and backwards looking, among other unsavory and wholly inaccurate descriptions.[11]

---

9 Emily Crane, "Awkward moment Jill Biden appears to tell Joe not to sit at D-Day ceremony, but he does anyway," New York Post, June 6, 2024, https://www.msn.com/en-us/tv/recaps/awkward-moment-jill-biden-appears-to-tell-joe-not-to-sit-at-d-day-ceremony-but-he-does-anyway/ar-BB1nKF50

10 Stephen Kokx, "Pope Francis again welcomes group of 'transgender' males, homosexuals at Vatican audience," LifeSiteNews, June 5, 2024, https://www.lifesitenews.com/news/pope-francis-again-welcomes-group-of-transgender-males-homosexuals-at-vatican-audience/

11 Svante Myrick, "Butler's misogyny is not unique, it's the conservative agenda," The Hill,

CHAPTER X: FAMILY LIFE

To our feminist-indoctrinated country, Butker's pushback against the daily bombardment of media propaganda aimed at young girls was simply intolerable and deserving of the utmost rebuke.

But as the days went by, I couldn't help but notice that almost every mainstream outlet was focusing solely on his comments about women, and practically nothing else. And it wasn't as if Butker didn't say other "controversial" things. After all, he criticized COVID lockdowns and pointed out how the recently passed "Anti-Semitism Awareness Act" could be used to throw you in jail for "stating something as basic as the Biblical teaching of who killed Jesus." So why did the media obsess over his remarks on marriage?

Reasons for the Media's Outrage

The first reason is that the family is the domestic church. It mirrors the universal Church, which has Christ as its head. The devil hates both "churches" and is seeking to destroy them. As Sr Lucy said, "the final battle between the Lord and the reign of Satan will be about marriage and the family."[12]

But more than that, the media is run by feminists, both female and male feminists. And feminism seeks to "liberate" women from submission to their husbands. It also encourages them to spend their most fertile, child-bearing years having abortions and slaving away at a job, which not only delays marriage (thus decreasing the number of children they will have) but convinces them to view their husband an equal "partner" who can be divorced at a moment's notice.

The second reason is because the Luciferian elite who run this morally depraved world want young American women—white, conservative women in particular—to not have children. Why? Because there is a massive number of illegal immigrants pouring in across the southern border from third-world countries and they want them to become the majority. In other words, the media is working to ensure that the "white replacement theory" that is derided as a "conspiracy" by the Jewish-run Anti-Defamation League comes to fruition.[13]

May 28, 2024, https://thehill.com/opinion/civil-rights/4688813-butkers-misogyny-is-not-unique-its-the-conservative-agenda/. Amanda Musa, "Kansas City Chiefs kicker Harrison Butker defends sexist, anti-LGBTQ+ commencement speech," CNN, May 26, 2024, https://www.advocate.com/sports/harrison-butker-sexist-commencement-speech

12 "Cardinal: 'What Sister Lucia told me: Final Confrontation between the Lord and Satan will be over Family and Marriage,'" Rorate Caeli, June 17, 2015, https://rorate-caeli.blogspot.com/2015/06/cardinal-what-sister-lucia-told-me.html.

13 "'The Great Replacement:' An Explainer," Anti-Defamation League, April 19, 2021, https://www.adl.org/resources/backgrounder/great-replacement-explainer

Both of these goals are carried out through different means of direct and indirect propaganda. I'd like to spend a few moments sharing how this has been done in recent decades.

How is the Anti-Family Agenda Advanced?

One of the most popular ways young girls are enticed to not have children is to set their dreams on professional sports.

Former University of Iowa basketball star Caitlin Clark was recently drafted as the number one pick for the Women's National Basketball Association. The league, which has never turned a profit in its history since being founded by former NBA commissioner David Stern in 1996, has several black players who disdain Clark, who is white. One of them hip-checked her to the ground in a recent game.[14]

When she was in college, Clark's popularity helped the women's Final Four obtain record viewership.[15] Nothing against her, but the corporate media is using her to entice little girls to think they should spend their entire childhood practicing sports so they too can be an athlete in their 20s, the decade of their lives when they would otherwise be giving birth to multiple children, or entering religious life.

This sort of programming happens with the Olympics and US women's soccer during the World Cup every four years. The ultimate goal is to "inspire" young girls to pursue athletic glory at the expense of raising large families.

Promoting a Low-Stress Life

Another weapon that has emerged in the battle against the family in recent decades is the normalization of the "child-free" lifestyle.

On social media platform Tik-Tok last year, users who were promoting their "DINKs" status went viral.[16] DINK is an acronym for Double Income, No

14 Kevin McCormick, "Is the WNBA a profitable league in 2023: Examining how the league is performing financially over the years," SportsKeeda, January 18, 2023, https://www.sportskeeda.com/basketball/is-wnba-profitable-league-2023-examining-league-performing-financially-years. Ryan Gaydos, "Caitlin Clark hard foul was 'welcome to the league' moment, NBA commissioner says," Fox News, June 6, 2024, https://www.foxnews.com/sports/caitlin-clark-hard-foul-welcome-league-moment-nba-commissioner-says

15 Will Graves, "Caitlin Clark set out to turn Iowa into a winner. She redefined women's college hoops along the way," Associated Press, April 8, 2024, https://apnews.com/article/caitlin-clark-ncaa-tournament-final-four-096ae2767eaad741196d1df384674603

16 Maria Espada, "TikTok Is Celebrating 'DINKs': Double Income No Kids Households," TIME.com, January 27, 2023, https://time.com/6250834/dink-tiktok-double-income-no-kids/

Kids. What was happening was that couples, usually white men and women in their 20s, were uploading videos of themselves walking on a nice sunny day explaining how they spend their money on vacations and Starbucks instead of on diapers. They would also boast about how they sleep in on the weekend.

This messaging was meant to instill jealousy in parents as well as single women by showing that they had low levels of anxiety and because they weren't burdened by the "drudgery" of taking care of infants.

Left-wing TIME magazine has been pushing this sort of anti-Biblical existence for years. On August 12, 2013, they released an issue titled, "The Childfree Life: When having it all means not having children." On the cover was a photo of a sunglass-wearing white male and female couple laying on the beach.[17] One has to wonder why the pair wasn't Hispanic, Black, or Indian.

Political Indoctrination

There is plenty of anti-family messaging in the world of politics as well. In 2013, then-MSNBC host Melissa Harris-Perry shockingly declared, "We have to break through our kind of private idea that kids belong to their parents, or kids belong to their families, and recognize that kids belong to whole communities."[18]

In August 2018, Chelsea Clinton bragged that Roe v. Wade was a boon to our nation's economy. "The net, new entrance of women [into] the labor force from 1973 to 2009 added three and a half trillion dollars to our economy," she proudly stated, seemingly forgetting that money is the root of all evil.[19]

During the 2020 Democratic presidential primary, socialist Senator Bernie Sanders tweeted support for publicly funded childcare. As I argued in an op-ed at the time, universal daycare is simply a tool liberals are using to separate children from their parents so they can brainwash them with LGBT ideology.[20]

17 Vaughn Wallace, "Behind the Cover: The Childfree Life by Randal Ford," TIME.com, August 1, 2013, https://time.com/75964/behind-the-cover-randal-fords-america/

18 LifeSite Staff, "MSNBC host: Children belong to 'whole communities', not their parents," LifeSiteNews, April 9, 2013, https://www.lifesitenews.com/news/msnbc-host-children-be-long-to-whole-communities-not-their-parents/

19 Calvin Freiburger, "Chelsea Clinton: Roe v. Wade freed women to add $3.5 trillion to US economy," LifeSiteNews, August 15, 2018, https://www.lifesitenews.com/news/chelsea-clinton-roe-v.-wade-freed-women-to-add-3.5-trillion-to-u.s.-economy/

20 Stephen Kokx, "Far-left demand for universal daycare is really about indoctrinating our children," LifeSiteNews, February 12, 2019, https://www.lifesitenews.com/opinion/far-left-de-mand-for-universal-daycare-is-really-about-indoctrinating-our-ch/

The Real Source of Women's Liberation?

Before his death, influential filmmaker and music industry insider Aaron Russo (1943–2007) was interviewed by InfoWars' Alex Jones.[21] Russo produced the 2006 anti-New World Order documentary *America: Freedom to Fascism.* He was also allegedly close with the Rockefeller family.

At one point during the interview, Russo revealed that he was recruited to join the Council on Foreign Relations by his friend Nick Rockefeller, who apparently informed him about his family's role in the feminist movement.

"Aaron, what do you think women's liberation was about?" Russo said, imitating Rockefeller. "That women have the right to work, get equal pay with men, just like they won the right to vote," he replied.

"And [Nick] started to laugh …. let me tell you what that was about. We, the Rockefellers, funded that. We funded women's [liberation]. We're the ones who got it all over the newspapers and television—the Rockefeller Foundation."

"And he says, 'you want to know why? There were two primary reasons. And one reason was we couldn't tax half the population … the second reason was now we get the kids in school at an early age—we can indoctrinate the kids how to think. It breaks up their family. The kids start looking at the state as the family.'"

Who knows if Russo and Rockefeller ever had that conversation. I am inclined to think he was being honest. Regardless, even if he wasn't, it is undeniable that the real goal of the feminist movement is to destroy the family and to ensure women spend their 20s and 30s being wage slaves and having less children.

Harrison Butker is a straight, white, Latin Mass-attending, married, wealthy, self-reliant male who is successful in his career. The anti-Christian media could have attacked him for any of those characteristics alone. The culture and faith he represents is what they desperately want to eradicate from the United States. But he won their fury because of the way he so eloquently defended traditional gender roles by encouraging young women to reject the "diabolic lie" they tell them and to instead embrace God's design for them. That alone tells us how much control the devil has in this "final battle" between himself and Our Lord. Fortunately, we already know who the winner is in this war. As Butker told graduates, "Christ is King!"

Catholic Family News • July 2024

---

21 "Reflections & Warnings—An Interview with Aaron Russo," InfoWars, June 8, 2022, https://www.infowars.com/posts/reflections-warnings-an-interview-with-aaron-russo/

SOUTHERN POVERTY LAW CENTER FORGETS HOW MUCH 'HATE' DEMOCRATS HAVE FOR UNBORN BABIES, CATHOLICS

The anti-Christian zealots at the Southern Poverty Law Center (SPLC) released their annual "Year in Hate and Extremism" report last Wednesday. The study claims to have found that under President Trump the United States has witnessed an increase in hate crimes and "hate group" membership.

The "study" also alleges that the number of hate groups in the United States has grown for four straight years thanks to increasing interest in so-called alt-right and white nationalist organizations. It cites an FBI report that alleges the number of hate crimes are up about 17 percent.

While reports like this might sometimes accurately summarize the despicable efforts of wholly un-Christian groups like the Ku Klux Klan, their real purpose is to discredit and ultimately destroy influential pro-life and pro-family groups by lumping them in with actual extremist movements. It's an obvious guilt by association tactic.

The Ruth Institute, the Family Research Council, and *Catholic Family News* have all been included in this year's report. Some of them have been in prior year ones as well. The SPLC's designation has caused real harm to them. In 2013, a crazed gunman entered the Washington, DC offices of the Family Research Council after learning the SPLC considered it "anti-gay." He nearly killed people. In 2017, the Ruth Institute saw its donations services discontinued by Vanco, a partner of Wells Fargo. Vanco told them it doesn't do business with those who promote "hate, violence, harassment and/or abuse."[22]

A coalition of more than 46 conservatives wrote a letter last year appealing to the media to stop citing the SPLC as an authority on "hate." They haven't listened. This year's report has received massive attention by mainstream outlets giddy to pass along its bogus findings.[23] NPR, for instance, referred to the SPLC as a "civil rights organization."[24] ABC described the SPLC (which

---

22 Doug Mainwaring, "Banking giant may be linked to cutting off services to Christian, pro-family groups," LifeSiteNews, September 6, 2017, https://www.lifesitenews.com/news/banking-giant-may-be-linked-to-cutting-off-services-to-christian-pro-family/

23 Chis Woodyard, "Hate group count hits 20-year high amid rise in white supremacy, report says," USA Today, February 20, 2019, https://www.usatoday.com/story/news/nation/2019/02/20/hate-groups-white-power-supremacists-southern-poverty-law-center/2918416002/. Charles Duncan, "Hate groups 'surge' across the country since Charlottesville riot, report says," Miami Herald, February 21, 2019, https://www.miamiherald.com/news/nation-world/national/article226562524.html

24 Leila Fadel, "US Hate Groups Rose 30 Percent In Recent Years, Watchdog Group Reports," NPR, February 20, 2019, https://www.npr.org/2019/02/20/696217158/u-s-hate-groups-rose-sharply-in-recent-years-watchdog-group-reports

has an endowment around $500 million) as a "legal advocacy group."[25] That's about as accurate as saying Hillary Clinton is a voice for the unborn. Robby Soave is an editor at the libertarian website *Reason*. He appeared on Tucker Carlson this week to throw cold water on the claim that the United States is experiencing a surge in hate crimes. "If you look very carefully, it is easy to misrepresent [the number of hate crimes]," Soave remarked. The increase in hate crimes is "actually because more agencies reported data to the federal government. So just counting the issue more accurately will make it look like the problem is getting worse when really there were just fewer people participating in this scheme to count hate crimes than the year before." Soave concluded that "a lot of the time it ends up being a hoax." He estimated that about half of all hate crimes in the United States could be made up. "Oftentimes they're just not solved."[26]

The SPLC is Not Being Honest About 'Hate'

As it stands currently, the Southern Poverty Law Center defines a hate group as an organization that attacks or maligns an entire class of people typically for their race, religion, ethnicity, sexual orientation, or gender identity.

If this is their operating principle, why is the Democratic Party not listed in its report? In 2017, Notre Dame law professor Amy Coney Barrett was viciously smeared by liberal US Sen. Dianne Feinstein, D-California, because of her Catholic faith. "The dogma lives loudly within you," Feinstein complained about her during a hearing. Socialist Senator Bernie Sanders likewise declared a Trump judicial nominee in June of that year unfit to serve because he was a Christian.[27] In April 2018, New Jersey's Democratic Senator Cory Booker grilled Mike Pompeo, Trump's current Secretary of State, for his views on same-sex "marriage."[28] Liberal Senators Kamala Harris, D-California, and Mazie Hirono, D-Hawaii, similarly went after a Trump judicial nominee in

25 Bill Hutchinson, "Hate groups grow more popular even as Ku Klux Klan membership plummets: Report," ABC News, February 20, 2019, https://abcnews.go.com/news/story/number-hate-groups-us-hits-time-high-report-61186850

26 Scott Morefield, "Reason Editor Explains How Hate Crime Statistics Are Misrepresented, Gives Shocking Guess On How Many Are Actually Real," Daily Caller, February 18, 2019, https://dailycaller.com/2019/02/18/robby-soave-hate-crime-statistics/

27 Jonathan van Maren, "Bernie's comments on Christians weren't just arrogant … they were unconstitutional," LifeSiteNews, June 13, 2017, https://www.lifesitenews.com/blogs/bernies-comments-on-christians-werent-just-arrogant-they-were-unconstitutio/

28 Jonathan van Maren, "Witch-hunt: Democratic Senator grills Trump nominee who says marriage is one man, one woman," LifeSiteNews, April 13, 2018, https://www.lifesitenews.com/blogs/has-supporting-same-sex-marriage-become-the-new-litmus-test-for-holding-pub/

January because he belongs to the Knights of Columbus.[29]

In light of these events, I propose that the SPLC include each and every one of these attacks in its annual study. I also call on them to include attacks launched against another class of people—unborn babies. That probably won't ever happen given that they are essentially a lap dog for the Democratic Party, but if they did, Planned Parenthood along with the legions of left-wing lawmakers promoting chemical and surgical abortions across the US would all be included in its "Year in Hate and Extremism" report. Only then will the SPLC provide an accurate depiction of the real level of hate in America.

GETTING RID OF PRIESTLY CELIBACY WILL NOT FIX CATHOLIC EDUCATION

According to Patrick McCloskey and Joseph Claude Harris, Catholic education isn't what it used to be. In fact, it's a disaster. The reason? Priestly celibacy. The solution? Getting rid of priestly celibacy.

In an op-ed for the *New York Times*, McCloskey, a project director at the Center for Catholic School Effectiveness at Loyola University Chicago, and Harris, author of *The Cost of Catholic Parishes and Schools,* argue the following:

> Catholic parochial education is in crisis. More than a third of parochial schools in the United States closed between 1965 and 1990, and enrollment fell by more than half. After stabilizing in the 1990s, enrollment has plunged despite strong demand from students and families...
>
> Until the 1960s, religious orders were united in responding to Christ's mandate to 'go teach.' But religious vocations have become less attractive, and parochial schools have faced increasing competition from charter schools. Without a turnaround, many dioceses will soon have only scatterings of elite Catholic academies for middle-class and affluent families and a token number of inner-city schools, propped up by wealthy donors.

McCloskey and Harris proceed to argue that the Catholic school system today can be saved if it gets innovative with fundraising, increases the percentage of funds the Church spends on its schools, and institutes reforms so financially strapped parishes can more easily seek help from wealthier ones. I think these ideas are quite good. McCloskey and Harris deserve to be applauded for their originality. But it's their final suggestion that deserves a closer look:

> After finances, personnel is the biggest challenge ... and one solution is in hand.
> In the late 1960s, the Vatican allowed men to be ordained as deacons, who are clergy with many but not all the powers of a priest. Today there are almost 17,000 in the United States, about the same number as active diocesan priests. Over the next decade, the diaconate will continue to grow, while the number of ordained priests is projected to decline to 12,500 by 2035.
> Many deacons have valuable professional, managerial and entre-preneurial expertise that could revitalize parochial education. If they were given additional powers to perform sacraments and run parishes, a married priesthood would become a *fait accompli*. Celibacy should be a sacrifice offered freely, not an excuse for institutional suicide.[30]

It is astonishing that McCloskey and Harris would regurgitate this age-old trope after writing such an insightful essay. After all, they offer no statistical evidence for their position. They—like the Roman Catholic Womenpriest movement—simply assume that opening up the priesthood to others will result in flourishing parishes.

While it might seem tempting to side with this logic, their solution only compounds the issue. Here is what Brother Andre Marie over at *Catholicism. org* thinks about their suggestion:

> Leaving aside the problems associated with a married clergy, this point needs to be made: By and large, the men under discussion have pay-checks from their non-ecclesiastical sources of employment. Will they all leave their jobs voluntarily to become full-time employees of the Church? Would they all want major mid-stream career changes? Where will the money come from to pay them, and won't the Church lose a substantial amount of support from the donations these deacons give? Will their wives want the social pressures of being the "priest's wife" and their children of being the 'preacher's kid'...? Would the cultural

30 Patrick McClosky and Joseph Claude Harris, "Can the Catholic Schools Be Saved?" The New York Times, January 13, 2013, https://www.nytimes.com/2013/01/14/opinion/can-the-catholic-schools-be-saved.html

and economic demands of this totally new status quo in the Catholic Church really fix more problems than it creates?

This is ideology parading as common sense. It was liberalism and progressivism that destroyed Catholic education in this country. Liberal progressive solutions will only worsen the matter, not fix it.[31]

McCloskey and Harris' essay reminds me of Chapter 8 of the Gospel of Matthew. The apostles were in a boat with Christ when a furious storm suddenly came over them, causing them to exclaim, "Lord, save us. We're going to drown!"

Christ responded by saying "You of little faith, why are you so afraid?" He stood up, rebuked the winds, and the sea was calm.

The Catholic Church is undoubtedly experiencing turbulent times right now. I agree that reforms in the school system are needed, but I reject the argument that those should adopt a means justifies the ends mentality.

What Catholics need to do, like the apostles didn't do in that boat, is to trust in God and know that He will always provide for His flock. This doesn't mean we should be ignorant of issues facing the Church, but we needn't adopt the apocalyptic view presented by McCloskey and Harris. Indeed, there are many encouraging statistics regarding the faith today that suggest positive changes are coming. Here are just a few:

- The number of seminarians, not only in the United States but worldwide, has been on the rise for the past several years.[32]

- The pro-abortion movement is less popular, especially among young women, than ever before.[33]

- Traditional Catholicism is gaining traction with young adults.[34]

31 Brother Andre Marie, "NYT's Ideological Solution For Catholic Education," Catholicism.org, January 8, 2013, https://catholicism.org/nyts-ideological-solution-for-catholic-education.html

32 Deacon Greg Sandra, "Here we grow again: more Catholics, priests, deacons, seminarians worldwide," Patheos, March 10, 2012, https://www.patheos.com/blogs/deaconsbench/2012/03/here-we-grow-again-more-catholics-priests-deacons-seminarians-worldwide/

33 Carol Tobias, "No Surprise Time Magazine Said Pro-Abortion Movement Losing," LifeNews, January 10, 2013, https://www.lifenews.com/2013/01/10/no-surprise-time-magazine-said-pro-abortion-movement-losing/

34 Thomas Peters, "The Economist Takes Note: It's Cool to be a Young 'Trad' Catholic," CatholicVote, January 5, 2013, https://web.archive.org/web/20130113083749/https://www.catholicvote.org/discuss/index.php?p=39394

Even if school closings continue to occur, the Church itself will not end. We must work to arrest this development, but the Catholic faith has survived World Wars and outlived genocidal dictators throughout history. Those who believe it must radically alter its ways in order to survive the present era reveal how little faith they really have.

CatholicVote • January 14, 2013

CLASSICAL EDUCATION IS THE FUTURE OF CATHOLIC SCHOOLING

It's no secret that there's been an identity crisis in Catholic education these past 50 years. More parishes closing, fewer vocations, and smaller families have left many wondering: what went wrong?

At the Bringing America Back to Life conference in Cleveland, Ohio last month, faculty, students, and alumni from several classical education academies told me they think they've found the solution.

Rocco Galizio is the headmaster of the Akron-based Chesterton Academy. He said that the way forward is focusing on the true, the good, and the beautiful.

> The ultimate goal of the academy is to make a well-formed human being who can go out into the world and actually interact with it and do good. We want them to be able to engage with their peers, engage with anyone they come across. And part of that is just knowing who you are and knowing where you've come from.

Vincent Ortiz, one of the students at Chesterton Academy, echoed his headmaster's remarks by praising the school's unique teaching methods:

> For the first 15 years of my life, I always had the same old lectures. You hear all these speeches, then you take tests ... I noticed I didn't really remember most of my classes and that I sort of forgot everything. But at Chesterton, they use something called the Socratic method, which is when the teacher constantly asks you questions. In order for you to answer any of them, you have to make sure that you're paying attention the entire time.

Other classical institutions were at the convention as well, including The Lyceum, an Ohio-based co-ed day school that offers the Traditional Latin Mass. I spoke with Luke Macik, the headmaster of The Lyceum, about its curriculum and what parents can expect for their children.

> We're educating the students in the great works of Western or Catholic civilization. So they're reading things from the ancient Greeks and Romans all the way up through medieval times and even a little bit into modern times … so our students are getting an education similar to that of the founding fathers of our country and certainly of the fathers of the Church.

"They also sing beautiful music," he said.

> They sing wonderful polyphony and Gregorian chant and even chant of the Eastern Catholic churches. All students at The Lyceum sing in choir. They also perform dramatic productions of Shakespeare and of ancient Greek plays tragedies. So they're getting a very well-rounded education and it's all grounded, of course, in the Catholic faith.

Lyceum senior Ted Macik also told me he appreciates the school's coursework. "It really helps you grow as a person and not only just in learning practical things that help in everyday life, but actually developing yourself as a man and your intellect," he exclaimed. "If you really want to grow as a man and be the best you can be and be what God created you to be, that's where it's at."

Mary Langley graduated from The Lyceum and went on to study at St Thomas Aquinas College only to return in order to teach ancient languages. "I think the students love it," she told me.

Brigid Coyne, an alumnus of the nearby Padre Pio Academy, also had nothing but praise for the classical education she received. "That love of truth and my faith that I gained at Padre Pio that made me want to continue that and continue looking at the liberal arts and truly Catholic colleges. And I think that's probably one of the biggest gifts that Padre Pio gave."

Coyne also remarked that contemporary Catholic education has gone wrong in two ways:

> I think it's a combination of modern parents and modern schools. I think parents kind of want theology to be taught in the schools and kind of to be hands off. And it's just something they do together on Sunday. And that it's not a big part of life. I think most modern Catholic schools

want to be well liked and want to be considered academically serious. And so theology is relegated to one class, hopefully every year, and it's not brought into all the other classes.

According to Michael Van Hecke, M.Ed., the president of the Institute for Catholic Liberal Education, there's reason to hope that there will be more classical academies popping up all over America.

"The big wave, the big trajectory, is diocesan parochial Catholic schools and high schools wanting to renew. A huge amount of what we're doing today is going into schools, running one or two-day programs for the faculty to renew the faculty in the [classical] methods and the curriculum that should be taught."

While some Catholic parents may still be on the fence about sending their child to a classical academy, Lyceum teacher Mary Langley's words should serve as a strong endorsement.

You will not regret it once you actually just try your best to give it a chance because it seems pretty foreign to you. It kind of seems old fashioned, maybe, but it's something that when I went to college and I look back at it and everyone says, 'oh, that was so impractical and how are you going to get a job' and all that kind of stuff? It's something that I'll never regret. And I am so happy I did it. And I would never I would not change that for the world.

LifeSiteNews • May 14, 2021

I WENT TO A DOWN SYNDROME DRAG SHOW: WHAT I SAW HORRIFIED ME

This past weekend I went to my first (and last) drag show. Normally, I'd never put myself in such a spiritually toxic environment. But I wanted to do my due diligence so my reporting would be accurate.

The show took place at Wealthy Street Theatre in Grand Rapids, Michigan, the city I grew up in and the town I currently reside in. It featured persons with Down syndrome from a U.K. drag troupe called "Drag Syndrome." It also had non-Down syndrome performers.

The event quite justifiably garnered international headlines. Local media was abuzz, too. But none of their reports mentioned the verbal abuse some of the event's supporters hurled at the peaceful protesters outside.

Who Hosted It and Why?

"Drag Syndrome" was part of ArtPrize, an annual art competition created and run by Rick DeVos, son of the current US Secretary of Education Betsy DeVos. The DeVos family are major Republican donors who practically own Grand Rapids. Members of the Christian Reformed Church in America, they have their name plastered over dozens of buildings in the area. To say they are influential power brokers in local politics would be putting it mildly.

You would think that the family's conservative views would compel DeVos to scrap the show. Apparently not. My guess is that he knew about it and simply let it happen out of fear of being labeled transphobic. Of course, I could be wrong. Worst case scenario, he actually supports this stuff.

Thankfully, Republican congressional candidate Peter Meijer canceled the event, which was initially scheduled to be held at one of his properties. He said that the performance was "exploitive." Good on him for doing what was right.

Persecuted for the Sake of Truth

When I arrived Saturday night for the 7pm show, I was astonished by the level of hatred that event supporters had for the nonviolent, two dozen or so protesters standing outside, almost all of whom were from local Protestant churches. It was like demonic possession was in the air.

Mere minutes after parking my car, I witnessed the co-host of the event, "Dice Santana," an African American who, from what I've gathered, is a woman who believes she is a man, lecture the protesters about how they "weren't acting lovingly" like Christ.

Most of them remained silent, taking the hatred head on. Others calmly responded with reasoned arguments.

Margaret Murphy, a married, middle-aged woman, was one of the protesters. She told me that while she was on the receiving end of "Dice's" tirade, she kept her eyes fixed on a statue of the Blessed Virgin Mary that was in the window of a soup shop across the street. She said she found comfort in that.

As "Dice" was busy lecturing Margaret and her family, I couldn't help but think that she probably wouldn't be that aggressive if a group of Muslim men or Jewish rabbis wearing yarmulkes were protesting. It's always for followers of Christ that liberals reserve their most intense vitriol.

A Den of Iniquity

Inside the theatre a "Content Warning" sign was taped to the wall. I laughed out loud when I saw that. It absurdly read, "PG-13: Adult Language." Really, "adult language"? That's what makes this event "PG-13"? I thought to myself. "Not the fact that grown men in dresses are prancing around like animals?"

Fortunately, less than a dozen children attended the performance, which seemed to take on a religious, almost liturgical nature.

I felt terrible for the kids who were brought there by their parents. Child protective services should be called on every one of them. Sadly, that won't happen in this day and age. Children are now allowed to get hormone injections and "transition" before puberty. It's their human right to do so, or we're told.

The show began with non-Down syndrome men wearing high heels, exotic costumes, and tons of makeup while lip-syncing songs they didn't write. The entire thing was, to quote Holden Caulfield from *The Catcher in the Rye*, "phony."

The production really is just one big fantasy for these people, who are obviously emotionally scarred. It's all very sad. The Down syndrome performers, who were featured during the latter part of the show, almost made me cry. I bet the same people in the audience who were cheering on these innocent persons would also be cheering on their mothers had they wanted to abort them because they have Down syndrome.

As the show pressed on, I kept wondering how "Dice" and others on stage got to this place in their life. The answer probably has to do with some sort of family trauma. Bullying in their teenage years, drugs, possibly even sexual addictions are also likely explanations. Parental indoctrination of LGBT propaganda is probably to blame as well.

I also wondered to what extent the Church could be faulted. I mean, millions of young people have been abused by priests over the past several decades.

Furthermore, how many priests today are actually telling adults who are living in sin to reform their lives and give up there wicked ways? Not as many as in years past, I imagine.

Fighting Back for Christ the King

The good news is that Christians are not letting this filth go un-noticed. I was pleased to see more than a dozen men protesting outside the theatre. Nothing against women—who tend to be more involved in these sorts of activities in the first place—but there needs to be strong male voices leading the fight on this and on many other issues. Simply put, society needs masculinity.

Tom Root of Flint, Michigan was a particularly inspiring figure on that front. Tom has a Down syndrome child. I could tell how sad he was when a woman with her lip-stick wearing son confronted him before going inside. Instead of over-reacting to her remark that she was "offended" by his presence, Tom spoke the truth with patience and calmness and easily dismissed her flimsy arguments.

I predict Down syndrome drag shows will grow in popularity in the years ahead, just as drag queen story hours have been popping up all over the place. Liberals will continue to use these performances to make pro-family conservatives appear uncharitable to the mentally challenged.

Regardless, Christians need to take a stand against these lurid shows so the common good of society is upheld. Not only are they an offense to the natural law but they violate the divine law in an especially grievous way. God will not be mocked. Christians need to defend His honor and His dignity, come what may. If not us, who? If not now, when?

LifeSiteNews • September 12, 2019

CATHOLIC HEALTH SYSTEM DEFENDS 'LGBTQIA+ CARE': HERE'S WHY THAT'S WRONG

A Midwest-based Catholic health system that has an annual revenue of over $18 billion dollars and employs more than 120,000 individuals is standing by its commitment to provide services for gender-confused college students living in West Michigan.

Trinity Health's medical center in Allendale, Michigan provides "LGBTQIA+ care" for persons who attend Grand Valley State University, a school founded in 1960 and has nearly 25,000 students.[35]

I was not aware of how long such services have been available for, or what they necessarily entail, so I emailed Trinity Health's media relations department with the following questions:

> Can you clarify to me what that sort of 'care' entails? Does it mean helping persons who are confused about their gender 'transition' into the opposite

35 Trinity Health, "Trinity Health Medical Group, Primary Care - GVSU," https://www.trinityhealthmichigan.org/location/trinity-health-medical-group-primary-care-gvsu

sex? Or even helping refer patients to sex 're-assignment' surgery, which has been shown to be very dangerous? As a Catholic organization, how does Trinity Health justify its services for 'LGBTQIA+ care'?

Senior Communication Specialist Amy Rotter replied to my email. She included her "preferred pronouns" (she/her/hers) in her response. She requested that the following quote be attributed to "Trinity Health Medical Group—West Michigan."

Trinity Health Medical Group does not have a multi-disciplinary program for gender-affirming care, but as a Catholic health system we honor the dignity of every person. Diversity is acknowledged and celebrated with a commitment to creating a culture where people feel safe and welcome. Our commitment reflects our core value of Reverence in the care we provide all people in our community.

According to its website, Trinity Health's mission is to "serve together in the spirit of the Gospel as a compassionate and transforming healing presence within our communities." Trinity Health also boasts that "we honor the sacredness and dignity of every person."[36]

Catholic teaching on sexual identity and human dignity firmly rejects these ambiguous statements. While it is true that every person possesses an innate, ontological dignity due to being made in the image and likeness of God, he or she loses their operative dignity when they embrace disordered lifestyles such as homosexuality, transgenderism, and other degrading behaviors. As St Thomas Aquinas teaches, "by sinning man departs from the order of reason, and consequently falls away from the dignity of his manhood ... and he falls into the slavish state of the beasts."

For Rotter to claim that Trinity Health is upholding "reverence" and honoring patients' "dignity" by providing services that affirm them in behaviors entirely opposed to God's laws, shows an off-the-charts level of unfamiliarity with Catholic teaching. What's more, far from creating a "welcoming" and "safe" environment for Grand Valley students, Trinity Health is encouraging them to continue down the dangerous and terrifying road to hell. As such, Trinity employees will be held accountable for being complicit in the destruction of souls.

36 Trinity Health, "Our Mission, Vision and Values," https://www.trinityhealthmichigan.org/about-us/mission-and-values

Catholics should pray but also attempt to persuade Trinity Health to reverse course so they can help persons who identify as "LGBTQIA+" live as the men and women God made them to be.

LifeSiteNews • November 17, 2023

'BRAIN DEATH' IS A MEDICAL FICTION INVENTED TO HARVEST ORGANS FROM LIVING PEOPLE

Is it morally permissible to harvest the organs of a person who has been declared "brain dead"? Why and when did organ transplantation first come about? And what are the Church's teaching on "organ donation"?

These questions and more were answered by Doyen Nguyen during an in-depth interview with Italian magazine *Radici Cristiane* recently.

In her remarks, Nguyen, a lay Dominican who teaches at the Pontifical University of St Thomas Aquinas in Rome, categorized "brain death" as an incoherent "medical fiction."

Nguyen explained that a committee at Harvard University in 1968 redefined the term "brain death" to mean someone who is in an irreversible coma. She says this was done to serve the interests of the organ transplant industry.

"Brain death" was coined to circumvent the phrase "irreversible coma" because someone who is in a coma is actually alive, she said. "It would be an oxymoron to say that a corpse is in coma!" she exclaimed.[37]

Nguyen appeared at a two-day conference in Rome from May 20–22 earlier this year titled "A Medicolegal Construct: Scientific & Philosophical Evidence," which was hosted by the lay-led John Paul II Academy for Human Life and the Family. Many attendees and speakers at the conference, including Austrian Catholic philosopher Dr Josef Seifert, were former members of the Pontifical Academy for Life. John Paul II founded the Academy in 1994 to combat what he called the "culture of death."

Lamentably, Pope Francis gutted the Academy in 2017 by replacing its members with clergy who support left-wing and social justice policies like immigration and environmentalism.[38] A pledge that previously demanded

37 Stephen Kokx, "'Brain death' is a medical fiction invented to harvest organs from living people: expert," LifeSiteNews, March 20, 2019, https://www.lifesitenews.com/news/brain-death-is-a-medical-fiction-invented-to-harvest-organs-from-living-people-expert/

38 Lisa Bourne, "Pope Francis guts Vatican pro-life academy of members chosen by. John Paul II," LifeSiteNews, June 15, 2017, https://www.lifesitenews.com/news/pope-francis-guts-vatican-pro-life-academy-of-members-chosen-by-st.-john-pa/

members uphold the Church's pro-life teachings was also radically altered.[39] Francis' actions compelled Seifert to found the John Paul II Academy for Human Life and the Family in 2017.

Throughout the conference's diverse and highly academic presentations, one discernible theme emerged, namely, that "brain death" has been invented to harvest viable organs from still-living people. Only when a person's heart stops beating and their breathing ceases for a certain amount of time can it be said that death has truly occurred.

Emceed by LifeSite co-founder John-Henry Westen and Lepanto Institute president Michel Hichborn, the conference featured lectures by some of the most accomplished Catholic scholars in the world, including Nguyen, who delivered three talks on the subject.

Blunt yet respectful, Nguyen maintained that John Paul's writings on brain death "made a mess" of Church teaching.[40] She also detailed the gruesome methods surgeons use when harvesting organs from a "donor" body. In 2018, she released a book titled, *The New Definitions of Death for Organ Donation*.

Dr Cicero Coimbra M.D. addressed the conference as well. He said apnea tests, a common procedure used on "brain dead" patients, actually *cause* irreversible "brain death." He also spoke about the importance of taking proper amounts of vitamin D and magnesium to have a healthy brain and immune system. For his truth-telling efforts, he has been ostracized by the medical community.

Other conference presenters agreed that "brain death" and "organ donation" are used by the medical community in order to convince people they are giving "the gift of life." In reality, as Dr Paul Byrne repeatedly stated in his talks, "you cannot take viable organs from a cadaver. The body needs to have a beating heart to maintain organ health."

During his two presentations at the conference, Byrne, a neonatologist and president of the Life Guardian Foundation, shared heartfelt stories about poor treatment that "brain dead" patients he has cared for received from mainstream doctors and hospitals.[41] He also showed a video of Zack Dunlap, a man diagnosed as "brain dead" who was minutes away from having his organs harvested but thanks to his cousin who showed obstinate nurses that his condition was improving he was spared from being killed. He eventually

39 Lisa Bourne, "Vatican pro-life academy widens mandate to include immigration, environment, arms control," LifeSiteNews, October 9, 2017, https://www.lifesitenews.com/news/vatican-academy-will-focus-on-immigration-instead-of-abortion.-pro-lifers-a/

40 John Paul II, Address to the 18th International Congress of the Transplantation Society, Vatican website, August 29, 2000, https://www.vatican.va/content/john-paul-ii/en/speeches/2000/jul-sep/documents/hf_jp-ii_spe_20000829_transplants.html

41 See Life Guardian Foundation, https://lifeguardianfoundation.org/

made a full recovery and is now married.

Byrne additionally played a clip of an "organ donation" procedure where the body cavity is opened up while the heart is still beating. Some members of the audience let out an audible grasp when the footage began. In an interview with LifeSite, Byrne said the following:

> What's really happening is that a multi-billion dollar industry has been created around the harvesting of organs. But organ damage occurs within minutes of death. Knowing they need to excise organs before a person dies, the medical community uses the term 'brain death' to say the person is dead. But these patients are not dead. The 'organ donation' procedure is what actually kills them. It stops their heart. Do not be an organ donor.

Other speakers at the conference included Fr Edmund Waldstein, a Cistercian monk from Austria; Illinois-based neurologist Thomas Zabiega; Dr Alan Shewmon, M.D. (via Skype); and Academy president Dr Josef Seifert. Bishop Athanasius Schneider appeared at the conference via a pre-recorded video message. In his address, His Excellency stressed the need for society to recognize the Social Kingship of Christ so innocent life will be protected.

At the conclusion of the conference, Seifert announced his desire to establish a Poland-based Academy for Human Life and the Family. He said he envisions a sort of "network" so its message can spread throughout the world.

LifeSiteNews • May 22, 2019

LOVING MOM SICK WITH COVID SAVES BABY'S LIFE WITH PREMATURE DELIVERY, DIES 10 DAYS LATER

I first met Jessica Hallgren a little over a year and a half ago. I noticed her the first time she came to our small chapel in Allendale, Michigan. It's not hard to stand out here. We're a rather tight-knit community. When someone new comes along, it's easy to spot them.

Jessica and I struck up a conversation in the parking lot after Mass. I forget everything we talked about, but she said something along the lines of how the Latin Mass is "just so beautiful" and that things in the mainstream church "don't seem right." I asked her where her family was and she told me her husband wasn't all that interested in coming yet. She wanted to "check it out" on her own before bringing everyone else along.

As the weeks went by, Jessica kept coming back. She and I became friends, often talking about Church-related topics but also my work at LifeSite. She immediately fit in at our chapel, especially with the women, with whom she made many friends. Jessica also happened to know two buddies of mine who attended the church. She was their boss 10 years prior when they were undergrads at a college she worked at in a nearby town.

What struck me most about Jessica—like all those who are interested in Traditional Catholicism—was her simple desire to know the truth. She had an inquisitive mind and never shied away from a question, or from sharing her opinion. She was a humble person who loved being a mom, wife, and friend.

I can't recall exactly when, but Jessica's husband Matt, a chef, and their kids, did start coming to our church. So did her parents. God was undoubtedly acting through her.

Jessica's children (she had a total of seven) are a riot. The youngest ones are extremely sociable and have fiercely unique and strong personalities. I always enjoy spending time with them after Mass. Some of them helped me move a married couple at our church into their new house not long ago. Jessica and her children also attended a bonfire I organized this summer. Children are so fun, especially when they know how to crack a joke. And Jessica's most certainly know how to do that.

About a month ago, COVID hit our church. Like many parishioners, Jessica got the virus. But unlike them, she was seven months pregnant. Many people began offering medical advice to her so she could improve with natural treatments. Her symptoms, however, soon got to the point that going to the hospital became a necessity. Her coughing hadn't stopped and her oxygen dropped to a dangerously low level. She even contracted pneumonia. "She was very concerned about the baby," her mom told me. "That's why she went to the hospital."

Everyone at our chapel prayed for Jessica's recovery. At the hospital, she told the staff, "I want you to take the baby if anything happens." Eventually, a C-section was performed. That procedure took place on Saturday, December 4.

Baby Margaret Hallgren entered this world prematurely by a full two months, weighing just 2 pounds 14 ounces. Margaret was given the middle name Barbara after Jessica's grandma and after St Barbara, on whose feast day she was born. Thankfully, Margaret continues to improve with each passing day.

Before being put on a ventilator, a priest gave Jessica Last Rites. "She was prepared to go, especially in order to save her baby's life," her mom told me.

Jessica Hallgren passed away on Tuesday, December 14, surrounded by her parents, loving husband, and eldest daughter. I will miss her very much.

Our church, and the world, lost a loving young mom who had a long life yet to live and a beautiful family yet to raise.

I believe Jessica may well be considered a saint one day for having laid down her life for her child, and that she could be remembered in the same way as St Gianna Beretta Molla (1922–1962).

If you don't know who St Gianna is, the short version of her story is that when she was pregnant with her fourth child in 1961 she was told by doctors that she had a fibroma on her uterus. They informed her that the only way to ensure that she would live would be to abort the child. She rejected that advice, telling them that the child "must come first." Gianna eventually gave birth to a little girl, dying a week later from complications. Her daughter, Gianna Emanuela, lived and is now a doctor.

I will continue to pray for the repose of Jessica Hallgren's soul. At the same time, I know that she gave up her own life, like Christ did for us, so Margaret could live. "What greater love have than this, than to lay down one's life for a friend," John 15:13 says. How could God not reward Jessica with anything other than eternal bliss for her sacrifice?

LifeSiteNews • December 16, 2021

Stephen Kokx is a journalist for LifeSiteNews. A former community college instructor, he has written and spoken extensively about spirituality, Catholic social teaching, and politics. Previously, he worked for the Archdiocese of Chicago. His essays have appeared on a variety of Catholic websites.

Also by Stephen Kokx:

St Alphonsus for the 21st Century: A Handbook for Holiness

Made in the USA
Monee, IL
15 November 2024